Teenage Dreams

Teenage Dreams

*Girlhood Sexualities in the
U.S. Culture Wars*

CHARLIE JEFFRIES

RUTGERS UNIVERSITY PRESS
NEW BRUNSWICK, CAMDEN, AND NEWARK,
NEW JERSEY, AND LONDON

Library of Congress Cataloging-in-Publication Data
Names: Jeffries, Charlie, author.
Title: Teenage dreams: girlhood sexualities in the U.S. culture wars /
    Charlie Jeffries.
Description: New Brunswick: Rutgers University Press, [2022] |
    Includes bibliographical references and index.
Identifiers: LCCN 2021041093 | ISBN 9781978806795 (paperback) |
    ISBN 9781978806801 (hardcover) | ISBN 9781978806818 (epub) |
    ISBN 9781978806825 (mobi) | ISBN 9781978806832 (pdf)
Subjects: LCSH: Teenage girls—Sexual behavior—United States. | Teenage girls—Sexual
    behavior—United States—Public opinion. | Reproductive rights—United States. |
    Teenage girls—United States—Attitudes. | Teenage girls—United States—Social
    conditions.
Classification: LCC HQ35 .J39 2022 | DDC 306.70835/20973—dc23
LC record available at https://lccn.loc.gov/2021041093

A British Cataloging-in-Publication record for this book is available from the
British Library.

References to internet websites (URLs) were accurate at the time of writing. Neither the author
nor Rutgers University Press is responsible for URLs that may have expired or changed since
the manuscript was prepared.

⊜ The paper used in this publication meets the requirements of the American National Standard for Information Sciences—Permanence of Paper for Printed Library Materials, ANSI
Z39.48-1992.

www.rutgersuniversitypress.org

Manufactured in the United States of America

This book is dedicated to young people involved in struggles for liberation of the past, present, and future.

Contents

Teenage Dreams

Introduction

"How Far Will You Go?"

In February 2007, the media entrepreneur, former model, and host of *America's Next Top Model* Tyra Banks interviewed the eighteen-year-old porn actress Sasha Grey on her eponymous TV talk show, for the episode "Teens in the Sex Trade." Above the strains of nightmarish intro music, Banks described in a grave voice-over how Grey had chosen her career. "Having been sexually active, and bombarded by pornographic materials in high school, porn has never been a stranger to Sasha."[1] In a prerecorded interview, shot as Grey drove through Los Angeles in her car, the porn star remembered it slightly differently. "I started watching porn when I was about 16 and a half," she said nonchalantly, "mostly online, internet stuff, but sometimes I'd steal DVDs from my friends."[2] As the opening sequence faded into a shot of Banks and Grey sharing a sofa on *The Tyra Banks Show* set, Banks fixed Sasha with the concerned expression of an older sister. "I'm looking at you right now, and you look like someone I went to middle school with," she told Grey breathily. "Someone at my school, eighth grade."[3] Though Sasha Grey was not in eighth grade, she appeared youthful in a pink T-shirt, blue jeans, and ballet pumps. Banks's discomfort with Grey's age did not stop her from directing a series of graphic questions toward her, on the exact nature of her work in porn. "How far will you go? What won't you do?" she asked. "So you'll have anal sex? On film?" she continued. "And I've heard that you do gang bang scenes? What's a gang bang scene?" Grey remained unflustered, offering calm explanations in response. After just a few minutes of conversation, Banks called for a commercial break. "This interview is actually really strange for me, Sasha, because I feel like I'm talking to a young girl, I am talking to a young girl," she told her. "I need to regroup a little bit and get this together, because this is very difficult for me."[4]

During the 2000s, conversations like this one—on the topic of young women's sexual choices—were happening everywhere in American society. From "hyper-sexualization" in the media to the potential impact of Gardasil, the HPV (human

1

papillomavirus) vaccine, on young women, the sex lives of teenage girls were an explicit, central battleground of the culture wars of the new millennium. The centrality of girlhood sexualities within the cultural politics of the Bush administration is already a part of our collective historical memory, owing to the outlandishness of abstinence campaigns, the titillating debates over "porn culture," and the accompanying imagery of high-profile abstinence pinups such as Jessica Simpson and Britney Spears.[5] However, this cultural obsession has a longer history, even if the debates of previous decades were more covert than the one between Tyra Banks and Sasha Grey. Throughout U.S. history, adults across the political spectrum have held racialized, classed conceptions of girlhood and believed that young women's sex lives hold the power to shape wider social mores and even impact American economic prosperity.[6] These ideas became increasingly important within the political battles that gained speed in the 1980s, as the New Right movement was bolstered by the election of Ronald Reagan. The central project of this book is to understand why girlhood sexual behaviors and identities became the focus of so much intense, divisive debate and discourse in the late twentieth and early twenty-first centuries. What about the economic and political climate of the United States in this period directed so much attention to the sexual lives of teenagers?

GIRLHOOD SEXUALITIES IN THE U.S. CULTURE WARS

Answering these questions is important, not only to better understand how gender and sexuality function in the modern United States, but to better understand this period of political turmoil as a whole. The sexual behavior of teenage girls was not only a battle fought by adults in the United States; it was critical in shaping the politics of both sides of the American culture wars and in carving out new lines of discord within these battles, from the 1980s onward.

Girlhood sexuality became such a central concern amid the U.S. culture wars because adolescent sexual and reproductive behavior mattered to both major strands of the New Right backlash to the social movements of the 1960s.[7] For religious, pro-family, social conservatives, ensuring the reproductive and marital conformity of white teenage girls was key to upholding their vision of the superior American family. For neoliberal, fiscal conservatives, dismantling welfare and advocating for interpersonal, familial practices such as individualism and personal responsibility—which involved supporting racist, sexist policies that punished young women who erred from this—supported their vision of American global economic dominance.[8] Crucially, the sexual and reproductive choices of teenage girls mattered to socially liberal adults in this period too. Teenage girls also represented the future of American values to them, one that would reflect the educational, professional, and bodily freedoms won for women in the postwar decades. However, as the episodes covered in this book detail, the positions of those on the right and those of more progressive factions often overlapped when discussing teenagers' sexuality in ways that defy the polarity of much of the political discourse of the culture wars era.[9]

Multiple groups of adults in the United States expressed a stake in teenage female sexuality in this period, including but not limited to Republican and Democratic politicians, feminist and antifeminist campaigners, the pro-family movement, sex educators, doctors, teachers, parents, artists, filmmakers, scholars, authors, and television executives. In many cases, the sexual lives of teenage girls fit within the expected moral stance of these groups and individuals. For example, to most social conservatives, the sex lives of unmarried teenage girls demonstrated the breakdown of traditional family mores in the wake of the sexual revolution and social movements of the 1960s and 1970s. Most liberal adults had a relaxed or neutral approach to premarital sex, supported teenagers' access to birth control and abortion, and believed that young people should receive comprehensive sex education in the wake of the AIDS epidemic.[10] The findings of the medical community were generally supported by those with progressive political values and were frequently dismissed by social conservatives. For instance, for many conservative Christians, the chance that the HPV vaccine would encourage young women to become promiscuous overruled its potential capacity to prevent cervical cancer.

However, adolescent sexuality presents anomalies in the opinions expressed by culture warriors, making it a particularly important case to explore, as it complicates and expands our understanding of contemporary political divisions in the United States.[11] For example, while studies of the battle over sex education often pit secular advocates against the religious Right's abstinence movement, many churches and religious groups campaigned for comprehensive sexuality education.[12] The Unitarian Church, for example, was instrumental in the late 1990s in drumming up support from over 140 leaders of communities of faith in a stand against the abstinence movement. In the same period, religious leaders within the Black Church began to reverse their position on sex education and birth control, which had been formed in resistance to eugenic control of Black reproduction by the state, in the face of the growing culture wars in America. Socially conservative administrations, particularly those of Reagan and George W. Bush, have correctly been assigned responsibility for inspiring large-scale abstinence movements in the United States. However, it was Democratic president Bill Clinton who signed into law the 1996 welfare reform bill, which introduced some of the most stringent abstinence education regulations in U.S. history and used racist imagery to strip the welfare provisions available for unmarried teenage mothers. Similarly, feminist positions on girlhood sexuality have been extremely diverse over the period of this study. For example, antipornography feminists such as Catharine MacKinnon and Andrea Dworkin collaborated with members of the New Right's antiobscenity movement in the 1980s in an attempt to ban pornography, and in doing so contributed to the idea that young women were inherently victimized by porn.

Tracing the theme of girlhood sexualities through the history of the culture wars reveals new ideological divisions within the culture wars themselves. It reveals a new culture war altogether in regard to adolescent sexualities—one between adults from across the political spectrum in the cultural mainstream who prioritized the desire to delay girlhood sexual experience and adults who remained culturally underground in their acceptance of teenage sexuality and their support for teenagers' access to frank sexual information, and who would advocate for this in public, alongside teenagers themselves who constituted a large and increasingly visible part of this activism. The story of teenage girls in the culture wars reveals that the traditionally established battle lines were perhaps more mutable than we have previously believed.

Despite the range in beliefs about what sexual information or images teenage girls should have access to, most adults agreed in this period, at least publicly, that young people should postpone their first sexual experience as long as possible.[13] Admitting that sex in adolescence need not be harmful remained contentious throughout the period that this book explores: very few took this position publicly, and those who did were chastised.[14] Scholars of sexuality have long warned of the conservative consensus that has emerged in the culture wars over sexuality in the United States.[15] This book details the way that conversations about girlhood sexualities in particular helped create these ideological overlaps between conservatives and many liberals over the late twentieth and early twenty-first centuries.

There are many social, cultural, and emotional reasons why most adults, even those on the political left, did not state in public that adolescent sex could be healthy. One might be the potential of appearing predatory or opportunistic, especially for adult men or queer people.[16] For others, their own past experiences of sexual harm, pervasive in so many people's pasts, may have made them hesitant to speak freely on—or even imagine—the potential for pleasurable and safe sexual exploration in youth. Another reason that some adults who are progressive in other areas might express more socially conservative views about teenage sex is because of how central protective politics toward young white women have been for the political Right: many liberals in this story perform conservatism in the areas of sex education or reproductive rights for teenage girls as a political machination. However, beneath the hesitation of many liberals to advocate for adolescent sexual and reproductive rights lay a fear of sex in American society that was tightly bound with systemic racism and attendant classism; sexual exploration, teenage sex, and sex outside of marriage or with multiple partners before marriage all contained layers of historical connotations that blamed such practices on economic and moral decline and associated these practices with people of color and with poverty—specifically, with young, poor women of color.[17] These implications made it difficult for Black Americans and for other people of color in particular to speak publicly about their advocacy without being punished for it, and influenced the hesitation of white liberals who did not challenge the origins of sex negativity that underpinned their blanket encouragement of delayed sexual initiation.[18] Though the reasons why liberal adults might avoid advocating for teenagers' sexual exploration are multifarious, a cultural fear of sex is interlinked with the history of white supremacy in the United States and was recharged with meaning in the rise of the Right and the pervasive logic of neoliberalism from the 1970s onward. In the late twentieth and early twenty-first centuries, this meant that speaking frankly about the sexual health and well-being of young women remained a firmly underground agenda.[19] Queer adolescence was also rarely mentioned in policy debates over young women's reproductive and sexual health, concerns regarding adolescent promiscuity, or the sexual vulnerability of young women.[20]

The racialized nature of the fear of adolescent sexuality in modern U.S. history is a reminder that all ideas about gender and sexuality are formed through ideas about race.[21] In the context of political debates over adolescent women, the New Right's backlash to the postwar-era civil rights movement was rooted in white conservatives' response to desegregation, in which they alleged that Black children would sexually corrupt their "innocent" white children should they be educated or play in the same spaces.[22] This fear would infuse all of the ensuing reactive politics over the sexual behavior of young people during the course of the late twentieth century. Racialized ideas about adolescent girls that combined racist fears about childhood sexual development with misogyny in the interest of pro-family politics were one manifestation of this reaction. Evidence of these beliefs was not, however, found solely in the rhetoric of the Right. Often, when white liberal adults spoke of protecting young women from sexual harm during this period, the imagined young woman in question was also often white, middle class, straight, and sexually "pure."[23]

Assumptions about race as it intersects with class also abounded in the policy conversations that feature in this book. In much of the discourse from the New Right, whiteness is conflated with a middle-class background. A white, middle-class, and straight girlhood emerged in this era as a pivotal gendered foundation to the future of the American family model that religious, social, and economic conservatives alike wished to preserve. Simultaneously, these were all too often the defining features of the young women that many liberal writers, politicians, and organizers put at the center of their advocacy. The teenage pregnancy panic itself—propagated by conservatives and liberals alike—arose in the 1980s primarily because it was young white women who were having sex earlier and becoming pregnant in higher numbers.[24] While much of the discourse on teenage girls in the culture wars revealed ideas about white and Black Americans to be bubbling just under the surface of the conversation, the diverse range of ethnicities present in the modern United States was rarely acknowledged.

Though young women of color faced immense sexualized racism throughout the period that this book covers, adolescent activists have consistently fought back against such discourses. Some contemporary narratives associate youth antiracist and feminist activism with the opportunities presented by today's social media platforms, and many popular accounts focus on the most visible, white, middle-class young women in the feminisms that emerged in the 1990s. In this book I point to the longer history of grassroots organizing, led by young people of color, that confronted the racism and sexism implicit in the culture wars that they were growing up in, including that which occurred "between the waves" of the women's movement as it has been traditionally historicized.[25] As Kimberly Springer writes in the pivotal essay "Third Wave Black Feminism?," "The wave model perpetuates the

exclusion of women of color from women's movement history and feminist theo-
rizing."[26] Despite the shortcomings of wave theory, however, Springer reminds us
that because "it is so deeply embedded in how we examine the history and future
of the women's movement, it remains useful for internal critique."[27] For this reason, I will cautiously use wave terminology to understand how women's movements
have developed in the United States, but I will continue the work of putting forward "new chronologies" of organizing around race and sexuality across and
between the waves.[28]

Public conversations about teenage female sexuality shifted over the three
decades that this book covers, from a discourse that subsumed debates about young
women's sex lives into other, less difficult topics to one that explicitly named adolescent sex as the topic under discussion. It was not always possible to acknowledge this subject matter in explicit terms, as the topic of sexuality in childhood
was so loaded to social and economic conservatives, and difficult for most adults
to discuss publicly, in the 1980s.[29] This was in part due to an ongoing backlash to
the social movements of the 1960s and 1970s; white children were frequently conjured by the Right as symbols of vulnerability to a changing society.[30] For many
progressive adults, who were aware of the politically incendiary nature of discussing young people's sexuality at this point in the culture wars, it was incredibly difficult to advocate explicitly for young people's reproductive and sexual rights in
public.[31] This was then amplified by the concurrent antipornography movement
and increased awareness of child sexual abuse that unfolded over the course of the
1980s. However, the impact of pro-sex feminisms, a gradual shift in sexual mores
in the wider culture, and the longer-term effects of sexual rhetoric surrounding
the scandal of Clinton's impeachment opened up a more explicit set of cultural conversations among adults about the appropriateness of sexual activity among young
people in the United States.[32] By the 2000s, the sex lives of young women were
explicitly named as a cause for concern by conservatives and liberals alike, and the
debate surrounding girls' behavior was entrenched as one of the central battles of
the culture wars.

THE LONGER STORY

By the presidential election of 1980, Americans were reeling. The previous two
decades had seen massive social upheaval, partly brought on by the movements
for civil rights, gay rights, and women's liberation. As a result of this progressive
activism, attitudes toward sex and relationships in the United States shifted substantially. Contraceptive options improved and were used more widely, sex and
childbearing outside of marriage increased, and nonreproductive sexuality and
homosexuality became more visible in public life.[33] But not everyone celebrated,
or even tolerated, these changes. Instead, from the 1960s onward, the United States
descended into a series of "culture wars" that reflected the nation's violently clash-
ing visions of what shape modern American society should take.[34] On one side were
proponents of the social movements that were demanding radical, revolutionary

change in America, and on the other were those who saw nothing wrong with what the United States had historically stood for, and felt fundamentally threatened by these movements.[35] Teenagers' behaviors, of course, were by no means the only topic up for debate. In the late twentieth century, battles raged over such a diverse range of topics as "abortion, affirmative action, art, censorship, evolution, family values, feminism, homosexuality, intelligence testing, media, multiculturalism, national history standards, pornography, school prayer, sex education, the Western canon," and more.[36]

Grasping at the exact periodization of the culture wars can be slippery.[37] When can we say that the culture wars "begin," when the nation's meaning and what it stands for have always been so consciously battled over?[38] I both take the term seriously and do not. It is true that the movements of the 1960s were unprecedented and led to uniquely charged battles in response to these movements, but it is also true that struggles for equality along the axes of race, gender, sexuality, class, religion, and other embodiments have always been a part of the story of the United States, and that they did not conveniently end in the new millennium. This book treats the culture wars as both the definitive period that historians have traditionally referred to and the consistent state of the American domestic scene. It begins by exploring how debates over girlhood sexuality intensified after the electoral success of the New Right in the 1980s and ends with a discussion of the presidency of George W. Bush, the period in which adolescent sexuality became the subject of so much national attention.

Though this particular story starts in the 1980s, it has a much longer history: racialized, sexualized girlhoods have always been constructed through moral-political battles in the nation's history.[39] White girlhood has been linked to narratives of vulnerability since the early American period, as white children's inability to consent owing to their "innocence" was written into early sexual consent laws.[40] At the same time, enslaved people, particularly enslaved women, were also denied the "capacity to consent" in early American lawmaking as they were seen by the law of the time not to have "reasonable will."[41] Later, enslaved people and white abolitionists drew attention to the pervasive sexual violence that white men subjected Black women to under slavery.[42] In the aftermath of the Civil War and Reconstruction, racist myths about Black sexuality were used to justify and reinforce racial segregation, as white journalists, politicians, and popular culture depicted Black men as violent and young white girls as victims.[43] This simultaneously denied young Black women the same vulnerability and perpetuated the ideas that they were promiscuous and that white men were entitled to their "sexual power" over all young women.[44]

Girlhood sexualities remained central to the construction of wider sexual mores in the United States in the ensuing decades. In the early twentieth century, societal fears about changing gender roles and immigration fed into debates about "girls' sexual delinquency."[45] The dating and consumer practices of teenage girls then became the focus of renewed public attention in the immediate postwar period.[46] In the same era, the earliest culture wars were about race, childhood, and sexuality.[47] As schools desegregated in the wake of *Brown v. Board of Education*, white southerners expressed a racist concern that their white daughters would be sexually corrupted through interacting with Black male children, and vocal anti-desegregationists were not the only ones to express this view.[48]

As the social movements of the 1960s unfolded, the culture wars that would rage across the late twentieth century took form. Sexuality became more public than ever.[49] As the Comstock Laws on decency that had been in place since the nineteenth century steadily loosened, sex outside of marriage became far more visible in film, television, literature, advertising, and porn.[50] Some white, middle-class youth benefited from the so-called sexual revolutions of this decade, as sex became increasingly distinct from reproduction in heterosexual dating practices.[51]

In the wake of these developments, many white, middle-class Americans amped up their promotion of traditional sexual morality and family structures.[52] One of the early conservative backlashes of the 1960s was against sex education. Though postwar comprehensive sex education programs had been adopted in schools across the country fairly easily at first, conservatives who were fighting to restore group prayer in public schools soon included the removal of sex education in their crusade, sparking a culture war that would continue for the rest of the twentieth century.[53] Additionally, while some forms of sex outside of marriage and some expressions of sexuality in the arts and in media were made possible in the 1960s, others were still very much punished—including homosexuality and any expression of Black sexuality.[54] This was exemplified by the publication in 1965 of the Moynihan Report, in which an assistant secretary in the Department of Labor, Daniel Moynihan, a Democrat, blamed family structures headed by young, single Black women for keeping African Americans from full equality in the age of civil rights.[55] By conflating Blackness and young motherhood in an attempt to scare white teenagers, Moynihan's report reified the beliefs of those who were fearful that white teenagers were having sex earlier.[56] Clearly, white young people and teenagers of color had vastly unequal access to sexual liberation in the 1960s. Women's access to the birth control pill in this era was also mitigated by race.[57] While the pill was liberating many white young women across the country, as Dorothy Roberts notes in *Killing the Black Body*, the same medical developments were used to continue a long history of controlling Black women's reproductive lives in "government-sponsored family planning programs" that "not only encouraged Black women to use birth control but coerced them into being sterilized."[58]

The culture wars over adolescent sexualities continued and gained pace in the 1970s. The explosion of women's rights and gay rights movements in the late 1960s continued into the 1970s, and reproductive rights were one of the main areas in which feminist groups gained ground, most notably with the success of *Roe v. Wade* in 1973.[59] These gains were unequal for white women and for women of color, and government-funded forced sterilization spiked in the 1970s. In the same year as *Roe*, two African American sisters from Montgomery, Alabama—Minnie Lee Relf, who was fourteen, and Mary Alice Relf, who was twelve—were forcibly sterilized after the Montgomery Community Action Agency told their mother they were going to have contraceptive injections, but they were instead sterilized.[60] Puerto Rican and Indigenous women were also subject to forced sterilizations in vast numbers over these decades.[61] Though many activists of color rallied against these racist programs, white feminist groups failed to mobilize quickly around this issue.[62]

In the 1970s, wider American society also became further sexualized, with pornography more available than ever before, and teenaged models increasingly featured in sexually graphic advertising.[63] In response to the increased visibility of sex in the mainstream, the conservative voices who opposed sex education in the 1960s and *Roe* in the early 1970s began to gain pace, form official groupings, and mobilize the electorate.[64] Anxiety over the impact of a sexualized society on white teenagers remained central to their politics. In the 1970s, many panicked over an "epidemic" of teenage pregnancies in the United States, reflecting new rates of sex outside of marriage and earlier sexual experiences among young Americans. Conservatives panicked, again, that this meant more sex among white teenagers. Social conservatives who had consistently pushed back against a more sexually open society were threatened by the gains for gay liberation, access to abortion, the availability of pornography, and the increased sexual habits of white teenagers and were outraged by the shape American life was taking.[65] Over the course of the 1970s, numerous groups of social and religious conservatives began to form under the rubric of a "New Right" in American politics. Organizations including the Conservative Caucus, the National Conservative Political Action Committee, and the Moral Majority were formed, and the Religious Roundtable united influential "television preachers" and conservative politicians.[66] In the late 1970s, these groups started to aggressively expand their memberships with an eye to the upcoming election, and opposing progressive social movements and a sexually open society was at the core of their recruitment.

Over the same period of time, the economic and political movement known as neoliberalism had also been rapidly gaining speed. In the late 1970s, the neoliberal movement saw banks and big businesses influence government spending, leading to cuts in spending on welfare in order to maximize profits and minimize taxes for corporations.[67] The wider New Right movement grew to include the university economists and big business leaders behind neoliberalism, and it became a many-pronged movement that catered to a number of conservative desires.[68] In this widespread backlash to changes in American social and sexual mores, opposing welfare funneled widely varied forms of conservatives, who used young predominantly Black and Latinx mothers as scapegoats to justify reorganizing government spending.[69]

If welfare was the issue that brought together the social and fiscal factions of this powerful New Right, then girlhood sexualities were at the center of conservative politics by the early 1980s. In this way, this book is in conversation with Laura Briggs's powerful argument in *How All Politics Became Reproductive Politics*. Briggs writes that the New Right framed those who were living in poverty as "responsible for their own poverty through their bad choices, involving that frequent object of horror in US society: rampant teenage sex. If all those slutty girls would just keep their legs shut, it insisted (however implausibly), there wouldn't be poverty in America."[70] I won't be explaining "how all politics actually became girlhood politics." Instead, I investigate the significance of those young people who were continually at the center of so many disparate political disputes. This book asks where and how the racialized images of sexuality in girlhood invoked here, at the start of the Reagan administration, traveled in the decades of culture wars that followed, and how these images were shaped by—and contributed to shaping—the social, cultural, and political discourse of the late twentieth and early twenty-first centuries.

Despite the fact that political and cultural battles over young women's sexual and reproductive lives started much earlier and were re-energized in the 1960s and 1970s, the story told in this book starts in the early 1980s. The New Right emerged over decades of discontent, but it was eventually legitimized through Reagan's election.[71] Conservative groups and individuals rallied consistently against a long list of issues including desegregation and the increasingly sexual public culture in the United States from the 1950s onward, and such political organizing escalated in response to the social movements of the 1960s and 1970s. However, it exploded into national politics via Ronald Reagan's presidential campaign in 1980. While Democratic incumbent Jimmy Carter, an evangelical Christian, had not taken the New Right movement seriously, Reagan rode the wave of their support for his moral and economic rhetoric straight to the White House.[72] On the campaign trail, Reagan garnered the New Right's support through a racist rhetorical focus on "welfare queens." Once he was in power, his policies and the grassroots socially conservative groups that he further enabled would continually focus on the sexual and reproductive choices of teenage girls in ways that built on this rhetoric. Covert political debates over adolescent sexuality continued throughout the 1980s but became a more explicit culture war over the decades of the late twentieth century, until discourse about purity and sexual agency was explicitly discussed—and representations of girlhood sexualities were everywhere in mainstream culture—by the early 2000s.[73] This book follows cultural and political debates from the moment in which teenage sex became unprecedentedly important to the changing tide of the national political scene, and from which point onward girlhood sexualities would become a significant battleground of the U.S. culture wars.

Conclusion

As the temporality of the culture wars is hard to grasp, so is that of "girlhood." The ethical, moral, and legal implications of regulating sexuality in adolescence, as opposed to childhood, have long been tricky for policymakers, cultural producers, and grassroots activists in American history. In *Sex and Harm in the Age of Consent*, Joseph Fischel makes the case for why we must be "attentive to differential distributions of vulnerability and autonomy" in the adolescent subject and in the child subject.[74] "What might it mean," he asks, "if we take seriously adolescence as that weird space-time between the fictions of the adult rational actor" and "the unknowing child?"[75] It is precisely the "weirdness" of adolescence that makes it important to understand as a part of modern American history. In this history of the culture wars, the terms I use throughout—"girlhood," "adolescence," "teenager," "youth," "young people"—are all used to imply different temporalities by the people speaking. Some mean just the specific "teenage" years of thirteen to nineteen, while others speak of a longer timeline. This book occasionally deals with histories of sexual and reproductive citizenship in the United States, in which teenagers' rights are enshrined at specific ages through age-of-consent laws, and in their access to abortion and birth control services or sexual information materials. In other moments in this book, teenagers of the same age are interpreted as vulnerable children by some and as agentic young adults by others. At other times still, "girl-hood" refers in the same breath to girls under ten and to women in their early thir-ties. This history tells the story of many different, sometimes conflicting, definitions of youth, which fluctuated depending on the politics and purpose of the speaker. It is also important to note the limitations of the term "girlhood." First, we should not assume that all the people affected by these discourses were cisgender.[76] As this book is excavating historical assumptions and beliefs about gendered difference, using the terminology that was being imbued with meaning at the time is a part of understanding how gender was constructed. However, when discussing the pre-sent, I opt to use more inclusive terminology.[77] As is the case for many contemporary historians, trans histories, activism, and scholarship have enabled my ability to cri-tique the way that essentialist and binary thinking constructed politicized girlhoods in the period that I depict in this book.[78]

This book is not exhaustive in its portrayal of political debates about adolescent sexuality in the late twentieth and early twenty-first centuries. I hope, however, that this book finds a place on the library shelves that contain global stories of young people's resistance to their politicized girlhoods, and that it inspires researchers and activists of all ages to keep expanding on these stories. It is my intention that the chapters that follow provide a context for understanding the histories and sup-porting the futures of young activists—and their critical antiracist and feminist work—today. The three decades that this story covers are divided into five chap-ters: two on the 1980s, two on the 1990s, and one on the 2000s. The first chapter examines the covert nature of discourse on teenage sex in the 1980s, particularly in political cultures. It explores the moral panic over the perceived spike in teen-age pregnancy rates in this period and the racism that infused this anxiety, and the Reagan administration's antiabortion efforts aimed at teenage girls. The sec-ond chapter looks in closer detail at the widely held idea in the 1980s that sexual speech constituted sexual action. In particular, it locates teenage girls in the con-current conversations around pornography and child sexual abuse, in conserva-tives' attacks on young adult fiction writers and on artists that used young women as subjects, and in the way that girlhood vulnerability and whiteness were con-flated in the rhetoric and imagery circulated in these debates. The third chapter is the first of two on the 1990s. It discusses the importance of sexuality within the so-called girl culture that emerged in this decade, from its queer, grassroots begin-nings, through the whiteness of how it was framed in popular culture, to its even-tual codification in the academy as "girl studies." The fourth chapter discusses the more explicit nature of political discourse on teenage sexuality from the 1990s onward and how this manifested in the Clinton administration, through the conversations surrounding Anita Hill, Dr. Joycelyn Elders, and Monica Lewinsky, through Clinton's extensive welfare reforms, and in the increasingly visible anti-racist and feminist activist efforts of teenagers themselves. The fifth and final chapter focuses on the hypervisibility of girlhood sexualities in the culture wars of the Bush administration, in battles over abstinence-only education, the HPV vaccine, and teen popular culture, and in youth activists' fight against the resurgence of conservatism in U.S. politics.

In "the struggle to define America," in which the progress made by civil rights, women's, and LGBTQ+ movements was attacked by the New Right's desire to reclaim American society and resurrect traditional gendered roles in private and in public, the sexual and reproductive behaviors of teenagers in the United States became invested with hope for the future of American society by adults across the political spectrum.[79] New divisions arose within these political struggles when debates turned to girlhood sexualities, and these political anomalies deserve greater attention. The unexpected political allegiances in the history of these debates suggest that the sides of the wider culture wars are not as straightforward as they might seem: the history of these moral-political debates must be re-examined in order to understand their persistence in the political landscape of the present. As the culture wars over adolescent sexual behavior became more explicit over time, it became increasingly clear how few adults, even those with otherwise liberal sexual politics, would outwardly support teenagers' access to sexual and reproductive health care and frank information about gender, sex, and sexuality.[80] The racism and classism that underlie the history of attitudes toward girlhood sexual behavior, in liberal as well as in explicitly conservative politics, persist today. Because adults in the United States still look at teenagers with hope and with fear, and still construct adolescence through race, gender, sexuality, and class to fit a myriad of political agendas, understanding this history is an important part of supporting the needs of young people in the culture wars of our present era.

CHAPTER 1

Teenage Girls and
the New Right

*In the age of just-say-no, as the focus of moral hysteria shifts from group to group—
AIDS sufferers, women who have abortions, pornographers, drug users—one target remains constant: sexually active teenagers. In the public mind, kids who have
sex are by definition "promiscuous."* —Ellen Willis, 1987

*Adolescence, as white people in this country appear to be beginning to remember—
in somewhat vindictive ways—is not the most tranquil passage in anybody's life.
It is a virgin time, the virgin time, the beginning of the confirmation of oneself as
other. Until adolescence, one is a boy or a girl. But adolescence means that one is
becoming male or female, a far more devastating and impenetrable prospect.*
  —James Baldwin, 1987

Teenage girls were propelled into the center of the American culture wars by the
New Right's economic and moral fixation on their sexual and reproductive habits.[1] A widespread social panic over a perceived swell in teenage pregnancy rates
brought national attention to young women's sexual behavior in the late 1970s,
but the revelation that the adolescent birthrate had in fact decreased brought no
comfort to social conservatives who were outraged at the new pervasiveness of
teenage sex. This was because the religious Right's ostensible reaction to the
increased sexual activity of teenage girls masked their actual concern over the
increased sexual activity of *white* teenage girls.[2]

The conservative fixation with the sexual and reproductive lives of teenagers
was born out of the Right's wider economic and political anxieties of the time. Ronald Reagan's presidential win in 1980 was celebrated by proponents of neoliberalism, an economic model that promoted privatization, an unfettered free market,
and the restriction of government spending on social programs.[3] For social and
religious conservatives, this ideology underscored their moral concerns about the
loss of traditional family structures in the wake of the revolutions of the 1960s, and
their belief that the government should not support such social shifts through welfare for single mothers, funding for sex education, or the endorsement of abortion.

It was in this historical and political moment that the sexual behavior of young people emerged as a focal point for the attendant "tensions and anxieties" of adults.[4] In their reactions to teenage pregnancy rates, social conservatives of the 1980s revealed their racialized and classed fear that promiscuity and nontraditional family structures would infiltrate white, middle-class America.[5] Their politics in the 1980s were reminiscent of the backlash against the desegregation of schools in the 1950s and the racist belief held by many white adults that Black male children would sexually corrupt their "innocent" white daughters if they studied or played together.[6]

Following the teenage pregnancy panic, young women's sexual lives would go on to become central to multiple ongoing culture war battles in the 1980s, including those over sex education, abortion, and parental control. Teenagers' sexual health and reproductive rights were also central to the work of progressive groups in this era, many of whom were concerned not only about teenage pregnancy rates but about the Right's response to them. At first glance, liberals and conservatives took the stances one might expect in these incendiary debates. However, a closer look at these conversations shows how the sexual and reproductive lives of teenage girls not only became the subject of various culture wars but also changed the shape of the culture wars. Conservatives and liberals sometimes showed surprising overlaps in this period in their support for certain measures.[7] This was evident in Reagan's ability to pass federal antiabortion legislation that affected those under the age of eighteen but not adult women: there was more support across the political spectrum when it came to controlling the reproductive lives of teenagers, whereas the wider abortion debate concerning adult women was more polarized.[8] Many of the debates over teenage girls' sexual behavior and subsequent policies in this era were highly coded. In this era, some ultraconservatives developed the position that the information relayed to young people through sex education was itself a form of sexual harm against them. This created an environment in which young women's sexualities had to be discussed tacitly through policy issues. This also impacted the liberal reaction to the rise in teenage pregnancies. A divide formed in the liberal response to teenage pregnancy rates in the 1980s, which meant that relatively few progressive sexual health advocates were willing to publicly advocate for teenagers, in the wake of the Right's covert crackdown on both teenage sex itself and talk about teenage sex.[9]

The Teenage Pregnancy "Epidemic" and Sex Education

Over the course of the late 1970s, a series of "widely publicized" surveys published by mainstream news sources revealed rates of drastically increasing teenage pregnancies in the United States, raising widespread alarm.[10] This concern permeated the halls of government, and in 1978 President Carter introduced the Adolescent Health, Services, and Pregnancy Prevention Act in an attempt to counter this trend.[11] Eager to uncover the reality of the crisis, the reproductive and sexual health research group the Guttmacher Institute published a report in 1984, *Teenage Pregnancy: The Problem That Hasn't Gone Away*, that substantiated the fears that had been circulating in the American public since the late 1970s: more than one in ten teenage girls were becoming pregnant each year, a total that had increased by 100,000 from 11 million in 1974.[12]

However, this report also sought to clarify some of the existing information on increasing teenage pregnancy rates that was being circulated by the federal government and by the press. Crucial to the Guttmacher Institute's findings was the revelation that the number of teenage women actually giving birth had in fact declined during the same period. "What is new and probably responsible for increasing public concern about the problem is its increased visibility," the report stated. "Fewer teenagers marry to legitimate out-of-wedlock pregnancies, more often choosing either to exercise their new option of legal abortion or to bear and keep their child outside of marriage."[13] What was accountable for increased teenage pregnancy rates was also revealed in these studies. "The increase in adolescent pregnancies stems largely from an increase in the number of teenagers who are sexually active," the report confirmed.[14]

It was this correlation, between the increased teenage pregnancies and the fact that teenagers were having more sex than ever before in American history, that was at the heart of the moral panic over teenage pregnancy in the 1980s, meaning that the decline in the adolescent birthrate was scant comfort for those in distress.[15] Evidence of the increased number of unmarried teenagers having sex was, for many, a tangible repercussion of the "revolution" in American sexual practices and social arrangements over the previous two decades.[16] Marie Winn, a *New York Times* journalist, expressed such anxieties in a 1981 op-ed. "The upheavals of the 1960s, television, family breakdown, youth protests and women's liberation have contributed to a generation of children whose worldliness has deprived many of their childhood," she wrote.[17] Socialist feminist organizer Ellen Willis, one of the few progressives willing to speak frankly about adolescent sex in this period, pointed out what she believed was riling the Right about teenage pregnancy rates. "The source of teen sex panic is not really teenage pregnancy," she argued in an essay for the feminist magazine *Ms.* in 1987. "A central aspect of the current panic is fear that if those liberal do-gooders have their way, pregnancy will no longer serve as a self-enforcing deterrent—or, failing that, punishment—for 'illicit' sex."[18] She continued by framing the panic as a crucial part of the Right's efforts to overturn the work of social movements in previous decades. "Whatever else the 1960s sexual revolution may or may not have accomplished, it destroyed the norm for (heterosexual) adults," she claimed. "Clearly, traditionalists' frustration and resentment at having lost this battle are being displaced with special vehemence onto teenagers."[19]

The desire of many conservatives to overturn the social movements of the 1960s and 1970s, and their impact on teenage sexual practices, was highly racialized. The teenage pregnancy panic revealed deeply embedded associations of early sex and reproduction with Blackness and with poverty.[20] Marie Winn's blaming of "the upheavals of the 1960s," her notion of "family breakdown," and her framing of childhood "worldliness" as opposed to childhood innocence exemplify the racism that underlined the reactionary stance on increased sex outside of marriage. Unmarried teenage motherhood was, for many white, middle-class Americans, seen as a societal problem perpetuated by low-income girls of color.[21] Such young women were frequently referred to as victims of circumstance, as "children having children," or as malicious and calculating "welfare queens" who purposefully became pregnant in order to live off the state.[22] Many Americans were increasingly "upset" by teenage pregnancy reaching "epidemic" proportions in the 1980s because of a crucial distinction disseminated in media coverage of the phenomenon: that rates of pregnancy had risen specifically among white teenagers.[23] In a 1981 *New York Times* article, the emphasis of the alarm was placed on the fact that "the increase was most dramatic among whites—especially those aged 15–17, whose rate of sexual activity doubled."[24] The conservative reaction to the reported increase in sexual activity among white, middle-class teenage girls shared its roots with the racist response to the desegregation of schools.[25] Charles Murray, a conservative sociologist and writer, was responsible for perpetuating these ideas in the early 1980s. He published a piece in the *Wall Street Journal* blaming welfare for encouraging the "spread" of the "Black problem" of teenage pregnancy to white girls.[26] In the same piece, he stated that "illegitimacy is the single most important social problem of our time," in that it drove "everything else."[27] Murray's response revealed that many white conservatives feared that the sexual practices they associated with Black, Latinx, and working-class teenagers were rubbing off on white, middle-class girls, and that they blamed these practices (and these teenagers) for causing widespread social problems.

The racialized reactions to teenage pregnancy rates drew a range of responses from African American women working in various contexts, who were deeply troubled by the framing of the crisis. In an article written for the liberal think tank the Family Impact Seminar in 1981, therapist and family counselor Dr. June Dobbs Butts berated American society's scapegoating of young Black women. "So, although teenage pregnancy is a fact of modern life, it is the black teenage mother who epitomizes the crux of the problem," she explained.[28] This, she noted, was similarly true of media depictions of young Latinx women.[29] Elsewhere, however, some Black women expressed shame and guilt over the intense visibility of their communities in the light of the teenage pregnancy "epidemic." "The problem of Black teenage pregnancy is *our* problem," insisted writer Peggy Taylor in an article for African American women's magazine *Essence* in 1985. "Whatever blame can be placed on the Reagan administration for the plight of many of us, it cannot be blamed for what goes on in the privacy of our bedrooms."[30] Taylor's frustration at her own community was echoed by the president of the National Council of Negro Women, Dorothy I. Height, in an article for *Ebony* magazine the same year. In "What Must Be Done about Children Having Children," Height named "the strong two-parent family" as African Americans' strongest "historical asset." "Our tradition of strong, extended families, more than anything else, has helped us cope with poverty and racism," she wrote. "Today we see families breaking down into smaller, poorer units with many young mothers living in isolation."[31] At the crux of these women's concerns about Black teenagers' pregnancies and single-parent families was their potential impact on the struggle for racial equality in the United States. "Think of the many middle-aged Black mothers who, instead of being able to channel their energies into the larger Black community must spend their mature years raising grandchildren," Taylor lamented in her article for *Essence*.[32]

For other antiracist organizers, the pregnancies themselves were less of a concern than the rolling back of services under Reagan's administration and the precarity that this caused for young people. Such activists were among those who dared to advocate for the sexual and reproductive well-being of teenagers in public, in the face of the increasingly restrictive political atmosphere.[33] Loretta Ross was one such organizer. An African American feminist and a lifelong activist across issues including tenants' rights, sexual violence, antiapartheid action, and reproductive rights, Ross was made the director of Women of Color Programs for the National Organization for Women (NOW) in 1985.[34] In a 1987 speech for Anti-Rape Week, Ross lamented "the loss of Medicaid funding for abortions through the Hyde Amendment, meaning that poor women lack access to abortion services; the miseducation of young people about sex, indicating the lack of sex education in the classrooms; the absence of school-based health clinics" and "a new initiative to improve children's health that's being opposed by the right wing."[35] Teenage pregnancy rates also concerned young people of color involved in the Washington, DC–based youth media collective Pyramid Communications International (PCI), an organization run by young people (predominantly young people of color) between the ages of four and twenty-five, in which they trained themselves in print, broadcast, and video programming.[36] Members of PCI as young as four hosted their own radio shows and used emergingly accessible video technologies to express their politics, a practice that AIDS activists in the same period were also undertaking. Troubled by the lack of structural support that led to the spike in teen pregnancies, children and teenagers involved in PCI organized their own "one day forum" in May 1986 called Teens Taking Charge, in order to brainstorm what it was that young people—particularly young women of color—needed to support their sexual and reproductive choices.[37] Adults were invited to the conference, but only if "accompanied by a teenager."[38] Echoing Loretta Ross, young people at the conference raised the issue of the importance of sex education as a way to "combat the epidemic teenage pregnancy rate."[39]

Though it was clear to many activists that sex education would give teenagers more agency in their sexual and reproductive lives, there was an ongoing culture war over what sexual information young people should receive that was becoming increasingly intense. In 1986, the director of the Sex Information and Education Council of the United States (SIECUS), Ann Welbourne-Moglia, noted that "with the possible exception of desegregation, no subject has aroused the passion that characterizes the debate on what schools should teach about sex education."[40] Welbourne-Moglia's comment, of course, also hinted at the racialized fear of youthful sexuality that underscored both the backlash to desegregation and the teenage pregnancy panic.[41] Over the course of the decade, the sex education issue assumed an increasingly central role within conservative organizations. It inspired the

attention of individuals and groups who had been politically active since the ascen-
dancy of the New Right, and gave rise to new groups.[42] This increased as liberals
called for better sex education in light of increasing teenage pregnancy rates.
Phyllis Schlafly, a notorious antifeminist conservative figurehead and the founder
of the Eagle Forum, wrote extensively on the evils of sex education. "The major
goal of nearly all sex education curricula in today's schools is to teach teenagers
(and sometimes children) how to enjoy fornication without having a baby and
without feeling guilty," she fumed in *Christian Life* magazine in 1982.[43] Another
faction of the Christian Right started to put forward a more extreme argument
against sex education, arguing not only that sex education encouraged immoral
premarital sex but that it was a form of sexual abuse in and of itself.[44] For instance,
such individuals accused the septuagenarian founder of SIECUS, Mary Calderone, of being a "raper and seducer of children in the classroom."[45] Increasingly,
protecting children and young people from sex education was viewed by the Far
Right as effectively protecting them from the harms of sexual abuse.

In this climate, there were also divides among progressives about how to approach
advocating for sex education as a response to rising teenage pregnancy rates. This
split proves that thinking about the culture wars as only between conservatives
and liberals does not provide a full picture of the tense political climate of this
period, and that these "sides" were not monolithic, particularly when it came to
navigating adolescent sexualities.[46] Some liberals were cautious of provoking the
ire of the New Right in their advocacy for sex education.[47] University of Pennsylvania sociologist Frank Furstenberg, for instance, described the efficacy of sex education in 1981 but acknowledged that it would be hard for traditionalists to swallow.
"There is the chance that some, thereby, may be encouraged to experiment with
sex somewhat earlier than they would have done otherwise," he admitted, "although
there is no evidence that provision of information about sexual decision-making
or contraception encourages teenagers to initiate sexual intercourse earlier than
they might have done without such information."[48]

While some liberals working in larger institutions were anxious about pushing
for wider sex education programs during the Reagan administration, grassroots
activists pushed forward with their own sex education programs in their communities. Unlike liberals contemplating governmental change, for these organizers,
accepting that teenagers had sex and being inclusive of those young people who
were pregnant or who already had children was not a problem. This included Loretta
Ross, who believed in "bringing reality to the debate."[49] Ross's activism was informed
by her own experience as a survivor of incest "by a distant relative," which led to
her having a child when she was fifteen. She lost a scholarship to study at Radcliffe
College as a result, though she would go on to study at the historically Black university Howard University instead.[50] The National Latina Health Organization
(NLHO), a bilingual English and Spanish organization formed in 1986 with the
needs of teenagers at its core, also took a realistic approach.[51] Another organization,
the National Council of La Raza (NCLR, now UnidosUS), supported sex education programs aimed at pregnancy prevention and those that were framed for

adolescent parents. These included the Centro de la Comunidad Unida / United Community Center's *Decisiones Para Jóvenes / Decisions for Youth*, which "focused solely on primary pregnancy prevention" and was circulated to youth via a "special collaboration with the Milwaukee school system." The NCLR also lauded the work of the Chicanos Por La Causa program *Via de Amistad* in Phoenix, Arizona, and the Guadalupe Center's *Westside Teenage Pregnancy Program* in Kansas City, Missouri, both of which focused their efforts on assisting teenage mothers "to complete their education and enhance their employment skills."[52] These programs show the resistance of many activists of color to the racialized government crackdown on both adolescent sex and sexual information in this era.

It was not only teenage pregnancy rates that drove progressives of all stripes to push for sex education in the 1980s. The impact of the emerging AIDS epidemic on young people, set against the backdrop of the New Right's campaign against sexual information, was of grave concern to advocates working inside and outside of government. In 1986, SIECUS director Ann Welbourne-Moglia expressed that in light of teenage pregnancy rates, the AIDS crisis, and the discussions in the media on "child sexual abuse, rape, pornography, and censorship," "never has the need for sex education been greater than now."[53] In 1987, Democrats in Congress formed a Select Committee on Children, Youth, and Families and released the report "A Generation in Jeopardy: Children and AIDS," recommending education on the use of condoms.[54] However, passing legislation to protect young people from HIV/AIDS was a formidable challenge in this era. HIV/AIDS, first known as GRID (gay-related immune deficiency) since it was initially discovered in communities of gay men, was allowed to escalate because of Reagan's negligence. Reagan even resisted acknowledging the disease publicly, let alone committing necessary funds and research to stop the spread of the disease or care for its sufferers.[55] The epidemiological timing of AIDS could not have been more cruel—for the New Right, it represented an act of "retribution from God" and a "gay plague" to stamp out the immoral and illicit activities of gay men following the liberation movements of the 1960s and 1970s.[56] The stigma and fear surrounding the AIDS crisis escalated the cultural chasm between underground sexual communities and those with already-policed sexual and reproductive lives—including LGBTQ+ people and young Black mothers on welfare—and the social and religious conservatives that formed the new Republican administration.[57] It is helpful to bear this embattled backdrop in mind in this history of attitudes toward adolescent sex in the 1980s: it was a climate in which the Far Right felt newly legitimized in their discrimination against historically marginalized sexualities, and in which many thousands of lives were lost as a result.[58] The use of the term "epidemic" to describe rates of teenage pregnancy in this sociopolitical context was therefore particularly loaded.

Alongside sex education, the teenage pregnancy "epidemic" also drew young women into a further incendiary battleground of the culture wars: the ongoing moral and political schism over abortion. "While abortion has served to conceal the growing sexual experience of teenagers, and to mitigate the potentially adverse effects of a rise in the adolescent birthrate, it has also drawn increased attention to

teenage sexuality," Frank Furstenberg worried in 1981. "In no small measure, opposition to abortion has forced attention to an issue that would previously have been
swept under the rug."[59] The panic over teenage pregnancy further revealed the racism of the New Right, as they were chiefly concerned with increased sexual activity among white teenagers. It also revealed diverging responses from liberals, in
their differing approaches to advocating for much-needed sex education. Meanwhile, the Reagan administration's ability to limit teenagers' access to abortions
while at the same time failing to curtail access for adult women proved that support for policing adolescent sex existed outside the bounds of the Republican Party
and the New Right movement.

ADOLESCENT WOMEN AND ANTIABORTION POLICY

There had been doubt among the Christian Right from the outset of Ronald Reagan's campaign that he could be an asset to the social and moral demands of their
movement. A former Hollywood actor, Reagan had signed the progressive Therapeutic Abortion Act as governor of California in 1967 and spoken out against the
1978 law designed to persecute gay teachers in his state, the Briggs Initiative.[60] Aware
of their mistrust of his legislative past, Reagan pointedly lent rhetorical support to
the Christian Right in their political agenda during his campaign, particularly on
the key issue of abortion.[61] It soon became clear, however, that not only did Reagan not have a personal investment in furthering the antiabortion movement from
the White House, but that he would actively avoid association with socio-moral
conservative groups and wedge issues, instead choosing to focus on neoliberal economic goals including taxation, cutting back on welfare, and Cold War foreign
policy—moral-political issues would have to fit within these neoliberal frameworks
in order to merit his attention.[62] Despite the symbolism of Reagan's electoral victory in 1980, it would not mean a wide-sweeping victory for the pro-life movement,
and women's access to abortion would not be substantively curtailed.[63] There was
an exception to this, however, when it came to teenage girls.

Through a series of legislative and legal developments over the course of the two
Reagan administrations, abortions became far harder to procure for women under
eighteen. This would therefore become one of the few battles of the culture wars
over abortion that the Christian Right could celebrate winning.[64] The ubiquity of
opinion on the need to regulate young women's sexual behavior in the wake of the
liberal social movements of the 1960s and 1970s, and these movements' impact on
teenage sexual activity and pregnancy rates, was such that this became the easiest
area in which to pass multiple restrictive policies and laws.[65] It provided antiabortion thinkers with strict and sometimes alienating views with a less controversial
platform, that of governing adolescent sexuality. Simultaneously, it became clear
in this decade that the majority of Americans wanted some access to abortion and
that the vocal Christian Right movement was matched by a powerful set of liberal
organizations and institutions that advocated for abortion rights.[66] However, where
proposed abortion regulations pertained to school-aged girls, such debates flattened

somewhat, making laws easier to pass. This was due to popular and deep-seated notions of "childhood sexual innocence" across the political spectrum in this period, the racialized implications behind the idea of preserving girls' innocence that were proliferating in New Right politics, and the difficulties liberals faced in advocating otherwise in the censorious atmosphere of the 1980s.[67]

From early in his presidency, Reagan demonstrated an understanding that racialized, classed fears of adolescent sexuality would mobilize support through his vocal opposition to welfare.[68] Doing so catered to the two major strands of the New Right: the social conservatives who believed harmful stereotypes about Black and poor young women on welfare, and the neoliberal thinkers who viewed this as an expedient economic move in that it limited government spending and promoted "personal responsibility."[69] Concern over the "epidemic" of teenage pregnancy in the United States was only one aspect of a wider uproar over the American "underclass," a term used by conservatives to describe those ostensibly living in an unending state of poverty and dependency on welfare.[70] American youth, and rates of pregnancy and drug use among them, were pivotal to these concerns. The First Lady, Nancy Reagan, engaged with the latter when she famously encouraged a group of school children in Oakland, California, in 1984 to "just say no" to drugs, a slogan that soon became synonymous with saying no to all aspects of permissive morality.[71] Reagan himself reacted to the former by vocally dismissing Nixon- and Carter-era welfare provisions under Title X family planning, which offered some assistance to single teenage mothers, lambasting the imagined character of the young, pregnant, African American "welfare queen" on benefits in a 1976 campaign speech and introducing welfare cuts in the 1981 budget that allowed states to implement new work-centered measures.[72] These supposedly "colorblind" initiatives in fact continued the long history of policing the sexuality of young women of color, following on from the forced sterilization of Black, Puerto Rican, and Indigenous girls that had peaked in the decade preceding the Reagan administration.[73] Reagan's initiatives did this while not explicitly naming race: this kind of coded racism and sexism would soon become characteristic of policymaking in his administration.

The centrality of adolescent sexuality to New Right policymaking was extended exponentially with the signing of the Adolescent Family Life Act (AFLA) in 1981, a rare advancement of antiabortion legislation that would give the Christian Right a sense of moving in the right direction.[74] Two religious conservative senators, Jeremiah Denton (R-AL) and Orrin Hatch (R-UT), were the major forces behind the introduction and writing of AFLA. They promoted the act as a corrective to the existing Title X family planning, which they disdainfully called a "safe-sex program for unmarried adolescents."[75] AFLA was the first piece of federal legislation to promote teaching young people abstinence from sex until marriage in place of contraceptive education, by offering federal funding to public schools that wished to bring in such a program. The act posited such education as a preventive solution to the perceived rise in teenage pregnancies and to the need for abortion. The passage of AFLA is also significant in that the president, so notably hesitant in putting his weight behind abortion policy, supported the bill—such was the political

concern for white adolescent women's increased sexual activity on the right. Crucially, the antiabortion motives of the bill were highly obscured. Though its aim
was to reduce the number of abortions performed in America, abortion was not
explicitly named in the act. The act was primarily devised to "(1) . . . find effective
means, within the context of the family, of reaching adolescents before they become
sexually active in order to maximize the guidance and support available to adolescents from parents and other family members, and to promote self-discipline
and other prudent approaches to the problem of adolescent sexual relations, including teenage pregnancy; (2) to promote adoption as an alternative for adolescent
parents."[76]

In these coded words, the text of AFLA conveyed the moral stance of its creators, Senators Denton and Hatch, on both abortion and the appropriateness of
sex before marriage. Their proposed approach to reducing teenage pregnancy rates
was prevention in the first instance, and adoption as an emergency measure in the
case of an unwanted pregnancy, both of which asserted an opposition to abortion
as an option for young people. Focusing only on the issue of teenage pregnancy
also ensured that, while maintaining gender-neutral language, the act emphasized
the sexual activity of teenage girls. Though disapproving of abortion does not necessarily denote a disapproval of teenage sexual activity altogether, for the writers
of AFLA, pregnancy prevention would not include increased access to birth control or comprehensive sexual education. Denton and Hatch's decision not to advocate for these approaches to preventing teenage pregnancy was emblematic of a
newly compounded cultural conservatism in this period. Before the formation of
an extensive Christian Right in national politics in the late 1970s and early 1980s,
it had not been uncommon for conservative antiabortion legislators to also support the need for increased access to birth control, "so as to make abortion unnecessary."[77] After the groundswell in their organizing activity around the election of
Reagan, however, such a position among conservatives vanished, and the antiabortion and pro-abstinence positions became synonymous, despite the efficacy of birth
control in preventing pregnancy.[78] This was characteristic of the sacred nature of
human sexuality to religious conservatives, who were newly dominant on the right
by the 1980s, and their reactionary response to increased sexual freedom resulting from the social movements of the 1960s and 1970s.[79]

AFLA's expression of core values of the New Right in coded language was symp-
tomatic of the Reagan administration's approach to policing adolescent sexuality.
This fit within conservative politicians' desires to limit explicit speech about sexuality and reflected Reagan's knowledge of the heightened culture wars over sexuality at this time and his wish to avoid becoming embroiled in them. Though AFLA
had at its core the desire to limit abortions among teenage women, this was to
become evident more in the discussion of the act in subsequent platforms as opposed
to within the text of the act itself, thus making it less contentious for Reagan to
put his name to. He celebrated AFLA as a source of personal pride in his essay for
the *Human Life Review* in 1983, "Abortion and the Conscience of a Nation."[80] In
the article, he praised AFLA for allowing "new opportunities for unwed mothers

to give their children life."[81] However, while the Christian Right were pleased with his uncharacteristic show of support for their movement through the publishing of this piece, it still allowed Reagan to keep a tactical distance, in that it did not require him to appear in person and be photographed with the "crazier" pro-life activists.[82] In press coverage of AFLA, Reagan's staff were also hesitant to explicitly name the act as an antiabortion policy, thus setting themselves apart from the socio-moral contingent of the Senate who pioneered such policy. One member of his administration, speaking anonymously to the *New York Times* in 1982, defined the act as having "an interest in helping teen-agers place babies for adoption" and not necessarily "having implications for the debate over abortion."[83] In the same article, Donald Underwood, grants management officer of the Office of Adolescent Pregnancy Programs, was reticent to herald the policy as a victory for the pro-life movement. Instead, he also urged the public to see the new program as one that "will emphasize counselling about adoption as an alternative to abortion." When pressed, he admitted, "Probably none of our money could be used for abortion counselling. Abortion would definitely not be encouraged."[84] By emphasizing the implications of the bill for pregnant teenagers and avoiding the discussions of abortion, the issue of teenage pregnancy was seen by Reagan and his staff as one with a much more unified base of concern than the incendiary issue of abortion, owing to the interest in tackling teenage pregnancy rates from across the political spectrum in this period of intense cultural debate.

Though they were aware of the ongoing controversy of debates over abortion, conservatives in Reagan's administration soon learned that the other major component of AFLA, abstinence education, would also require some tact in the climate of the culture wars. The act that was initially proposed became known derisively among Democrats in Congress and sexual health advocates outside the government as the "teen chastity program" because of the original wording of the policy, which stated that the primary purpose of the act was "to promote self-discipline and chastity, and other positive, family-centered approaches to the problems of adolescent promiscuity," and then later went on to define "promiscuity" as meaning any sexual activity outside of wedlock.[85] Because the wording caused an uproar with members of Congress and adolescent sexual health organizations, the text was reworded to the more ambiguous aim: "to promote self-discipline and other prudent approaches to the problem of adolescent sexual relations, including teenage pregnancy."[86] A closer examination of who protested the inclusion of the word "chastity" is illuminating: the shared vexation of many members of the clergy, sexual health advocates such as Planned Parenthood and the Guttmacher Institute, and Democrats in Congress depicts a moment of consensus in opposition to conservative socio-moral policy.[87] Such maneuvering and editing viscerally demonstrates the way that the culture wars were at play in Congress. Though putting forward an abstinence bill was less controversial than other outright abortion policies put forward in the Reagan administration because it dealt with teenage girls, there was a moralistic tone that still bothered more progressive groups and individuals. Though the inherent intent and meaning behind the act remained the same, the rewording allowed for Christian Right members of Congress such as Denton and Hatch to put forward a very socially conservative idea of what they considered inappropriate sexual behavior among young women.

Planned Parenthood and other such advocacy groups protested the act because they believed that teaching abstinence to young adults in the place of contraception education put young people in unnecessary danger. They were also wary of the influence of the Christian Right within the Reagan administration. In 1981, the same year that AFLA was passed into law, Planned Parenthood was subject to a series of government audits on its use of funds, launched by Senators Denton and Hatch, that accused it of using federal money to "promote abortion as a means of birth control."[88] This infuriated Faye Wattleton, who in 1978 had been made the youngest and first African American president of Planned Parenthood. She saw these audits as "an abuse of the power and machinery of Government by people philosophically opposed to abortion."[89] Wattleton was also highly aware of the ways in which the New Right government tried to enact laws that curtailed the sexual citizenship of teenage girls and punished African American young women in particular. It was her work with teenage mothers in the 1960s that led Wattleton, originally trained as a nurse, to realize the urgency of allowing teenagers access to sex education, birth control, and abortion services and made her change direction on her lifelong calling to work as a missionary nurse in Africa and instead focus on a career in health policy in the United States.[90] In the early 1980s, as president of Planned Parenthood, she was all too aware that, along with poor women, "teenagers" were majorly "vulnerable to the assault of the opposition" that had taken over "*both* the House and the Senate in the 1980 elections" and was beginning to be expressed in policy like AFLA.[91]

Despite this initial contestation of the language of the act, AFLA would go on to further multiple points of the Christian Right's political agenda in addition to discouraging abortion. One such area was that of abstinence-only sex education. The federal funding attached to AFLA was offered to schools that chose to teach abstinence from sex until marriage in place of educating students about safe sex, including contraception. This meant that in order for a school to receive any federal funding to teach its students sex education, it must only teach students the virtues of sexual abstinence until marriage.[92] By 1985, this funding had been distributed not only to interested school districts but to new organizations that were developing abstinence-only curricula to "compete" with that of comprehensive sex education advocates such as SIECUS.[93] Kathleen M. Sullivan, the founder of one such organization, named Project Reality, started her group because of her concern "for all children . . . who might be negatively affected by so called 'comprehensive' sex education which many times advocated sexual activity among teens."[94] AFLA therefore led to a substantive change in the nature of federal funding for sex education. However, the quantity of funding available and the ambiguity of the language of what was to be taught allowed a certain amount of room for maneuver from schools that received this funding. Later federal abstinence policies such as that contained in the Clinton administration's welfare reform bill were far more explicit in what was to be taught and put forward a far larger sum of money for this task, raising AFLA's $4 million of annual funds to $50 million, which led to a much wider use of abstinence materials in schools in the 1990s.[95]

The potential threat of white teenage girls' sexual activity outside of marriage to the strength of the American family unit was also implied by the writers of AFLA. Written into the bill was the proposal that education about sexuality should ideally take place in the home. In this way, the site of the discussion was seen to reinforce the family-first substance of the conversation. "Services encouraged by the Federal Government should promote the involvement of parents with their adolescent children, and should emphasize the provision of support by other family members, religious and charitable organizations," it read.[96] The text of the act even suggested a particular family model that inherently encouraged the reproduction of that style of unit—namely, one headed by a set of married, heterosexual parents. The inverse of this suggestion was that pregnant teenagers were a societal problem not just in the governmental care they would require as young mothers but also in the subversive family unit that that mother and baby then formed. Many historians have over the past few decades charted the way that historical efforts to instate "family values" through welfare have inevitably chastised low-income families, particularly in communities of color.[97] AFLA's endorsement of one specific kind of family unit implicitly derided family units that did not conform to that model: in particular, families headed by a young, Black, unmarried mother.[98] Such young women have consistently found themselves subject to federal intervention and condescension, which was particularly exacerbated by President Lyndon B. Johnson's assistant secretary of labor Daniel Patrick Moynihan, a Democrat, through the publication of his damning report, *The Negro Family: The Case for National Action*, in 1965.[99] The Moynihanian methods of the Right in the 1980s led Black feminist theorist Hortense Spillers to pen the essay "Mama's Baby, Papa's Maybe" for *Diacritics* in 1987. In it, she laid out the ways that Moynihan specifically made social problems in America "the fault of the Daughter, or the female line" in Black communities, and how, according to his report, "those persons living according to the perceived 'matriarchal' pattern are, therefore, caught in a state of social 'pathology.'"[100] Spillers called the discourse around welfare that was reinvigorated in the late twentieth century a symptom of a much older, deeply entrenched "American grammar" surrounding Blackness and gender that was formed through the violence of colonialism, the middle passage, and slavery in the United States.[101]

AFLA's pro-family politics therefore continued this historical scapegoating of sexually active Black teenage girls for a long list of social woes, blaming them for perpetually raising children without fathers. "In a high proportion of cases," the opening statement of AFLA reads, "the pregnant adolescent is herself the product of an unmarried parenthood during adolescence and is continuing the pattern in her own lifestyle."[102] Though race is not explicitly mentioned in AFLA as it was in Moynihan's report almost twenty years earlier, the utterance of the single-parent family signaled the same ideology. AFLA stoked the fears of such a "pattern" influencing the sexual, reproductive, and marital practices of white young people, which was at the core of early culture wars over desegregation in the 1960s and which was resurfacing amid the rise of the New Right. Here, the unspeakable nature of adolescent sex for conservatives in the 1980s also allowed such policy language to insinuate racialized meaning in an already coded and covert discussion of adolescent women's sexual practices. By chiding the low-income young women and families for whom Title X family planning funding was originally intended when it was written in 1970, AFLA constituted a significant refiguring of federal public health provision and set a precedent for future welfare reform that would continue to punish young women of color for their sexual and reproductive choices. It also suggests why Reagan was able to put his name to this act over other pro-family, antiabortion policies, in that it had implications for welfare and thus the economy, a priority of his from the outset. It therefore did not alienate his neoliberal, economic conservative base who were less concerned with the moral implications of teenage sex. The disproportionate social attention to white young women's increased sexual activity in this historical moment meant that the pro-life movement was able to carry through antiabortion legislation pertaining to teenagers while failing to substantially curtail abortion access for adult women.

Promoting Parental Control

In the years after the introduction of AFLA, white, married parents were implored by extra-governmental conservative thinkers to set an example for their teenage children. In the introduction to his pamphlet *What's Wrong with Sex Education*, the conservative doctor and writer Melvin Anchell dedicated the booklet to "decent people—loving people in our nation," who he believed "exemplify the life sustaining nature of human sexuality" by teaching their children through example "the wonder of sexually fulfilled man/woman monogamous love—the meaning of life itself."[103] Though Anchell's beliefs and writings fell on the extreme end of the scale when it came to recommending such an invasive role for parents in their teenagers' sex lives, they were representative of a branch of socially conservative pro-family activism that suggested a family-centric model of sex education with incestuous undertones, more recent examples of which include the "purity balls" wherein teenage girls take their own fathers as their dates.[104] Like the text of AFLA, Anchell's propaganda also suggested that, for young people, witnessing a successful heterosexual monogamous marriage would serve as a replacement for sex education.

As the 1980s progressed, parents of teenagers would play an increasingly important role in the Christian Right's attempts to control the sexual behaviors of young women and promote a heterosexual nuclear family model that was also imagined to be white. In 1985, Judie A. Brown, president of the American Life Lobby, stated in a speech that Title X funding had created "a lot of promiscuity" among adolescents, which had in turn "divorce[d] them from parental authority."[105] The suggestion that teenage girls had been newly "divorced" from parental control as a result of Title X implied that this policy, in supporting young low-income mothers predominantly from communities of color, had inadvertently also caused white teen-

TEENAGE GIRLS AND THE NEW RIGHT

age girls to become more sexually active.[106] By criticizing wider use of Title X services, Brown was implying that it was white teenagers' increased use of family planning services that really concerned her. Brown's statement also re-emphasized the role of the parent that was espoused in the Moynihan Report, which positioned a child's promiscuous sexual behavior and pregnancy before marriage as indicative of a substandard moral example set by the parents.[107]

AFLA had been seen by congressional conservatives as an attempt to control the problem of white teenagers behaving outside of parental control, and this effort was reified by a series of Supreme Court cases that expanded the rights of a parent to control their child's access to an abortion. Like AFLA, the escalation of parental notification and consent laws for minors' abortions during this period made adolescent sexuality the central issue in order to put forward antiabortion and pro-family legislation.[108] The three major cases that allowed states to require parental notification or consent from parents for minors' abortions were *H. L. v. Matheson* in 1981, *Planned Parenthood of Kansas City v. Ashcroft* in 1983, and *Planned Parenthood of S. E. Pennsylvania v. Casey* in 1992. These cases were preceded by *Bellotti v. Baird* in 1979, which struck down a Massachusetts statute that required parental consent for minors' abortions as unconstitutional.[109] These three cases, then, demonstrated an increasing acceptance in this period of young women as unable to make informed decisions about their sexual and reproductive health. That these were signed into law, over restrictions for abortions for adult women, shows how unifying restricting teenage sexual activity was for conservatives of all stripes and for some liberals.[110] Not all progressives blithely accepted the emergence of these laws, however. Faye Wattleton was appalled at this development in the curtailing of teenage girls' reproductive rights, reflecting on this development in 1996: "No one who was aware of the tragedies that befell women of all ages before *Roe*, when they were forced to face hospital review boards or turn to illegal means, should have been surprised that the same result would come of demanding that teenage girls disclose their illicit acts to their parents or face a court of law."[111]

The stringency of these Supreme Court decisions increased with each case, each one reinforcing the expectation that parents were responsible for their daughters' sexual behavior, and in turn that they should be able to refuse them the right to obtain an abortion. In 1981, *H. L. v. Matheson* upheld that requiring parental consent for a minor's abortion was unconstitutional but maintained that requiring the minor to notify their parent was not. The statute confirmed that a state could require "a physician to 'notify, if possible,' the parents or guardian of a minor upon whom an abortion is to be performed."[112] The court's chief justice Warren E. Berger delivered the decision, stating that the statute was not believed to be "unconstitutionally restricting a minor's right of privacy to obtain an abortion or enter into a doctor-patient relationship."[113] Maintaining "family integrity" was mentioned in the *Matheson* decision as an important rationalization in allowing states to introduce parental notification laws, corroborating the effectiveness of invoking girlhood sexualities in uniting antiabortion, pro-marriage, and antiwelfare sentiment during this period.[114] By 1983, the *Planned Parenthood of Kansas City v. Ashcroft* decision reflected the growing impact of pro-family politics at the national, federal level. Expanding the ability of states to require parental notification from *Matheson*, it ruled that a state wishing to require "parental consent or consent from the Juvenile Court for an abortion" was constitutional.[115] This was reinforced by the 1992 ruling in *Planned Parenthood of S.E. Pennsylvania v. Casey*, which upheld state parental consent laws as entirely constitutional. In the plurality opinion put forward by Supreme Court justices O'Connor, Kennedy, and Souter, the *Casey* decision reiterated the importance of such laws in fortifying the roles of both parents and children: "It is reasonably designed to further the State's important and legitimate interest in the welfare of its young citizens, whose immaturity, inexperience, and lack of judgement may sometimes impair their ability to exercise their rights wisely."[116]

This renewed focus on the parents' role in the sexual and reproductive decisions of their teenage children reached far wider than conservative lawmakers, demonstrating again the unexpected overlaps in culture wars debates over girlhood sexualities.[117] Faye Wattleton noted that parents' desire "to pretend" that they could still influence their teenage daughters' decisions was "part of the reason that most Americans, pro-choice and anti-choice alike" were "ambivalent about or in favor of parental consent laws."[118] Some culture war progressives argued that encouraging discussions about sex to occur more frequently between parents and their children could potentially help lower teenage pregnancy rates. In Kristin Moore and Martha Burt's 1982 study *Private Crisis, Public Cost*, they found that "intervention is easier and less costly earlier in the decision-making process," meaning "before pregnancy and within the family or local community, rather than after pregnancy or at the national level."[119] However, Moore and Burt's study differed from the claims of conservatives in that it positioned frank conversations in the home as being important *in addition* to sex education as school and did not see these two approaches as ideologically opposed. "Sex education in conjunction with contraceptive services and follow-up appears to be a particularly effective approach," they wrote.[120] This issue, like other matters of reproductive and sexual health, presented an anomaly in the traditions of classically conservative and liberal American thought, in that those on the right uncharacteristically mandated for more extensive government control, and those on the left found themselves advocating for less government involvement in private lives. Henry Waxman, the Democratic congressman for California, demonstrated this paradox in his comments on the parental notification laws in 1984. "Suddenly, the most private decisions are a public controversy," he complained.[121]

However, even those liberals who had been "ambivalent" about parental consent for abortion and who agreed that parents should be more involved with their teenagers' reproductive decisions drew a line when the most stringent parental notification was suggested, and which subsequently failed to pass into law.[122] In 1983, members of Reagan's administration put forward a "squeal rule" that would have forced all medical professionals to notify parents whenever their unmarried minors sought contraceptive services or advice from medical professionals. The proposed

law sparked outrage. The policy was struck down in the same year that it was written, in the case *State of New York v. Heckler*. In delivering the decision, the presiding judge Henry F. Werker determined that it was unviable because "the deterrent
effect of the regulations will cause increased adolescent pregnancies" that were
"fraught with dangers to the health of both the young mother and her child."[123] In
their support for the squeal rule, social conservatives within the Reagan administration again demonstrated that at the core of their concern over the rate of teenage pregnancy was not the medical danger of childbirth before full physical
development but rather the racist association of childbearing out of wedlock with
Blackness and poverty, and a desire to better allow white parents to control the
sexual lives of their adolescent children in order to ensure that they would re-create
nuclear, heterosexual families such as their own.[124]

Beyond the belief that this policy would actually serve to increase the number
of teenage pregnancies, opponents saw the potential for the squeal rule to harm
those most in need of government-funded sexual health services.[125] Kathleen
Carscallen, director of the Buffalo General Hospital Family Planning Program,
noted that the desire of conservatives to "bring the teen and parent back together
again" was redundant in family planning, as "a good number of young women
already involve their parents," and that the squeal rule would therefore "hit those
most in need of confidential services, those from troubled homes."[126] Faye Wattleton even claimed that if the squeal rule were to pass, her organization would "look
for other ways to fund the programs" so that they would not have to comply in
alerting parents of young people who sought help from them.[127] Many doctors also
found themselves opposing the squeal rule and supporting the rights of teenage
girls to privacy, even when they disagreed with the sexual conduct of the young
women in question; this was due to an increasing move toward confidentiality
within the medical profession.[128] As information and misinformation about the
AIDS virus spread, this trend of conservative medical practitioners making excep-
tions to their beliefs in order to ensure medical safety was widespread. This trend
was even demonstrated by the surgeon general of the Reagan administration, the
antiabortion Christian conservative C. Everett Koop, who would stand his ground
in resistance to those on the Christian right who stood in the way of providing
information to teenagers. Though his proposed sex education plan was blocked in
Congress, he insisted that education about sex, though from a conservative moral
standpoint of course, was medically prudent in the age of AIDS.[129]

Despite their many efforts, antiabortion activists were only able to celebrate
minor policy successes in this decade.[130] Ronald Reagan, despite the backing of the
Christian Right during his election, was hesitant to align himself with niche social
and moral movements among his support base, preferring instead to leave his legacy as president in the realm of economic affairs and global relations and align himself more with the neoliberal fiscal movement that made up the other major faction
that contributed to his rise to power. For this reason, it is hugely significant that those
"small legislative victories" for the Christian Right, the policies and laws that gained
enough momentum and support from within the administration and that Reagan

chose to endorse publicly, were abortion laws that pertained to the sexual lives of teenage girls, as it shows their presumption that even many liberal adults would not object to attempts to discourage teenage sex.[131]

The teenage pregnancy "epidemic" of the 1980s brought girlhood sexualities into the center of the culture wars. The New Right's response showed that their real concern was the increased sexual activity of white teenage girls, and that discouraging and punishing sexualities, reproductive choices, and family models that they associated with Black and Latinx teenagers were key to both economic and social conservatives' political objectives.[132] Liberals split over how to respond: many were unwilling or unable to advocate publicly for the realities of teenage girls' sexual lives in a political climate wherein sexual speech was so policed.[133] In this period, the sexuality of children and adolescents was highly taboo in public discourse, meaning rates of pregnancy and abortion stood in for more explicit conversations about adolescent sexual practices. This covert approach to discussions of teenage sex was underscored by a desire among the pro-family movement to limit young women's access to sexual speech or information, a cause that over the course of the 1980s spilled over from a debate about formal sex education to one over the literature that young people were exposed to in public and school libraries, and advertising and artworks that depicted teenage girl subjects. Alongside the policy debates discussed in this chapter, the 1980s "obscenity wars" would make innocence in adolescence even more closely associated with whiteness and would proliferate even more unusual political collaborations, the kind that frequently arose in the culture wars when girlhood sexualities were under discussion.[134]

CHAPTER 2

Women and Children?

SEXUAL SPEECH AND SEXUAL HARM

The idea that "sexual speech enacts an emotionally abusive type of sex" was pervasive in the 1980s.[1] Many Christian Right groups reacted to increased rates of teenage sexual activity in the 1980s by placing blame on the exposure of young people to sexual information in comprehensive sex education. Beliefs such as Anchell's were underpinned by an increasing nationwide concern over rates of child sexual abuse in this decade, including a "satanic panic" over ritual child sexual abuse.[2] However, the significance of Anchell's sentiment extended far past the Right, and to much broader issues than that of sex education. Young adult literature, artworks depicting teenage girls, and music, television, and magazines with an adolescent audience all came under intense scrutiny and censorship in the 1980s as conservative groups and the federal government cracked down on teenagers' access to "obscene" materials.

A highly organized antipornography faction of the American women's movement joined forces with government officials dedicated to banning obscenity in American culture. This unlikely alliance was characteristic of the way that debates over adolescent sexuality blurred the traditional lines of the culture wars.[3] The "performativity of sexual speech" was central to these discourses—despite coming from very different ideological traditions, these politically disparate groups were united by a commitment to the idea that sexual speech and imagery could constitute sexual harm, especially when young people were depicted.[4] So pervasive was the conversation about protecting children from sexual harm in U.S. society that advocating for teenagers' rights to access sexual information became almost impossible to do publicly, especially given the context of social panic over the teenage pregnancy "epidemic."[5] This could be seen in the way that adolescence was frequently subsumed into childhood in antipornography activism, as teenagers sat complicatedly between the notions of "women" and "children" that these feminists conjured in debates.[6] This further entrenched the covert nature of debates over adolescent sexuality during this period. In the face of this, so-called pro-sex feminists opposed the work of antipornography feminists and pointedly centered teenage girls in their organizing. A "sex war" ensued between these factions of the American women's movement, with teenage girls at the center of many of the battles. A further culture war emerged out of these mixed feminist responses to sexual violence, in which a mainstream stance, made up of adults across the political spectrum, dissuaded all forms of talk about teenage sex, and candid discussions about the diverse sexual experiences of teenage girls were pushed underground.

The collaboration of antipornography feminists with antiobscenity conservatives made childhood innocence further synonymous with whiteness in public conversations about "women and children" and sexual harm.[7] The children alluded to in obscenity war debates were often white: for instance, young adult novels that were banned in the 1980s centered mostly on the narratives of young white women with new levels of sexual freedom. For social conservatives who held racist associations of promiscuity with Black and Latinx teenage girls, books by Judy Blume and her ilk were dangerous, and white teenage readers were vulnerable to being negatively influenced by these texts. At other times, the racial neutrality of the teenage girls described in obscenity debates was often revealed to signal whiteness. In this decade, mainstream media coverage of the social debates over pornography, child sexual abuse, and depictions of girlhood sexuality in American culture continued to focus on protecting white teenage girls. This made it even more plain that it was white young women that conservatives—and some liberals—were predominantly concerned about protecting from the shifting sexual culture of the late twentieth century.[8]

BANNING JUDY BLUME

The genre known as young adult (YA) literature had only come to be a "publishing phenomenon" as late as the 1960s and 1970s, and within this a subgenre of so-called problem novels quickly emerged.[9] These were most often aimed at young women and focused on "a teenager with a problem—divorce, drugs, alcohol—or problems associated with social life, sexual experience, and physical development."[10] By the early 1980s, writers such as Judy Blume and Norma Klein, who wrote frank, relatable, and often gritty fiction on the trials of puberty, started to gain recognition for their literary contributions.[11] However, just as quickly as their novels came to be accepted by many as worthwhile literature for young people, others began efforts to have such works removed from bookshop and library shelves and kept away from young eyes.

Conservative culture warriors of the 1980s were concerned not only with the impact of formal sex education on the sexual behaviors of the young. Their anxiety— and their action—extended to all forms of sexual information and imagery that teenagers might access. This resulted in a "wave of censorship" over the course of the decade that targeted, in particular, authors of YA fiction.[12] Writers whose work dealt with themes of adolescent sexuality immediately noticed the impact of Reagan's election on antiobscenity conservatives. "Almost overnight, following the Presidential election of 1980, the censors crawled out of the woodwork, organized and determined," recalled Judy Blume, one of the authors whose coming-of-age narratives would come under the most scrutiny.[13] It was around this time that signs of a growing conservative focus on YA fiction began to emerge. In Missouri in 1980, a family destroyed their library cards "to protest the presence of (Judy Blume's) *Forever*" on its shelves, and Blume's novel *Blubber* was "pulled from school libraries in Maryland and Arizona."[14]

Blume was aware of which theme in her novels most commonly set off alarm bells for censors: adolescent sexuality. "The reasons given are always the same," she explained. "Language, sexuality (which means anything to do with puberty) and something called 'lack of moral tone' which I think means, evil sometimes goes unpunished."[15] In 1981, *New York Times* writer Colin Campbell penned a special report on the frenzy of YA book banning taking place across the nation. In it, he described how limiting teenagers' access to sexual information was central to the censors' moral agenda, listing book banners' most common complaints as "vulgarity" or "descriptions of sexual behavior," followed by "depictions of unorthodox family arrangements, sexual explicitness even in a biological context, speculations about Christ, unflattering portraits of American authority, criticisms of business or corporate practices, and radical political ideas."[16] A group of anti-"no-God" books' campaigners were interviewed in the *Pittsburgh Post-Gazette* in 1981. "They occasionally have words as 'damn' or 'b-tch' or 'rat face.' They don't teach home values," claimed one. In the same article, Mel Gabler, the prodigious Texan campaigner against immorality in public school textbooks and cofounder of the Christian Right organization the Gabler Family, added that it troubled him how divorce appeared as "acceptable and natural" in these books.[17] "The problem with realism is it is realistic to only a few children but teaches all children unhappiness," he proclaimed.[18] It was not only descriptions of sex itself but descriptions of reproductive and familial practices outside of heterosexual, nuclear families that conservative censors thought would influence or harm the young white children they were fighting to protect.

Judith F. Krug, the director of the American Library Association's Office of Intellectual Freedom, was at the forefront of liberal efforts to counter the censorship of YA literature. She witnessed the ways that the censorship campaigns were intrinsic to the political organizing undertaken by national conservative organizations that gained ground in the lead-up to Reagan's election. "The same factors that led to the increase in censorship also led to the election of Reagan," Krug noted.[19] Many of the major New Right groups rallied around this cause. Jerry Falwell, "on behalf of the Moral Majority," signed a letter stating their opposition to YA fiction such as Blume's.[20] Other prominent national conservative groups, including the Heritage Foundation, Phyllis Schlafly's Eagle Forum, the Pro-Family Forum, and the Gabler Family (an organization that "analyzes textbooks"), reached out to conservative thinkers on school boards, in libraries, and in bookshops, encouraging them to pay more attention to what children and teenagers were reading.[21]

In addition to the censorship efforts launched by national conservative organizations, many of the disputes over YA fiction were "of local origin."[22] A local case in Peoria, Illinois, in 1984 caught the attention of the national press and mobilized further action on both sides of the battle over sexual information—for authors of fiction that treated teenage sex with frankness and honesty, it would provide a clear-cut answer to the age-old question: Will it play in Peoria? In November of that year, trustees of the school district of Peoria, Illinois, voted to ban three novels by Judy Blume—*Blubber, Deenie,* and *Then Again, Maybe I Won't*—from the city's public school libraries, "on the ground that the books' strong language and sexual content were inappropriate for children under thirteen who might gain access to them."[23] Parent and Peoria resident Bruce Dunn defended the decision. "It's not as if we're taking all the Judy Blume books and putting them in a bonfire," he said, before commenting that the books were still "available in city bookstores."[24] In this way, those banning the books were keen to assert that they were merely expressing a natural concern for the well-being of the children in their community, and that they were not advocating for total censorship in a way that would impinge on the First Amendment right to freedom of speech, or that which echoed McCarthy-era book burning. However, this decision proved to be far more divisive than Peoria School Board members initially assumed. In the same month that the ban was announced, Judy Blume arrived in Chicago to receive the Carl Sandburg Freedom to Read Award from the Friends of the Chicago Public Library. This juxtaposition of values within the same state brought the incident in Peoria to national attention. In the wake of the outrage that followed the discovery of what had happened to Blume's books in Peoria, the case was reviewed the following month, and the books were returned to the shelves.[25]

However, not all attempts at book banning were as public as the Peoria case, which often made it hard for those fighting against censorship to interrupt these efforts. In a guide for English literature teachers written by education scholars Alleen Pace Nilsen and Kenneth L. Donelson, they outlined the challenges teachers might face in tracking and reversing the censorship of young people's reading materials. "Most censorship episodes do not result in legal hearings and court decisions," they warned, continuing by explaining that such censors "almost never operate under any definitions of obscenity that a court would recognize."[26] In 1993, Judy Blume spoke at the conference "The Sex Panic: Women, Censorship, and Pornography" at the Graduate Center at the City University of New York (CUNY), an important event for feminists fighting against conservative censorship in its various forms in that period. In her speech, she told the assembled crowd that she had "lost track of how many incidents there have been involving [her] books since 1980—hundreds, probably thousands."[27] She gave examples in her talk of an unofficial censorship system, wherein concerned individuals in positions of control over libraries and curricula could simply remove a book without needing to have their decision appraised by any other authority or through a group decision. She recalled giving three copies of her 1970 coming-of-age novel *Are You There God? It's Me, Margaret* to her son's elementary school, then later realizing that they had "never reached the shelves" as "the male principal decided on his own that they were inappropriate for elementary school readers because of the discussion of menstruation."[28] "Never mind that many fifth and sixth grade girls already had their periods," she added.[29]

In her speech at "The Sex Panic" conference, Blume also discussed the amplified alarm that was raised among censors when the adolescent sexuality depicted in her novels was that of a young girl: "There was the young librarian who was told by the male principal at her school that *Deenie* was unsuitable for young readers because in the book Deenie masturbates. *It would be different if it was a boy*, he'd said. . . . I told her that I wrote those scenes right out of my own childhood experiences. . . . She listened, wide-eyed, and then she said, 'Could I tell my principal that Judy Blume masturbated when she was twelve?' I said, 'Sure, why not?'"[30] Blume elaborated that "masturbation is the ultimate taboo in kids' books," particularly if the subject is a girl. Blume's most upsetting experience of censorship was when she was forced to censor herself. In a meeting with her editor before the 1981 publication of *Tiger Eyes*, which tells the story of a teenager grieving the death of her father, she made the difficult decision to remove a scene wherein the main character, Davey, "allows herself to *feel* again after months of numbness following her father's death." "I saw that a few lines alluding to masturbation had been circled," Blume recalled. "The scene was psychologically sound, he assured me. . . . But it also spelt trouble. Everyone is too scared. The political climate has changed."[31] The political climate in which Blume was experiencing a new crackdown on her work was the same in which the New Right movement, bolstered by a new Republican president, panicked over teenage pregnancy rates, adolescent access to abortion, and the advent of AIDS. Using these flashpoints, strict moral conservatives were able to pathologize marginalized sexualities with renewed fervor and support. Though Blume did explore the issue of racism in her work, most of the main characters in her YA novels were white teenage girls, who were those that morally conservative culture warriors were committed to protecting from increased sexual experience, which they associated with gay men and with Black and Latinx teenage girls. Protecting teenagers from sexual speech, whether through sex education or sexual themes in YA literature, was a part of how such conservatives sought to limit the sexual activity of white teenage girls in this era.[32]

Norma Klein was another successful author of YA fiction whose books were consistently banned in this period for their depictions of sexually active teenage girls. In 1983, one of Klein's most frequently protested novels, *Breaking Up*, was "banned in Salem, Oregon."[33] During this period, Klein received a letter from a parent listing the reasons the novel was found to be inappropriate for young readers:

1. Girl dates without asking her parents' permission. She is 15.
2. Girl gives a strange man her phone number
3. Mother of girl says it's good for her to read *Playgirl* magazine and view naked men's bodies
4. 15 year-old girl makes a big deal about how special it was that she "saved" herself for a boy she really loved. . . . I always thought girls were to save themselves for the man they married!
5. The author makes it seem as if it's perfectly okay that the girl lives with her gay mother and her lover.[34]

The letter's author was concerned about the loss of parental authority over young women's sexual behavior in ways that were similar to conservatives in federal government, who were writing this into law through the introduction of AFLA and parental consent and notification clauses. However, the complaints that Klein received from this concerned parent also reflected a number of the wider concerns moral conservatives had about changing sexual behaviors in the wake of the sexual revolution, including the audacity of young women's sexual empowerment and agency and the decreasing importance of heterosexual marriage or traditional gender roles to a younger generation. Reactionary voices such as the one above reflected a concern for the vulnerability of young women to the specter of strange adult men—one that would be revealed as reserved only for white girls as the decade wore on.[35]

Notably, many of these novels, which came under such contention in the 1980s, were first written and published in the 1970s, during the "brief moment" in American history wherein there appeared to be "few sexual constraints on sexually active girls."[36] Blume's and Klein's fiction often included themes that were central to Second Wave feminist activism, including abortion and birth control rights, women in education, and gender roles within families. The time of writing is also significant in the lack of negative outcomes the teenaged characters face in novels by Blume, Klein, and their peers, wherein "two nice kids, in love, have sexual intercourse and no one dies," a fact that incensed conservatives who saw such writing as irresponsible in the age of the teenage pregnancy "epidemic" and AIDS.[37] In both Blume's frequently censored novel *Forever* and Klein's *It's OK If You Don't Love Me*, the young male love interests are abandoned by their teenage girlfriends, the young female lead characters having lost interest or behaved in what censors might have understood as traditionally "masculine" ways. "I've gone out with boys I don't like very much out of sheer horniness," brags the bold protagonist of *It's OK If You Don't Love Me*.[38] In this way, Klein's fiction sought to reverse the narrative of "victimization" that was often seen in historical depictions of sexually active teenage girls in popular culture.[39] Finally, the characters written by these authors often were described as seeking out sex education and information, such as the central character Katherine in *Forever*, who talked through her contraceptive options with her grandmother. Their characters are described as having an almost utopian level of support from their families, teachers, and friends in their quests for sexual knowledge. However, much of the freedom the young women are afforded in these novels is due to their privileged backdrop of middle-class households in East Coast cities. For instance, *Forever*'s Katherine is able to take public transport into Manhattan in order to visit Planned Parenthood and obtain birth control on her own.[40] The world created by the writers of YA fiction in the context of 1970s social movements was thus one that galled social and religious conservatives of the 1980s.

Critics and censors' biggest concern regarding teenage women's literature was that the actions of the characters in the books would influence the behavior of young readers, an anxiety similar to that expressed by anti-sex-education campaigners in the same period. In 1989, Barbara Nosanchuk of Ithaca, New York, wrote a letter to the *New York Times* complaining about a positive review the newspaper had published of the emerging YA fiction writer Francesca Lia Block's "punk, young adult fairy tale," *Weetzie Bat*. "Is Weetzie Bat a good role model?" Nosanchuk asked doubtfully. "Scarcely," she retorted, "since in many respects friendship and sexuality are quite distorted."[41] She continued: "There are far better choices available for impressionable readers than this superficial novel."[42] Other such claims were more strongly worded. In Leesburg, Florida, in 1981, a Baptist minister launched a campaign to "purge school libraries of novels by Judy Blume," incensed that "some of the stories amount to a sexual 'how-to' lesson for young students."[43] The autonomy and rationality of young people were defended by many progressives, including the authors of *Literature for Today's Young Adults*, who criticized censors for having "limited faith in the ability of young adults to read and think."[44]

However, the conservative position on young people's access to "sexual speech" only hardened over the 1980s and developed in such a way that many conflated sexual speech with actual sexual harm.[45] This concept became a pervasive trend in 1980s social conservatism, and the censorship of sexually frank YA novels was only one part of a much larger cultural trend, particularly in efforts to protect children.[46] Conservative doctor Melvin Anchell was one of the main proponents of this idea in its earliest form, writing that "seduction is not limited to actual molestation," and that children "can be seduced" by "overexposure to sexual activities, including sex courses in the classroom."[47] This belief represented an extreme subset of the morally conservative faction of the New Right that were committed to protecting young women's sexual innocence. Phyllis Schlafly was among these numbers, and in a 1981 article titled "What's Wrong with Sex Education?" she contended that sexual information in textbooks and other sources "shred girls of their natural modesty" by "forcing them to discuss sexual acts, techniques, devices, and parts of the body."[48]

Censoring novels and textbooks in order to protect children and teenagers from sexual harm was also a major goal of some organizers in the New Right who were opposed to "secular humanism."[49] To these individuals, speaking about sex to minors was akin to forcing sex on them.[50] "Secular humanism" was a term used to describe the impact of progressive social movements of the 1960s and 1970s on the norms of sexuality in American culture. Conservatives fighting against these perceived evils believed that "faith" in secular humanism was espoused most commonly through school-based sex education.[51] By encouraging parents to be aware of what books their children were exposed to in school, they believed they could prevent exposure to such ideas. This was encouraged by religious educator and prominent pro-family, Christian Right leader Lottie Beth Hobbs in the 1981 pamphlet *Is Secular Humanism Molesting Your Child?* In her guide to secular humanism, Hobbs urged parents to "examine your child's library and textbooks for immoral, anti-family, and anti-American content." She continued: "Voice your views to the state school board, state legislators, governor, and U.S. Congressmen," compelling parents to further the movement against sexual information in schools.[52] Judy Blume noticed the emergence of "secular humanism" as a label for progressive views that were perceived to be dangerous in American society. "Thanks to

Jerry Falwell and his Moral Majority I went from being called a 'Communist' to being labelled a 'Secular Humanist,'" she wrote.[53] The numbers in which Blume's books were banned made her consistently one of the top five most censored authors in the United States, from the 1970s onward. For reactionary culture warriors of the 1980s, communism and "humanism" were interchangeable as bad influences on a younger generation's political and moral choices. The importance of Blume's writing to opponents of both was characteristic of how teenage girls arose in the politics of both contingents of the New Right: the religious conservatives who wished for a return to the social mores of an earlier decade, and the neoliberal thinkers who were ideologically opposed to socialism in the context of the Cold War.[54]

The authors of YA fiction fought back against censorship in its various forms, but the Right's highly mobilized response to discussions of adolescent sexuality in this era, particularly their emerging claims that sexual speech directed toward children constituted a form of sexual abuse, made it difficult for authors to directly defend their forthright depictions of girlhood sexual experience in the 1980s. There-fore, the significance of including sexual content in their books, and the impor-tance of young women being able to access these narratives, was not at the forefront of the authors' retorts to censors. Instead, they focused their anticensorship activ-ism on the breach of First Amendment rights. Both Judy Blume and Norma Klein became deeply involved as campaigners with the American Library Association's Office of Intellectual Freedom during this period. "I am horrified to see my own teenage daughters come of age at a time when the books to which they have access in libraries and schools are being scrutinized in a way we would deplore were it described as taking place in the Soviet Union," Klein stated.[55] Blume also noted that some feminists, whose work focused on what they saw as the necessary cen-soring of pornography that degraded women, berated these authors' activism, call-ing them "First Amendment Fundamentalists."[56] In the context of the conservative war on obscenity and the growing feminist war on pornography, authors of YA literature were forced to be covert in their activism and could not be outright advo-cates for teenage girls' sexual autonomy or their rights to sexual information until the battles had cooled down significantly.[57]

TEENAGE GIRLS IN THE SEX WARS

In the late 1970s, feminists in the United States became irretrievably divided over the issue of pornography. As Lisa Duggan and Nan Hunter write in their history of the sex wars, these battles were "no party and no joke."[58] Many feminists saw pornography as a harmful act of speech that should thus not be protected under the First Amendment. In reaction to the formation of such groups, a second group-ing emerged that considered itself "pro-sex" in its challenging of what they saw as antipornography feminists' repressive ideals. In very different ways, teenagers were central to the politics of both groups. For antipornography feminists and for con-servative antiobscenity campaigners in this era, "women and children" were framed as the central victims of the pornography industry and sexually graphic advertising campaigns. Antipornography feminists' concern for both women (via pornography) and children (via child sexual abuse) often deliberately obscured the intersection of these figures, the teenage girl.[59] The opposing group of feminists defined themselves as "pro-sex," as a statement of their belief that the antipornography position on sexual violence was in fact antisex. Pro-sex activists explicitly named teenage girls as those who would suffer the most from the obscuring of sexual information and from the belief that sexual speech and imagery were forms of sexual violence.

The sex wars themselves were mainly academic and activist in nature in the late 1970s, shifting to a national, political platform from 1983 onward.[60] From the earliest conversations about sexual violence and pornography, experiences of sexual harm in girlhood were connected to adult sexual inequality. The original writings and organizing that sparked the sex wars came from women in the New Left who had become "discontent with their subordination by male radicals."[61] Andrea Dworkin was one such woman. A radical feminist activist and writer, Dworkin went on to become a leading figure in the feminist antipornography movement and produced some of the most powerful polemics against women's oppression.[62] She was an instantly recognizable public figure, always seen in "her uniform of denim overalls and sneakers, militant and unmitigated by a single capitulation to feminine beauty standards."[63] When remembering the origins of her involvement in antipornography feminism, Dworkin recalled that she encountered socialist men who denied the existence of incest "under the rubric of free sexuality for children" and defended pornography as "liberated sexuality."[64] The realities of sexual trauma in the lives of women and children were therefore a formative part of anti-sexual violence and eventually antipornography feminisms in the late 1970s.

Many other feminist writers and thinkers mobilized against the persistence of rape and sexual abuse in various geographic contexts despite the gains made by women's movements, and young people were the focus of much of this initial organizing. Black feminist organizer Loretta Ross, active across many leftist social movements of this period, became drawn to the antirape movement because of her own experience of childhood sexual abuse.[65] Owing to the growing antirape feminist movement in the United States, rape crisis centers opened across the country over the course of the 1970s, and in 1979 Ross became executive director of the first rape crisis center in the world in Washington, DC, and the only woman of color director of such a center at that time.[66] As feminist conversations on sexual violence honed in on pornography, the sexual vulnerability of female children emerged as an underlying theme. Susan Brownmiller, a New York–based feminist activist and author, drew attention to the "remarkable number of accounts of childhood molestation and rape" that had emerged in literature "by and about" women, including Virginia Woolf, Billie Holiday, and Maya Angelou, in her 1975 publication *Against Our Will: Men, Women, and Rape*.[67] It soon became clear to feminists writing about rape and sexual abuse that the increasing prevalence of pornography in American cities, and the intensification of the violence depicted in such films and magazines, was at the heart of the perpetuation of male violence toward women and children.

In 1976, Women Against Violence in Pornography and the Media (WAVPM) formed in San Francisco and began to galvanize the link between sexual speech and action in their activism, developing the refrain that "pornography is the theory, and rape the practice."[68] In 1978, WAVPM held one of the first major conferences to address pornography's role in sexual violence against women and children, and published the speeches two years later in the anthology *Take Back the Night*. Vulnerable girlhoods threaded through these early expressions of antipornography thought. African American author and activist Alice Walker contributed an essay to the collection in the form of a fable, in which she outlined what she saw as a prototypical pornographic narrative of "a young blonde girl from Minnesota" who finds herself "far from home in New York," who Walker notes is "probably kidnapped."[69] In Walker's imagined scenario, the African American woman viewing such pornography cannot help but liken the woman in the porn film to "the young girl who, according to the *Times*, was seduced off a farm in Minnesota by a black pimp and turned out on 42nd street," and in turn finds it *"depressing."*[70] Walker's story describes historical, racist tropes perpetuated by both pornography and the news media in this era. It was also prescient in revealing that despite the critique of Black antipornography feminists, it was white young women's vulnerability to sexual harm that would eventually capture the attention of antiobscenity campaigners and the wider public in the Reagan administration.[71]

Despite an increasing focus on women and children, as opposed to adolescents, in the activism of antipornography feminists, teenage girls frequently arose as the focus of their campaigns against the mainstream media for creating and disseminating harmful imagery. Dworkin worked alongside Catharine MacKinnon, a feminist lawyer and legal scholar who began her contribution to antipornography feminism from within the academy, in collecting and documenting evidence of the news media's complicity in the sexual exploitation of young women.[72] Among their findings were sensationalist articles about "teen hookers" in publications like the *New York Post*, and obsessive tabloid coverage of the lives of teenage actresses Jodie Foster and Brooke Shields, whose appearances as teenage sex workers in *Taxi Driver* and *Pretty Baby*, respectively, drew criticism from adults across the political spectrum. Shields was also, during the early 1980s, the focus of much controversy owing to her appearance in a series of advertisements for Calvin Klein jeans, in which she was depicted seductively whispering to the camera, "I've got seven Calvins in my closet . . . and if they could talk, I'd be ruined."[73] Another ad that troubled antipornography feminists was one for Baby Love soap, which featured a five-year-old girl dressed up as Marilyn Monroe.[74] Despite the fact that teenage actresses, as well as child models, came up in their activism, antipornography feminists did not explore any differences between children and teenagers in their arguments. Instead, antipornography feminists "stuffed" teenage girls into childhood to suit their politics, as it would not serve the aims of those advocating for the protection of children on the basis of their sexual innocence to extend their concern to adolescent women, a slightly older group with potentially more sexual agency.[75]

Foster and Shields were thin, conventionally beautiful, white teenagers, embodying the kind of young womanhood that has historically been seen as vulnerable
and in need of protection from exploitation.[76] The vast media coverage of their sexual lives in this period indicated that it would be white young women's sexual exploitation that would concern the conservative antiobscenity movement when they
eventually collaborated with antipornography feminists. Black feminists who contributed to early antipornography activism, such as Tracey A. Gardner, acknowledged the specific ways that women of color in the United States and elsewhere
were particularly affected by sexual exploitation, and yet at the same time were omit-
ted from the dominant writing against pornography. "But doesn't she realize how
we're being hurt? If she'd only look at what they're doing to Black women too," Gardner wrote in her contribution to the antipornography *Take Back the Night* anthology in 1980.[77]

Both in writing at the time and in more recent criticism, the pornography wars
were understood to have occurred predominantly within the white women's movement.[78] Though the most visible, white antipornography feminists did discuss race
in their analysis, Black feminist scholars including Jennifer C. Nash and Angela P.
Harris have shown since that these feminists "mobilized claims about race to bol-
ster their arguments about the *gendered* harms of pornography."[79] Meanwhile, as
L. H. Stallings has detailed, Black antipornography feminists' writings showed "very
different concerns" from those of white antipornography feminists and focused
instead on "white supremacy and its construction of sexuality as a tool of power."[80]
Black feminists involved in antipornography feminism, such as spiritual teacher
and writer Luisah Teish, wrote that young Black women were at a particular dis-
advantage in such a cultural climate as their exploitation often did not happen as
visibly in mainstream Hollywood films or in the tabloids but in ways that were far
more systemic and widespread: "Facing the greatest degree of discrimination in
education, jobs, and federal aid, some poor Black women have been forced to the
streets."[81] Teish was joined by other major Black feminist thinkers, including Audre
Lorde, Alice Walker, Tracey Gardner, and Patricia Hill Collins, in their discussion
of the historical, eroticized racism that underscored Black women's treatment in
pornography.[82] However, despite this important body of thought on white supremacy and its impact on sexuality, white antipornography feminists would go on to
work with the Right in order to achieve their goals through policy, and in doing
so, the vulnerability of young white women would become increasingly central to
the society-wide panic over pornography.

As momentum gathered in the antipornography movement, there were political rumblings among other feminist and queer thinkers and activists who purported
that antiporn campaigns were not only antiporn but antisex. A further feminist
grouping started to form that labeled itself "pro-sex," and various organizations
began to form under this rubric. From the earliest stirrings of this retort to antiporn feminists, the discourse of the pro-sex camp acknowledged and centered the
liminal experience of the teenage girl that antipornography feminism often obscured

within the evocative rhetoric of "women and children" and challenged the notion of a childhood ideally absent of sexuality that this binary suggested. One of the first women to react to the increase in antipornography groups was Ellen Willis, the rock critic, journalist, and founding member of NYC socialist-feminist group Redstockings, whose "personal venn diagram" included "rock music, women's lib, and grand, deliberately non-Washington politics."[83] Willis was alarmed at the symbolic alignment of the arguments against pornography of WAVPM and the New York–based Women Against Pornography (WAP) with the New Right's position on obscenity and the regulation of images. She was disturbed by the ways that both groups cast experiences of sexuality in girlhood as always or only the result of assault, coercion, or a highly eroticized ideal created by advertisers.[84] In her early journalism on the subject, Willis distinguished between the sensationalist girlhoods depicted by a misogynist mainstream popular culture and a potential radical revisioning of erotic liberation: "This revolution, the erotic revolution, the real thing not Playboy bunnies, has to begin with children."[85] bell hooks, the Black feminist scholar and activist, also urged American feminists to move away from mere criticisms of "negative aspects of sexuality as it has been socially constructed in sexist society" and to actually "change the norms of sexuality."[86] Doing so, hooks believed, would "have many positive implications for women and men, especially teenagers who are at this historical moment most likely to be victimized by sexist sexual norms."[87]

Many pro-sex thinkers were concerned with the potential ramifications of the antipornography movement on teenagers' access to sexual information and the impact of this on existing race and class inequalities in the United States. In 1981, Gloria I. Joseph and Jill Lewis published *Common Differences: Conflicts in Black and White Feminist Perspectives*, in which Joseph detailed the importance of young Black women's "early childhood and adolescent upbringing" in their "sexual socialization."[88] Joseph saw the potential for sexual information to be further censored in the atmosphere of the 1980s as one that could have particularly dangerous consequences for Black teenage girls: "What is common and true in most homes is that regardless of whether or not sex is an open or discreet issue, Black women do not receive necessary and accurate information about sexual matters."[89] The Chicana lesbian feminist activist and writer Cherríe Moraga also described her own experience of adolescent sexuality as critical to her adult sexual politics in the conversation between Moraga and Amber Hollibaugh published in *Heresies* in 1984, "What We're Rolling Around in Bed With," which details the implications of the sex wars for lesbian feminists. For Moraga, this included the "particular pain" of growing up identifying "as a butch queer" and unrequited desire for another girl at age fourteen.[90] In closing, Moraga and Hollibaugh emphasize their concern that the mainstream of the feminist movement was not hearing the arguments of "working class and Third World women" and that these were particularly crucial in debates about sexuality "because we are the ones pregnant at 16 (and straight *and* lesbian), whose daughters get pregnant at 16, who get left by men without childcare, who are self-supporting lesbian mothers with no childcare, and who sign forms to have our tubes tied because we can't read English."[91] However, given the measures taken to repress sex education and information by conservative "family values" campaigners and the focus on the harm of sexual speech to women by white antipornography feminisms, those fighting to make the voices and sexual and reproductive experiences of marginalized teenagers heard faced increasing difficulty in this era.[92]

The difficulty facing those advocating for more extensive, frank discourse on teenage sex in the midst of the obscenity wars and the feminist sex wars became apparent at the Barnard Scholar and Feminist Conference of 1982. Held annually at the all-women's Barnard College in New York City, the conference that April chose as its theme "Women and Sexuality." From early on in the planning meetings for the conference, the pro-sex organizers hoped to include discussions in the event on the consequences of the sexuality debates for teenagers.[93] The way that mothers can pass fear about sex onto their daughters was raised in one particular meeting. "Mother is the voice of caution: 'stay inside, the world is dangerous, men will get you,'" they noted in the meeting's minutes. The organizers also wondered: "How is the mother/daughter dialogue being replayed in the anti-pornography movement?"[94] The conference planners hoped to bring together those in opposition to the antipornography position but did not wish to provoke antagonism between these factions, hence "sexuality" was chosen as a less incendiary theme than "pornography" for the event.[95] Nonetheless, antipornography groups caught wind of the event. They staged a protest outside of the conference, and a "coalition" of such groups including WAP, WAVPM, and New York Radical Feminists signed and delivered a letter of protest to the conference organizers, in which they reiterated the nature of their work: protecting "women and children." "Excluded from this conference are feminists who have developed the feminist analysis of sexual violence, who have organized a mass movement against pornography . . . and who have worked to end the sexual abuse of children," the letter read.[96] Despite the furor unfolding at the gates, the conference at Barnard's Morningside Heights campus went ahead. A number of conference speakers stressed that the sexual well-being of teenage girls was particularly at stake within the denial of their autonomy, and the conflation of adolescence with childhood, in the antipornography position.[97]

From 1983 to 1985, the pornography debates shifted irrevocably through their entrance into mainstream political culture. Via this move, teenagers became further obscured in the rhetoric of antipornography feminists. Instead, the sexual vulnerability of female childhood was centralized in the work of antipornography feminists as a result of their collaboration with members of the New Right, and white children would become increasingly prioritized in national conversations about vulnerability to sexual harm. In the fall of 1983, Catharine MacKinnon invited Andrea Dworkin to co-teach a seminar on pornography at the University of Minnesota Law School.[98] It was here that the two feminists forged their political bond—Dworkin contributing polemical rhetoric and grassroots activist experience, and MacKinnon bringing with her theoretical and legal knowledge, and years of teaching experience.[99] During this tenure, they fused and put forward their central idea that pornography was a harmful act of speech and thus a harmful action, one that constituted a civil rights abuse toward women and children. For them, it then followed that pornography should not be considered protected speech. "First Amendment logic has difficulty grasping harm that is not linearly caused in the 'John hit Mary' sense," wrote MacKinnon in her characteristically acerbic style.[100] This belief inadvertently echoed that of culture wars conservatives campaigning at the time to ban sex education in schools and in children's literature on the premise that sexually explicit speech directed toward young people was a form of child abuse. While MacKinnon and Dworkin would go on to collaborate with the Right in order to try to enact policy change, they disputed claims that their own politics were in any way conservative: in MacKinnon's early writing on the subject, for instance, she admonished lawmakers in the Reagan administration for their disproportionate attention to children over women.[101]

MacKinnon and Dworkin's alignment with the Right, however, quickly moved from theoretical to practical. It was while teaching the Minnesota Law School seminar in 1983 that they were employed by the city of Minneapolis to write a draft amendment to the Minneapolis Civil Rights Ordinance to address the creation of "adult-business zones" in the city.[102] They conducted a series of hearings in Minneapolis to provide evidence for their ordinance. Over these two days in December, MacKinnon and Dworkin took a number of statements that focused on the perceived interrelationship between pornography and child sexual abuse. Though MacKinnon, as described above, had once chastised Reagan-era lawmakers for their inability to care about the impact of pornography on adult women, the focus of the Minneapolis statements on either the "infantilizing of women" or the "Brooke Shields-ing of children" suggested that she and Dworkin were aware of the persuasive political power of childhood innocence in the age of the New Right's obscenity wars.[103] Charlotte Kasl, a private therapist, gave one such testimony. "It has been my experience that pornography is an integral part of sexual addiction, and sexual addiction is an integral part of child abuse," she stated.[104] The deliberate emphasis on female childhood in the Minneapolis hearings, framed in a way that would cater to conservative concerns for the safety of children over that of women, entrenched the omission of adolescence from the antipornography position.

The Minneapolis Ordinance passed, but the city mayor, Donald M. Fraser, a liberal Democrat who had worked toward human rights and women's issues in the 1960s and 1970s, immediately vetoed the law on constitutional grounds.[105] A further ordinance that MacKinnon and Dworkin worked on in Indianapolis passed briefly into law but was also quickly struck down as unconstitutional in *American Booksellers v. Hudnut*. The presiding judge Frank H. Easterbrook cited a critique of MacKinnon and Dworkin often used by pro-sex feminists, that the graphic descriptions of rape and child pornography given in the writings of antiporn feminists often did not differ substantially from the content of violent pornography designed to titillate.[106] Pro-sex feminists Carole Vance and Gayle Rubin, who had been key organizers of the Barnard Conference two years earlier, formed the Feminist Anti-Censorship Taskforce (FACT) in reaction to the ordinances and filed an amicus brief in support of the American Booksellers' case.[107] Through FACT and in other instances, pro-sex feminists formed their own unlikely coalitions with First Amendment groups to defend the freedom of sexual speech. One instance of this was the action over banned YA literature, such as the defense of Judy Blume's novels, though this collaboration also took unexpected turns, such as when pro-sex feminists aligned with editors of the men's magazine *Hustler* in 1988.[108] This presents one of the key problems with this unlikely culture war coalition: often, pro-sex feminist contributions to the fight for sexual liberation involved bolstering a version of sexual liberation that was designed by heterosexual men. The mainstreaming of feminist debates over pornography had meant serious political compromise on both sides of the battle.[109]

One of the largest compromises was antipornography feminists' decision to work towards the protection of young people alongside social conservatives in the New Right, who had consistently perpetuated the idea that it was white young women who were vulnerable to exploitation and harm and deserving of protection.[110] However, this is also a historical problem in white women's movements and occurs whenever ostensibly universal claims are made about women and children by white feminists. Black feminist and critical race theorist Patricia Hill Collins notes that "whites typically view themselves as being 'raceless', yet they perceive Blacks, Latinos, and indigenous peoples as having a 'race' or an ethnicity," and she observes a "racial continuum" between "White *individuals*" and "an intensely raced Black *group*."[111] In her influential writing on intersectionality, Kimberlé Crenshaw has also described the way that white feminists overlook the experiences of women of color when "*white* women speak for and as *women*."[112] This occurred within the antipornography movement through the frequent use of the universal language of "women and children." This, however, was not typical of MacKinnon's approach. In her earlier work toward the introduction of sexual harassment law, she acknowledged the leadership of Black women in such activism and considered how sexual violence specifically affected the lives of women of color.[113] However, working in coalition with conservatives in the Reagan era would inevitably mean excluding young women of color from discussions of vulnerability. Conservative frameworks of innocence were, and are, highly racialized, meaning that the vulnerable "universal" girlhoods evoked in antipornography arguments and policy would symbolize explicitly white girlhoods to social conservatives.[114]

The co-option of antipornography feminism by the antiobscenity Right was most evident in the 1985 Commission on Pornography, launched by Reagan's attorney general Edwin Meese. Antipornography feminist group WAP provided a list of twenty-eight witnesses to the commission, for which WAP received "a certificate of appreciation" from the U.S. Department of Justice.[115] The subsequent Meese Report, released in 1986, was over 900 pages in length. Despite MacKinnon and Dworkin's contributions to the report's research, their polemical feminist writings on porn had been pushed aside for a general endorsement of censorship and a specific focus on the influence of child pornography on child sexual abuse. Though teenagers were mostly missing from the discourse, as was standard within the antipornography position, they did get a small mention when the report discussed the age that many performers started to work as porn actors. The report included evidence given by a police officer who had "extensively investigated the production of commercial pornography." "They (the producers) are looking for models that look as young as possible," he stated. "They may use an eighteen-year-old model and dress her up to look like she is 15 . . . most whose age we have been able to gauge began their careers in their late teens."[116] Finally, as well as recommending the outright banning of "sexually explicit depictions" of "performers under the age of twenty-one," the report recommended a move to critically examine non-pornographic materials, to "seriously consider how we can effectively discourage proliferation of these destructive messages which reach out to children on television, in theaters and even by way of their toys and comic books."[117] The Meese Report therefore reified the conservative and antipornography belief in sexual speech as not only an instigator of physical sexual harm but also as a form of sexual harm to children in and of itself. In the years immediately following the release of the report, many states keenly passed its recommended regulations pertaining to child pornography, which in many cases meant further cracking down on depictions of children and young people in art and media.

Pro-sex feminists were outraged that, in the climate of moral panic it engendered, the Meese Report effectively pushed sexual information further underground for teenagers.[118] They fought back through the publication of Caught Looking, which featured commentary and collages of pornographic images that the writers found empowering.[119] Pro-sex feminists who contributed to this collection highlighted the seeming encouragement of sexual "ignorance" in children that the Meese Commission implied was desirable, and linked this to their initial position that the antipornography movement punished desire and discredited the possibility of pleasure in adolescence. In Ellen Willis's contribution, she stated that in the conservative/antipornography feminist alliance, "teenagers were obvious targets" and would suffer the most from the ensuing impact on sex education.[120] Patrick Califia, a prominent member of the queer pro-sex movement on the West Coast and a writer of essays and sadomasochistic erotica, contributed an essay to Caught Looking that described his experience of growing up under such a culture.[121] "None of the adults I knew would talk to me about sex, beyond sketching the anatomy of reproduction," wrote Califia. "I needed to know much more than that, I needed to know about pleasure."[122] In a separate analysis, Califia also wrote that, during the commission hearings, "any sexually explicit material which adults might show to children to teach them about sex or seduce them into sexual activity was referred to as 'child porn,'" thus further silencing possibilities for sexual education of young people.[123] Califia also noticed the characteristic treatment of adolescents in the commission's conception of childhood. In the report, Califia noticed, "commissioners coined a new phrase—'children between the ages of 18 and 21'—who presumably need as much protection as prepubescents."[124] Young people had been "stuffed" back into childhood in the collaboration of antipornography feminists and the New Right, to sound as vulnerable as possible to the potential harm of sexual speech.[125]

Ultimately, the heat came out of the sex wars. The failure of MacKinnon and Dworkin's ordinances to pass into law and the widespread poor reception of the Meese Commission caused the wars to cool toward the end of the decade, at least in their 1980s iteration.[126] The alliance of antipornography feminists with the Christian Right and the Reagan administration had been a misguided gamble for the campaigners involved. Antipornography feminism started as the identification of girlhood as a time of unique vulnerability to sexual trauma, an idea that men on the left had belittled. Their position on pornography as a form of sexual speech that caused real sexual harm to women and children had led them to ill-advisedly collaborate with social conservatives who saw all sexual information as a form of sexual harm to children. The conservatives they had worked with relied heavily on the research, testimonies, and rhetoric of feminists to put forward their own goals. However, conservative policymakers failed to secure any of the demands of WAP, WAPVM, or other individual campaigners and ignored not only teenagers but also adult women in their work against porn.[127] As a product of their interactions with the New Right, antipornography feminists increasingly focused on protecting children and erased the specific needs of teenagers, which also ultimately centralized the protection of white children because of these conservative politicians' priorities. The desire to uphold the sexual innocence of white children—which had driven the earliest culture wars over desegregation—echoed throughout conservative approaches to "obscenity" in this era. Though this alliance was not a fruitful one for feminists, the overlap of their politics with conservative politics is a reminder of the flexible lines of the culture wars that are revealed in the history of debates over girlhood sexualities.[128]

AWARENESS OF CHILD SEXUAL ABUSE AND THE SPOTLIGHT ON SEXUAL SPEECH

The Meese Commission made it more necessary than ever for public debates over the sexual and reproductive well-being of teenage girls to happen as covertly as possible, and as a widespread concern over child sexual abuse transformed into an unsubstantiated frenzy over "satanic ritual abuse," the needs of children and young people in the United States were further obscured by moral panic.[129] The focus on child sexual abuse within the obscenity wars did not occur in a vacuum. Over the course of the 1980s, there was an unprecedented concern for child sexual abuse rates in the United States. The coexistence of the obscenity wars alongside and in relation to this society-wide conversation further compounded the fervor in which sexual imagery and speech that children might have access to was policed. While it was crucial that child sexual abuse was finally being taken seriously in medical and therapeutic circles, a side effect of the media treatment of this issue, however, was that adolescent sexual expression was suppressed by an overarching narrative of childhood victimhood, with little room for the distinction of teenagers as a legal and developmental category.[130] Many of the public conversations on this topic also entrenched the racialized and classed notions of what kinds of people were most often perpetrators, and which kinds of children and young people were vulnerable to abuse.

The link between the prevalence of child pornography and increased incidences of child sexual abuse across the nation was made from the earliest days of the pornography debates, in the late 1970s. In 1977, during a series of raids designed to "clean up Times Square" for the upcoming Democratic National Convention in 1980, police officers discovered that child pornography was easy to buy in the area.[131] The officers concerned made these findings public, and a "sudden concern with child pornography swept the national media."[132] Though the extent to which child pornography had become readily available was unmeasurable, the belief was widely held that "child pornography had become a highly organized, multimillion dollar industry," and was met with a "crusade"-like response.[133] Within weeks, in response to a national outcry, Congress passed the Protection of Children against Sexual Exploitation Act, "prohibiting the production and commercial distribution of obscene depictions of children younger than sixteen."[134] This sentiment was echoed in the courts in 1982 in the case of New York v. Ferber, which clarified that child pornography was not protected under First Amendment rights.[135] These statutes began the process of enshrining the sexual vulnerability of children in law and policy, which would continue throughout the decade. By the early 1980s, there was a renewed fear in adults across the political spectrum for the ways in which children and adolescents were vulnerable to sexual predation.[136] As in the concurrent obscenity debates of this era, adolescence was frequently collapsed into childhood in these discussions, and the children at the center of the media coverage of the problem were most often white.[137]

In the ensuing years, the media increasingly reported allegations of incest, pedophilia, and abuse committed by numerous celebrities, including Michael Jackson and Woody Allen.[138] Within this climate, the Catholic Church also started to face accusations of widespread sexual abuse of children.[139] Celebrities began to come forward with their own testimonies of surviving such abuse. In 1985, Oprah Winfrey opened up during an interview with a survivor of childhood sexual abuse on her eponymous talk show that she, too, had experienced that form of trauma. She would go on to become "an activist for all incest survivors."[140] Increasingly, therapies were developed that were aimed at uncovering abuse in people's pasts, and multiple guides for therapists and survivors were published.[141] Many aspects of this burgeoning industry provided support and empathy to those who were survivors of child sexual abuse. Over the course of the decade, however, media attention to cases of child sexual abuse increased, as did the sensationalism of what was being reported. The stories became increasingly large-scale and "entered the literary terrain of the gothic."[142] By the mid-1980s, the media concern over individual cases of missing children was supplanted by reports of mass sexual abuse, performed as a satanic ritual, in Sunday schools and daycare centers across the country. One major trial was that of Peggy Buckey, her son Ray, and six other adults at the McMartin preschool in Manhattan Beach, California, who in 1983 were accused of sexually abusing countless children as part of devil worship.[143] Though the case was eventually thrown out, the media coverage it received led to countless other increasingly dramatic cases across the country, producing widespread investigations and extensive media attention in a so-called satanic panic.[144] Media coverage of the satanic panic was often unnecessarily graphic in its descriptions of alleged child sexual abuse. As in the obscenity wars and the feminist battles over pornography, sexually graphic language was contrarily often used by those who alleged that providing sexual information to children and young people was itself a form of child sexual abuse.[145] This phenomenon is detailed in Foucault's *History of Sexuality*, in which he describes how the historical "tightening up of the rules of decorum likely did produce, as a countereffect, a valorization and intensification of indecent speech."[146] Within the ensuing panicked media atmosphere, meaningful cultural and policy debates over the sexual and reproductive health needs of adolescents were nearly impossible to have.

In the graphic news coverage of these stories, racialized and classed stereotypes of typical perpetrators of child abuse were constructed, and a media atmosphere developed that was increasingly hostile to those who might advocate for children's access to sexual information and education.[147] Nontraditional family models were blamed for perpetuating sexual harm, in ways that mirrored the blame that was also being placed on nonnuclear families for teenage pregnancy rates in this period. A journalist at the time, Richard Wexler, was concerned by this development and wrote that by scratching the surface of many narratives about childhood sexual abuse, a much larger problem of widespread poverty could be found. "The broad definitions of neglect used in most state statutes are virtually definitions of poverty," he noticed.[148] Much of the treatment of child sexual abuse in the media upheld a historical stereotype of impoverished families or nonnuclear families as typical perpetuators of such abuse and played on reactionary anxieties surrounding welfare recipients that the Reagan administration perpetuated over the course of the 1980s.[149] Even some critics of the national conversation on child sexual abuse perpetuated these stereotypes. Mary Pride, an evangelical writer, stated at the time that the newly heightened awareness of child sexual abuse was driving families apart, and that "what the child abuse industry fails to tell us is that *the vast majority of sexual abuse occurs in non-families or broken families.*" "We even have a profile of the typical perpetrator," she wrote: "Promiscuous, often remarried and even more often not married (ie., a live-in boyfriend), alcoholic, often with a criminal record, a heavy porn user. Hardly the picture of the traditional family."[150] By insisting that child sexual abuse only happened in divorced or single-parent families, and conflating a criminal record with the use of pornography, Pride was contributing to a portrait taking shape in American conservative discourse of what socioeconomic background and what kind of family would include abusive adults. These were, not coincidentally, the same families that social conservatives claimed were to blame for increased teenage sexual activity and pregnancy rates.

In this political atmosphere, engendered by both the feminist pornography wars and the increasing awareness of child sexual abuse, the appearance of underage women in pornographic films came under newly strict legislation.[151] One particularly public case was that involving the pornographic actress Traci Lords. In 1987, her agent and two producers were indicted for producing child pornography, when it emerged that the star of such films as *Sex Shoot, Lust in the Fast Lane*, and *Harlequin Affair*, was only sixteen at the time of their filming.[152] The publicity the trial received made campaigners against child pornography hopeful that it would serve as a deterrent to other pornographic filmmakers considering working with underage performers, or to ensure that more producers knew for certain the ages of their employees. "We hope that the message will go out loud and clear to the pornographic film industry that if they do use minors in their productions, they will be prosecuted to the full extent of the law," California U.S. attorney Robert C. Bonner told a press conference after the trial.[153]

Some antipornography and anti-child-abuse campaigners, however, did not limit the remit of their investigations to porn alone. In the years after the publication of the Meese Report, the work of visual and musical artists caught the attention of both feminist activists and conservative legislators and became highly scrutinized as potential forms of child pornography, and thus as potential forms of child abuse.[154] In 1981, social worker and antipornography feminist Florence Rush gave a speech on child pornography laws, urging Americans to cast their nets more widely in what they considered to be abusive sexual speech or imagery. "Child pornography is notorious for its ability to disguise itself (thinly or otherwise) as educational, artistic or, in the name of sexual freedom, as political," she warned.[155] New laws introduced as a result of the Meese Report's recommendations gave renewed power to those who wanted to crack down on "artistic" or "political" representations of young people that they viewed as child pornography. Some censorship took place in the local, individualized way that YA book censorship occurred, but in addition, a series of policies were introduced that restricted not only the kind of images that could be made of young people but also how they could be exhibited and distributed. For those antiobscenity and antipornography campaigners that viewed sexual speech as akin to sexual action, any images that explored childhood or adolescent sexuality were seen as tantamount to the sexual abuse of the subjects.[156]

The increase in censorship efforts in American culture was extensive. It was not restricted to outright pornography, textbooks, fiction, or images but extended to any material that could feasibly be obscene. This meant that those invested in these efforts were exhaustive in the material they scoured for possible indecency. In 1981, various conservative groups including the National Federation for Decency and the Moral Majority, along with "about four hundred other Christian organizations," came together to form the Coalition for Better Television.[157] Another prominent campaign was that of Mary Elizabeth "Tipper" Gore, wife of Senator Albert Gore (D-TN), who alongside multiple other wives of powerful Washingtonians started an organization under the name of the Parents' Music Resource Center (PMRC) in 1985.[158] Gore's complicity in the antiobscenity movement as an ostensibly socially liberal Democrat is indicative of the power of adolescent sexuality to trouble the lines of the culture wars as they have long been understood.[159]

The work of the PMRC often aligned with that of the antipornography movement, though there were some important distinctions. The group's main concern was with the lyrical content of popular music, particularly with a vaguely defined genre they referred to as "porn rock."[160] "Porn rock," according to Gore, included a wide variety of rock and pop performers such as Prince, AC/DC, Judas Priest, Great White, Dokken, and the female metal performer Wendy O. Williams.[161] What drew these disparate acts together, to Gore, was the overt sexuality of their lyrics and performances. Like the antipornography feminists such as Andrea Dworkin, and the rhetoric of the Meese Commission, Gore frequently reprinted the offending content under discussion, in a way that was sometimes seen as gratuitous or as producing a certain kind of pornography in and of itself.[162] However, unlike many in the antipornography movement, Gore drew particular attention to the category of "adolescence" within childhood, and to the plight of teenage women in particular. "Can anything be worse than being a teenage girl," Gore wondered, "having to cope with teenage boys who are psychologically primed to cut, slice, and shoot with their 'guns, knives, and swords'? Yes—being a teenage girl programmed to *accept* it."[163] In addition to porn rock, the group criticized other media culture consumed by teenage women, such as teen girls' magazines. "One teenybopper magazine presented its young readers with a Top Ten list rating the size of the genitals of certain male rock stars," wrote an appalled Tipper Gore.

The work of the PMRC echoed the socially conservative focus in this decade on including parents in adolescent sexual decision-making. Gore believed, for instance, that parents "have a right to know what their children are buying."[164] PMRC was successful in its campaign to make major record companies emblazon "obscene" records with a sticker reading "Parental Advisory: Explicit Content" by persuading the Senate Committee on Commerce to hold hearings on this issue.[165] Though Gore and the PMRC were mostly concerned with rock and pop in their campaign, and predominantly white recording artists, in practice the parental advisory stickers were often seen emblazoned on rap records by Black performers.[166] In 1989, the rapper Ice-T retaliated to Gore and the PMRC on the track "Freedom of Speech" by drawing attention to the fact that these stickers in fact validated the music as rebellious and helped to sell records.[167]

However, despite having similar motivations to those in the wider antipornography campaign, Gore and the PMRC did not align themselves with censorship efforts in this era. According to Gore, First Amendment rights to freedom of speech were at the core of their beliefs. Instead, Gore's goal for the PMRC was to encourage greater "corporate responsibility," wherein businesses took morals into consideration when creating and marketing products. Nonetheless, the case of Tipper Gore and the PMRC sheds light on the socially conservative values that have historically appeared in many liberal organizing efforts aimed at teenage girls.

As the antiobscenity movement gained pace over the course of the 1980s, important legal changes enabled their work. The precedent for antiobscenity law had been set in 1973 in *Miller v. California*, the Supreme Court case that created a "three prong" test for deducing whether materials could be deemed obscene. According to the "Miller test," a work had to lack "serious literary, artistic, political, or scientific value," "depict or describe" sex or bodily functions in a "patently offensive way," and consist of material that the "average person" would find "prurient" in order to be classified as obscene.[168] In 1982, however, this legal precedent was shifted in the Supreme Court case of *New York v. Ferber*. This case was brought by the State of New York against a bookseller found by an undercover police officer to be selling child pornography.[169] Because of the precedent set by *Miller* and its three-pronged approach to defining obscenity, existing New York laws against child pornography did not categorize the bookseller's material as obscene. The court concluded that when child pornography "bears so heavily and pervasively on the welfare of children engaged in its production," it "is permissible to consider these materials as without the protection of the First Amendment."[170] *Ferber*, therefore, allowed "greater leeway in the regulation of pornographic depictions of children" because of its "harmful" effects on the "physiological, emotional, and mental" health of the child subject.[171] Therefore, in the new precedent set by the *Ferber* decision, any depiction of a "sexual performance" by a child would not need to be subjected to the *Miller* test for obscenity.[172] *Ferber* would go on to have a major impact on the regulation of images of nude children. The case demonstrates that by the early 1980s, a greater sensitivity to the impact of sexual images of minors was already entering into public and legislative discourse.

The legal developments that followed the release of the Meese Report in 1986 further enabled antipornography campaigners to target and prosecute the creators of "obscene" materials, and as a result investigations into artists who worked with young models increased dramatically over the late 1980s and into the early 1990s. A central argument of the report was that "sexual imagery and sexual behavior are linked," and on this basis it called for "stricter regulation of the distribution and sale of erotic materials."[173] Its recommendations for the control of images of children resulted in two amendments to Title 18 of the U.S. Code—the Child Sexual Abuse and Pornography Act of 1986 and the Child Protection and Obscenity Act of 1988. The act of 1986 amended Title 18 with a more exhaustive list of the ways one could be criminalized for involvement in producing or distributing child pornography, including "to receive, exchange, buy, produce, display, distribute, or reproduce" such images.[174] The act of 1988 extended this list further to include emerging technologies such as distribution "by any means including by computer." The 1988 act also added a "warrant of seizure."[175] Artists who worked with nudes immediately worried about the implications of this bill, "arguing that such burdensome record-keeping provisions and severe forfeiture penalties would, in effect, ban constitutionally protected art books, photography, and motion pictures that have sexual content."[176] Both of the acts introduced in the wake of the Meese Report introduced strict new regulations for photographers and those working in art publishing and would have both an immediate and lasting impact on the careers of artists working during this period.[177]

The first high-profile investigation in the wake of these legal changes was that of Virginia-based artist Alice Sims, who was accused of "producing child pornography" after sending in film containing images of nude children to be processed at a local drugstore.[178] The photographs were part of a series titled "Water Babies," which featured nude images of her one-year-old daughter Ariel and a friend, superimposed onto photos of water lilies "to create arcadian scenes."[179] The photography lab "reported her, as required by new laws."[180] On 14 July 1988, her house was raided by police and other officials, "including US Postal Inspector Robert Northrup—who testified before the Meese Commission."[181] They "searched Sims house, carted away three bags of 'evidence' (her art), and removed her children, including the still-breast feeding daughter, to foster care."[182] If convicted of a felony charge for making "sexually explicit" material of children, she would have faced up to ten years in prison.[183] However, the children were returned to their parents the following day, and the case was eventually dropped by the state of Virginia.[184]

Though photographer Robert Mapplethorpe's black-and-white homoerotica and suggestive flower portraits were surrounded in controversy and censorship attempts over the course of his career, it was his images of children that raised alarm in June 1989. Along with over one hundred other members of Congress, Representative Richard Armey (R-TX) sent a letter to the National Endowment of Arts criticizing the use of public funds for an exhibition of such images at the University of Pennsylvania's Institute of Contemporary Art, titled *Robert Mapplethorpe: The Perfect Moment*, because of its inclusion of "several images depicting explicit homosexual acts or nude children."[185] Judith Reisman, the associate director of research for the American Family Association, a conservative fundamentalist Christian group, had been a committed campaigner against child pornography and exploitation, working alongside antipornography feminists such as Florence Rush, and was commissioned to conduct research for the Meese Commission.[186] Reisman argued that "in the midst of pandemic reports of child sexual abuse, the art community needs to ask itself why 'artistic' child pornography has too often been accepted."[187] In her protests against Mapplethorpe's images of children in *The Perfect Moment*, Reisman appropriated the writings of feminist photographer and theorist Susan Sontag, who argued in her landmark 1977 monograph *On Photography* that through consistent exposure to violence and suffering in photographic images, humans flatten such events in their imagination and therefore fail to respond adequately to the injustice depicted. Reisman's reference to Sontag was unexpected, given the two women's vastly different politics, but it is typical of the blurring of the traditionally understood battle lines of the culture wars in debates over youth and sexuality. Sontag, Reisman asserted, "implies that unless one protests such photos one is an accessory. In this case, it could be argued that Mr. Mapplethorpe enlists us in the child's photographic molestation."[188] This case exemplified the conservative discourse on sexual speech and imagery as a form of abuse to young people. According to Reisman and her contemporaries, to create an image of the nude form of a child not only rendered it pornographic but also made the photographer an abuser. The controversies around Sims's and Mapplethorpe's work pivoted on the young age of the subjects of the photographs. However, the newly punitive atmosphere facing artists in the wake of the Meese Report would equally impact artists working with adolescent models, further subsuming adolescence into childhood within the antiobscenity fight.

Such controversies continued to escalate. In 1991, the artist Sally Mann came under fire for her nude portraits of teenage and prepubescent girls, including her own daughters. Though Mann was never charged and did not have her work or children taken from her, debates over the use of nude, mainly female children in her work were highly publicized, owing to the cultural climate of the late 1980s and early 1990s. Her collection *At Twelve*, released in 1988, demonstrated her interest in the young female subject. The introductory essay by short-story writer Ann Beattie hinted at the photographer's attraction to the ambiguous sexual power dynamics present in capturing the adolescent subject. "Consider the two girls sitting at the base of a tree that, split and repaired, now looks like a vagina in brick and bark," she reflected. "Though the girls probably did not see the sexual implications of the background, the photographer did, and because of that the viewer cannot help but interpret the girls in terms of the tree."[189] Many of the images in *At Twelve* suggest that Mann was drawn to the 1980s ideal of white adolescent feminine beauty in America, as many of the young women pictured boast sporty, tanned, white bodies, long blonde hair, and Keds sneakers. Appearing occasionally in the book were sporadic images of visibly less privileged, unkempt girls, the only models with tragic stories printed underneath. One such image shows a young girl posing with her stepfather, who, it was later revealed, was also her abuser.[190] As with so much of the art, culture, media, and advertising produced in this period, Mann's work contributed to the construction of an image of a white, middle-class teenage girl who was simultaneously the most desired subject and the most vulnerable to corruption.[191] In the context of an era of heightened fear over child sexual abuse rates, her work also contributed to the insinuation that nonnuclear families living in poverty were those most likely to be abusive, both in the explicit statements accompanying pieces portraying young women from such families and in other places in her work, in her styling of her own children in settings that were contrived to simultaneously display poverty, early sexuality, and apparent harm.

It was Mann's exhibition *Immediate Family*, in 1991, that proved to be her most incendiary, partially because the nudes were of her own children. She was warned by a federal prosecutor in Roanoke, Virginia, that at least eight of her photographs that she had selected for the exhibition "could subject her to arrest."[192] While she was never prosecuted under the new child pornography laws, media responses to her work revealed some of the major concerns in the post–Meese Commission climate. The photographer, art professor, and critic Charles Hagen worried that Mann was using her children to toy with the dominant culture, fully aware of the cultural discourse on child sexual abuse and battle over obscene images and how her work would stir up these debates.[193] "Ms. Mann seems to want to flaunt the troubling suggestions of her pictures," he wrote in regard to her photograph *Damaged*

Child. "Given current awareness of the problem of child abuse, Ms. Mann's title lends her photograph another meaning, suggesting that the girl may have been beaten."[194] Hagen's criticism of Mann is further evidence of the instability of previously assumed culture wars battle lines when it came to the representation of childhood sexuality, as concern for victims of child abuse ran across the political spectrum—it was not only within the PMRC, the American Family Association, or Reagan's administration that adults were worried about children's vulnerability to abuse. While a major theme of Mann's work seemed to be the posturing, experimental sexuality of girls in transition to adulthood, she did not in any way advocate for the existence, let alone the free expression, of childhood sexuality. Mann admitted that the photographs were not candid snapshots and were contrived by her, but firmly stated in a 1992 interview, "'I think childhood sexuality is an oxymoron."[195] Despite the assertions of Hagen and others, she has insisted that the fact that *Immediate Family*'s release occurred simultaneously alongside "a moral panic about the depiction of children's bodies" was "a case of comically bad timing."[196] Her previous collections had not garnered nearly as much attention as *Immediate Family* did. "Those pictures," Mann recalled, "had the unlikely effect of delivering the kind of overnight celebrity that so many people, including threadbare artists, desire."[197]

The way that the law and cultural critique struck out at artists with similar fervor regardless of the differing ages of their subjects shows the way in which adolescence was sublimated into childhood in the legal structure of post-Meese child pornography efforts, without a consideration of the differing levels of agency an adolescent model might have compared with that of a much younger child.[198] The fact that almost all of the children depicted in the contested art and photography of this period were white also demonstrates the centrality of white girlhoods within the mainstream media coverage of debates over sexual speech and sexual harm during this period. The gender of the artist in each case, however, was significant in the nature of the criticism they garnered, and in the attitudes toward adolescent sexuality that they revealed. Mapplethorpe was described and pursued as a potential child molester: pernicious stereotypes about Mapplethorpe's homosexuality undoubtedly intensified the scrutiny he came under for depicting nude children in his oeuvre. For Sims and Mann, women photographers who used their own children as models, their maternal transgression was at the center of the outrage directed at them.[199] Sims's daughters were removed from her care when it was suspected that she was producing child pornography. Though Mann's children were not taken from her, many critics publicly doubted her fitness as a mother because of how she portrayed her children in her work. The *New York Times* art critic Richard B. Woodward wrote of her in 1992: "If it is her sole responsibility, as she says, 'to protect my children from all harm,' has she knowingly put them at risk by releasing these pictures into a world where pedophilia exists?"[200] Pro-sex feminist artist Carol Jacobsen saw the censorship of women's art as a historical problem of which accusations of child pornography were merely one facet. She called this "the automatic lockout of women and artists of color by art-world systems of education,

exhibition, funding, publication, criticism, hiring, and tenure, and the construction of history."[201] The gendered nature of the attacks on these artists also compounded ideas about predation. For the women artists, the strikes taken against
their work were, importantly, against their *work*: it was not only the images they
created but the fact that they were working at all that raised pro-family hackles during this period. Ellen Willis noted that this escalation of conservative responses to
child sexual abuse rates was in fact a "collective anxiety" about "the exodus of
women from the home."[202] The fear of mothers leaving the home for work was just
one facet of the association of nontraditional family structures with child sexual
abuse in the pro-family conservatism in this era.

The censoring of women's artistic production was a part of the same political
climate in which YA fiction writers such as Judy Blume and Norma Klein had their
work dismissed as "smut" without literary value and censored or banned across
the United States for constituting a form of child abuse, and in which the New Right
moved within and outside the Reagan administration to curtail sex education in
schools.[203] The idea that gained speed from the late 1970s onward that children and
young people would experience sexual speech and imagery as forms of sexual harm
intensified the culture wars over young people's rights to sexual information. As
evidenced by the movement of antipornography feminists and the organizing of
Democratic women such as Tipper Gore against sexual obscenity in music, it was
not only social conservatives who took this stance, and the culture wars continued
to take on new shapes when the debates centered around adolescent sexuality.[204]

Conversations about adolescent sexuality were necessarily covert in this intense
climate, in which it became increasingly difficult to advocate frankly for the sexual and reproductive well-being of teenagers in the mainstream of U.S. culture.[205]
Pro-sex feminists convened in the early 1990s to discuss and organize against this
state of affairs. At the 1993 "Sex Panic Conference" at the Graduate Center at CUNY,
Ellen Willis summarized the scared silence on youthful sexuality that had resulted
from the pornography wars and the coinciding national conversation on child sexual abuse. "On childhood sexuality," she stated, "we are all but mute. If an artwork
even suggests kids are sexual, the artist risks ridicule, professional exile, and even
criminal charges."[206] At the same conference, Judy Blume commented that the climate had changed so much since she began writing in the early 1970s that she could
not imagine writing those books had she begun her work in the late 1980s or early
1990s. "I might find it impossible to write honestly about kids in this climate of
fear," she told the audience.[207]

Over the course of the 1990s, this climate would seismically shift. Some pro-
sex feminists claimed that these cultural changes proved they "won" the sex wars,
as American society became increasingly resistant to the idea of censorship.[208] However, it became clear over the course of the ensuing decade that this was not strictly
true. The collaboration of some pro-sex feminists with pornographers and First
Amendment groups enabled mainstream sexual culture to become more graphic,
and occasionally informed by pro-sex feminisms, but ultimately in the flow of male
advertisers' desires. Despite the fact that pro-sex feminists had focused on adoles-

cent women's need for sexual information in their arguments against censorship, this would be ignored in much of the cultural mainstream, in favor of increased imagery of adolescent women designed to appeal to adult men. As a result, popular culture and politics in the 1990s would embrace a vision of sexual liberation that centralized the image of the white, thin, sexually appealing teenage girl.[209] One of the most pernicious effects of the obscenity wars climate of the 1980s was the association of predation and promiscuity with Black and Latinx communities and with poverty, and a concept of childhood vulnerability that was afforded only to the white young women affected by Hollywood, porn, art photography, and the news. This racialization of girlhood sexualities would plague the emerging "girl cultures" of the 1990s and take on new forms. However, as new sexual cultures formed in the 1990s, so did a new culture war over girlhood sexualities, in which teenage girls themselves fought back. A culture war division was emerging that would continue into the early twenty-first century—one that pitted underground, activist conversations about adolescent sexuality against mainstream depictions of teenage girls within a newly sexually explicit culture.

CHAPTER 3

Explicit Content

CULTURES OF GIRLHOOD

As the 1990s unfolded, a new sexual politics dawned in the United States. The New Right lost its hold on the executive office, as George H. W. Bush failed to secure re-election. Meanwhile, the fervor of the antiobscenity movement and the moral handwringing of the Parents' Music Resource Center gave way to a more explicit sexual culture, albeit one that mostly benefited straight men.[1] Young women played a central role in the shift to a more frank discussion about sexuality in American public life. By the end of the 1990s, the sexual lives of teenage girls were no longer unspeakable: they were a major matter of public debate across multiple platforms, from local, underground activist and punk communities to national organizations. While in the 1980s adults spoke about teenage female sexuality through debates around outcomes such as teenage pregnancy or the issue of parental consent for abortions, the question, raised more pointedly in the 1990s, was more explicitly behavior focused and saw adults asking outright whether increased sexual knowledge and experience in young women was a matter for celebration or concern.

In this new era, where adolescent sex became more explicitly spoken of, the culture wars concerning the sexual practices of young people would shift yet again—with one side continuing to see sexual imagery and speech as harmful to young people, and a sexual underground emerging, led for the first time by young women themselves, which advocated for sexual self-expression, an acknowledgment of sexual diversity in young people, and access to sexual information and education. As in the previous era, the categories of culture war "progressives" and "conservatives" weren't always adequate at explaining these divisions in debates over sexuality.[2] Rather, as the category of "teenage girl" became newly prominent within feminisms and in the wider culture wars, the cultural and political debates of the 1990s became defined by mainstream and underground approaches to adolescent sexuality.[3]

Because of the relevance of the debates about sex in the 1980s to the lives of young women coming of age in that epoch, and changing access to technologies that enabled young people to create their own forms of media and communication, teenagers increasingly entered these debates themselves in the 1990s via zine- and music-making, which shifted the nature of public discourse on adolescent sexuality and the nature of women's movements in America. However, the "girl culture" that resulted was quickly co-opted and deradicalized by the mainstream media. Attempts to monetize or more widely circulate this kind of activism—exemplified in the case of *Sassy* magazine—were quickly shut down by still-powerful conservative organizations. Despite moving into the spotlight of American culture and political debates of this period, teenage girls ultimately still needed to turn to the cultural underground to find honest and informative discourse on adolescent sex.[4] The version of girl culture that was used to sell clothes, music, and TV shows mainly took its cues from the most visible underground girl cultures, and centered a white, middle-class girlhood, ignoring the young women of color who were extremely active in mobilizing girl cultures but were not seen as part of the twin zeitgeists of either "girl power" or "girl in crisis" that were circulating in the media, the academy, and policymaking circles during this period.[5]

This chapter follows the development of this girl culture from its grassroots, youth-driven beginnings, through its movement into mainstream culture, and ultimately into academic cultures and neoliberal rhetorics of girlhood.[6] As adolescent sexuality became increasingly important in the development of American feminisms, it would expose the fluidity of culture wars actors when it came to the sexual practices of young people, and the continued concern over the increased sexual and reproductive activity of white teenage girls that had underpinned the modern culture wars since their inception.

"Girls to the Front!"

The increasing inclusion of and focus on teenagers' and young women's voices became characteristic of feminist conversations of the 1990s.[7] A new wave of activism emerged, one that was keen to reclaim terms such as "girl."[8] Sexuality, having been a major concern of feminist debate in the late 1970s and throughout the 1980s, would continue to be central to young activists in the 1990s, though there was more of a focus on the intersection of discourses of sexual violence with race, class, and queerness compared with earlier mainstream women's movements. Girlhood was at the fore of this feminism, the definition of which would be expansive and elastic, sometimes including both girl children and the reclaimed girlhoods of women in their twenties and early thirties. Within these grassroots movements, teenage girls and young women were able to advocate for their own sexual safety, desires, and identities in ways that remained impossible in the cultural mainstream, even as American society became more sexually open.[9]

From 1989 to 1991, one such movement, Riot Grrrl, began to form. In these years, young feminists who were enrolled at the progressive Evergreen State College in Olympia, Washington, and involved in local punk communities came together over twin concerns—on the local and personal level, misogyny within their own musical communities, and more broadly, continuing violence against women on the national and global scale.[10] The name Riot Grrrl was conceived by two of the movement's founding figures, Molly Neuman and Allison Wolfe, who met while studying together at the University of Oregon. Neuman had recently moved to the Pacific Northwest from DC.[11] She was impressed by Wolfe, a local who had been raised by a lesbian feminist mother and whose edgy looks stood her apart from the hippy crowd in Eugene, Oregon.[12] Together, they took a series of women's studies courses, developing their critical approach to gender and sexuality, and simultaneously discovered the local Olympia music scene.[13]

Neuman and Wolfe soon formed their own band, Bratmobile, and started to make and circulate a small fanzine, or "zine" (a handmade and photocopied pamphlet), bearing the name *Riot Grrrl*, which would come to define a movement.[14] The zine created a space wherein the writers and their contemporaries shared stories of sexual harassment and abuse they had experienced at punk shows and in their childhoods.[15] Soon, those contributing to the *Riot Grrrl* zine decided to bring the readers and contributors together and held "an initial experimental all-girl meeting," which soon turned into a "weekly forum for girls to discuss political, emotional, and sexual issues."[16] Out of these meetings arose the idea that the strongest resistance to the sexism they were facing in the present, and the abuse they had suffered in the past, would be to form women-only punk bands that addressed these issues lyrically and create safe spaces at shows for women to watch them play.[17] A number of girl bands sprung up in these communities and were united for the first time at a special event, "Girl Night" at the International Pop Underground Festival in Olympia in August 1991, a night that was remembered as "the unofficial beginning of the Riot Grrrl movement."[18] At the same time, a second major chapter of the Riot Grrrl movement formed in Washington, DC, which consisted initially of a small group of young women who met weekly to discuss feminist politics and plan direct actions, and to start to make music and art together.[19] A gregarious recent high school graduate from Virginia, Erika Reinstein, was a key early member of Riot Grrrl DC and was responsible for distributing zines and recruiting young women to the meetings from punk gigs across the city.[20]

Over the following year, the musical and political roots of Riot Grrrl developed and extended geographically from the two coasts as the girl bands toured, a plethora of zines were hurriedly made and distributed, and local and national networks were created through this culture.[21] By 1992, there were chapters of the movement in cities and towns across the United States.[22] This increased momentum led to the first Riot Grrrl Convention in Washington, DC, in July 1992. Women in their teens and early twenties traveled from as far as California and Washington State for two days of discussion and performance.[23] In the workshops, which covered such topics as sexuality and rape, grrrls taught each other about "domestic violence, and self-defense," as well as "unlearning racism," a workshop that led to some discomfort as young white women present at the convention realized that they, too, functioned as "oppressors."[24] The convention also included two shows of all-female bands and spoken-word performers, and an "All-Girl All-Night Dance Party".[25] The impact of the previous decade's proliferation of public abuse narratives was evident in the confessional, testimonial style of the convention. A writer for the feminist publication *Off Our Backs* reported that, at the convention, "many girls recounted their experiences with sexual abuse," from ongoing sexual inequality with "older, 'cooler' boyfriends" to memories of childhood sexual abuse.[26] Kathleen Hanna, an energetic Evergreen State College student and frontwoman of the major Riot Grrrl band Bikini Kill, had moved to DC shortly before the convention.[27] Hanna's art and writing at college, as well as her songwriting in Bikini Kill, were shaped by past experience of sex work and of sexual abuse. She relished the experience of coming together with other young women through Riot Grrrl to work through these issues in a productive way. "I'm so f-cking proud of myself," she stated at the event, "because to be somebody who has experienced the sexual abuse that I have and to be somebody who's experienced the kinds of things I've experienced and who's doing sex trade work and who's able to talk about it in this really legitimate way is pretty amazing."[28]

Returning, emboldened, to their respective cities, Riot Grrrls continued their commitment to attesting to previous sexual harm by writing such testimonies into their bands' songs. Hanna saw this as being reflective of the divergent developmental experiences of young men and women and positioned the songs as retributive action. "I saw a lot of guys playing music I didn't understand," she recalled, "songs I couldn't relate to . . . the whole chicks and car thing. I sing about rape and child abuse, because that's what my life was made up of."[29] Early Riot Grrrl bands included Hanna's Bikini Kill and Neuman and Wolfe's Bratmobile, Washington's Heavens to Betsy and Excuse 17, and Babes in Toyland, born out of the Twin Cities.[30] These bands played songs whose lyrics reflected, as Hanna emphasized, themes that resonated with young female fans in their exploration of the darker side of adolescence. A collective memory of sexual trauma also influenced the organization of early Riot Grrrl events. Flyers advertising the bands' shows made interested young women aware that, unlike experiences they might have had previously, these performances would be safe spaces. For instance, a poster made for a performance by bands Bikini Kill and Huggy Bear read, "At this show we ask that girls/women stand near the front . . . this is an experiment . . . Why?? because I am a female performer who has been verbally/and physically assaulted while being on stage."[31] It was clear from the flyers posted around Riot Grrrls' towns that sexualized violence had followed these women from childhood through to their young adult communities. Another stated, "Being alienated is going to a show and seeing a sign taped to the wall that says 'no head, no backstage.'"[32]

In addition to the bands, another major vehicle for Riot Grrrls' politics and aesthetics was their handmade and distributed zines. In their print culture as well as their music, Riot Grrrls grappled with the debates over sexuality in recent feminist history. Many of these women were learning of their recent feminist heritage by undertaking college courses in the emerging field of women's studies, or taking part in local rape crisis or pro-choice activism.[33] They were influenced in turn by both sides of the sex wars. The impact of antipornography feminists such as Catharine MacKinnon and Andrea Dworkin, and the graphic descriptions of sexual harm toward women they employed in their arguments for a ban against pornography, could be seen in the rhetorical style favored by Riot Grrrls in their songs and in their zines. Erika Reinstein, a key member of the DC Riot Grrrl chapter and a major distributor of zines, demonstrated a commitment to the anti-sexual-violence activism of Second Wave feminists in her own publication.[34] "We need to acknowledge that our blood is being spilt," she wrote in 1993, "that right now a girl is being raped or battered and it might be me or you or your mom or the girl you sat next to on the bus last Tuesday."[35] A continuation of this kind of Second Wave politics also influenced the activist practices of early Riot Grrrl events, such as the forming of women-only "safe spaces" at the front of gigs.[36] At the same time, Riot Grrrls could be decidedly pro-sex. While they had both an intellectual and lived comprehension of sex and gender inequality, they nonetheless pursued the belief that this was not inescapable, seeing instead a liberating potential in sex for girls and women. In the first zine by Kathleen Hanna's band Bikini Kill was a list of instructions for a "girl-led revolution." "MAKE PORNOGRAPHY," the writer demanded, "that includes more than just hetero sex. This can be queer girl sex or boy + boy sex or hetero sex where more than just dumb conversation and f-cking take place."[37] Riot Grrrls' belief that pornography did not necessarily need to be harmful, while simultaneously acknowledging their experience of sexual violence, demonstrated the ways in which both sides of the 1980s pornography debates were essential to the activism of a younger generation.

Referencing and fusing former feminist approaches to sex, and embracing the contradictions of this duality, gradually became a defining characteristic of Riot Grrrl.[38] "SEX ISN'T DIRTY AND BAD UNLESS SOMEONE'S FORCING IT ON YOU," one teenaged Riot Grrrl scrawled in bold in her zine, capturing the fusion of pro-sex and antiporn feminisms adopted by these young activists.[39] In Kathleen Hanna's zine Bikini Kill, which shared a name with her band, she demonstrated the merging of Second Wave principles on sexuality. "It doesn't have to be this intense dramatic self righteous thing to affect change," she wrote. "It can be fun to talk about scary issues."[40] These early musings in print were then personified in the distinctive performance style of young women in Riot Grrrl bands. On stage, the Grrrls played up their femininity and sexuality while singing songs about past sexual abuse.[41] The performers were consciously evoking this dissonance in their performances—Hanna, for instance, coined the term "hypocrobrat" to describe "a girl who wears lipstick and tight clothes and is boy crazy, and yet is still into girl culture and feminism."[42]

It was through the reappropriation of terms such as "brat" and "girl," and the focus on youth in the movement, that Riot Grrrls contributed to the history of women's activism in new ways, as well as continuing the work of previous feminisms. Though many of these young women were leaving their teenage years, and some were well into their twenties, their aesthetics and identities were based on the image of a rebellious teenage girl.[43] Riot Grrrls' choice to identify more with teenage girls than with adult women in their feminism demonstrates the importance of this category to the women's movement as it moved into the 1990s. Identifying as "grrrls" also positioned the voice of the teenage girl as one imbued with

power, instead of victimhood, and thus it allowed young women to reclaim girlhoods lost to sexual abuse, reclaiming not only a term but a temporality.[44] This
was emblematized by the mantra of the Riot Grrrl movement—"Revolution Grrrl
Style Now."[45] Young women in the movement embodied this mantra in their personal aesthetics. A recognizable grrrl style emerged, which included baby-doll slip
dresses, accessories featuring children's cartoon characters such as Hello Kitty, and
tiny, multicolored hair clips usually reserved for the fine hair of little girls.[46] Before
going on stage, Grrrls in bands scrawled "SLUT" and "RAPE" on exposed skin in
permanent marker, further subverting the childlike outfits worn on adult bodies.[47]
These, too, were terms that Riot Grrrls sought to reclaim and repurpose. Hanna
argued that "girl, slut, and d-ke all need to be taken back, and taken away from the
men that use them as weapons."[48] The practice of reclaiming language as a political
tool was one inherited from earlier social movements in the United States, including that of Black Power and LGBTQ+ activism.[49] Slightly older Riot Grrrls started
this practice, with the intention of proving to teenagers that they could "be a feminist and still dress up and be whoever you want to be."[50] This resonated with some
teenage Riot Grrrls, one of whom wrote in her zine, "SLUT. yeah, I'm a slut. My
body belongs to me."[51]

Many young grrrls of color, however, expressed that this practice felt less empowering to them, when their bodies were already marked as subversive in society in
a way that was unwelcomed.[52] This was just one of the ways in which the whiteness of the founding members of the Riot Grrrl movement shaped their engagement with punk and with feminism. Many of the wider punk music scenes that
Riot Grrrl bands were situated within were dominated by white musicians and fans,
and young people of color were frequently excluded by those involved in organizing these spaces. In a contribution to the zine *Not Even 5*, Ani Mukherji, for
instance, discussed the "white pride" in songs by hardcore bands Minor Threat and
Downcast.[53] Lauren Martin, reflecting on her early years as a zinester, recalled how
quickly these spaces revealed themselves as exclusionary to people of color. "In 1993,
I discovered zines, riot grrrl, punk rock and the DIY ethic," she wrote. "I quickly
realised that even so-called progressive and radical groups can be embedded with
nasty little things like racism, sexism and xenophobia."[54] Mimi Thi Nguyen, now
a scholar of transnational feminisms, grew up in punk and Riot Grrrl scenes in
Minnesota and California and was a prolific zinester in the 1990s.[55] Nguyen, who
was born in Vietnam, had by the late 1990s rejected the punk scene she had come
of age in for its racism. "I'm over it like I'm over puberty, like I'm over ripped fish-
nets and barracudas and Asian fetishes," she wrote in the introduction to *Evolution of a Race Riot*, a 1997 compilation zine that she put together featuring writing
by people of color involved in punk and Riot Grrrl scenes across the United States.[56]
In addition to the explicit forms of racism that Mukherji noted existed in some
punk and hardcore music, Nguyen was attuned to the ways in which "white punk
antiracist discourses" perpetuated inequality.[57] She has since written that white Riot
Grrrls imagined that the "aesthetics of access" and the "aesthetics of intimacy" that
they cultivated—via consciousness-raising and "girl love"—would be a "pathway

to social bonds and from there, racial justice," but "when viewed in light of histories of desire for access and attachment to racial, colonial others" would "turn out
to be the reiteration of those histories in new idioms."[58]

Punk and feminist consciousness-raising were not the only cultural movements
that informed Riot Grrrls' artistic production. Their politicized aesthetics were
partly informed by older Riot Grrrls' knowledge of feminist history but also by the
artistic and literary styles that they were exposed to in their own cities and the colleges they attended, particularly the work of other women.[59] Female punk bands
and performers in the "Do It Yourself" (DIY) musical subculture such as Marine
Girls, Lydia Lunch, and the Slits influenced them with their sparse, minimalistic
musical style. College-aged Riot Grrrls also read sex-positive journals and zines
such as *Frighten the Horses*, which contained art, collage, poetry, erotica, and long-
form essays on subjects such as the satanic panic of the 1980s and the introduction of feminist therapy.[60] Many grrrls read and admired the literary style of punk,
avant-garde writer Kathy Acker, particularly her novel *Blood and Guts in High
School*, the nonlinear, collaged prose and graphic illustrations of which provided
a model to Riot Grrrls for artistic self-expression on experiences of sexual abuse.[61]
They admired the queer, feminist video art of experimental filmmaker Sadie Ben-
ning, including her short *Girl Power*, and the narrative films of Sarah Jacobsen,
who often focused on adolescent sexuality in works such as *Mary Jane's Not a Virgin Anymore*. The frantic, hastily assembled aesthetic that these young women
admired in the work of women across the feminist avant-garde was thus as important to their practices of zine writing and songwriting, dress, and performance as
was their academic and activist feminist understanding.[62] Zines, in particular, were
a place where the grrrls re-created the punk feminist politics and aesthetics of
women like Acker, including handwritten, stream-of-consciousness polemics,
poetry, cut-and-paste collages, and quotation.

The artistic influences listed here also point to the whiteness and middle-class
backgrounds of the majority of Riot Grrrls—while the wider movement of zinesters
and activists involved teenage girls from across the United States and from a range
of backgrounds. Some of the most prolific and widely known zinesters were themselves just out of their teens and were middle-class college students who had access
to the DIY subcultures of college towns and the artistic and literary texts they were
exposed to at their respective colleges, the creators of which were also mostly white.[63]
Grrrls of color, in contending with this problem, circulated reading lists of feminist theory, historical writings, and fiction by writers of color in their zines. One
list of "books, zines, and films to consider" was put together in the zine *eracism*,
which was circulated at a workshop on racism at the Santa Barbara Girls Convention, run by young people in the California DIY scene in June 1996, and included
critical antiracist feminist texts such as Cherríe Moraga and Gloria Anzaldúa's
edited collection *This Bridge Called My Back* and *Yearning: Race, Gender &
Cultural Politics* by bell hooks.[64]

As the circulation of *eracism* suggests, zines were far more than a mode of artistic expression for Riot Grrrls. They were one of the principal modes in which Riot

Grrrls entered the culture wars, proliferating a subversive, raw, gritty discourse about young women's sexuality directly from such women, to an extent that was unprecedented in American history. These handmade, photocopied, and stapled publications had long been an extension of underground cultures, but for Riot Grrrls they were critical in allowing young women across the country to stay in touch with one another, to advertise meetings and gigs, and to continue to redefine their feminism. They enabled college-aged Riot Grrrls to disseminate knowledge to teen-agers across the country whose socioeconomic background or geographic location might not allow them to be as physically involved in the movement.[65] Riot Grrrl print culture, including zines, posters, and flyers at gigs, therefore functioned as a form of DIY sex education. For example, in *Fuckooth*, a zine by then-student Jen Angel, the writer reprinted a Canadian sexual health guide called "DIY gynecol-ogy" and urged readers to "share information." "If you're raped by someone," she urged, "get the word out."[66] These efforts were in reaction to changes in mainstream politics; older Riot Grrrls were seeking to compensate for escalating restrictions on sex education in this period.[67] The first *Bikini Kill* zine instructed young women with access to information and materials to "MAKE FLIERS around the issues that're important to you" and to "put them inside newspapers, library books, leave them on buses."[68] At one show, the band Bikini Kill distributed flyers on "a vari-ety of herbal abortifacients" and noted that it was becoming "absolutely necessary to gather and trade secret, safe alternatives" in the face of legal abortion becoming increasingly difficult to obtain.[69] The explicitness of sexual and reproductive advice that Riot Grrrls advocated for and created within these materials hints at the way the culture wars themselves were shifted by these young women's underground net-works. By the early 1990s, a Democratic administration was under way, and even in the more liberal political climate and more sexually graphic social climate that unfolded, access to feminist-informed sexual health information—on both "plea-sure" and "pain"—remained an underground, subcultural discourse that went head to head with liberal sexual and reproductive health policies.[70]

The noncommercial nature of zines also enabled a level of sexual explicitness that would certainly have been subject to censorship in mainstream publications.[71] Grrrls often explored their sexuality within the pages of their zines. Like the lyr-ics of many Riot Grrrl songs, zines sometimes functioned as a confessional space where young women released anger over their experiences of rape and sexual assault. "I thought it was common to not remember my childhood," wrote one zinester in the fourth issue of the *Riot Grrrl* zine.[72]

However, these zines were also spaces where positive experiences of sexuality, of discovery, experimentation, and excitement, were discussed.[73] "I masturbate every day before and after school," declared one fifteen-year-old in *Girl Germs*, another zine by Molly Neuman and Allison Wolfe of the band Bratmobile.[74] In her zine *Aperture*, Maine teenager Eleanor Whitney described her growing understanding of her own sexuality as she entered her teens. "I am not ashamed," she wrote decid-edly. "I've noticed the power of sex, sexuality and how often it is denied and repressed."[75] Zines also allowed girls to safely explore sexual feelings toward other girls, whether they were confusing or exciting. In 1996, one zinester raged about the impact of pervasive homophobia on her process of coming out as queer. "i hate how i'm kissing a girl and it feels totally right but there is a voice in my head telling me i'm disgusting," she wrote. "i hate how i want to tell my mom all of this but i'm afraid."[76] In other zines, queer teenagers celebrated their love. "Teen love is real and teen girls in love is real," declared one young queer grrrl in the fourth issue of *Girl Germs*.[77]

The widespread network of zines that proliferated during this period reflected the diversity of the young people involved in this DIY print movement across the United States. However, the majority of the Riot Grrrl movement, and particularly those in the most high-profile bands, were white and middle class.[78] Some people of color used their zines to critique the amount of space given to discussions of sexuality by white zinesters, without an understanding of how these issues intersect with those of race or class. In *Bamboo Girl*, Sel Hwahng commented that "putting so much energy into trying to define lesbianism vs. bisexuality is putting more energy into privileging sexual orientation, again and again."[79] Further, Sel expressed hope that "more whitegirls/lesbians would do more work around how their own race—white—has been constructed through history and the European immigration process, instead of feeling like because they are white, they have nothing to do with race."[80] Though white members of the movement expressed on stage and in their zines that antiracism should be central to Riot Grrrl's feminist politics, many grrrls of color felt that while the promise of the grrrl-led revolution was exciting, white grrrls in the movement failed in ensuring their inclusion.[81] In the fourth issue of their zine *Gunk*, the African American New Jersey teenager Ramdasha Bikceem, for instance, wrote that while "I am totally for revolution grrrl style now," it "shouldn't just be limited to white, middle-class, punk rock grrrls 'cuz there's no denyin' that's what it is."[82] Prolific zinester Lauren Martin echoed this sentiment in *You Might As Well Live 4*: "Sisterhood, yes. Revolution, yes. But what is a predominantly white suburban upper-middle class girl revolution going to accomplish?"[83] The experiences of teenagers of color within the "white-dominated" Riot Grrrl movement sadly forecasted the whiteness of the resulting "girl culture" that would take off in the mainstream of American culture as the decade progressed.[84]

It is important to recognize the feminist, DIY activism of young women of color within, and sometimes necessarily outside, the Riot Grrrl movement, particularly in the way they fused antiracist thought with their writings on sexuality.[85] This is something that those who lived through and those who are scholars of Riot Grrrl are still contending with—in the accompanying statement to her donation to the POC Zine Project at NYU Fales Library in 2012, Mimi Thi Nguyen discussed the politics of seeing the work of zinesters of color as "mere addition or supplement to the archives." She went on to write that the zines by people of color that she was donating "point to not a side story in riot grrrl movement, but the story of encounter and contest, exchange and challenge."[86]

Within Riot Grrrl zine culture, girls of diverse racial and class backgrounds, without the social capital of Hanna and others, were extremely active in zine-making and forms of local activism and used this platform to voice their particular experiences of adolescent sexuality as young women of color. Tasha Fierce's zine *Bitchcore* is one such publication. "I'm half black and half white," they wrote in an opening statement to their first zine. "I'm fat. I'm female. I'm vegetarian. I'm a rape survivor. I'm a feminist. I like punk music and I support the Riot Grrrl ideals."[87] Much of zine culture was driven by young Asian American women. One zinester wrote of her transformation as a teenager "unable to flirt with Korean boys" to a political lesbian in college, where she had access to a Riot Grrrl email mailing list. "The trooperlist was a place where I could not only come out as a d-ke, but as a political d-ke, a feminist queer, a radical lezzie," she recalled.[88] It was also where she realized the "limitations of Riot Grrrl, especially with issues surrounding race."[89]

Because of these limitations, cultural forms of resistance of women of color in this period occurred in a range of other spaces. A lot of punk bands made up of or including women of color did not consider themselves part of Riot Grrrl but were active across DIY music and zine cultures, especially those that made up the early "queercore" music movement. This was true of Tribe 8, a band from San Francisco made up of "five tough d-kes" who wrote "raucous, exuberant punk rock."[90] Durham, North Carolina's the Butchies saw their "mission" as "to offer hope and comfort to lesbian teens doing time in small towns to a groove that mixes punk and Fleetwood Mac-style anthems."[91] In her important 2015 article for *Broadly* on Black women in and outside of Riot Grrrl, "Alternatives to Alternatives," Gabby Bess describes the Black punk "Sista Grrrl Riots" that Tamar-kali Brown, Maya Glick, Simi Stone, and Honeychild Coleman organized in New York starting in 1997, "playing to a packed crowd who could finally see versions of themselves onstage."[92] Bess writes of the important distinction between these "lifelong punk outsiders" and the Riot Grrrl movement: "They were girls. They were angry. They were tired of playing shitty gigs and taking a backseat to the boys. But these women would scoff at the thought of designating themselves 'Riot Grrrls.'"[93] According to Tamar-kali Brown, "*This* was a Sista Grrrl's Riot."[94] Importantly, Bess highlights, the Sista Grrrl Riots made clear a historical fact that was lost in the white punk scene: that "rock music is black music."[95] Within zine culture, too, young women of color who did not feel included in the Riot Grrrl movement were prolific in their art and activist practices and pointed to the fact that these had a much longer lineage than that of Riot Grrrl. As Lauren Martin wrote in Mimi Thi Nguyen's compilation zine *Race Riot 2*: "I was critical long before I ever did a zine, discovered punk rock, or went to college. . . . My anger is a legacy passed down from immigrant generations, yellow ancestors, queer patriots, centuries of marginalized peoples, who were f-cked by The Man and did everything they could to f-ck back (to paraphrase activist Loretta Ross)."[96] The way that artists and zinesters of color were frequently not understood to be a part of the movement of underground musical activism by young women foreshadowed the way that the evolving mainstream "girl culture" would also exclude young popular musicians of color from its oeuvre.[97]

The explicitness afforded to young women by the underground nature of zines, and by their communicative circulation, created a dialogue on race, sexuality, and politics among teenagers that was unprecedented—and that would prove hard to replicate in popular culture, even in the newly sexually explicit media climate of the 1990s.[98] The grassroots, anticapitalist approach of Riot Grrrl allowed them to discuss both negative and positive aspects of their sexuality in graphic detail without censorship or intervention, or adults attempting to provide the narratives for them.[99] From the earliest days of the movement, Riot Grrrls were aware of the importance of remaining underground, in order to have these unfiltered conversations about sexuality. Kathleen Hanna expressed concern in early meetings and musings that even talking to mainstream music press might allow critics to misconstrue and dilute their message. "Will RG even *deal* with w/corp/ publications/ businesses ie SPIN, elle, Rolling ST?" Hanna wondered.[100] It was not long, however, before the mainstream music press and wider American news outlets began to take notice of Riot Grrrl and react in shock at the sexual content of the movement.[101] Their music was often reviewed poorly, or viewed merely as a vehicle through which to promote their politics, as reflected in feminist music journalist Kim France's 1993 article "Grrrls at War" in *Rolling Stone*. "To the teenage girls who flock to Bikini Kill shows to experience Hanna's rage on stage," she noted, "technical prowess is not the point."[102] While Riot Grrrls were aware of the inherent contradictions in their feminist politics and deliberately crafted this duality, mainstream media often misrepresented the activists' inconsistencies in a way that undermined the women involved. "Rock's current female style makers are facing the contradiction of their demand for both equality and the right to be provocative," reported one piece of notorious Riot Grrrl coverage in the *New York Times* in 1993.[103] Another much-hated article, this time in *Newsweek*, noted that "they've set out to make the world safe for their kind of girlhood: sexy, assertive, and loud."[104]

Misrepresentation in the media continued to increase with the growing commercial success of some Riot Grrrl bands, including Bikini Kill and Bratmobile. Many of the women in these bands were offended by the claim made in the *Newsweek* piece that Courtney Love, the provocative lead singer of the commercially successful grunge band Hole, was "the patron saint of Riot Grrrls," as she performed in "vintage little girl dresses that barely make it past her hips[—]all the better to sing songs about rape and exploitation."[105] Courtney Love was in fact a contentious figure for Riot Grrrls.[106] Her music and aesthetics mirrored those of Riot Grrrls, particularly in the ways she subverted imagery of girlhood innocence, in her juxtaposition of playing thrashing, scream-filled pop-punk while wearing hyperfeminine baby-doll dresses, and through the cover image of a tear-stained beauty queen on Hole's 1994 album *Live Through This*.[107] However, she was openly antagonistic toward the Riot Grrrl movement—particularly Kathleen Hanna, who had been close friends with her husband, Nirvana frontman Kurt Cobain—and she regularly decried these women in the mainstream music press.[108] The misunderstanding of these subtleties by the *New York Times* and *Newsweek* riled Riot Grrrls and eventually led to them putting in place a press embargo in 1993, urging young Riot Grrrls not to talk to major publications.[109]

Despite the ban on talking to the press, many continued to do so, and the widespread media coverage of Riot Grrrl became one of the reasons that the movement faded into nonexistence before the end of the decade. The overproliferation of images of the grrrls prompted cynicism by critics. "They have to move forward or else get sucked into a vortex of itty-bitty barrette self-parody," commented *Village Voice* writer Natasha Stovall in 1996. "It's a slick slope between girl power and baby-doll dresses that show your ass," she continued, and expressed concern that "it hides the potentially much greater power in being a woman behind a fantasy of childhood strength."[110] Even though the Riot Grrrls in the public eye were adults representing adolescent sexuality, mainstream media portrayals understood teenage girlhood as implicitly weak, vulnerable, and corruptible. At this moment in history, despite the increasing sexual explicitness allowed in wider American culture, raw, unfiltered representation of the perils and pleasures of adolescent sexual experience remained resolutely underground.[111]

By 1996, "it was common knowledge among punks and indie rockers" that Riot Grrrl was dead.[112] The major bands that had spearheaded and defined it had split up, and most of the women involved were moving on to other, more aesthetically "mature" musical projects.[113] Riot Grrrl chapters continued to meet, though online mailing lists and forums increasingly took the place of physical meetings in the second half of the decade.[114] It was in these online spaces that discourse between Riot Grrrls became more critical of the movement, in particular the lack of visibility for nonwhite grrrls.[115] The conversations initiated by Riot Grrrls about the importance of girlhood sexuality for the feminist project continued to take place. Their ideas would have an impact on wider American culture, though the version of "girl culture" that flourished in such spaces would reflect mainly a white, sanitized version of Riot Grrrl that was palatable to the mainstream: mainstream media coverage of white Riot Grrrl band members failed to portray activism by young women of color inside and outside the movement, meaning that it was only the most visible white factions of the movement that would be represented in the mainstream "girl culture" that followed. Over the course of the 1990s, the wider U.S. culture wars over sexuality took on a new division: between teenagers in underground cultures and the young adult women who advocated for their sexual well-being, and the advertisers, television producers, and policymakers who supported a glossy, attractive version of girlhood sexuality and empowerment.

GIRL POWER IN THE CULTURAL MAINSTREAM

Riot Grrrls had been prescient in their fear of the mainstream media. "We need to make ourselves visible without using mainstream media as a tool," read an urgent notice in a zine in 1993. "Under the guise of helping us spread the word, corporate media has co-opted and trivialized a movement of angry girls."[116] By the mid-1990s, as the raw anger of the early movement dissipated, the reclamation of the language and aesthetics of girlhood taken on by Riot Grrrl was becoming increasingly visible in mass culture.[117] "Girl Power," a phrase once seen splashed across a zine by Hanna's band Bikini Kill, was used as the catchphrase by British pop group the Spice Girls.[118] Riot Grrrls' punk stylings, including slip dresses and piercings, became popular dress for adolescents across the country.[119] Shrunken T-shirts known as baby tees came into fashion, emblazoned with slogans like "Girls Rule!" In 2001, the girls' chain store Claire's Accessories stocked patches for jeans or backpacks reading "SLUT."[120] This shift of the ideas, rhetoric, and aesthetics from underground to mainstream culture is not historically exceptional.[121] What is exceptional about the flow of punk ideas into the mainstream via the Riot Grrrl movement is that it initiated a newly explicit discourse on the sexual desires and travails of teenage girls in American media. However, despite the sexual explicitness of the resulting mainstream girl culture, the radical conversations about girlhood sexualities happening in subcultural spaces would prove not to be possible in popular media.[122]

The tumultuous story of the short-lived teen magazine *Sassy*, which ran from 1988 to 1997, illustrates the growing explicitness of the public conversation about adolescent sexual behaviors in America in the 1990s and, at the same time, the sustained power of conservative groups that took issue with speech that could be seen as endorsing sexual activity in young women outside of marriage.[123] *Sassy*'s demise proved that a progressive, feminist voice on adolescent sexual citizenry would be perpetually pitted against mainstream culture in the culture wars of this decade. The nature of the conservative response to *Sassy* magazine also proved that the conversation over whether young women should be sexually active had taken an explicit turn, no longer to be discussed merely in the covert terms of the preceding decade.[124]

Sassy originated when Sandra Yates, a single mother who had founded the popular Australian teen magazine *Dolly*, decided that American teenagers were in need of a similar publication, "one that would discuss issues like sex, fashion, or suicide, without cloaking them in euphemisms, one that would take a tone of . . . 'Hey guys, we're in this together.'"[125] While establishing the publication in New York, she sought out a young editorial team, which she believed would be crucial for the magazine's success—the *Dolly* staff in Australia were in their early twenties, and for Yates this was the key to the youthful voice of the magazine.[126] The woman Sandra would hire as editor, Jane Pratt, was only twenty-four at the time and had the funky, youthful aesthetic, feminist politics, and raw ambition that Yates was seeking in her staff.[127] Yates's approach to staffing *Sassy* followed a similar dynamic to the one established by Riot Grrrls, wherein women just out of their teens coached slightly younger girls—they were close enough in age to remember and understand adolescence but had gained experience and knowledge, as well as social and cultural power that teenagers living at home did not have.[128] This editorial decision inadvertently mirrored the dynamic of the most prominent, adult factions of the Riot Grrrl movement with the teenage print movement that propelled them. *Sassy* staffer Elizabeth Larsen recalled that, in the first meeting of *Sassy*'s young, mostly female editors and writers, "the unanimous first priority was to provide sex education."[129] This was in part an effort to set themselves apart from the competition, as "the sex information published by teen magazines was scarce and usually couched in judgmental terms."[130] However, this was also a politically motivated decision by the self-proclaimed feminist staff. Writers were aware that the United States had "the highest teen pregnancy rate of any similarly industrialized western nation," and were angry that abstinence was getting increased attention in policy as being "the only sure way to prevent AIDS."[131]

In the early years of its publication, the *Sassy* team endeavored to make their magazine an essential mode of sex education to its young readers. The first issue in 1988 ran a piece that had previously been included in *Dolly*, titled "Sex for Absolute Beginners."[132] The magazine's initial advertisements for subscriptions drew attention to the inclusion of sexuality within its pages. "It's about time you had a magazine that's really in touch," they read. "We'll be giving you the lowdown on everything from boys to looks, from schools to careers, from dating to sexuality."[133] Initially, the magazine did just that. The tone set *Sassy* apart from other teen magazines. While sex was discussed in regular, short advice columns as in other publications, *Sassy* also included extensive features on various aspects of burgeoning sexuality, and the language used in both was colloquial and youthful. For example, the June 1988 issue included a piece called "Getting Turned On":

> It happens like this. You're sitting in front of the television . . . And a Terence Trent D'Arby video comes on. (I don't care which one. They're all sexy.) All of a sudden your ears flush and you start to feel like someone turned up the thermostat and you're all excited and you really, really wish your parents would leave because this feeling, while very nice, is very embarrassing. . . . Anyway, you know the feeling, right? But if you're like most of us, what you probably don't know is *why* you get turned on. Well the next time it happens to you, don't assume you're some kind of pervert. There's an explanation for it. Honest.[134]

A similarly youthful tone and pro-sex approach to common issues surrounding teen sexuality could be seen in August 1988's article "Hot for Teacher," which advised young women on what to do if they found themselves attracted to an authority figure: "It's totally normal to like an older, smarter, more experienced guy who takes an interest in you and is maybe even good-looking, too. I mean, it's fun to have a crush—it gives you something to think about while you're doing your sit ups. But what should you do about your undying love?"[135] With articles such as these, the writers were deliberately attempting to provide a narrative for young women that described relatable sexual experiences without the "shame" or "just say no" approach they saw heralded in other magazines previously, and while refraining from moralizing.[136]

Another aspect of *Sassy*'s coverage of sexuality that was important to its writers was its encompassing of queer sexualities, which were rarely, if ever, mentioned in other teen magazines at the time.[137] As with other discussions of sexuality in the magazine, one way that staffers included queer teens was through the advice letter section. "Since a really young age, I've known that I'm a lesbian," read one letter, signed "In Pain," in March 1994. "Recently I've started to like a female friend of mine whom I have always been close to . . . the problem is, she is not a lesbian.

What should I do?"[138] It was also an issue addressed in some full-length articles, such as the July 1988 special feature on young gay couples, the headline of which read: "Laurel and Lesli and Alex and Brian are your basic kids. They're dating. They go to movies and concerts. They fight over stupid things. They make up. They're sad sometimes. They're happy. AND THEY'RE GAY."[139] Similarly to the music and writings of Riot Grrrls, *Sassy* embraced aspects of both sides of the 1980s sex wars, in a way that was becoming characteristic of the grassroots of girl culture and of 1990s feminisms. Despite the tone of sex positivity that most of their articles took, writers for the magazine also acknowledged sexual and gender inequality. Unwanted pregnancy, rape, incest, and abuse were also discussed in *Sassy*'s pages. Unlike other popular teen magazines at the time, including *Seventeen* or *YM (Young and Modern)*, *Sassy* approached these issues in explicitly feminist terms and was careful to avoid language that might inspire fear or shame.[140] For example, in June 1989's "Real Stories about Incest," the writer tells young women who have experienced abuse that "the first step to telling your story of incest is learning to believe in yourself. To know in your heart that you're right; that none of the fault lies with you. There is *never* an excuse for sexual abuse."[141]

The immediate reader response to *Sassy* confirmed teenage girls' desire for this accessible and explicit information on sex and sexuality. From its first issue, *Sassy* received hundreds of letters in which teenage girls expressed their gratitude to the magazine for speaking to them in a relatable voice.[142] The writers, disconcerted by the negative experiences many of these teenagers relayed, tailored their research and writing to respond to the worries these young women expressed in their emotional letters, and sometimes even phone calls to the *Sassy* offices.[143] Among its desired readership, *Sassy* was instantly beloved. It was also heralded by those adults who acknowledged its critical importance in interrupting the status quo of enforced silence around adolescent sexuality. As a result, it soon took on a cult popularity that was rare among teen publications—it was championed by adults such as Kim Gordon and Thurston Moore, whose band Sonic Youth released a special record for *Sassy* for the publication to give away in a competition in one of the issues.[144] *Sassy* served as a bridge between underground and mainstream cultures. It celebrated independent music, film, and fashion but also deconstructed mass culture and celebrity, all from an explicitly feminist perspective.[145] Drawing together underground cultures including punk and feminist activism with what was popular in the mainstream, and actual teenagers with adults who supported their need to access frank sexual information and advice, was becoming a defining characteristic of the girl culture aesthetic.[146]

Part of this ethos meant that *Sassy* also played a role in Riot Grrrls' proliferation, though for many Riot Grrrls this was not a welcome platform. The bands and activism launched by the movement were covered frequently in *Sassy*, mostly by Christina Kelly, a precocious teenage music journalist when hired by editor Jane Pratt, never seen without her grandmother's leopard-print coat.[147] The trends page "What Now?" documented Riot Grrrl gigs, including powerful images of the performers with "SLUT" and "RAPE" written on their bodies, and regularly interviewed

Riot Grrrl band members.[148] Christina Kelly dedicated a section of the music page to a "zine corner," which profiled a different Riot Grrrl zine each month and gave details of how to order them.[149] This helped teenagers based in rural areas find and access underground cultures. Writer Sarah Maitland, who would go on to found Richmond Zine Fest, first discovered zines through *Sassy*: "I first became aware of zines when I was 11 or 12 and would check out back issues of *Sassy Magazine* from the library," she wrote. "I grew up in a small rural town," she continued. "With no older friends or siblings, I was left to find out about the underground on my own."[150] Not all Riot Grrrls were happy about press coverage in *Sassy*, however, even if the magazine did seem to have the movement's best interests at heart. In issue 5 of the zine *Riot Grrrl NYC*, one grrrl complained that despite the fact that *Sassy* wrote "good articles about incest survivors, rape, witchcraft, how to make clothes, etc.," they had a format and visuals "the same as all other magazines with a female audience—thin, VERY attractive models AND the 'lose weight so boys will like you' advertisement in the back."[151] *Sassy*'s connection with Riot Grrrl occasionally came off the page. They "sponsored several all-age events in New York at the politically active nightclub Wetlands, featuring all-women bands."[152] These events sometimes exemplified the major differences between *Sassy* and Riot Grrrl, as when, during a Bikini Kill set Kathleen Hanna "used a microphone as a penis substitute" and music editor Christina Kelly wished to herself, "Oh God, let there be no parents here!"[153]

Though Riot Grrrl and *Sassy* shared a "confessional, stream-of-consciousness style," the aesthetic and content in zines were far more radical in their revelation of teenage girls' sexual desires and experiences. Because they were noncommercial, they did not have to worry about attracting advertisers or stockists or about being censored. Christina Kelly, speaking to an alternative music magazine in 1992, acknowledged that Riot Grrrl music and zines were "more radical" than *Sassy*, but that ultimately they shared the same underlying punk feminism, "because, of course" she argued, "we're a business. We do have the same philosophy, we just can't express it."[154] This distinction was hugely significant in its implications for the culture wars of this period—it proved that the self-published, teen-written print culture of zine-making and the DIY venues and nights that played host to Riot Grrrl bands and activist meetings were crucial to the frank exploration of adolescent women's sexual lives in this period. Though writers for *Sassy* held the same commitment to these politics as those involved in Riot Grrrl, and though sexual explicitness in the media was increasingly becoming the norm in American culture, both the continued sway of conservative groups in the mainstream and the incendiary nature of discussing adolescent sexual agency in a positive light would soon be made clear to them. Even in a more liberal political climate, discussions about the sexual and reproductive needs of teenage girls could still only take place in the cultural underground.[155]

Ultimately, the commercial setting of *Sassy*'s intervention into American sexual politics would make its teen-centered feminist project impossible. Despite its popularity among alternative-culture-loving teenagers and adults, the publication

faced controversy over its treatment of girlhood sexualities from its first issue
onward. Reactions to *Sassy*'s portrayal of teenage desire would see involvement escalate from concerned parents to some of the most well-known conservative figureheads in the country.[156] In 1989, as letters poured in from teenagers desperate for
more advice on sexual issues, so did countless complaints from infuriated parents.[157]
One such concerned mother, Jan Dawes from Wabash, Indiana, and two of her
friends petitioned the closing of the magazine and successfully persuaded the Kmart
and Hooks drugstores closest to her to stop selling *Sassy*.[158] Soon, larger, more for-
mally organized pro-family conservative groups that had originated with the dawn
of the New Right discovered and reacted to the portrayal of sex in the new publication. In July 1989, Focus on the Family's monthly newsletter *The Citizen* called
Sassy "without question the most sexually provocative magazine ever published."[159]
Founder and New Right figurehead James Dobson took particular grievance to articles such as "The Truth about Boys' Bodies" but also mentioned articles that had
never actually appeared in the magazine, such as "Good Manners for Good-
Mannered Sex."[160] Following suggestions listed under "what you can do," a socially
conservative women's group named Women Aglow helped initiate a letter campaign aimed at *Sassy*'s major advertisers, threatening a boycott of their companies
if they did not withdraw their advertisements from *Sassy*.[161] Reverend Donald Wildmon, head of the American Family Association, joined in urging a boycott, as did
the Moral Majority, who started their own campaign on the basis that *Sassy* encouraged homosexuality and teenage sex generally, and that the magazine undermined
parental authority.[162] Over the course of a few months in 1989, *Sassy* lost almost all
of their advertising accounts, including major advertisers Procter & Gamble and
Tampax, and editors referred jokingly to the thin publication that remained as "The
Sassy Pamphlet."[163] *Adweek* reported that as many as twelve chain stores had stopped
stocking the magazine.[164] The attacks on *Sassy* revealed a critical distinction within
the teenage years that allowed conservatives room to operate—while much of the
writing was aimed at slightly older teenagers who were over the age of sexual consent in their state, all that these conservatives saw was that teenage readers of the
magazine could theoretically be as young as thirteen, and thus viewed the content
of the magazine as a form of sexual harm to children.

The reader-advertiser boycott set the tone for the struggle that *Sassy* editors would
constantly be immersed in as they attempted to put forward a useful source of sex
education for teenage women. In order to survive the boycott, *Sassy* editors were
forced to make constant editorial compromises. This included removing a response
to a "help" letter about contracting HIV from oral sex, and a "story debunking the
myths of masturbation." After the writer of the masturbation piece, Karen Catchpole, heard about the removal of her article, she threw things in rage but eventually gave the piece to the Riot Grrrl zine *Girl Germs* to publish instead.[165] This proved
again the extent to which it was Riot Grrrl's noncommercial, underground circulation that allowed them the freedom to discuss sex, and that the mainstream of
American culture was still a hostile environment for frank but basic information

about adolescent sexuality.[166] Importantly, however, it was not the corporations advertising in *Sassy* that took issue with the magazine's frank approach to sexuality: editor Jane Pratt and creator Sandra Yates toured the country after the boycott attempting to convince "advertisers and wholesalers" of *Sassy*'s importance and were met with widespread support.[167] Rather, companies that responded to the boycott and continued to ask *Sassy* to remove sexual content over the rest of the magazine's run were worried about the loss of customers that would result from upsetting such powerful conservative groups that had strong public platforms and a strong influence on consumers.[168] Liberal actors, here, were making conservative decisions based on a fear of retaliation from the still highly mobilized socially conservative factions of the New Right. Despite *Sassy*'s popularity in certain groups, the organizational power of the Right on issues affecting "the family" continued to prevail into the 1990s. While Riot Grrrls and *Sassy* girls were calling for a more explicit discourse on the sexual lives of teenage girls, social conservatives were tightly organized around such issues and were able to exercise this weight in their activism and to affect what more progressive adults were willing or able to advocate for. In doing so, a culture war schism between underground and mainstream representations of adolescent sexuality widened further. The battle over *Sassy* showed how the previously established sides of the culture wars were complicated once teenage sex was at stake.[169]

What remained by the end of *Sassy*'s life was far removed from what its creators had envisaged. The continual threat of losing advertising meant that the sexually explicit content the writers had hoped to emphasize was constantly monitored and removed. The increasing pressure led to the original editor, Jane Pratt, leaving in 1992, and the rest of the original editorial team leaving together after the publication of the October 1994 issue. Under the new editorial team, the magazine was completely unrecognizable, most notably in its discussion of sex. One noticeable change was that sex was only discussed in negative terms. One of the final issues, from April 1996, demonstrated how far the publication had drifted from its initial sex positivity. Articles included "I Got HIV after My First Sexual Experience: One Girl's Tale of Fatal Infatuation" and "Special Report: Teen Moms Tell It Like It Is (if you don't want to become a statistic, read this now)," the tone of the reportage now echoing the fear tactics and shaming of the abstinence-driven curricula the founders of the magazine had initially sought to counteract.[170] The last issue came in December 1996, before it was bought by the owners of *Teen*, a magazine that rarely mentioned sex, and disappeared.[171]

The story of *Sassy* emphasizes the desire of young women in the United States, in addition to many adults, for adequate sexual information by the 1990s, and concurrently the impossibility of such a thing in the mainstream of that culture. Following the new awareness of child sexual abuse in the U.S. in the 1980s, social conservatives were aware of the political salience of accusing a publication of perpetuating this problem. So top-down and unifying was this discourse that it is hard to imagine how progressive or feminist groups could counter this censorship at

the same level. Thus, in such a climate, it was only within subcultures that teenagers were able to circumvent restrictions in writing and reading information about
sex.[172]

Two other magazines emerged in the mid-1990s that also contributed to the
developing girl culture within that era's feminism. These publications, *Bust* and
Bitch, were aimed at women ranging from just out of their teens to their early thir-
ties and were thus protected from the censorship that *Sassy* had been subject to.
Both of these publications started as underground, noncommercial zines and were
eventually transformed into traditional magazines, though both maintained the
punk aesthetic of zines and continued to espouse the progressive sexual politics
of Riot Grrrl.[173] Girlhood was central to these publications. Both publications continued in the spirit of merging artifacts of underground and mainstream girlhood
cultures that *Sassy* had begun and that would come to be a defining characteristic
of so-called Third Wave aesthetics.[174] Though founders of both magazines "grappled" with "how far feminism can be mainstreamed before selling out," ultimately
the development of accessible technologies in the 1990s meant that the young women
who started the magazines could remain in charge, through desktop publishing
programs.[175]

Bust was the first of these publications to form, at the same time as Riot Grrrl
was noticed by the mainstream media and as *Sassy* began to fade into nonexistence.
In 1993, two women in their late twenties working for the children's television channel Nickelodeon met and discovered a shared love for *Sassy*, despite not being in
the publication's target readership, and a desire for an equivalent publication for
women their age.[176] They soon began to steal office supplies from Nickelodeon in
order to start making *Bust*, the name of which, referencing breasts, denoted their
sex- and body-positive politics and humorous approach, first as a traditional, handmade zine.[177] Both women had explicitly feminist aims in this project, and the kind
of sexual politics they were espousing was characteristic of the feminists that were
beginning to describe themselves as Third Wave—they engaged with the 1980s feminist sex wars but saw young women as having been missing from these debates,
despite being central to them.[178] Both women had formal training in feminist theory: Marcelle Karp had studied film and television at Queen's College in 1982, and
Debbie Stoller had earned a PhD in social psychology from Yale in 1988, having
written a thesis on media representation of women.[179] From the outset of their project, they had a strong focus on "the pleasures, rather than the pain, of growing up
girl" that they believed *Sassy* had captured.[180] With their publication aimed at a
slightly older audience, this meant a strong focus on sex, and they were decidedly
pro-sex in their approach.[181] *Bust* often featured articles on female sexual pleasure,
including regular reviews of sex toys and erotica; the erotic literature column was
titled "The One-Handed Read."[182]

Despite the fact that this magazine was aimed at adult women, its focus on sexuality was a part of what Stoller and Karp were beginning to define explicitly as
"girlie culture."[183] Girlie culture, though inspired by teenage sexual exploration and
rebellion, was increasingly proliferated and enjoyed mostly by adult women. *Bust*

and spaces of "girlie" or "girl culture" allowed for women with feminist politics to explore the underground activism and aesthetics of Riot Grrrl with mainstream fashion and visual culture trends, and for these women to re-examine their own sexual experiences as teenagers with the feminist knowledge and sexually open platform they now had as adults. Crucially, what enabled these women to access this in the 1990s when *Sassy* readers could not was the fact that they were legally adults— while mainstream publications for adults became more sexually explicit in the 1990s, teenage girls remained without sexual citizenship, their bodies falling instead under the self-proclaimed jurisdiction of social conservative groups still pursuing anti-obscenity and pro-family activism. The experience of growing up as a young woman in the political climate of the culture wars of the 1970s and 1980s, and of being at the center of these battles, fed the explorations of politicized girlhoods by the adult writers of *Bust* in the pages of their magazine, and the desire for similarly aged readers to seek out these stories.

Sexuality in youth culture was also a recurring theme in *Bust*. The fifth issue of *Bust* took the special theme "My Life as a Girl," though teenagers were the focus of many of the magazine's early issues.[184] In the Winter 2000 "feminism issue," for instance, *Bust* featured an interview between Second Wave feminist writer and activist Gloria Steinem and founding Riot Grrrl Kathleen Hanna, wherein they discussed the younger generation of feminists and their activism. *Bust* also had a regular "Buffy Watch" column that deconstructed the major themes in *Buffy the Vampire Slayer*, a show aimed at adolescent audiences. These themes were often sexual in nature. "Season Three could have been called *Sex and the Slayer's City*, it was so hot," read one of the articles. "We LOVED the overload of S/M: bondage, torture, and Willow as a dominatrix."[185] In 1999, the editors of *Bust* published *The BUST Guide to the New Girl Order*, which codified girl culture and positioned representations of youth and young women at the center of 1990s feminisms. In the book, Stoller and Karp declared that "from those T-shirts proclaiming that 'Girls Rule' to pseudo-feminist bubblegum bands preaching about 'Girl Power' to 1997's 'Girl Issue' of *Spin* magazine, girl has gone from being a profanity among feminists to becoming practically a rallying cry," and even stated, "Women, step aside: the time of the girl is on us."[186]

Bitch was the next publication to form in the wake of *Sassy*, in 1996, contributing to the spreading "girl culture" among feminist adults of the period.[187] Founders Lisa Jervis and Andi Zeisler, a pair of young writers, friends, and fans of girl culture including both *Buffy* and *Sassy*, started the project, a "feminist response to pop culture," originally as a handmade and distributed zine.[188] *Bitch* shared *Bust*'s focus on girlhood sexualities as a part of "girlie" culture.[189] Like *Bust*, *Bitch* also dedicated a special issue in 1998 to the location of youth within feminism, this time called "The Puberty Issue."[190] In the editor's letter, Jervis and Zeisler named young women as a priority for a new wave of American feminism. "Pubescence and adolescence are the years when girls *most* need feminism's support," they asserted.[191] In doing so, the editors of *Bitch* were contributing to the growing focus within feminist activism and in mainstream culture on the conditions of teenage girls' sexual initiation in America. Though *Bitch* became a commercial publication, its writers saw their efforts as being distinct from the wider mainstreaming of girl culture. In 1997, *Bitch* ran an article by editor Andi Zeisler that derided the newly fashionable baby tees, which she claimed "eighty-sixes the underlying rage of Riot Grrrl fashion-as-politics, opting instead for the straight-up shill of barely pubescent flesh as titillation." Instead of urging a critical rethinking of girlhood sexuality, she argued, the mainstreaming of girl culture merely "cashes in on familiar fantasies of the young girl as budding sex plaything."[192] Zeisler had noticed that the representations of agentic adolescent sexuality that did not get quashed in this period were those that commodified the rebellious teenage girl and simultaneously catered to the male observer by embodying societal standards of thin, white beauty and desirability—these realities suggested that the pro-sex celebration of "victory" at the end of the 1980s was premature, as it was predominantly a heterosexist version of sexual liberation that dominated the mainstream in the 1990s.

Because of this, writers at *Bitch* struggled in particular to decipher the political importance of what was becoming a very visible articulation of "girl power" in mainstream popular culture: the teen TV show *Buffy the Vampire Slayer*. In an article from issue 10, "The Buffy Effect," author Rachel Fudge discussed the show's feminist potential as an offshoot of mainstream girl culture. Namely, she weighed up the titular character's sexual agency against her conforming attractiveness as a white, thin, feminine teenage girl. She named the most important aspect of the show as the teenage protagonist's ability to "survive her sexual mistake" in losing her virginity to a vampire, and celebrated that "as cute and perky and scantily clad as she is, she's not overtly sexualized within the show."[193] These factors situated Buffy as a character that could not have been portrayed at any other moment in American history, as conversations about girlhood sexual experience happening among feminists in the media were becoming more explicit than ever before. However, Fudge was concerned about the "diluted imitation of female empowerment" that *Buffy* could be seen to represent. "She's feisty and moody and won't let anyone push her around," Fudge noted, but also remarked that "her ever-present tank tops showcase her rack quite efficiently," before asking, "Is Buffy really an exhilarating post-third-wave heroine, or is she merely a caricature of '90s pseudo-girl power, a cleverly crafted marketing scheme to hook the ever-important youth demographic?"[194] What Fudge was addressing was the shift of the "girlie" aesthetics of Third Wave feminism, as initiated by Riot Grrrl and codified by magazines such as *Bust* and *Bitch*, into wider popular culture.

What the heated discussion of *Buffy*'s feminist merits in *Bitch* also denoted, however, was the focus on white women within the girl culture that was reaching the American mainstream by the end of the decade. Readers of color reached out to the magazine's editors to point out this problem. "I would like to respond to the question 'What do you like least about *Bitch*?,'" wrote "An Urban Girl Who Wants to Remain A Loyal Reader." "It is the fact that it is so WHITE!" she continued. "I can't recall one article in the two years I have been a reader, other than the Gina Gold interview in #11, that was written from a black perspective about black women's issues. It made me feel really shitty, and I know I will be less enthusiastic about buying *Bitch* in the future."[195] Another letter pointed out the magazine's hypocrisy in accusing the teenage magazine *CosmoGirl!* of being "mighty whitey" when, according to the author, "that's the impression I get of *Bitch*": that it was "the white feminist's response to pop culture."[196]

The author of the letter went on to mention how they had been "spoiled" by another publication, *HUES (Hear Us Emerging Sisters)*.[197] *HUES* was another DIY zine turned magazine that was "started by three 19-year-old University of Michigan students in 1992": Dyann Logwood, who is African American, and twin sisters Ophira and Tali Edut, who are Israeli American.[198] The idea for the magazine came when the trio, self-dubbed "vending machine philosophers," were "trapped in a snowy dorm cut off from main campus."[199] As they discussed the way that popular media made them feel excluded both "culturally" and "physically," they decided to create the "perfect magazine."[200] *HUES* started as a zine for a class project and grew into a nationally distributed glossy magazine with major feminist activists Gloria Steinem and Rebecca Walker on the board.[201] It was run by a team ranging from eighteen to twenty-four in age, with a focus on "self-esteem among women of all cultures, classes, religions, sexual orientations and experiences."[202] It featured articles such as "HIV: Three Women's Stories" and "Black Men against Sexism," and in the experience of the person who wrote to *Bitch* about the magazine's hypocrisy, *HUES* was "really multi-cultural, not just in talk but in action."[203] This was aided by the freedom the publication had because of its grassroots foundations. Unfortunately, the magazine's small distributor, New Moon Publishing in Duluth, Minnesota, "didn't have the capital needed to sustain or mass-market *HUES*," yet another example of the ways in which truly radical conversations about race, gender, and sexuality in American culture remained underground in the 1990s.[204] Though it ran for only seven years and could not stay in circulation as *Bitch* and *Bust* have, *HUES* constituted a part of the diverse girl cultures of the 1990s that were sidelined by a mainstream representation of girl culture that centered mostly on the sexual coming-of-age stories of middle-class white teenagers.

This could also be seen in the increase in explorations of young women's sexualities in mainstream film and television. *My So-Called Life*, which starred teenage actress Claire Danes as the lead character Angela Chase, was viewed as an "alternative" television show and heralded by writers at *Sassy* as being relatable and realistic; *Bust* editors called it "the TV equivalent of Judy Blume's books."[205] The "loss of virginity episode" became an institution among television for teens, alongside shows such as *Buffy* and *Beverly Hills, 90210*.[206] Additionally, queer characters gained an unprecedented visibility in teen programming, as in the hugely popular *Dawson's Creek* and the Canadian teen drama *Degrassi*, which was also widely viewed in the United States.[207] The ability of adolescent characters to come out on screen was in turn a reflection of more acceptance toward homosexuality in American popular culture: a number of actors and performers announced their sexuality over the course of the 1990s, including Ellen DeGeneres and Jodie Foster.[208] One of the main characters in *Buffy*, Willow Rosenberg, was a bisexual character who had a two-year relationship with another woman, Tara, which to some feminist critics made her one of the most well-rounded and thoughtfully represented queer female characters on TV.[209] To others, however, these representations were still problematic, as the sex scenes of the straight main character Buffy were shot at far greater length and with more detail than those of Willow, whose romantic scenes remained fairly chaste.[210] Therefore, while the legacy of pro-sex feminism and the movement of new activist cultures out of the underground and into the mainstream had made representations of sexuality in girlhood in America more explicit than ever before, the feminist politics behind these representations muddied as they became more commercialized. Beyond this, as is evidenced by the above examples, that which was deemed a part of girl culture in the mainstream mirrored the whiteness of the Riot Grrrl movement that it had taken its cues from.[211] Despite the concurrent feminist organizing and cultural production of young women of color in the same era, these girls were not given the same platform as a part of the dominant teen culture. For instance, teenage celebrities of color that starred in TV shows centering on their characters' emotional experiences and complex coming-of-age stories— such as Tia and Tamera Mowry of sitcom Sister, Sister and R&B singer Brandy Norwood, who played the titular role in the sitcom Moesha—received only a fraction of the media attention that white adolescent celebrities did.[212] The whiteness of girl culture's heroines as portrayed by the mainstream press in the 1990s both reveals the perpetuation of societal standards of beauty and desirability by TV and music industry executives, and suggests the pernicious continuation of a historical exclusion of Black and other girls of color from experiences of girlhood and of innocence.[213]

The uncertain empowerment to be found in mainstream girl culture could also be seen in the popularity of teenage celebrities such as pop singers Britney Spears and Christina Aguilera, about whom the term "sexualization" came into use to describe the anxiety many adults felt about the erotic nature of these young women's performances.[214] Spears, for instance, was launched into the public eye with the debut of the video for her 1998 single ". . . Baby One More Time," in which she sports a revealing version of a private school girl's uniform.[215] The limitations of 1990s girl power as it was represented by the mostly male-run mainstream media have recently been brought to light, in both the accusations that the stars of Buffy have made against the show's creator, Joss Whedon, for misogynistic treatment on set, and the revelations about the realities of Britney Spears's struggles for financial and personal freedom in the years since she became famous.[216] Despite the unprecedented discourse on adolescent sexuality in the mainstream of American culture in this period, it was only within grassroots, youth-driven spaces that teenagers could access stories and information about sex that did not also cater to the desires of adult men in positions of power.

In the same period, a wave of young female talent took hip-hop by storm.[217] Sex and sexuality were central themes in their music, and these young women, all of whom were in their late teens, displayed degrees of self-knowledge and sexual empowerment in their recordings and were seen as figureheads of the Third Wave of feminism in the United States.[218] Despite these artists' commercial success, they were considered less frequently as a part of 1990s "girl culture."[219] Among these recording artists were rappers Roxanne Shanté, who began rapping at age thirteen, and Queen Latifah, who while eschewing the label "feminist" nonetheless was heralded by young women as such, including the young DC Riot Grrrl Molly Neuman.[220] Lil' Kim, an artist discovered at the age of nineteen, attracted controversy for showing a lot of skin in her stage and red carpet outfits, and for the unapologetically frank lyrical content of her raps.[221] In May 1997, bell hooks interviewed Lil' Kim for the independent culture magazine *Paper*—the intellectual was excited by the potential for young Black women's sexual liberation that simmered in Lil' Kim's art, if frustrated by the male-led music industry that framed her work. In the article, hooks noted the "boring straight male porn" vision Lil' Kim portrayed when "the boys in charge package her," but spent the interview giving the young star credence for her personal sexual autonomy and the emphasis she put on pleasure.[222] "My mother and older generations felt that in exchange for the p-ssy, you should get marriage, you should get something," hooks relayed. "I'm not that kind of girl, though. I think real sexual liberation means that you're in charge of your p-ssy; you don't have to exchange it for anything." Lil' Kim concurred, adding "and sometimes it's not just exchanging; sometimes it's just having a sexual orgasm 'cause you love it and you need it."[223]

The cross-generational conversation between hooks and Lil' Kim revealed the new space for young Black women to be forthright about their desire in mainstream music. However, as the music industry was controlled by men, of course it remained mitigated by these figures. Additionally, as with the white young women represented within girl culture, it was still only possible for outrightly heterosexual expressions of these young women's desire to be upheld by the music industry. Despite being in their late teens and early twenties at the start of their careers—as were the Riot Grrrls, white female pop stars of the decade, and the writers of *Sassy*, *Bitch*, and *Bust*—these artists were, however, not framed at the time or in histories of the period as being central to "girl culture," either as teenagers or as young adults reclaiming girlhood. The girl culture that moved from the underground to being celebrated as such in the mainstream over the 1990s was a white girl culture, despite the existence of diverse girl cultures in the United States in the same period. Though cultural representations of girlhood sexual experiences were enabled in American popular culture in the 1990s in ways not seen before in history, they were predominantly those that continued to perpetuate historical ideas of who was entitled to a protected girlhood.[224]

GIRLS IN THE ACADEMY: SEXUALITY, SELF-ESTEEM, AND SCHOLARSHIP

As the mainstream of American culture became increasingly sexually explicit and included increasing representations of girlhood sexualities, the culture wars over adolescent sex in turn became increasingly explicit. The question of whether the new girl culture was empowering or potentially dangerous for teenagers in the 1990s was debated by a number of adult feminists in this period. A growing concern for the impact of American culture on the mental and physical health of teenage girls was expressed through a wave of academic publishing on the subject, birthing an interdisciplinary approach known as girl studies over the course of the decade. During the 1990s, the most popular and widely read feminist texts began to focus on the impact of a changing society on teenagers and to see young women as a priority for the movement, bringing them into the center of even adult feminisms in unprecedentedly explicit ways. Through documenting the rise of girl culture as it happened, such writers were also contributing to the mainstream iteration of this culture.[225] In particular, the binary debate that emerged in the new literature, described by some as a narrative of "girl power" versus one of "girls at risk," became a fragment of mainstream girl culture in this period.[226] On the one hand, some feminists celebrated the new and promising "youth feminism" of this era.[227] Changing fashions for young women, which included new emphasis on self-expression and on comfort, were also seen as indicative of shifting mores.[228] Simultaneously, however, a slew of books on the harmful effects of these shifts in society on teenage girls were published in both the United States and the United Kingdom.[229] Though "girls in crisis" and "girl power" were posed as polar approaches in these works, both frameworks offered quite surface analyses of the needs of teenagers in the 1990s, and both bodies of writing tended to centralize white, middle-class teenage girls.[230] Those adult feminist thinkers who took a more nuanced approach toward the problems and pleasures of girlhood sexualities formed a fringe, less popular front of the culture war battle that crystallized in this period, which ultimately pitted the ever-expanding mainstream representations of and reactions to adolescent sex against more realistic considerations of the needs and feelings of teenage girls.

Leading the body of work that believed young women to be at the mercy of the social changes of this period was psychologist Mary Pipher's 1994 study *Reviving Ophelia: Saving the Selves of Adolescent Girls*. Pipher researched and wrote *Reviving Ophelia* based on her work as a therapist with teenage girls, and the alarm she felt at what she saw as a "girl-poisoning culture" that had led young women in America to suffer from a widespread, chronic lack of self-esteem. "As a therapist, I often felt bewildered and frustrated," Pipher somberly remembered. "These feelings led to questions: Why are so many girls in therapy in the 1990s? Why are there more self-mutilators? What is the meaning of lip, nose and eyebrow piercings?"[231] The book was hugely popular and remained on the *New York Times* bestseller list for more than two years.[232] It was also influential to other scholars and researchers, so much so that it "spawned a new generation of best-selling critique and social interest in girls" that cited Pipher directly.[233] The influx of titles on teenage girls and self-esteem that emerged after Pipher's publication is comparable to the self-help "empire" that emerged in the 1980s as the nation became newly aware of the extent of child sexual abuse. Pipher and others writing about "girls in crisis" also began to proliferate the term "sexualization" to describe exploitative representations of young women in mainstream media in this period, an idea that remained in consistent use to describe fears surrounding teenage female sexuality.[234] Pipher and her cadre were right to draw attention to the needs of teenage girls in a culture that enjoyed only the most titillating images of their sexual empowerment, but in which their sexual and reproductive rights were not enshrined in policy and law. In the 1990s, most teenage girls were not politically active around their sexuality in the way that Riot Grrrls were or were connected through these kinds of feminist networks. However, the focus on mostly white subjects in these works and the majority white voices pioneering these efforts meant that those researching "girls in crisis" further perpetuated the historical inequality of vulnerability only being afforded to white children.[235]

Pipher's attention to a self-esteem problem in young women both inspired and reinforced an increasingly institutionalized approach to teenage girls in America. In her book, Pipher hinted at the institutional appeal of addressing girls' self-esteem. "I believe that most Americans share the concerns I have for our daughters," she stated, supporting this by explaining that "Hillary Rodham Clinton, Tipper Gore, Janet Reno, Marian Wright Edelman and many others" were also "sounding the alarm."[236] The list of Democratic women Pipher was referring to illustrates again the fluid lines of the culture wars when it came to girlhood: it was not only the social and religious conservatives who shut down *Sassy* magazine who believed that the newly sexually explicit culture was harmful to young women.[237] Coinciding with the publication of *Reviving Ophelia* were various studies and programs, launched by national liberal think tanks and nongovernmental organizations, that also addressed the issue of self-esteem in girls and demonstrated a concern for a variety of pressures facing young women in their development.[238] For instance, in 1993, the National Organization for Women (NOW) Legal Defense and Education Fund and the Wellesley College Center for Research on Women produced research that showed that "sexual harassment was rampant in elementary and secondary schools."[239] A theory of "girls in crisis" was becoming popular across the liberal establishment, as the framework of "self-esteem" aligned a protected period of sexual coming of age with education and career ambition.

Popular American feminist Naomi Wolf, meanwhile, was one of many writers of girl studies who viewed the 1990s as an era of "girl power."[240] In the early 1990s, twenty-eight-year-old Wolf published the master's thesis she wrote as a Rhodes Scholar as the book *The Beauty Myth*, to great academic and popular acclaim.[241] Her next book, *Fire with Fire: How Power Feminism Will Change the 21st Century*, was published in 1994; here, Wolf distanced herself from what she described as a "victim feminism" perpetuated by antipornography feminists, and argued that women such as MacKinnon and Dworkin feared "that to have too much fun poses a threat to the revolution."[242] Instead, Wolf argued that women should proceed with "power feminism."[243] Wolf's work was perpetuating a divide in feminist approaches to young women's experiences of sex that continued the schism of the sex wars. Accordingly, in 1998, Wolf's *Promiscuities* explored what it meant, culturally, for a teenage girl to be described as a "slut". "If we were out of line sexually we could become sluts; if we became sluts, we could die several deaths," she grimly recalled.[244] This revisiting of previously harmful terminology furthered her critique of "victim feminism" and situated her within the similar tradition of reclaiming that was popular in Riot Grrrl.[245] Though Wolf's "power feminism" or the notion of "girl power" was ostensibly opposed to notions of "girls in crisis," both emerged from the American political economy of the 1990s, in which girlhood was becoming further politicized by liberals as a formative time for the construction of financial or political success as an adult woman.[246] Direct links between young women's sexual experiences and their future citizenship were growing over this period, whether the discourse was one of "girl power" or "girls in crisis." Further, the literature on "girl power," like that of "girls in crisis," was also predominantly penned by white researchers and focused on the behaviors of white teenage girls.[247] As with the pop cultural aspects of girl culture, popular girl studies literature centered its concern on white teenagers.

Outside of these widely read reactions to teenagers' sexual lives, some feminists studying girlhood resisted the polarized, popular accounts of girlhood in the 1990s that described them as either powerful or in crisis. Such writers included sociologist Janice Irvine and Sharon Thompson, who had been involved in pro-sex feminism in the 1980s. Both Irvine and Thompson believed that the political and economic realities underpinning cultural representations of girlhood in this era and the presence of HIV/AIDS required widespread research on the diverse experiences of teenagers. For reasons that diverged from Naomi Wolf's, they felt that a narrative of "victimization" was not an adequate framework through which to view teenage sex.[248] Thompson, who had spoken out about the needs of teenagers as a pro-sex feminist in the 1980s, urged "anthropologists, psychologists, and literary critics" to better understand "the issues that absorb girls themselves" rather than approach their research with "adult preoccupations."[249] Another thinker who resisted the media-centric debate over whether girls were in crisis was historian Joan Jacobs Brumberg, who published *The Body Project: An Intimate History of American Girls* in 1998. She argued that in the 1990s, "American girls are both the beneficiaries and the victims of a century of change in sexual mores and behaviors."[250] Brumberg's assessment witnessed both the exciting emergence of teenage girls' politicized voices about their sexualities into pockets of American culture, and the detrimental effects that the mainstreaming and commercialization of teen spirit was having on girls.

These writers' assertions, less titillating than the extreme of either the empowered girl or the teenage victim that was espoused in the mainstream media and girl studies texts, took notes from the more complicated realities of teenage sex that young women involved in underground girl cultures described in their songs, zines, and other activism. The co-optation and misinterpretation of underground girl cultures by mainstream television, music, and feminisms, and the whiteness and straightness of this resulting culture, proved that despite the newly explicit con-versations about adolescent sex in the United States in the 1990s, it was not a main-stream culture that could contend with frank, honest discussions of the realities of being a teenager.[251] As the next chapter will detail, the explosion of mainstream girl culture was not the only route through which teenage girls became central to the culture wars of the 1990s in newly explicit ways: adolescent sexual behavior was also becoming increasingly pivotal within the policy and legal debates of the same period.

CHAPTER 4

The Third Wave and
the Third Way

On 25 October 1991, teenagers and young people filled the Hollywood Palace in Los Angeles to see a lineup of grunge and post-punk bands including Nirvana, L7, Hole, and Sister Double Happiness. The scale of the gig could be attributed to more than the popularity of the bands on stage—the event, Rock for Choice, was a benefit to raise money for pro-choice groups and to encourage voter turnout to counter antiabortion laws.[1] Organized by members of the all-female grunge band L7 and Sue Cummings, the associate editor of *LA Weekly*, the event was modeled after both Bob Geldof's Live Aid concerts and the Rock the Vote gig the previous year. "Why couldn't it be cool for people into rock to support feminism," Cummings had wondered, "as it was to care about farmers or famine or environmentalism?"[2]

While Cummings was referring to large-scale, well-publicized events by musicians with recording contracts, her statement came at the same time that young women in towns and cities across the country were, through their music and other creative practices, organizing around feminist issues as a part of the Riot Grrrl movement. Whether attending massive Rock for Choice gigs in LA or tiny spoken-word nights in Olympia, Washington, young women at the beginning of the 1990s were aware of the need to rock the 1992 elections in order to secure reproductive—and other—rights for women. Growing up under two Republican presidencies left many young women on the cusp of voting age desperate to impact federal policy in whatever way they could. Writing in the zine *Girl Germs* in 1992, one Riot Grrrl raged that "we might as well burn the constitution and the bill of rights (the only Bill I'll ever love) because most all of us are being denied our rights. . . . We have white males in office telling us what to and not say . . . how and what to do with our bodies, and on and on." Most of all, she was furious that she couldn't do anything about it. "I can't vote (in November I'll turn 15)," she bemoaned, "so I can't kick Georgie Porgie out of office."[3]

The movement of girl culture, as depicted in the previous chapter, from its punk, grassroots beginnings into the cultural mainstream, was consistently shaped by developments in national political culture. Despite the anarchic nature of DIY cul-

ture, many Riot Grrrls encouraged young women to notice and respond to electoral politics during this period, sometimes by protesting, through providing
education and services that they saw as being restricted by national policy, and at
other times by speaking out about the sexual politics of Washington and how they
affected young women. This chapter details the national political events that shaped
the sexual and political identities of young women in the 1990s: the experiences of
African American lawyer Anita Hill and the first Black surgeon general, Joycelyn
Elders, the development of welfare and abstinence education policy under Clinton, and the treatment of White House intern Monica Lewinsky following the exposure of her affair with the president. It reveals the conversations that took place at
the level of national politics regarding young women and sex, and in doing so pro-
vides a backdrop to the cultures and activism of teenagers.

Following on from the story of 1990s girl cultures, it further positions the decade
as a pivotal period in the culture wars. Tracing the presence of adolescent sexuality
within policy and political discourse of the era reiterates that there were newly
explicit conversations about adolescent sexual practices in this era, but also reveals
the vast limitations of the ostensible sex positivity of the 1990s for teenage girls.[4] The
ways that racialized misogyny both sparked and perpetuated the culture wars are
central to this history, both in the experience of women in positions of power and in
the case of the young women of color who were targeted and scapegoated by welfare
reform.[5] This further frames the margins of the decade's celebratory "girl culture."
Treatments of girlhood sexuality within political culture in the same decade revealed
how girls of color and working-class girls were construed separately from white,
middle-class girlhoods within political discourses, as a subversive, disruptive, social
problem to be managed, which reinforced the whiteness and relative privilege of
girl culture.[6] The concurrent discourse on sex and pregnancy among young Black
women on state benefits, alongside one on young white "victims" in "girls in crisis"
literature and abstinence education curricula, saw the racial divides in conceptions
of teenage female sexuality re-emerge in the 1990s with exceptional clarity.[7] However, this period also saw the mobilization of organizations led by young women of
color, which became increasingly visible in their response to social injustice.

This inequality was reified in this period by federal policy under President William Jefferson Clinton. Clinton's presidency encapsulated the flimsy promises of
1990s mainstream feminism for the sexual and reproductive health of young people.
Despite signaling success for progressive demands, he would ultimately continue
and exacerbate the long-running scapegoating of poor young women of color, passing welfare reforms that reiterated the imagery evoked by Reagan's notion of "welfare queens" in the 1980s. What is revealed here is the way in which Clinton's
presidency, and his neoliberal, "Third Way" centrism, consistently resulted in a conservative and punitive approach to the sexual and reproductive health of young
women as a measure through which to deflect from his own sexual transgressions,
and remain in government.

National political culture during this period saw consensuses form and dissent-
ers emerge, frequently in ways that were unexpected or inconsistent, furthering

the influence of adolescent sexuality on culture wars alliances as a whole.[8] Adults with a stake in adolescent sexuality became increasingly outspoken on the topic in this era, whether advocating for abstinence until heterosexual marriage or for a more realistic approach to young people's sexual behavior in the age of AIDS. Young people themselves also became increasingly politically active around issues of social justice that affected them and their communities. The debates over what legal sexual and reproductive rights teenagers should have saw a new culture war divide emerge: between those who would dare to advocate frankly for the needs of teenagers—which now included many teenagers themselves—and those who explicitly prioritized the delaying of sexual activity over all else, a collaboration of old members of the New Right and many Democrats, including Clinton himself.[9] Through these shifts, the sexual lives of teenage girls played an increasingly central role both within the American culture wars and in reshaping them.

THE BACKLASH AGAINST ANITA HILL AND JOYCELYN ELDERS

In the fall of 1991, as young feminists around the country devoured Susan Faludi's *Backlash* and became involved in abortion-rights organizing in the form of Rock for Choice or Riot Grrrl, events in Washington further revealed the extent of the unfinished fight for gender equality to young people coming of age in the United States. In the wake of the retirement of Supreme Court justice Thurgood Marshall, the eminent civil rights lawyer, activists from various progressive movements balked at the nomination of Clarence Thomas to the bench by George H. W. Bush.[10] The African American federal judge had spent most of his career opposing policies such as affirmative action and abortion rights, which Marshall had upheld during his tenure in the Supreme Court.[11] In September 1991, the thirty-five-year-old legal professor and lawyer Anita Hill accused Thomas of sexually harassing her at work at the Department of Education and the Equal Employment Opportunity Commission (EEOC). Hill's testimonial served as a cross-generational antiracist feminist clarion call in the United States.[12] Shirley Gutierrez wrote of this shift in 1992 in the zine *Frighten the Horses* that "1991 was a banner year for the forces of reaction." She continued: "The national sympathy for Thomas and his eventual confirmation underlined the obvious: the backlash against women's rights had reached new heights."[13]

The Hill-Thomas hearings presented to women, particularly African American women, how rampant race and gender inequality remained at this point in American history.[14] On 11 October 1991, Hill testified before the Senate. She recalled how, at the Office of Civil Rights at the Department of Education, "he would turn the conversation to discussions about his sexual interests."[15] These, she told the Senate, included "acts that he had seen in pornographic films involving such things as women having sex with animals and films involving group sex or rape scenes."[16] Hill noted that the harassment began again when they worked together at the EEOC: "He would comment on what I was wearing in terms of whether it made me more or less sexually appealing and he commented on my appearance in terms of sexual attractiveness."[17] In the grueling questioning Hill received by an almost all-male, all-white Senate, the accomplished young Black lawyer was rendered isolated and disbelieved. "Did you take, as Senator Biden asked you, all steps that you knew how to take to prevent being in the witness chair today?," Senator Howell Heflin (D-AL) asked her. Comments such as these made Hill feel "like a child who was being chastised for wandering into traffic."[18] Despite the evidence presented and the feminist support that was roused by Hill's accusations, Thomas's nomination was approved by the Senate, and he was appointed as a Supreme Court justice on 23 October 1991. For many young women following the confirmation hearings in the news, Hill's testimony demonstrated the difficulties still facing women, particularly women of color, in their attempts to succeed in the halls of power. This was compounded further by the fact that evidence of Thomas's sexual mistreatment of a female colleague did not prohibit him from succeeding in his career.

Though Anita Hill's mistreatment, by Thomas and in the Senate hearings, did not have a material impact on the career of the conservative judge, Hill's highly publicized testimony moved and angered women of all ages, and a groundswell of feminist action rose in the United States in response, frequently under the rubric of the Third Wave.[19] The history of the term, however, as with all categorization of the American women's movement in "waves," is not straightforward. While historians have used the term "Third Wave" mostly to refer to the younger generation of activists who started organizing after the Hill-Thomas hearings on the "terrain" of "age," it was first used by adult activists in the late 1980s who wished to move forward as an "anti-racist, women-of-color led feminism for the coming decade," and was used to define their critique of racial inequality in the women's movement in the "First" and "Second Waves."[20] Anita Hill's treatment was noticed by those already working along these Third Wave intersections of antiracist and feminist thought in 1991. Hill's experience epitomized the writing of feminist scholar and lawyer Kimberlé Crenshaw, who had introduced the term "intersectionality" to critical race theory not long before, in her 1989 article "Demarginalizing the Intersection of Race and Sex." In this pivotal piece, she described the exclusions that Black women faced both from white women within feminist activism and from Black men within antiracist movements, and in their interpersonal relationships.[21] Crenshaw's theory of intersectionality also specified that Black women were doubly oppressed in that they experienced sexism both externally from white men and from men within their own Black communities: Hill's alleged harassment in the first instance by Clarence Thomas and then subsequently by white men in the Senate demonstrated the urgency of Crenshaw's text. This was clear to Crenshaw herself, who joined the legal team representing Hill during the hearings. It is important to understand that the terms "Third Wave" and "intersectional" that underpinned the multiracial, multigenerational organizing of this era had their roots in women-of-color-led feminisms of earlier years.[22]

While young people would mobilize politically in reaction to Hill's treatment, it is also crucial to understand that youth feminisms of the 1990s built off the ongoing work of older Black feminists, many of whom had grown up experiencing sexism within Black Power organizations.[23] The response from these women was almost instantaneous: "within minutes" of C-SPAN broadcasting the confirmation hearings, Black feminists Elsa Barkley Brown, Barbara Ransby, and Deborah King began to form a group named African American Women in Defense of Ourselves.[24] The group then published a statement in the *New York Times* in support of Hill's testimony against Thomas's nomination, which was signed by 1,603 Black women. The celebrated African American author and playwright Toni Morrison swiftly assembled a collection of academic responses to the hearings that grappled with the variant meanings of Hill's testimony and Thomas's confirmation for the intersecting politics of race and gender in American life.[25] It included an essay by Wahneema Lubiano that focused on how Anita Hill had been constructed as a threatening, single, "Black lady," one half of the two-pronged tropes of "Ms. Black Professional/the welfare queen" that were simultaneously deployed as "signs for and of everything wrong with the United States" and used to "not only perpetuate racism and sexism but guarantee the continued unequal distribution of economic resources."[26] Lubiano's analysis was prescient—the historically scapegoated figure of the Black or Latinx "welfare queen" would be deployed for further "ideological war by narrative means" under Clinton's presidency as the 1990s wore on.[27]

Hill's experience also reignited earlier debates among adult feminists over the issues of pornography and censorship. The reluctance of some pro-sex feminists to outrage over Hill's treatment would not be echoed by a younger generation of feminists coming into their political awakening via news coverage of the trial. For instance, Ellen Willis was hesitant in her reaction toward the hearings. Willis thought it "was unclear if it was really harassment or just C.T. being a jerk" and worried that the "conflation of C.T's interest in pornography with sexual harassment" would work towards the anti-pornography goal of, as she viewed it, "expanding sexual harassment law into a weapon of censorship."[28] Despite Willis's claims that pro-sex feminism had won the hearts and minds of a nation by the close of the 1980s, the mobilization of younger activists against sexual harassment that would ensue following Hill's testimony, despite or even in tandem with the more sexually graphic popular culture, suggests a reinvigoration—and reinvention—of feminist activism that focused instead on the sexual harm facing women in their work, relationships, and daily lives. This was also true for sex education campaigners concerned with young people's right to sexual knowledge, many of whom saw the event as a turning point in their advocacy against the growing tide of abstinence-only education at the federal level. Elsewhere in Washington on the same weekend of the hearings, Debra Haffner, president of the Sexuality Information and Education Council of the United States (SIECUS), was launching a task force to develop a framework for "the life criteria of a sexually healthy adult," which would describe sexual health at each developmental stage. To Haffner, the timing was perfect. "All week America had been focused on how confused we were about sexuality issues, and we got up and used that," she recalled. "Don't we want something better for our kids?," she asked the gathered sex educators and researchers.[29]

Haffner was not the only one to notice the political implications of Anita Hill's testimony for young people coming of age in the early 1990s. Though Hill's ordeal touched many women, it was a catalyst for young women's feminism in particular.[30] Some historians argue that before the early 1990s, there had been a lull in the formation of feminist activist groups among young women—that those born in the millennial generation (1982–2000) or Generation X (1964–1982) inherited the rights secured for them by the era of social movements, which had been fought primarily by those in the baby boomer generation (1946–1964).[31] The organization of progressive politics, as the story goes, was not largely felt to be as urgent by many who grew up in the 1980s. While this was indeed the narrative of white, neoliberal success presented through advertising to young women, this view obscures the ongoing activism that receives less coverage—often that of people of color—that occurs "between the waves."[32] However, youth-driven movements certainly were not as visible in the 1980s, and it was harder for young women wishing to seek out feminist action to find such groups.[33] Hill's experience marked a turning point for a younger generation of activists, convincing many that further action needed to be taken to displace the deep-seated sexism and racism that remained in American society and sparking new organizing across the country.[34]

The resurgence of feminist activism among young women in the wake of the Hill-Thomas hearings was emblematized by Rebecca Walker's diatribe for *Ms. Magazine* in the fall of 1991. In it, the twenty-two-year-old Yale senior and daughter of the prominent African American author Alice Walker described how she and her peers were "becoming the Third Wave" through their fury over Hill's treatment.[35] Walker had been thoroughly depressed by what she saw the weekend of the hearings, including "a Black man being grilled by a panel of white men about his sexual deviance" and "a Black woman claiming harassment and being discredited by other women."[36] However, she was also determined that this event, rather than "silencing" her, had instead "radicalized, politicized, shaken awake" her feminist spirit.[37] Walker asserted that young women now had to turn their "anger and awareness" into "tangible action" and to pay attention to the interrelationship between mainstream politics and intimate sexual politics. "I write this as a plea to all women, especially the women of my generation," she implored. "Let Thomas' confirmation serve to remind you, as it did me, that the fight is far from over. Let this dismissal of a woman's experience turn you to anger. Turn that outrage into political power. Do not vote for them unless they work for us. Do not have sex with them. Do not break bread with them."[38] Walker's essay was an impassioned call to arms to young Black women, in particular, to pay attention to the violence they faced, and to galvanize personally and politically in response.

Not long after, Walker joined forces with a white recent Harvard graduate and activist, Shannon Liss, to form what was then called the Third Wave Direct Action Corporation (and what would become the Third Wave Foundation in 1997), in order to prompt and support such political action by young women.[39] Those involved in Third Wave Direct Action saw American racial and gender inequality as critically intertwined in their activism.[40] It was not only Anita Hill's mistreatment that drove Walker to start the organization: the police brutality that African American construction worker Rodney King was subjected to the same year, the acquittal of the police officers who assaulted him, and the ensuing riots that "set LA ablaze" also left Walker "feeling powerless, confused, and immobilized."[41] The murder of fifteen-year-old African American high school student Latasha Harlins by shopkeeper Soon Ja Du in 1991, and the lack of justice for her killing, was one of the mounting instances of racist violence that led to the LA riots.[42] The events following her murder showed that while Black teenage girls were extremely vulnerable to violence, they were not viewed as vulnerable either by individuals or by the U.S. legal system.[43] Walker wrote in an early newsletter for the Third Wave Foundation, reflecting on Rodney King's experience: "At that time, Spring of '92, there seemed to be very little we could actively do to fight for an end to sexual harassment and other kinds of gender violence; and even less we could do to stop the racist police brutality which continues to suppress and terrorize many of our communities."[44] Finding no existing organizations that put young women at the center of antiracist and feminist action, Walker and her fellow organizers rallied together to set about registering new young voters in what would be dubbed the Freedom Summer of 1992.[45]

This action was timely. The 1992 presidential election was fast approaching, and Thomas's ability to assume the role of Supreme Court justice despite a history of sexual harassment reminded newly awakened feminists like Walker of the impact of Washington politics on young women's lives, and of the limitations of the supposedly more sexually liberated 1990s. As proven by the popularity of the Rock for Choice concert in 1991, legal access to abortion had been consistently under threat since the beginning of the Reagan administration. This particular issue was fresh in the minds of teenage girls and their parents after the death of Becky Bell in 1989.[46] Planned Parenthood president Faye Wattleton was told this story by Bell's mother at one such musical rally on a rainy day in Portland, Oregon, in October 1991, with an Indigo Girls set "in full swing" in the background.[47] Wattleton was "filled with fury" at what she heard: seventeen-year-old Bell had been too frightened to tell her parents she needed an abortion, which was required under Indiana's parental notification laws, and so she obtained an illegal abortion from which she developed sepsis and died.[48] "How was it possible that fifteen years after abortion was legalized, a young girl could suffer such a fate?" Wattleton wondered.[49] To young feminist activists in the early 1990s, it seemed imperative to direct activist energy toward the political system, and for those of age, to vote in a Democratic government that would secure more liberal appointees to the Supreme Court, in order to secure young women's reproductive and sexual rights. As a result, in April 1992, Planned Parenthood, the National Organization for Women, and over 750,000 pro-choice women and men came together in the March for Women's Lives in Washington, DC.[50] Enraged by the Hill-Thomas trial and consistent threats to abortion rights, Riot Grrrls from across the country descended on Washington, DC, for the march, including members of the bands Bikini Kill and Bratmobile, and college and high-school grrrls, many of whom traveled by bus or train to meet the night before the march for a benefit concert.[51]

The presidential race gave young women another glimpse of how important the upcoming election would be for them, as the Right continued to galvanize voters by villainizing the sexual and reproductive lives of young women of color as they had in previous decades. While on the campaign trail in 1992, Bush's vice president Dan Quayle gave a speech on the dangers of single motherhood so vitriolic that it received a "widespread negative reaction" across the political spectrum.[52] While speaking at the Commonwealth Club of San Francisco, Quayle echoed the moral values of Lyndon B. Johnson's assistant secretary for labor Daniel Patrick Moynihan, whose report in 1965 placed the blame of many of America's social problems on young Black mothers raising children on their own.[53] "The underclass," according to Quayle, was "dependent on welfare for very long stretches." He stressed that it was "teenage girls" who "lacked sufficient motive to say no to this trap." He also lambasted the irresponsibility of the popular TV show *Murphy Brown* for its depiction of a young working woman who raises a baby on her own. Quayle damned the titular character for failing to demonstrate that "a welfare cheque is not a husband."[54] The speech drew criticism from feminists, journalists, and even the writers of *Murphy Brown*, who retorted through the medium of the TV show itself, in an episode titled "Murphy's Revenge."[55] Despite the widespread discomfort at Quayle's remarks, the issue of family values remained at the fore of the Republican campaign.[56] In just one moment within the flurry of campaign activity, Quayle had pulled back the curtain to reveal that simultaneous desires to uphold the supremacy of the white, nuclear family, to define wider sexual and reproductive mores in the context of that model, and to punish sexualities outside those frameworks remained at the core of reactionary forces within the culture wars. These motives continued to fuel moralizing efforts to crack down on government spending in the 1990s, just as they had in the early culture wars over desegregation and in the surge of New Right activity under Reagan.[57]

Democratic nominee Bill Clinton, however, was not the ideal star upon which young feminists could hitch their political wagon. Clinton also played to fears about spending on welfare in his campaign, promising to "end welfare as we know it," though he avoided using the kind of Moynihanian language that Quayle employed.[58] "Welfare" remained scrawled and underlined on a whiteboard in his campaign headquarters, and while he was unclear about the specifics of how he envisioned welfare reform on the campaign trail, he had been inspired in 1979 by Carter's "workfare" initiatives in Arkansas, in which "able-bodied food-stamp recipients were required to register for work."[59] "The experience sparked my abiding interest in moving towards a more empowering, work-oriented approach to helping poor people," he recalled.[60] His personal sexual politics were also under scrutiny from early in his run for the presidency. During his campaign, a model named Gennifer Flowers came forward to claim that she and the Democratic nominee had been in a sexual relationship for twelve years, during which time he was married to the

successful lawyer Hillary Rodham Clinton.[61] His campaign communications director George Stephanopoulos and lead strategist James Carville successfully diverted
attention away from the affair. Carville reminded Clinton throughout the campaign to focus on the credo "it's the economy, stupid!," which was an approach to
changing welfare that distanced him from moralizing.[62] Nonetheless, most feminists viewed Clinton as a better choice than four more years of Bush-Quayle.[63] Forty-
five percent of his vote came from women.[64] Clinton's campaign organizers were
also aware of the importance of the youngest voters in his successful run for president. Stephanopoulos, looking over a draft of Clinton's acceptance speech, pointed
out that he had to include a sentence thanking "the young people," who "had voted
in record numbers."[65]

In the immediate wake of becoming the forty-second president of the United
States, Bill Clinton gave young liberal feminists hope. This came first in the image
of the numerous female hires in his administration, and in Congress. He appointed
Miami state prosecutor Janet Reno as attorney general (the first woman to serve
in this role), Donna Shalala as the secretary of health and human services, Hazel
O'Leary as the secretary of the Department of Energy, Madeleine Albright as the
ambassador to the United Nations, Carol Browner as the director of the Environmental Protection Agency, and Dr. Joycelyn Elders, an outspoken advocate of sex
education, AIDS prevention, and abortion rights, as surgeon general of the United
States (the first African American woman to serve in this role).[66] The number of
women in the Senate went from four to seven, and from twenty-eight to forty-seven
in the House.[67] His nomination to the Supreme Court, Judge Ruth Bader Ginsburg,
was the first self-defined feminist to be confirmed in the role.[68] Additionally,
his wife, Hillary Clinton, was the first outwardly feminist First Lady, though her
inhabitation of both identities was met with some controversy by liberals and
conservatives during the campaign.[69] Clinton's apparent commitment to women's
advancement in American society earned him the moniker "the first feminist president" in media coverage of his early presidency.[70] In addition to what he symbolized, his substantive policy moves impressed young feminists in the early days of
the administration.[71] The twentieth anniversary of *Roe v. Wade* came two days after
his inauguration, on 22 January 1993, on which Clinton overturned Reagan's "gag
rule" that disallowed federal funding for international nongovernmental organizations that provided abortion services.[72] The first bill he signed into law was the
Family and Medical Leave Act, which provided leave for workers to care for a new
baby, and in 1994 he introduced the Violence Against Women Act.[73] In the first
two years of his administration, he increased spending for family planning by
11 percent, and federal spending on contraception rose to $715 million by 1994.[74]
Also in 1994, he challenged the long-standing ban on gay men, bisexuals, and lesbians serving in the U.S. military, replacing the restriction with the policy "Don't
Ask, Don't Tell."[75] Though this would soon be critiqued by gay rights activists as a
discriminatory policy in and of itself, it demonstrated Clinton's initial commitment
to at least demonstrating a challenge to existing forms of governance over gender
and sexuality in the United States.

This initial influx of feminist-friendly hiring and policymaking, however, was not to last. The midterm elections of 1994 saw the GOP gain fifty-four seats in the House and eight additional seats in the Senate, in a sharp conservative shift in Congress deemed the Republican Revolution.[76] The so-called revolution was a direct confrontation to Clinton's liberalism, which saw Republican candidates mobilize behind Georgia congressman Newt Gingrich's proposed "Contract with America," a document that laid out the proposed changes to what they saw as a worryingly big-government approach in the Clinton administration.[77] In the tense days that followed the election, a swift and expansive welfare reform emerged as a priority for Republicans, and Clinton publicly agreed that this was an area in which he and Republicans would "get an agreement."[78] In light of this shift, and with the importance of re-election already looming, the Clinton administration immediately began to curtail its liberal policies and endorsements.[79]

Activists were alarmed by the implications of the "Contract for America," particularly for young women of color, and immediately began to organize in retaliation to the proposed changes in welfare policy.[80] "The supposed intention," wrote Linda Burnham, a journalist, activist, and cofounder of the Women of Color Resource Center, "is to reduce teen pregnancy and welfare dependency. But the punitive and coercive nature of the bill is perfectly clear. It is a government-sanctioned, all-out assault on the right of the poor to even the most minimal requirements for survival."[81] Burnham circulated examples of local organizing against the "Contract for America" in the center's newsletter, including rallies, meetings of welfare recipients and activists, and a policy paper prepared by the National Asian Women's Health Organization, and encouraged other women to join these efforts or to "get something going" themselves.[82] On 9 April 1995, the National Organization for Women held the Rally for Women's Lives in Washington, DC, in protest against the "Contract" and "the war on poor women," with the Young Feminist Summit on Violence held in the days leading up to it.[83]

Many other women, however, would continue to view Clinton as a feminist president, as would be evidenced later by sympathetic reactions from some feminists to his affair with White House intern Monica Lewinsky. Clinton did not change tack on such highly contentious or visible issues for women as abortion policy. Instead, he made a number of policy moves toward the right in an area that resonated both with New Right Republicans in Congress and with many liberals: the policing of girlhood sexualities. From 1994 onward, Clinton would become emblematic of the anomalies in the culture wars that are revealed when we trace the history of attitudes toward adolescent sexuality. Liberals, the history of talk about teenage sex shows us, are capable of deeply reactionary politics.[84] Clinton's decision to perform conservatism by protecting middle-class white children from sexual harm and scapegoating poor women and young women of color demonstrates how unifying this historic approach was for adults of varying political affiliations, and how difficult it remained to push back against such politics even in the ostensibly sexually liberal 1990s.[85] His most conservative moves in this area would take place in his introduction of strict abstinence-only sex education guidelines and major cuts to welfare in the 1996 Social Security Act, though he would first perform social conservatism when he fired his longtime friend and colleague Surgeon General Joycelyn Elders later in 1994.

The events of the U.N.'s World AIDS Day conference on 1 December 1994 provided an opportunity for Clinton to demonstrate to pro-family Republicans in Congress, and to the powerful lobbies behind them, that his "feminist" policy agenda did not include a desire to encourage sex among young people. However, he would sacrifice one of the most progressive members of his administration, and one of his closest allies, in doing so. On the day of the conference, Surgeon General Joycelyn Elders gave a talk on the specificities of protecting youth from HIV/AIDS to a room of sex educators. In the question-and-answer session that followed her paper, the psychologist Dr. Rob Clark asked whether "a more explicit discussion and promotion of masturbation" might be considered useful in limiting the spread of the virus among young people.[86] After describing herself as "a very strong advocate" of teaching sex education in schools "at a very early age," she replied that she considered masturbation "a part of human sexuality" that "perhaps should be taught."[87] This brief statement was met with uproar by members of Congress, who met to discuss the immediate termination of her tenure. Republican Dan Burton of Indiana berated Clinton for hiring a woman who was part of a movement "killing the moral fiber of America."[88] One week later, she was forced to resign from her role as surgeon general for espousing "values contrary to the administration."[89]

The firing of Joycelyn Elders was further proof to American feminists of the limitations of the newly sexually explicit culture of the 1990s.[90] Frank conversations about the sexual health needs of teenagers could still not take place on a major platform, and Black women faced particular resistance when advocating for teenagers' sexual and reproductive health in American politics.[91] Before the event that led to her dismissal, Elders had already been considered an outsider in Washington. Born Minnie Lee Jones to a family of sharecroppers in Arkansas, Elders had worked hard to achieve success, first joining the army and then training as a medical doctor, going on to become a professor of medicine.[92] She carved out her career through a commitment to multiple controversial issues, including the legalization of some drugs and strong support for access to abortion.[93] By the time of her resignation, she had worked alongside Clinton for six years, as his pick for director of the Health Department of Arkansas during his tenure as governor. During his candidacy for president, Clinton had advocated that young people should be told in "blunt, clear, but sensitive terms how people get AIDS and how to avoid it."[94] Upon Elders's appointment, Clinton had commented that she was ideal for the role because of her expertise on children and AIDS, and her "dedication to improving the lives of all Americans, especially the children of America."[95] Part of Elders's commitment to public health involved supporting the idea of in-school sexual health clinics and the distribution of contraception in schools, issues that brought her under intense criticism as Clinton's nomination for surgeon general, which had led to a lengthy confirmation process.[96] Clinton's dismissal of Elders signified a move to the right, as it showed him rejecting frank advocacy for the sexual welfare of teenagers.[97]

A letter to the president signed by members of the pro-choice group Women of African Descent for Reproductive Justice, which included activist Loretta Ross, stated that they had "watched as you appointed the courageous, no-nonsense Dr. Joycelyn Elders, a woman who dared to speak forthrightly about delicate issues, to be Surgeon General, only to abandon her when it became politically expedient to do so."[98]

Of the list of divisive issues she advocated for, it is significant that acknowledging "healthy sexuality" in teenagers provided Republican members of the House with the opportunity to remove her from office, for what was called "preaching the gospel of free sex" in a congressional debate.[99] The Republican reaction to Elders's comments on masturbation, and Clinton's decision to fire his friend and colleague, marked the shift of adolescent sexualities to the forefront of moral-political debates in American politics—though the reactionary desire to protect the sexual innocence of white childhoods had been foundational to and a driving force throughout the culture wars themselves, this conversation would become newly explicit and urgent for the rest of Clinton's presidency. Abortion had long been an issue of such fundamental importance to its detractors and defenders: the 1990s saw similar divides coagulate over the issue of young people's access to sexuality education and information.[100] Elders was aware of the difficulty of being surgeon general during the culture wars, but it "never occurred" to her to "tone down" her ideas. "I was doing what I thought had to be done," she said of her advocacy.[101] A strong contingent was forming in Washington with a clear agenda to impede giving voice to childhood sexuality, whether it was through Elders's discussion of the issue or through comprehensive sex education.[102] However, while sexual speech was being denied, for the first time in American history the individuals involved were speaking in explicit terms about why young people's sexual behaviors were important to them.[103] This differentiated the political discourse on adolescent sexuality of the 1990s from comparable debates of the 1980s. Adults' positions on teenagers' sexual activity were no longer covertly discussed in public through broader social issues such as the American family, teenage pregnancy rates, or "secular humanism." The relevance of the Hill-Thomas hearings for young women, and the amplified stigma of female masturbation that underpinned conservative reactions to Elders's speech, brought girlhood sexualities to the center of the culture wars debates across the early 1990s. With Clinton, many Democrats, and the Right on one side, and sexual health advocates and newly politicized young feminists fighting against them, the battle between mainstream and underground treatments of girlhood sexuality thus became entrenched in political as well as media cultures over the course of the decade.

In the immediate aftermath of firing Elders, Clinton retreated for a few days into a brief silence that alarmed some Democrats.[104] He eventually emerged, and the very next item on his agenda was a meeting scheduled a few weeks later in January 1995, aimed at "overhauling" the welfare system to an unprecedented extent.[105] The sexual behavior of young women, and ideas about this behavior rooted in race and class difference, would thus remain at the center of Washington politics as the decade progressed.

CLINTON, ABSTINENCE, AND WELFARE

The context of the culture wars meant that Clinton needed to convincingly perform his centrism in time for a successful re-election in 1996. His election had
already galvanized opposition to what he represented as a person: a draft dodger,
a member of the 1960s counterculture, a pot smoker, and a womanizer.[106] His early
policies on abortion and gay rights exacerbated the culture wars, and the Republican Revolution in Congress in 1994 made his shift to a more centrist position all
the more urgent.[107] Clinton was not the only Democrat who wished to demonstrate
a more centrist position in the context of the culture wars. Donna Shalala, secretary of health and human services, had initially been viewed by some feminists as
a "sop" to the left.[108] However, within the first two years of the administration she
was at pains to visibly demonstrate her allegiance with cultural conservatives on
the issue of sex education, even writing to the popular Ann Landers advice column in the *Chicago Sun-Times* to advocate for the teaching of abstinence.[109] She
also reached out personally to Joycelyn Elders, warning her to be "more discreet"
in her remarks on the topic.[110] In congressional hearings on welfare reform, Shalala stated that no one "in public life today ought to condone women having children
born out of wedlock, even if the family is financially able," earning her the nick-
name "Dan Quayle's poster girl" from Ellen Willis.[111] The forced resignation of
Elders, by contrast, served as an example of what might happen if you did not move
toward the center in the Democratic Party in the heat of the 1990s political climate. In firing Elders and moving rightward on welfare, Clinton performed a
punitive approach toward sexual liberalism—and specifically those forms of
nonconforming sexualities that were associated with young, unmarried women of
color—to curry favor with Republicans.[112] Clinton's choice to demonstrate conservatism in this area of policymaking suggests the long-standing centrality of racialized and classed adolescence to reactionary forces in American politics.[113] Such a
performance, through both welfare reform and its attendant abstinence-only education stipulations, also conveniently helped rehabilitate his own lecherous
reputation.

Within this tense political atmosphere, the Clinton administration set about
constructing a welfare reform act that took a conservative approach to the sexual
behavior of young people in order to demonstrate the Democrats' moral and
political centrism, and Clinton's own mores. What would become the Personal
Responsibility and Work Opportunity Reconciliation Act (PRWORA) of 1996
was unprecedented in the centrality of the sexual teenager in its rhetoric. The
PRWORA used the issue of teenage childbearing to justify complete overhauls of
two massive tenets of American social policy: sex education and welfare provision. Clinton had put forward his first proposal to the 103rd Congress for such
reform in June 1994, emphasizing the centrality of teenage pregnancy prevention in
this effort, occasionally referring to this as a "national mobilization or crusade."[114]
Here, Clinton was already demonstrating a commitment to smaller government
and to social conservatism to Republicans, in the knowledge that midterm elections

were looming.[115] Having a plan for welfare reform in place served him well after the Republican Revolution in Congress in the midterm elections in November 1994 and in his run for re-election in 1996. In his State of the Union Address in 1996, Clinton seized the chance to assert his commitment to welfare reform, drawing attention to "the link between teen childbearing" and misspent federal funds and announcing the bipartisan efforts under way to address this.[116] Over the course of that year, the bill would go through a rigorous redrafting process by both Republicans and Democrats in Congress.[117] Conservative pro-family organizations such as the Heritage Foundation were consulted and were responsible for connecting the dangers of sex before marriage, teenage pregnancy, and dependency on welfare in the language of the bill.[118] Some Democrats took issue with the strictest moral language in the draft, which was amended in the final version of the bill, though a bipartisan group of governors agreed that states should be able to withhold welfare from the children of unmarried mothers under the age of eighteen.[119] Despite the lengthy debates over exactly what would be included, the act that was finally agreed upon in August 1996 demonstrated the complicity of many Democrats in racist reproductive health policies aimed at teenagers, and the flexibility of culture war actors where girlhood sexualities were concerned.[120]

Historical, racist stereotypes of sexually active girls were at the heart of the abstinence and welfare provisions of the PRWORA. The act both earmarked $400 million in federal funds for abstinence-only education and redefined in strict terms what could be taught with this money, and gave states the power to deny benefits to babies born "to unwed women under the age of eighteen."[121] The new welfare provision, titled Temporary Assistance for Needy Families (TANF), was proclaimed by Senator Howell Heflin (D-AL) as being essential for ending "welfare as a way of life." It was in this kind of language, surrounding the act as much as that encoded within it, that racist stereotypes of young women of color were circulated by ostensibly liberal politicians, malignantly reaching across the aisle.[122] TANF limited the time period in which young mothers were able to access public welfare support for their families, in addition to placing "real work requirements" on further welfare after this temporary period.[123] The finalized text of TANF included a detailed promotion of the institution of marriage over that of welfare, and in doing so seemed to respond to Dan Quayle's statement in his "Murphy Brown speech" of the 1992 elections that "a welfare cheque is not a husband." "Marriage is the foundation of a successful society," it proclaimed.[124] The act specifically named "young women 17 and under who give birth outside of marriage" as those who were most likely "to go on public assistance and to spend more years on welfare once enrolled."[125] The language of the act evoked the historical, racist association of poor Black and Latinx teenage girls with welfare, using the language used by Moynihan in 1965 and the myth of the "welfare queen" circulated by Reagan in the 1980s.[126] In so doing, the PRWORA reified the pernicious moral panic of the late twentieth century that such young women and their alleged reliance on the state was in fact draining the state and perpetuating poverty across the United States.[127] That such policy was developed in the same era of mainstream "girl power" is further proof of how working-class, teenage girls of color were excluded from the sex positivity of the girl culture that beamed into middle-class living rooms on MTV or Nickelodeon each week.

A part of what Joseph Fischel has called the "underpinning, breathtaking logic" of the PRWORA was the way in which it wove statutory rape into its conception of how poor teenage girls of color ostensibly exploited the state and caused wider poverty in the United States.[128] By including a statutory rape provision, the PRWORA suggested that the increase of teenage pregnancies among younger girls was "linked to predatory sexual practices by men who are significantly older."[129] Criminalizing the adult men who fathered the children of unmarried teenage girls would, according to the act, decrease teenage pregnancies and in turn reduce government spending via welfare.[130] While some language in the PRWORA interpreted sexually active young women as knowing manipulators of the state, in the discussion of statutory rape the same such individuals were instead cast as victims of abusive older men, playing on the reawakened public concern over childhood sexual abuse that had risen in the previous decade.[131] "I'm particularly proud of my role in fighting for child abuse programs," commented Senator Barbara Mikulski (D-MD) in the final hearing for the PRWORA.[132] Though the welfare reform bill cited childbearing among younger teenagers in order to justify these measures, research by the Alan Guttmacher Institute in 1998 revealed that only 1 percent of teenage mothers receiving benefits were under eighteen.[133] A number of feminist scholars found fault with the inclusion of a statutory rape provision in the PRWORA, including legal scholar Michelle Oberman, who noted that the link between statutory rape and teenage childbearing in the act "flies in the face of everything we know about why girls get pregnant."[134] The statutory rape provision in the PRWORA failed to reduce teen pregnancies, criminalized the pregnant teenage girl's relationship, meaning she was less likely to implicate the father by reporting him, and did not pay attention to the needs of "prepubescent and non-pregnant teenage girls in sexually coercive relations."[135] While feminist legal debates over how to theorize and encode the sexual citizenship of teenage girls into law most inclusively continue apace to this day, those that were put forward in the PRWORA in no way took into account or created support for vulnerable young women.[136]

Critics of welfare reform noted how explicitly the language in and around the PRWORA laid the blame of social decline and the poor economy on young, poor, sexually active Black women.[137] Though the most overt allegations toward young Black women did not make it into the final bill, early drafts included statistics that demonstrated rising "illegitimacy" among African American families, criminality in Black men raised by single mothers, and the correlation of single motherhood and poverty, echoing the language of the Moynihan Report.[138] Reflecting on the bill in a report to the U.N. World Conference Against Racism, Racial Discrimination, Xenophobia and Related Intolerance in 2001, director of the Women of Color Resource Center Linda Burnham commented that the "deep historical roots" of the "public conversation immediately preceding passage of PRWORA" resulted in "the simultaneous evocation and denial of racist content," which brought about "a profoundly regressive policy palatable to a distressingly broad swath of the political spectrum."[139] The intentional recipients of these welfare changes were also denoted through recurring images of young women of color that accompanied media reports on the reforms.[140] For instance, as Clinton's welfare reform was announced, one news reporter showed an image of the Chicago 19, a case in which five Black mothers of nineteen children were found living on welfare in a "filthy, rat- and roach-infested apartment," and said, "Here's an example of the problem."[141] The process through which the bill was drafted and received by the American public thus made it apparent toward whom these reforms were aimed, and that the culture war over adolescent sexual behavior was becoming increasingly explicit in the late twentieth century.[142]

Black thinkers responded swiftly to these developments, alarmed by the focus on the sexual behavior of young Black women in the PRWORA's provisions and its historical roots. Critical race theorist Patricia Hill Collins saw the handing of social welfare programs "back to the states" included in the PRWORA as a "retrenchment from federal social welfare programs" and one that would dash the hopes of civil rights activists who had believed that "the opportunities for Black working-class children would continue after the victories of the civil rights and Black power movements."[143] Legal scholar Dorothy Roberts named the welfare reforms as the pinnacle of "modern day racist ideology," in that "Black mothers are portrayed less as inept or reckless reproducers in need of moral supervision, and more as calculating parasites deserving of harsh discipline."[144] In their reception of the PRWORA, these scholars called attention to the tactics that Clinton was using to scapegoat young Black and poor women's sexualities. This simultaneously turned the spotlight away from his own, by drawing on historical racist, classist, and sexist discrimination. The oppressive, punitive treatment of young Black women on welfare during the Clinton administration moved Cathy Cohen, a Black feminist, activist and political scientist then based at Yale, to publish her groundbreaking essay "Punks, Bulldaggers, and Welfare Queens: The Radical Potential of Queer Politics?" in 1997. In it, she challenged queer activists to expand their analysis and action to include "progressive transformative coalition work" with those outside the queer community whose sexualities are still deemed "*nonnormative* and *marginal*," asking, "How would queer activists understand politically the lives of women—in particular women of color—on welfare, who may fit into the category of heterosexual, but whose sexual choices are not perceived as normal, moral, or worthy of state support?"[145]

Grassroots activists also fought back against the ways in which teenage girls of color were impacted by welfare reform, and continued to organize against the unfolding politics of the Clinton administration. Nina Perales, of the Latina Rights Initiative at the Puerto Rican Legal Defense and Education Fund, expressed outrage at the lack of understanding in the bill as to the lived experience of pregnant and parenting teenagers, and at the harm it would bring to them: "A policy that cuts benefits on the theory that poor teens give birth in order to get their own apartment or to get out of school is not going to significantly reduce teen childbearing and will place these young mothers at even greater risk of homelessness and star-vation." Writing for *Instantes*, the newsletter of the Latina Initiative of the organ-ization Catholics for a Free Choice, she urged others to "take a vocal stand, as Latinas, against harmful welfare policies."[146] Linda Burnham reflected on the hypocrisy of U.S. domestic policy under Clinton in the year following the 1995 World Confer-ence on Women in Beijing, and noted the irony of Hillary Clinton's insistence in her speech in Beijing that "women's rights are human rights," given the president's ensuing welfare reforms.[147] Burnham pointed to Clinton's betrayal of women, in that he had framed his administration in feminist terms at the outset, only to become so socially conservative in the years following that Republicans might even be happy to see him stay in office after the 1996 election: "Could it be that the Republicans have chosen such an ineffective and uninspired campaigner as Bob Dole because they are reluctant to change administrations when this one is so enthusiastically implementing Reagan's domestic and Bush's foreign policies?" she wondered.[148] Burnham's critique shows how Clinton's treatment of teenage girls of color in domes-tic policy belied his liberal, feminist politics, and recasts him and many other Demo-crats of this era as in league with social conservatism.

In addition to the resistance formed by adult scholars and activists, teenagers themselves played an increasingly large role in the growing response to racist and sexist policy developments in the Clinton administration. As with the formation of Third Wave Direct Action earlier in the decade, many youth activist groups that mobilized as the administration progressed prioritized intersectional antiracist and feminist issues in their work. Some responded with their own grassroots, community-based support systems in response to teenage pregnancy rates, which also encouraged more teenage girls to engage in political activism. Women in Sup-port of Each Other (WISE) was a program started at UCLA in which college stu-dents of color acted as mentors for girls of color aged twelve to fourteen in the local area, which then grew to see other WISE branches formed at UC Berkeley and Yale. WISE was initially started "as a response to the high teenage pregnancy rate and drop-out rates seen among young women of color" but developed to focus on "issues of self-esteem, social and political climate for women of color, and goalsetting for future options," and to encourage teenage girls "in community education and activ-ism so that they can take an active role in changing their environment."[149] This was mirrored in the work of Brigette M. Moore, whose organization Black Grrrl Revolution, which she started in Brooklyn, New York, in 1998, helped to make "Grrrl-feminist awareness and tools accessible to every womyn and grrrl of color within communities of color by way of grassroots community activism, artist out-reach, and education."[150] Politically active teenage girls across the country took part in the National Young Women's Day of Action (NYWDA) on 22 October 1998, which that year took the theme "Use Your Voice/Usa Tu Voz, Claim Your Power/Usa Tu Poder, Create Choices/Tienes Opciones, Take a Stand/Puedes elegir." In Boston, "welfare reform, affirmative action and dating violence were just a few of the issues addressed by an outstanding group of young performers," including "low-income activist, Linda Carney," who "performed excerpts from her poignant 'Secret

Diary of a Welfare Mother'" at the Boston Community Church.[151] In New York, the Teen Outreach Reproductive Challenge of New York City ran a "workshop/discussion on judicial bypass and parental consent" but held their NYWDA activities on 21 October, "because October 22 is also the Day of Protest to Stop Police Brutality."[152]

This move shows how politically minded young people across the country responded to a range of challenges from the Clinton administration outside of and intersecting with reproductive politics. The effects of Clinton's 1994 Violent Crime Control and Law Enforcement Act, which legal scholar Michelle Alexander has shown led to the current levels of mass incarceration of African Americans in the United States, were also noticed by young antiracist activists, who retaliated against police brutality and incarceration rates during the 1990s.[153] This was a focus of the Raza youth movement, where high school students organized school "blowouts" in the style of 1960s Chicanx walkouts. Elizabeth Martinez, a Chicana activist who had been a part of the movement of the 1960s and 1970s, noticed how teenage girls were central to the leadership of this new wave, and that antipatriarchal politics were key to their activism.[154] In California, Raza youth walked out "in response to repressive new anti-crime laws" and "above all fighting Proposition 187 with its brutal call to deny educational and health services to anyone, including children, merely suspected of being undocumented."[155] Again, the painful irony of having to address such violence under the presidency of a proclaimed liberal was noticed by these activists.[156] The Third Wave Foundation, which had partly been formed in response to the Rodney King trial, continued to organize against police brutality as a part of their feminist praxis as the decade wore on—on 26 February 1999, they marched alongside thousands of others in New York City, demanding justice for the murder of Amadou Diallo, a twenty-two-year-old Guinean immigrant who was killed by police "in the doorway of his apartment building."[157] These examples of feminist and antiracist activism by young people across the United States show how mobilized teenagers were in the 1990s in response to regressive policies in the Clinton administration. As teenagers became increasingly vocal in the culture wars of this period, their activism started a critique of the nature of the culture wars themselves—that adults with voting and policymaking capacities and public platforms were impacting the lives of teenagers without their input, and by calling attention to the ways a Democratic president was a threat to a wide range of social justice issues, their input into political conversations also critiqued the culture war assumption that social conservatism could only be seen in a Republican administration.[158]

Clinton's socially conservative domestic policies were not unique in this era—they were a part of a global trend within neoliberal governments of a "third way" of doing politics between progressivism and conservatism, by moving toward the right where it was politically and economically expedient to do so.[159] The PRWORA put forward a deeply neoliberal set of policies in its emphasis on individual responsibility for personal economic well-being in the name of bolstering the wider U.S. economy.[160] In 1998, gender studies scholar Cris Mayo commented that the requirement for students to "attain self-sufficiency before engaging in sexual activity" in the abstinence provisions encouraged "students to see the link between sex and money."[161] Outside of policymaking, the growing literature on "girls in crisis" during the 1990s concluded that "the key to happiness and success for women was economic and emotional self-sufficiency."[162] However, such studies predominantly focused on how this was possible for white, middle-class teenage girls.[163] This was reiterated in the way that welfare and abstinence policy coexisted in the PRWORA. The public discourse on adolescent female sexual behavior in the United States in the 1990s was thus divided along racial lines. The recognition of high rates of teenage pregnancy resulted in two contemporaneous narratives. Concerns for young white women were voiced through a literature on "girls in crisis" that connected teenage pregnancy to low self-esteem, poor mental health, self-harm, and other individual problems.[164] The "crisis" in relation to young white women as perceived by the writers of such texts lay, therefore, in these women's inability to succeed financially or become "productive" members of society as adults.[165] Meanwhile, through welfare reform, sexually active young Black women, other young women of color, and poor young women who bore children outside of marriage were positioned as burdens to the state. To social conservatives, the image of a pregnant teenager denoted a lack of progress, a nation in development—not a global superpower with the ability to educate and empower its students and make all young people productive members of the workforce.[166] The inequality in these discourses demonstrated both the limitations in the girl culture that was gaining ground in mainstream popular culture and the significance of teenage girls to Third Way, neoliberal policymaking in this decade.

Alongside welfare reform, teenage girls of color were further implicated by policy in the 1990s through the coercive programs that pushed the use of controversial, long-lasting contraceptives Norplant and Depo-Provera as a solution for teenage pregnancy.[167] Policymakers targeted schools with student bodies primarily made up of Black students, starting in Baltimore's inner-city clinics and in schools.[168] Activist groups responded vehemently, focusing on the fact that the contraceptive implant Norplant (approved by the Food and Drug Administration [FDA] in 1990), as well as the injectable Depo-Provera (approved by the FDA in 1992), had a number of potential physical side effects of which the long term consequences were not yet known, especially for teenagers. The National Latina Health Organization (NLHO) launched a research project among Latinx women who had had the drug administered. NLHO used a survey model designed by the Native American Women's Health Education and Resource Center in South Dakota, which had surveyed forty-two Native American women who had used Depo-Provera and delivered a report of their results to the FDA.[169] The central goal of the NLHO study was to "at the very least, keep Depo-Provera from being used on adolescents."[170] Some activists of color agreed that the drug could potentially be useful, but disagreed with the coercion and force used, and the implication behind the programs that teenagers of color were drains on the economy. "We are not against Norplant per se," stated Eleanor Hinton Hoytt, then program director of the National Council of Negro Women, "but Norplant does not answer all of the problems for poor women, women of color or teenagers."[171] In 1993, Hinton Hoytt embarked on a weeklong, five-city tour speaking about reproductive issues for women of color, including the use of Norplant and Depo-Provera; she was joined on this tour by Luz Alvarez Martinez, executive director for the NLHO; Olga Morales Aguirre, executive director for San Antonio's Mujeres Project; and Mary Chung, state coordinator for Asian/Pacific Islanders for Choice.[172] These organizers were "unhappy about the use of Norplant to control teenage pregnancy," when, as Aguirre noted, "no one really knows the long-term effect of Norplant for women under 20." "The solution," she concluded, "is comprehensive, mandatory sex-education in the schools."[173]

Unfortunately, this, too, was under attack in Clinton's welfare reform bill, which also included new guidelines and funding for abstinence-only sex education. There was far less public fanfare about this, partially because of its last-minute inclusion in the bill. It was dropped from one version, then suddenly added back.[174] In an extremely unusual scenario for a final version of a bill draft, two congressmen from Oklahoma persuaded House Speaker Newt Gingrich to include the previously drafted abstinence education provision. The Abstinence Education Grant Program made $50 million available annually to public schools willing to adhere to an abstinence-only sex education curriculum.[175] This was an unprecedented program, in that it extended both the amount of funding and the specificity of Reagan's Adolescent Family Life Act of 1981, which had been the first federal program to promote abstinence education. For a public school to receive these funds, it was required to teach a curriculum that fulfilled the eight criteria of the act's A-H definition of abstinence education, a set of standards that explicitly stated what constituted normative teenage sexuality during the Clinton administration:

> For the purposes of this section, the term "abstinence education" means an
>   educational or motivational program which:
> A. has as its exclusive purpose teaching the social, psychological, and
>   health gains to be realized by abstaining from sexual activity;
> B. teaches abstinence from sexual activity outside marriage as the expected
>   standard for all school-age children;
> C. teaches that abstinence from sexual activity is the only certain way to
>   avoid out-of-wedlock pregnancy, sexually transmitted diseases, and
>   other associated health problems
> D. teaches that a mutually faithful monogamous relationship in the
>   context of marriage is the expected standard of sexual activity;
> E. teaches that sexual activity outside of the context of marriage is likely to
>   have harmful psychological and physical effects;
> F. teaches that bearing children out-of-wedlock is likely to have harmful
>   consequences for the child, the child's parents, and society;
> G. teaches young people how to reject sexual advances and how alcohol
>   and drug use increase vulnerability to sexual advances, and
> H. teaches the importance of attaining self-sufficiency before engaging in
>   sexual activity.[176]

These guidelines made clear the kind of girlhoods that were supported in the domestic policy agenda of Clinton's allegedly "feminist" presidency, and those that were most excluded from the girl culture and sexual liberalism of the 1990s. The stipulation of marriage within these guidelines for healthy sexuality meant that sex education programs that discussed homosexuality could not receive this funding, as "the context of marriage" was not a secured right for same-sex couples in 1996. This was underscored by Clinton's introduction a month later of the Defense of Marriage Act (DOMA), which allowed states to recognize only a marriage between a man and a woman as legally binding. In addition to the Don't Ask, Don't Tell policy for gay men, bisexuals, and lesbians in the military and its discriminatory implications, Clinton's welfare reforms and DOMA contributed to an increasingly socially conservative domestic policy over the course of his administration.[177] Though this abstinence program was ostensibly gender neutral, its stated intention was to "promote abstinence from sexual activity, with a focus on those groups most likely to bear children out of wedlock."[178] Read alongside the changes to welfare, this also further implicated poor teenage girls of color. In addition to the impact that these young women's sexual and reproductive lives were accused of having on the economy through alleged reliance on the state for welfare, the centrality of these young women in the reforms and the timing of these policy changes reflected the importance of the white, middle-class, heterosexual family to conservative politics, and the apparent role of teenage girls in upholding these sexual and reproductive norms within this that had been a core part of the New Right's politics since their ascendance. The PRWORA, through punitive welfare reform and stricter abstinence education, therefore enabled Clinton to perform conservatism to both profamily, social conservatives and the New Right forces in Congress who framed their concerns over teenage pregnancy rates through a neoliberal ideology of prioritizing smaller government.[179]

These racialized discussions of teenagers in domestic policy, which saw young women of color as manipulative "welfare queens" and young white women either as victims or as potential contributors to the economy, whose potential worth to society must be protected through abstinence, were not born in the 1990s. This act saw the eruption of a sex education war that had been brewing across the United States for almost twenty years by the time of Clinton's welfare reforms.[180] Various New Right groups had designed and circulated abstinence-only sex education materials in the early 1980s, but the limited federal funds available for schools wishing to teach these syllabi meant that use of these materials was not widespread. The $50 million dedicated to abstinence-only education set aside by the PRWORA enabled these materials to be used far more widely in schools. While the welfare bill's A-H guidelines for appropriate sexual behavior among young people were fairly brief, the materials of the abstinence-only sex education programs were not.[181] Thus the bill increased the explicitness in discourse around the sex lives of teenagers in public life, even where the language of the act itself had been edited to not be so explicit.

The content of these new abstinence programs, which included True Love Waits and Silver Ring Thing, was explicit, yet explicit about *not* having sex.[182] Cris Mayo called the virginity movement that received funding under the PRWORA "a Foucaultian frenzy of talking sex under the guise of not talking sex."[183] Foucault's conception of a "veritable discursive explosion" of talk about sex, despite, and growing out of, restrictions to discussing sex in public indeed resonates with the extensive discourse on abstinence during this era of the culture wars.[184] In addition to the newer initiatives, older programs such as Sex Respect: The Option of True Sexual Freedom and Teen Aid: Me, My World, My Future, both of which were designed in the early 1980s by anti-secular-education campaigners, received funding from the PRWORA, meaning that despite being written and designed almost twenty years previously, they were circulated most widely in the late 1990s.[185] These materials were more discursive versions of the moral code expounded in the A-H definition of abstinence-only education. The Sex Respect syllabus not only used language that essentialized gender roles but also defended their importance. It perpetuated derogatory stereotypes of girlhood and boyhood sexualities and asserted a rigid gender binary: "Boys tend to use love to get sex. Girls tend to use sex to get love."[186] Like Clinton's federal abstinence guidelines, these materials ignored sexual pleasure and the possibility of same-sex attraction and focused only on monitoring potentially reproductive sex. Abstinence-only materials also implicated young people of color, which extended the scapegoating of young Black people that occurred throughout the development of the welfare reform act itself. In Sex Respect, the only illustrations of Black teenagers in the workbooks showed them "in a clinic, accompanying a description of sexually transmitted diseases," in contrast to images of young white students holding hands in pastoral surrounds.[187] The fictional scenarios in the teaching material were deliberate in their use of names that sounded African American—for example, LaWanda and Calvin—to give examples of sexual mistakes and tragedy.[188] As with the wording of the welfare reforms that led to the expansion of such programs, these materials revealed the prioritization of keeping young white women safe, while young Black women were assumed to be doomed to harmful sexual and reproductive futures and to be a burden to public services.

Just as the PRWORA enabled abstinence education campaigners to circulate materials that explicitly discouraged sexual activity, it reignited comprehensive sex education groups, who in turn became more explicit in their advocacy for the needs of teenagers. In the early 1990s, the executive director of the Sexuality Information and Education Council of the United States (SIECUS) was Debra Haffner, a religious woman who would go on to join the clergy as a Unitarian minister, but whom then at only thirty-three years old was an energetic and ambitious woman who was driven by her belief that children and young people had a right to medically accurate sexual information in the age of AIDS.[189] She also believed that such a stance was fairly "conservative" or "mainstream" and set out to prove this as she developed a massive task force of "the most mainstream people" she knew.[190] By 1995, she and the task force had created the National Coalition of Adolescent Health.

They had spent two years compiling a lengthy report detailing a model of a "sexually healthy adolescent." The report, titled *Facing Facts: Sexual Health for America's Adolescents*, dismissed abstinence-only curricula as moralistic and factually baseless, concluding that, instead, "public policies on sexual health should be based on knowledge of adolescent development" and "accurate data."[191] It asserted the importance of developing and funding curricula that teaches young people that "sexuality is a natural and healthy part of life," and that acknowledges the "variety of contexts and communities" that young people grow up in in America, including those defined by race and socioeconomic factors. It also urged that curricula not limit the definition of sexual behavior to "hetero-sexual penile-vaginal intercourse."[192] While Haffner saw this as a fairly "mainstream" approach to basic comprehensive sex education, she would soon learn that in the political climate of the 1990s this was a surprisingly radical proposal.[193]

For Haffner, SIECUS, and the many groups in the coalition, the *Facing Facts* report would be remembered as "a really important project whose timing could not have been worse."[194] The report was released in the same year as Clinton's sweeping welfare reforms, rendering the work of the group futile against the money made nationally available for the teaching of abstinence.[195] These simultaneous events, the unveiling of Clinton's welfare bill and the SIECUS report, would lead James Dobson, founder of Focus on the Family, to declare that teenage sexuality was "the battleground of the culture wars."[196] "Really?" Debra Haffner responded. "Abortion makes a little more sense as a divisive issue, but why education?"[197] That there could be such division on sex education was particularly shocking to Haffner, as major institutes including the World Health Organization and the American Medical Association had also recently released consensus statements that corroborated what *Facing Facts* had argued: that the wide use of abstinence-only education was not based in evidence for its efficacy in ensuring the sexual and mental health of young people, and that its incompetency in this regard was dangerous, given the context of HIV/AIDS prevalence in America in the 1990s.[198] In the midst of the culture wars, in which teenage sexual behavior was a key battleground, the research driven by Haffner and SIECUS was both ignored by the federal government and actively targeted by historical conservative groups formed in the rise of the New Right. Soon after *Facing Facts* was released, the socially conservative evangelical Christian women's group Concerned Women for America launched a letter-writing campaign aimed at SIECUS, which saw them receive in excess of 35,000 letters of complaint in their New York City offices, some of which were death threats.[199] The inability of Haffner and her organization's ostensibly politically moderate research to gain any traction in mainstream policymaking in this period reflected the new culture war trend emerging around adolescent sexuality, in which frank discussions of the topic could take place only in the cultural underground.[200] In the case of sex education, this was increasingly so because of Clinton's decision to exploit the racist and misogynist tropes of girlhood sexuality and childbearing historically held by social conservatives in order to stay in office longer, and to appear more chaste himself.

Not everyone working at SIECUS shared Haffner's view that comprehensive sex education was as mainstream or noncontroversial as she believed it was. Leslie Kantor, who was hired in 1992 by SIECUS as their first director of community advocacy, was a recent graduate of Barnard College who had been a peer-to-peer AIDS educator as a student and then a sex advice worker at the Columbia University Health Service after graduating. Kantor was more aware than Haffner of the significance of an organization like SIECUS in the culture wars, as part of the "broader progressive movement" working against the "movement on the far right."[201] Kantor even took pleasure from the knowledge that what they were doing was somewhat radical or incendiary, in particular when Focus on the Family published a report with her name on it, which to her proved she was "doing something really useful" in irritating such groups.[202] Though research produced by SIECUS and other organizations corroborated Haffner's belief that a large majority of Americans supported comprehensive sexuality education, this did not take into account the political clout of the socially conservative groups who backed the teaching of abstinence.[203] Despite widespread opposition to abstinence-only sex education in schools, in Clinton's bid for re-election in 1996 he tactically acquiesced to the wealthy and powerful lobbies and conservative policy positions that centered the white, middle-class, and heterosexual American family and associated immorality, broken families, and sexual promiscuity with poverty and with Black and Latinx communities. In drawing on these historical, racist conceptions of Black adolescence, Clinton had set the scene for future political machinations that pivoted on adolescent sexuality and that George W. Bush would continue. Through public debate and policymaking about welfare and abstinence, the sexuality of young people became one of the most politically and morally charged national public debates in the culture wars of the late 1990s.

"THAT WOMAN": MONICA LEWINSKY AND THE DEBATES OVER YOUTH AND SEXUALITY

The extent to which young women's sexuality had become an explicit battleground of the culture wars was starkly revealed when news of President Clinton's affair with a young White House intern named Monica Lewinsky emerged in the national press in January 1998. The hypocrisy of such behavior by a man whose major policy moves had involved demonizing sex outside of marriage was almost too painfully obvious to mention, though of course many commentators did. This was not Clinton's first sexual scandal, and those policies—particularly the ones that cracked down on the behavior of young women—had been put in place to convince voters and Republicans of the president's family values. The conversations that occurred nationally in the "frenzy" that followed showed little public consensus as to how to process the event or the power dynamics at hand.[204] Nevertheless, despite the maelstrom of opinion, the political potency of young women's sexuality played a central role in the debates.[205] Questions that arose from this frantic discourse often dealt with sexual power: the public asked, was Monica Lewinsky a "victim or a tramp"?[206] Was Clinton "a good or bad man, in the terms of progressive/feminist ethics"?[207] In such debates, the attitudes of feminists, liberals, and social conservatives regarding young women's sexuality from the preceding twenty years were crystallized over the course of 1998, as the American public contended with the power dynamics of an apparently consensual sexual relationship between the president of the United States and a twenty-two-year-old intern. The question of whether young women could escape victimization and enact sexual autonomy was at the heart of the ensuing public discourse. Clinton's affair with Monica Lewinsky also tied into wider culture wars over sex education and welfare that had been raging throughout the 1990s. Their relationship represented the disparity between the relative sexual freedom of the upper-middle classes and the association of premarital sex with young Black women, teenage pregnancy, and dependency on the state as written into the PRWORA.[208] The public condemnation Lewinsky received in the wake of the affair, despite her privilege, reminded feminists of the inequality still inherent in heterosexual relationships and the prejudice facing even the most financially stable young white women.

Despite the mass political mobilization of feminists, particularly young feminists, after the Thomas-Hill hearings at the beginning of the decade, there was far less concurrence in the reactions of similar groups to allegations against Clinton, most likely because of the discussion of consent that took place.[209] Lewinsky, unlike other women Clinton had allegedly been sexually involved with, did not bring this information to light on her own. She had confided in her colleague and friend at the Department of Defense, Linda Tripp, who secretly recorded their phone conversations in order to submit them to the attorney Kenneth Starr, who was investigating alleged corruption within the Clinton administration. These allegations included the sexual harassment of Paula Jones, an employee of the State Government of Arkansas. Clinton initially denied the affair, but when Lewinsky submitted a dress bearing a semen sample, he was forced to admit to their sexual relationship. Starr then added the charge of perjury to the list of claims against Clinton, and he was impeached in December 1998. Throughout this process, the sexual relationship between Clinton and Lewinsky was never deemed abusive or nonconsensual in legal terms. However, the power relations between the president of the United States and a twenty-two-year-old intern were well noted in feminist debates.

It's important to note here that Lewinsky herself has in recent years re-entered the public conversation about her experience. Following the launch of the global #MeToo and the Time's Up campaigns against all forms of sexual harassment, assault, and abuse that emerged in 2017, she wrote in an essay for *Vanity Fair* that though she had consistently maintained their relationship was consensual, she now views it as a "gross abuse of power." "I'm sorry to say I don't have a definitive answer yet on the meaning of all of the events that led to the 1998 investigation," she wrote. "I am unpacking and reprocessing what happened to me. Over and over and over again."[210] She also credited the broader feminist movement against harassment and abuse for helping her to start to rethink her own experience twenty years prior:

"I now see how problematic it was that the two of us even got to a place where there was a question of consent. Instead, the road that led there was littered with inappropriate abuse of authority, station, and privilege. (Full stop.)"[211] Within the mainstream feminist conversations of the 1990s, however, discussions of young women's sexual pleasure and sexual harm were more immediately imbued with the ferocity of the feminist sex wars of the 1980s. "So often have I struggled with my own sense of agency versus victimhood," Lewinsky has said. As she remembers it: "In 1998, we were living in times in which women's sexuality was a marker of their agency—'owning desire.' And yet, I felt that if I saw myself as in any way a victim, it would open the door to choruses of: 'See, you did merely service him.'"[212]

Lewinsky's recollection reflects how her story became caught up in the conflicting narratives of girl power and victimization within feminisms of the period. The sex wars of the 1980s were never far from the surface in discussions of young women's sexuality in the wake of the scandal. Some women went as far as to defend the affair as liberated sexuality: polemical "feminist" writers Kate Roiphe and Camille Paglia complained that critiques of the scandal were prudish.[213] For feminists who had long been involved in pro-sex activism, there was a danger in comparing the sexual relationship between Clinton and Lewinsky as akin to the blatant misogyny of Clarence Thomas. "Monica is young, but she is not a child, and she has not accused the president of force, harassment, or intimidation," wrote Ellen Willis in *Newsday*.[214] Willis was among the old guard of feminists who believed the reception of the Clinton-Lewinsky affair among many feminists was proof of the lasting triumph of pro-sex approaches, arguing that it "reflects salutary second thoughts about moralistic, anti-sexual tendencies in the women's movement, including the impulse to expand the definition of sexual harassment beyond all reasonable bounds."[215] Willis also saw the opportunism of conservatives to berate Clinton for his affairs as "a rather amusing conversion to a Catharine MacKinnonoid view of male-female relations which holds that there can't be such a thing as consensual sex between people of unequal power."[216]

Catharine MacKinnon did indeed weigh in on the scandal, keen to defend herself against reductive readings of her politics as "neo-puritan" and to distance her reading of Lewinsky's experience from that of social conservatives.[217] To MacKinnon, Clinton and Lewinsky's relationship was an opportunity to consider a sexual harassment policy that would criminalize vastly unequal sexual relationships in the workplace, and that such a law could be "the beginning of liberation: ending the inequality between the sexes."[218] In a piece for the *New York Times*, she reminded the reader of the inherent "inequality" between the president and Lewinsky, in that "being an unpaid intern at the White House was more like being at school than being at work," and she strongly reasserted her belief that the law could be used to mitigate potential abuses of power against young women.[219] People had to "face the fact," she stated, that "a comparatively young person in a vulnerable position can be sexually exploited, even if she wanted a sexual relationship, whether or not she had a legal claim for sexual harassment."[220] Fundamental to Willis's and MacKinnon's disparate readings of Clinton and Lewinsky's relationship was in their conception of the progress of feminist sexual politics by 1998. For MacKinnon, while she acknowledged that no one had brought forward a claim of harassment or abuse in this case, historical sexual and gender inequality and the imbalance of political and social power was so entrenched in this relationship that both par-ties' fully informed consent to sex was, she believed, theoretically impossible. Willis, in contrast, saw the relationship as exemplary of the ability of young women in the 1990s, even in relationships with much older men, to exercise sexual agency and decision-making without coercion or harassment.

Many feminists stayed loyal to Clinton in the wake of the affair for fear of the Republican alternative, including many organizations of younger, politically engaged feminists. Gloria Steinem, the media-savvy and well-known feminist activ-ist and founder of *Ms. Magazine*, was among the more vocal feminists who con-tinued to support Clinton, as an "ideological friend."[221] In March 1998, she declared her position on the affair in an opinion piece titled "Why Feminists Support Clin-ton" in the *New York Times*.[222] She argued that the "common-sense guidelines" agreed upon by the women's movement "30 years ago" that "no means no" and, importantly, "yes means yes" made it obvious to young women in particular that Clinton had committed no sexual crimes against Lewinsky.[223] Steinem's article was a retort to conservative writers such as the *New York Post* columnist Steve Dun-leavy, who had berated feminists for being partisan and hypocritical in not damn-ing Clinton as they had Clarence Thomas.[224] Partisan interests informed some younger feminists' reaction to Clinton's behavior—in October 1998, a number of young women's organizations including "AAUW, CyberGrrrl, La RAZA, Third Wave Foundation, US Student Association" and "White House Interns" joined together "because the media wanted to know what young women of America" thought of the events unfolding in Washington. "We're disappointed in Bill Clin-ton, but it's what's above the collar, not below the waist, that really counts," they stated.[225] The coalition held a number of "events and actions" to demonstrate their belief that he had not committed "an impeachable offense," driven by the motive that "Republican legislation is bad for young people."[226]

Regardless of varied levels of feminist support for Clinton during his impeach-ment, the hypocrisy of his affair in light of his conservative, pro-marriage poli-cies, which framed premarital sex among the young as a societal ill, proved difficult for many to ignore.[227] While Ellen Willis had defended the president against alle-gations of sexual harassment in this case, she soberly reminded her readers that Clinton had "never hesitated to pander to the right by wrapping himself in the family-values flag." "If revelations of his sexual proclivities cripple his ability to indulge in pious blather about the evils of illegitimacy," she concluded, "I can only cheer."[228] The scholar Simone Weil Davis also commented on the social and sex-ual inequality in the United States that was brought to the fore by Clinton and Lewinsky's relationship. Clinton, she wrote, was able to "grandstand about family values" in Congress, introducing restrictive social policies such as DOMA, Don't Ask Don't Tell, and the PRWORA, while conducting the kind of extramarital sex-ual relationship his policies condemned.[229] She noted that "those in our society who

are sexual minorities and marginalized by class or race are under fire in a completely different way than were Bill and Monica in the aftermath of their 'outing.'"[230]
What the hypocrisy of Clinton's affair revealed was the instrumentality of teenage girls, particularly young, poor girls of color, to his political agenda and ability
to progress as a politician, despite his personal detachment from the implications
of welfare and sex education restrictions, and in turn the continued significance
of teenagers' sexual and reproductive lives to the social conservative forces in U.S.
government throughout the 1990s.[231] Clinton's ability to demonize nonheteronor-
mative adolescent sexualities, penalize Black, Latinx, and poor teenage girls for their
reproductive decisions, and block all young people's access to sexual information
while enjoying his own sexual freedom encapsulated the limits of the "girl culture"
that was being celebrated in popular culture, and of the wider sense that a truly
inclusive "pro-sex" sentiment had made any kind of sweeping impact on American social life—unless you were the president of the United States.

Amid the public conversations about Clinton's behavior and the nature of his
relationship with Lewinsky, the nation's attitudes toward a young woman's assertive sexuality were laid bare. The vilification of Lewinsky in the nation's press united
feminists of various stripes in solidarity with her. The pathologizing of Lewinsky
revealed how shocking a sexual transgression still was in a young woman in America at this moment in history. Her body and her sexuality were picked apart at length
by political pundits, who exoticized her physicality, her Jewish heritage, her makeup,
her youthfulness, and her perceived sexual voraciousness in ostensibly seeking out
and seducing the president.[232] Much of the language used to describe her focused
on the intersection of her relative youth, at twenty-two years old, with her perceived
sexual aggression, positioning her as a calculating Lolita. The *National Examiner*
called her plan to seduce the president an "oversexed teen's scheme," labeling her
a "sex-crazed vixen" with an "insatiable lust."[233] On *Fox News*, she was called a
"young tramp looking for thrills," and Representative Charles Rangel (D-NY) called
her a "poor child" with "serious emotional problems."[234] These examples also illus-
trate how the mainstream perception of girlhood in the girl culture of the 1990s
conflated young women from puberty through their twenties. Cruel, lowbrow
humor abounded in the national press and on the talk-show circuit, focusing on
such crude details as the president's semen stain on her blue shift dress.[235] Details
on what happened between Clinton and Lewinsky featured in the national news
invited a newly explicit discourse on oral sex in the United States; this would have
implications for the way scandals over the sexual practices of teenage girls would
be discussed in the years following.[236]

Lewinsky initially appeared to trouble the idea of the All-American good girl
that 1990s studies such as Mary Pipher's *Reviving Ophelia* urged parents to raise.
Her apparent sexual desire and prowess discounted the ideas of those who saw girls
in the 1990s as being victims, or in crisis, including the creators of abstinence-only
sex education materials who saw girls as "using sex to get love."[237] However, she
eventually might have served as a cautionary tale to such writers, as the public reception of her sexual behavior ultimately impinged on her ability to succeed in her

career. Feminist critics at the time noted that Lewinsky faced the classic "double standard" that applied to school-aged girls who participated in sexual encounters with an enthusiasm equal to that of boys.[238] Clinton would overcome impeachment and move past the scandal, his reputation as a womanizer just another Washington tradition, while "Lewinsky will spend the rest of her life in the shadow of her tarnished reputation." This evaluation proved to be prescient.[239] If Monica Lewinsky, a white, upper-middle-class young woman at the start of a promising career, could have her life effectively ruined by the same affair that failed to materially impact on the life of the man she was involved with, then how much progress could feminists claim had been made in American sexual politics? By the end of the 1990s, young white women's bodies were still held up as the litmus test for whether girls were in crisis or infused with girl power, and historically racist tropes about the sexualities of girls of color were still used to legitimize punishing teenagers who failed to uphold the norms of abstinence until heterosexual, monogamous marriage.[240]

The curtains on the Clinton administration, and the twentieth century, drew to a close over one of the most explicit conversations about the sexuality of young women in the nation's history, in which teenage girls were at the center of many major culture wars debates. However, as graphic as the mainstream discourse was, it did not allow for the sexual health needs of teenagers to be discussed in any real way, which was of course exacerbated by the president's stringent welfare and sex education policies during this era.[241] Under the next presidency, a widespread concern over the "hypersexualization" of American young women, again ranging from childhood through a woman's twenties, would grip American culture. However, some would respond less with panic and more with a focused concern for how young women who had come of age during a sexually conflicted era—including witnessing the treatment of Anita Hill, Joycelyn Elders, and Monica Lewinsky—would discuss these events and learn from them.[242]

Even Bill Clinton himself would admit that the bombardment of explicit details of his affair in the national press in 1998 exposed young people to sexual information and ideologies whether or not parents, schools, or the federal government thought young people deserved access to sexual knowledge.[243] Clinton remembered that Carol Browner, the director of the Environmental Protection Agency, told him that "she had been forced to talk with her son about subjects she never thought she'd have to discuss with him."[244] The sex education campaigners who had been called to arms during the Clinton decade would mobilize over this issue. Susan Wilson was one such woman. A sex educator in New Jersey since the 1970s, Wilson saw the scandal as an ideal "teachable moment" for students of all ages and urged other teachers to seize the chance to discuss the affair and its fallout with their pupils. She believed that the affair would open up an important dialogue for young people who urgently needed a space for such discussions. "Most want the opportunity to talk about the emotional, social, and psychological aspects of sexual relationships," Wilson said. "Many are beginning to engage in romantic and sexual relationships themselves. Many are not significantly younger than

Monica Lewinsky was when she was engaged in an affair with the President."[245] She also believed that leading students in various grades through a discussion of the sexual politics of the era was a rebellious act, one that retaliated against Clinton's federal abstinence-only policy and the powerful lobbies behind it, because while sexual talk in public was more explicit, it was still infused with misogyny, and talking frankly to teenagers about sex in the 1990s was still only possible in the cultural underground. She encouraged other teachers to tell them "that they are wrong" by "boldly and clearly encouraging discussion of the Clinton-Lewinsky story."[246] Wilson would not be alone in her retaliation. Over the decade that followed, those advocating for young people's sexual health across American society would be more vocal than ever in order to confront the intense racist, heterosexist, and classist discrimination evident in mainstream discussions—and policy—surrounding girlhood sexualities in the United States under the administration of George W. Bush.

CHAPTER 5

Medicine, Education,
and Sexualization

It was only a matter of hours before the FBI had identified the individuals who, working on behalf of the global terrorist organization al-Qaeda, plotted and executed the terrorist attacks on the World Trade Center and the Pentagon on 11 September 2001.[1] Not far behind the nation's calls for justice came an internal war cry against those within American society who might be tangentially responsible for the lives lost in the attacks.[2] Specifically, a number of prominent religious conservatives placed sexual liberalism at the center of moral decline in America, which they argued had in turn led to the weakening of America's borders.[3] On Thursday, 13 September 2001, the prominent Southern Baptist televangelist Jerry Falwell and Pentecostal minister and media pundit Pat Robertson discussed the traumatic events of the week on the Christian Broadcasting Network's show *The 700 Club*. In a grave tone, Falwell remarked that Americans must allocate some blame for the terrorist attacks on "the pagans, and the abortionists, and the feminists, and the gays and the lesbians who are actively trying to make that an alternative lifestyle," and "the ACLU [American Civil Liberties Union]," who, in trying to "secularise America," had "helped this happen."[4] "When we destroy 40 million little innocent babies," he chided, "we make God mad."[5] Though he came under a great deal of public criticism for these widely circulated remarks, he was not alone in these views. The socially conservative women's group Concerned Women for America (CWA), for instance, published a series of articles on their website that speculated that the sexual misconduct of American "elites" had "hijacked" American values, and that the war between good and evil that they believed was taking place on a global scale similarly took place on American soil, and in American souls.[6]

Gender and sexuality would become increasingly prominent in American public discourse and debate in the wake of 9/11, and adolescent sexualities would be at the center of many of these conversations.[7] The newly instated president George W. Bush and his wife, Laura, would draw attention to the plight of Iraqi and Afghani women under the Taliban in their endorsements of sending American troops to the Middle East, while American feminist groups scoffed that they had fought to bring attention to these women for years without response, until a war against terror was at stake.[8] American feminisms, including those of young women across the country, would emphasize women's global plight for equality in new ways.[9] Over the course of the 2000s, American sexual politics took on a newly transnational and visible character. As suggested by the reactions of Falwell and the CWA, international events in this period symbolized for many Americans a moment to reflect on the sexual and cultural state of the Union. It was upon such reflection that many on both sides of the culture wars, and from both sexually liberal and conservative backgrounds, found themselves concerned.[10] Mass culture was more sexually graphic than ever before in American history. Writing on the change of culture in 2001, sex education advocate and sociologist Janice Irvine described the media coverage of the Clinton impeachment trial as being pivotal in opening up a more sexually explicit discourse in the United States.[11] This newly provocative culture saw the term "hypersexualization" appear in popular parlance to describe the new media atmosphere and, in particular, the impact it might have on young women. The term's popularity uncovers the centrality of girlhoods within cultural debates over gender and sexuality in this period, which saw long-standing arguments over young women's sex lives become explicit and important in the public sphere at an unprecedented level.

This final chapter uncovers how America under the Bush administration has come to be associated with the most virulent abstinence and purity movements aimed at teenage girls, despite the fact that the roots of these movements had been growing for years as a result of financial and rhetorical support from presidential administrations from Reagan through Clinton. It also discusses the ways that these newly explicit and highly visible campaigns made obvious the racism and sexism that had always underpinned the discourse around sex education in schools, and adolescent purity more broadly—through the explicitness of language used in these campaigns, and their increased use of imagery of white young women's bodies to demonstrate idealized pure girlhoods. At first glance, the traditional lines of the culture wars seemed more entrenched than ever during the Bush years. The attendant religiosity and social conservatism of his presidency, and the Islamophobia and nationalism that surged after 9/11, was met with a fierce response from activists and advocates of all ages, and from scientists, medical researchers, teachers, politicians, and lawyers alike. However, exploring this era of the culture wars through the lens of girlhood sexuality again reveals unexpected moments of consensus across these known battle lines, changing the way we understand the larger shape of political debate in this period.[12]

TEENAGE GIRLS AND THE BUSH ADMINISTRATION

The entry of George W. Bush into the White House following the general election of 2000 spelled trouble for young feminists. Over the course of the decade, as a result of the administration's policies and the socially conservative movements they bolstered, the racialized, misogynistic discourse on girlhood sexualities that had simmered for decades of the culture wars became more explicit than ever before. This was not immediately clear at the outset of the administration, however. After all, Clinton's presidency had been hugely disappointing for advocates of reproductive rights. For many feminist organizers, the consequences of his welfare reform bill for young Black and Latinx women in particular and his unprecedented funding for abstinence-only sex education revealed the limitations of blanket partisan support for Democrats in American politics. Further, because Congress had instituted the "charitable choice" provision during Clinton's presidency, which allowed religious organizations to apply for public funds, Bush's identification as a "compassionate conservative," an ostensibly centrist position, was not in and of itself particularly alarming.[13] During his campaign for the presidency, he couched his open religiosity in caveats that he was not aligned with the religious Right.[14] However, sensing the desire in the electorate for a more explicit religiosity, he began to expand his vision of compassionate conservatism to include increasing references to his own faith in the years leading up to 2001.[15] Within days of Bush's administration commencing, the implications of a Republican in the White House for women became apparent in his renewed focus on antiabortion measures.[16] Bush spent his first full day in office re-introducing Reagan's "global gag rule," which banned federal funds being distributed to any international organization that provided abortion services globally.[17] He set about instating pro-life supporters to high-profile roles in his administration, including the stringently antiabortion Missouri senator John Ashcroft as attorney general.[18] Bush continued in this vein in the early years of his presidency, bringing in a partial-birth abortion ban in 2003 and signing the 2004 Unborn Victims of Violence Act, which named the fetuses of murdered women as "second victims" and supported the pro-life movement's push for fetal personhood.[19]

As the dangers that the Bush administration posed to reproductive rights in the United States became abundantly clear—particularly for young women of color—advocates leapt into action. In 2003 in Washington, DC, legal scholar and reproductive rights advocate Dorothy Roberts spoke at a conference held by the National Black Women's Health Project, the Congressional Black Caucus Health Braintrust, and the U.S. Senate Black Legislative Staff Caucus. She emphasized in her paper that the "lack of financial support for abortion has converged with welfare child exclusion policies, decreases in Medicaid coverage, and cutbacks in funding for contraception to especially burden the reproductive health and rights of economically disadvantaged Black women."[20] The new conservative government also buoyed state and local antiabortion action. In 2005, a "coalition of grassroots activists" worked to shut down Proposition 73, a "parental notification ballot initiative" in California, "despite the wishes of Governor Arnold Schwarzenegger."[21] Activists involved in this struggle included Dolores Huerta, the civil rights activist and cofounder of United Farm Workers, and Rocio Córdoba, executive director of California Latinas for Reproductive Justice, and their concern was primarily for the inevitable impact this law would have had on Latinx teenagers in the state, "thereby endangering our most vulnerable young women."[22]

The sexual and reproductive lives of teenagers were indeed critical to Bush's domestic and foreign policies. The president's explicit commitment to extending abstinence education at home and abroad has contributed to our understanding of this era as one in which teenage girls were central to conservative politics. However, developments of federal abstinence policy in the Bush administration would not have been possible without the financial and rhetorical precedents set by Clinton's 1996 welfare reform bill.[23] Title V of the bill created a $50 million annual budget for the teaching of abstinence in public schools and specified with unprecedented clarity the responsibility of the individual in the maintenance of abstinence, the connection between abstinence and personal economic success, and the perceived dangers to health from sex outside of marriage.[24] Bush's abstinence policies extended both the fiscal and moral tenets of the abstinence policy established in 1996. This process began early in the administration: the federal government allotted $30 million of funds through the first Community-Based Abstinence Education (CBAE) program to become available in October 2001.[25] Unlike previous federal abstinence funding, CBAE bypassed states' approval of which programs would receive funding, instead awarding funding directly to community-based programs.[26] By fiscal year 2006, CBAE funding had increased to $113 million.[27] The Bush administration continued to increase funding for abstinence education as time went on, especially financial support for conservative programs and initiatives directed at teenagers. In 2002, an organization that produced literature claiming that condoms were ineffective, the Institute for Youth Development, received $71,000, and a range of crisis pregnancy centers received grants of up to $800,000.[28] By December of that year, information on Centers for Disease Control (CDC) websites had been amended to remove any mention of the correct use of condoms, replacing such information with data on condom failure rates and abstinence promotion.[29] As a Republican president, Bush was able to explicitly display his desire to limit sex outside of marriage, though this would not have been possible to the same extent without the decades of abstinence education funding that had been more covertly introduced in previous administrations.

The Bush administration's fresh commitment to promoting abstinence soon expanded to include international affairs, which also made the culture wars over adolescent sexuality increasingly visible. In 2002, U.S. delegates to the U.N.'s Special Session on Children opposed any reference to "reproductive health services for youth" in the resulting resolution, joining nations including Iran, Iraq, and Sudan in an unlikely alliance.[30] The U.S. delegates confirmed that no American sex education efforts abroad would include anything other than abstinence-only education.[31] Bush put his own weight behind this kind of initiative in his 2003 State of the Union address, in which he proposed the President's Emergency Plan for AIDS Relief (PEPFAR), "an act of mercy," thus aligning it with his campaign promises of compassionate conservatism.[32] "I am asking Congress for $15 billion over the next five years," he announced, "to turn the tide against AIDS in the most conflicted nations of Africa and the Caribbean."[33] The ensuing bill, known as the Global AIDS Act, was drafted by Congress that same month. The bill lauded a Ugandan program, spearheaded by the country's president Yoweri Musevini, known as "the ABC model," short for "Abstain, Be faithful, use Condoms" (listed in order of priority).[34] PEPFAR had a mixed reception among liberals, some of whom viewed the policy as the most positive contribution of Bush's presidency.[35] Elsewhere, however, it recharged the long-running sex education debates that would rage throughout the 2000s. Writing in *Conscience* magazine, Rosemary Radford Ruether, a feminist theologian at the Pacific School of Religion in Berkeley, criticized the measures as an attempt "to impose Western sexuality on Africans in the AIDS crisis," claiming that these values would not work in African countries because they "have never 'worked' in the United States or indeed any place in the Western world."[36] The way that the sexual and reproductive choices of teenagers were folded into Bush's foreign policy agenda—which was already highly visible after 9/11—played a part in making the debates over girlhood sexualities more explicit than ever before.

In 2005, abstinence policy under Bush took an even sharper conservative turn. From this point onward, the administration became more overt in its promotion of adolescent abstinence, through both increasing funding for and expanding the requirements of abstinence-only sex education.[37] By transferring control of Title V abstinence funding from the Maternal and Child Health Bureau to the far more conservative Administration for Children and Families (ACF), the Bush administration was able to build on the guidelines given in the A-H definition of abstinence education, first written into Title V of Clinton's welfare reform bill.[38] The ACF now also demanded additional documentation, requiring applicants to be "consistent with the definition of abstinence education pursuant to A-H of Section 510 (b) (2) of the Social Security Act," as well as address "each of the elements" given in the new program announcement. The act's "scope" shared the vision of sexual propriety put forward by Title V, but in far more explicit terms, even advising young people not to associate with sexually active teenagers.[39] The document acknowledged the fact that young women are likely to physically suffer more from teenage sex. It also made explicit the essentialist, gendered division of sexuality implicit in Title V by insisting that successful applicant programs instruct "that males and females may view sex, intimacy, and commitment differently."[40] In outlining the importance of essential, binary genders in adolescent sexual development, the ACF's revised Title V policy completely dismissed the existence of transgender and nonbinary young people.

The newly detailed policy reinforced the exclusion of all LGBTQ+ teenagers that Clinton's Title V had begun to articulate.[41] The ACF endorsed heterosexual marriage in the new guidelines, insisting that programs receiving funding define marriage only as "a legal union between one man and one woman as a husband and wife."[42] This sent a message to LGBTQ+ youth that they could never experience sex in a way that the government defined as healthy.[43] Youth activist organizations responded to the homophobic developments under the Bush administration by working to provide support for LGBTQ+ teenagers across the United States.[44] The Audre Lorde Project, a New York City–based community organizing group for "Lesbian, Bisexual, Two Spirit, Transgender & Questioning Young Women of Color" aged sixteen to twenty-one, ran the Young Women's Leadership Training Program, which sought to recruit fifteen to twenty LBTSTQ young activists of color for an eight-week summer program to learn "leadership," "communication," and "analytical skills" to "effectively address multiple needs/challenges facing young LBTSTQ women of color and their peers."[45] The Third Wave Foundation also encouraged LGBTQ+ teenagers to fight back, and urged young people wishing to "make a difference now" to "check your school's curricula" and to "demand that your administration allow teachers to use diverse materials in the classroom and that your library includes books specific to LGBT history and issues."[46] In 2006 the same organization also moved to become more inclusive in the young people that they supported by redefining their mission statement to include transgender youth and providing grants to organizations including the Silvia Rivera Law Project, the legal aid organization for low-income trans people and trans people of color, and FIERCE!, "a community organizing project for Transgender, Lesbian, Gay, Bisexual, Two Spirit, Queer, and Questioning youth of color in New York City."[47] They also introduced new initiatives to support transgender youth in the 2000s, asking young people to fill out and send in "I SPY TRANSPHOBIA" postcards when they or someone they knew experienced discrimination, including "obstacles because of your perceived gender when using public bathrooms."[48]

In addition to abstinence programs, the Bush administration promoted heterosexual marriage to teenagers. In 2006, Bush dedicated $500 million to the initiative Healthy Marriage and Responsible Fatherhood Grants, which funded programs that included "education in high schools on the value of marriage, relationship skills, and budgeting."[49] Concerned with the way that nontraditional families were coming under further fire as a result of these developments, the Bay Area–based Women of Color Resource Center released a report on marriage promotion under Bush. "The George W. Bush Administration came to Washington representing a disciplined, ideology-driven, right-wing social movement," they concluded, which was exemplified "by the Administration's initiatives to promote marriage and fatherhood for welfare recipients in order to 'cure' their poverty."[50] The steady financial and administrative expansion of abstinence and marriage promotion policies over the course of the Bush administration, and the adjustment of the language within them, demonstrates its commitment to a strictly gendered and sexually delayed adolescence, necessary for the perpetuation of the white, heterosexual nuclear family. Reinforcing the economic and moral importance of this kind of family, and teenagers' role in upholding this model, had been central to the politics of social conservatives since the rise of the New Right.

Feminist and LGBTQ+ organizations working on behalf of young people had to fight hard in this era against the reactionary politics that were buoyed by the Bush administration: the surge in federal financial and moral support for abstinence programs allowed for a widespread extra-governmental abstinence movement and industry to flourish in this decade.[51] Leslee Unruh, a chirpy antiabortion campaigner from South Dakota with a trademark blonde bouffant, founded one of the central organizations of this movement in 1997, the abstinence "affiliation network" National Abstinence Clearinghouse. In 2000, she boasted that groups such as hers were by then receiving "nothing but support from the Bush administration," allowing abstinence to become a "business."[52] Though many of the abstinence groups operating in this decade had been formed in the 1980s or 1990s, using funding from Reagan's Adolescent Family Life Act or Clinton's welfare bill, they began to grow in size and visibility from the early days of the Bush administration, where they could tap three large sources of funding: the ACF, CBAE, and the newly formed Office of Faith-Based Initiatives.[53] Leslie Kantor of the Sexuality Information and Education Council of the United States (SIECUS) remembered despairing at how, for schools and communities, it was becoming "harder and harder to not take that kind of money."[54] As Kantor and other comprehensive sex education advocates feared, the abstinence movement's influence expanded far wider in the 2000s than it had in any previous decade.

Notably, this reach did not end at the walls of the classroom.[55] The abstinence industry utilized new pedagogical tools and ostentatious methods in this decade to reach out to teenagers. The evangelical abstinence group Silver Ring Thing (SRT), founded in the mid-1990s and named for the silver abstinence "promise rings" they sold to teenagers to wear until their wedding night, is one such example. As well as producing educational material for schools, SRT toured the nation's stadiums with their "concert-style approach," in which their trademark ring-exchanging ceremonies and testimonials were set to blazing lights and blaring music.[56] SRT received almost $1.5 million of CBAE funding from 2003 onward, until it was withdrawn two years later as a result of an ACLU lawsuit that successfully claimed the group were using government funding for evangelistic purposes.[57] Another group established in the 1990s that continued to expand in the 2000s was True Love Waits. True Love Waits also developed a theatrical and memorable style of delivering an abstinence message outside of schools, including "purity balls," glamorous gala events wherein young women donned gowns and attended as the dates of their fathers, to whom they would "pledge" to uphold their virginity until marriage.[58] The father would then promise the young girl to help "keep" her virginity intact until she found her husband, sometimes also presenting her with a promise ring.[59] As well as using rock and hip-hop acts and prom-style dances to appeal to the young, these programs had a commercial element designed to connect to American teenagers through their consumer identities.[60] At events like those described above, teenage girls could buy clothing bearing slogans such as "CHASTEGIRL" and "NO TRESPASSING ON THIS PROPERTY, MY FATHER IS WATCHING."[61] The vastly increased visibility of these campaigns in mainstream culture caused unprecedented media attention to the abstinence movement, which contributed to the sense that these kinds of purity politics were a new phenomenon in the United States. However, they were in fact the result of decades of pro-abstinence organizing, increasingly funded by presidents from Reagan onward, and impossible without the major expansion of federal abstinence support from Clinton. In the abstinence movement as elsewhere in American society, public representation of ideas about adolescent sexuality—whether in positive portrayals of teenage sexual experiences in popular culture or in the proclamation that sex before marriage was harmful—was becoming increasingly explicit and graphic over time.[62]

A controversial aspect of these groups' attempts to appeal to youth in an era of increasingly graphic public discourse on sex was their more sexually charged aesthetics and language, marking a departure from the more fearmongering rhetoric of earlier abstinence programs.[63] This incongruity, which feminist writer Jessica Valenti in 2009 called "fighting sexualization with more sexualization," has also contributed to the increased attention that the Bush-era abstinence movement received both at the time and in histories of the period.[64] The graphic language used by abstinence campaigners mirrored Foucault's "repressive hypothesis," in which the "whole restrictive economy" of sexual speech and the "policing of statements" that developed in the seventeenth century were simultaneously accompanied by an "institutional incitement to speak about it, and to do so more and more."[65] This took multiple forms in the abstinence movement of the early twenty-first century. To chime with a more sexually graphic mass media culture, conservative abstinence campaigners put a new emphasis on the existence of sexual pleasure but framed it as achievable only through the institution of marriage. In one SRT event, for instance, the host led the audience in the chant "sex is great!" before adding the qualifier that "it *is* great, in the context of marriage."[66] An extension of this new sexual frankness in abstinence campaigns was a more forgiving, evangelical approach to "secondary virginity," or welcoming nonvirgins to the events.[67] "I don't care if she starts over seven times, or twenty times," Leslee Unruh said of girls who were unsuccessful in maintaining their virginity pledges. "I'm going to believe in her each time she comes back."[68] From the inclusion of a certain kind of religiously sanctioned, marriage-centric sex positivity within the abstinence campaigns of the 2000s, it becomes apparent that pro-sex feminism from the 1980s was co-opted not only by a misogynistic mainstream culture but also, more strangely, by certain factions of the pro-family religious Right.

A further manifestation of this new incorporation of desire by the pro-abstinence movement was the promotion of abstinence through young celebrities. A generation of teen pop stars made famous by the Disney TV channel, including Miley Cyrus, Demi Lovato, Hilary Duff, the Jonas Brothers, and Selena Gomez, publicly proclaimed their virginity and sported purity rings.[69] The pressure on young pop stars to highlight their virginity in the media demonstrates the intensity of the public gaze on the sexuality of famous young people in this era, and the wider cultural obsession with adolescent sexual behavior.[70] It also shows how delaying sexual behavior had become a critical component of how neoliberal, middle-class success was seen to be achievable for young women.[71] As evidenced by this list, as in the 1990s, young people of color and queer young people were present and a part of the dominant girl culture, but they were not celebrated as such.[72] Instead, the values historically attributed to white, middle-class, heterosexual girlhoods were upheld in an ostensibly "color-blind" media culture and erased or sidelined the specific girlhood experiences of queer teenagers and young people of color.[73] Further, young, straight, attractive but sexually well-behaved white women remained the most visible and the most lauded for representing what Sarah Projansky has called "acceptable girlhood."[74]

This was exemplified by the visibility of abstinence pinup Jessica Simpson, a blonde and curvaceous pop singer who sang at True Love Waits events before finding mainstream success, and who was the daughter of a Baptist youth minister.[75] The popular appeal of such abstinence spokesmodels was a further factor in how the work of the abstinence movement became more conspicuous than ever before in Bush-era sexual culture. Simpson's presence was intended to represent to teenaged onlookers a vision of young womanhood idealized by abstinence campaigners: conventionally sexually attractive but, importantly, sexually pure.[76] In her memoir, Simpson later described the way she was viewed as a "sexy virgin."[77] The newly commercialized and spectacularized abstinence movement in the 2000s entrenched the racism and misogyny that informed school-based abstinence programs by positioning predominantly young white celebrities at the forefront of their movements. The promotion of these simultaneously lauded and lusted-after young people made plain the ill-covered fact that over the prior two decades, when white social conservatives promoted the teaching of abstinence, condemned young mothers (especially when they sought welfare to support their family), and decried abortion, the idealized girlhood that they sought to protect was also white, middle class, cisgender, and heterosexual. In 2008, political scientist Alesha Doan called this the "ethnocentrism" of the abstinence movement, wherein "white, middle-class, social and religious conservatism" was upheld as the "cultural standard and ideal."[78] The continued relevance of a critique of the abstinence movement's racism, originally leveled against Clinton's abstinence policy in the 1990s, is exemplary of the deepening of the debate over teenage sexuality in the Bush years. Though such social conservatism had its ideological roots in the previous century, its public prominence in the Bush administration led to the exaggerated visibility of sexual practices in American public life. In confluence with an increasingly sexualized mass media in the 2000s, these developments led to a more explicit set of public conversations on the sexual behaviors of teenage girls in this era than ever before, even when the conversation focused on *not* having sex.[79] As we have seen, that discussion also fueled the explicit nature of the historical, racial implications of "innocence" in purity campaigns.

Advocates Fight Back

The relative ease with which evangelical Christian activists discussed issues of sexuality bothered former SIECUS president Debra Haffner, who had left the organization in 2001 to enter the Unitarian ministry.[80] "The organized religious right has no reluctance to address sexuality," she warned religious liberals in her 2006 guide for churches, *A Time to Speak*, in which she emphasized the need for an increased presence of "progressive religious voices" in public debates.[81] The abstinence movement may have received federal support and that of conservative organizations, but it did not represent the sexual politics of all Americans at the turn of the century. There were many groups and individuals involved in a fight for young people's right to sexual information in this period. As abstinence warriors became more vocal, comprehensive sex education campaigners were correspondingly reinvigorated. The resulting battle brought the long-running culture wars over girlhood sexualities to the forefront of public consciousness in the early twenty-first century.

Many of these youth sexual health organizations, including SIECUS and Advocates for Youth, had been campaigning since the 1960s. In the 2000s, these groups responded to the overt attack on the sexual and reproductive rights of teenagers by the Bush administration via new media forms, focusing their energies on debunking the misinformation that the federal government condoned and produced. In 2005, SIECUS called on the Department of Health and Human Services to take down their new website, 4parents.gov.[82] They criticized the site for ignoring the health needs of "sexually active youth, youth who have been sexually abused, and lesbian, gay, bisexual, transgender, and questioning youth."[83] The work of public health organizations sometimes included releasing freely available sexual health information for teenagers, to counter what was being withheld from them in schools. The nonpartisan health research group the Kaiser Foundation did so in a project named Sexsmarts, through which they joined forces with the girls' magazine *Seventeen* to provide "a guide to the head and heart" and "sexual health issues."[84] This partnership was particularly significant given *Seventeen*'s reputation in the preceding two decades for failing to provide any frank discussion of sex and sexuality to its teenage readership. Despite the magazine's chaste history, the October 2000 issue featured the official launch of the project.[85] A Sexsmarts website was also eventually launched, featuring more exhaustive information available to an even wider readership. *Seventeen*'s shift to providing candid sex education to its readers reflected both the newly sexually explicit mainstream culture of the post-Clinton era and the ways in which the conservative abstinence movement of the 2000s inspired many liberals to take an unequivocal position on sex education in response.

Outside of the major sex education advocacy groups, smaller local efforts also ramped up in this period, many of them led by young people themselves. In 2002, at Cesar Chavez High School for Public Policy in Washington, DC, five teenage girls—Lauriel Patterson, Ari Humphries, Zakiya Jones, Monique Jackson, and Cherry Wooten—turned a semester-long policy research project with the organization Choice USA into a "year-and-a-half dedication to bring comprehensive sex education to their school."[86] Jones said of their first attempts to do so, "Even though some students were pregnant, the principal didn't think the kids were having sex and didn't think sex ed was necessary," but after "twenty-five students showed up at 7.30 A.M. on a Saturday" for the first seminar that they had organized, the administration of the school agreed "to offer human sexuality as an elective class every Thursday afternoon." It soon became "the most popular elective" held at the school.[87] In 2005, Choice USA recognized young activist leaders for their efforts in fighting against the growing attacks on reproductive rights under the Bush administration, including access to sex education. Hannah Owens-Pike, a high school senior in

Minneapolis, won the organization's Next Generation Award "for her work to educate both parents and high-school students about sexual and reproductive health
and sex education." Owens-Pike had worked for her local Planned Parenthood from
the age of thirteen, and by the end of high school she was "a peer educator with
Planned Parenthood's Teen Council."[88] As Crystal Plati, executive director of Choice
USA, noted, "the work of young people" was "crucial to the struggle for reproductive freedom and justice" in the 2000s, and fighting for and creating comprehensive sex education where there was none was one major contribution that teenage
activists made in this period.

   Susan Wilson, a New Jersey–based sex education advocate who had worked at
the Network for Family Life for twenty-three years, was inspired by young people's
demands to make *Sex Etc.* in 1994. While speaking to a group of eleventh graders,
Wilson tentatively asked those who might be interested in participating in a newsletter about sex "written by teens for teens" to come speak to her afterward, hop-
ing to gauge potential interest. Wilson was shocked when, upon finishing her speech,
she was "struck by a tsunami" of over 200 teenagers demanding "you've gotta do
this, this is what we need, this would be so helpful."[89] The Network for Family Life
ensured that the publication made it into "schools, community centers, Planned
Parenthoods, school libraries, college libraries," and even "one florist," who put out
the publication to get teens engulfed in the literature and out of her flower shop.[90]
The teenage contributors met on Saturdays in the organization's New Brunswick
offices, some of whom "took three kinds of transport" just to be involved.[91] In the
mid-2000s, the newsletter became a sleek magazine with a corresponding website.
Its tone was serious but sex-positive—answers were sought to such queries as "the
condom broke last night" and "I'm not sure if it was rape," though it also featured
articles such as "I'm Perfect," where teenagers of all genders wrote in discussing
what they loved and hated most about their bodies.[92] The teenage writers often
appealed to their contemporaries with humor. The Spring 2006 issue featured an
article on how teenagers could handle "the big question" posed to them by a parent, beginning with the ice-breaking joke: "Are you having sex? / No mom, I'm
having breakfast."[93] Wilson ensured there would be no charge for the magazine,
knowing that they would never get it into schools otherwise, and that this would
help the publication to stay "under the radar."[94] However, conservatives were certainly aware of the publication. Carol Platt Liebau, a libertarian attorney and political pundit, mentioned *Sex Etc.* in her 2007 book *Prude: How the Sex-Obsessed
Culture Damages Girls (and America, too!)*, accusing it of antiabstinence "prosely-
tizing."[95] Liebau's attack on the magazine demonstrates the heightened charge of
the culture wars over teenagers' sexual lives in this era.

   The 2000s also saw many religious groups emerge as forthright defenders of comprehensive sex education, in response to the newly visible attack on the sexual health
of teenagers by the Bush administration. Many Black churches were a part of this
fight. From the late 1990s into the early 2000s, the Black Church transformed their
former "silence" on issues including "teen pregnancy, domestic violence, and HIV/
AIDS."[96] Baptist minister Carlton W. Veazey, who would go on to become presi-

dent of the Religious Coalition for Reproductive Choice, came to the realization that "black clergy, myself included, did not know how to talk about sexuality prayerfully and realistically." He recalled that "if sex was mentioned at all, it was in a shaming, negative way," and that "it seemed that talking about teen pregnancy and AIDS meant we were doing something morally wrong."[97] Through the Religious Coalition for Reproductive Choice, Veazey began the Black Church Initiative, which ran a series of Black Religious Summits on Sexuality and opened the conversation around sexual health from within the Black Church. Many African American parishioners were particularly moved to take part in such conversations because of the increase in funding for abstinence education in the Bush administration. "We had to admit that most were already sexually active and that we could not help them, or others, with abstinence education," said Veazey.[98] Therefore, the Black Church Initiative also developed a comprehensive sex education program to be taught in their communities, titled Keeping it Real!, one of the first efforts launched by the Black Church to deal with sexual health, particularly that of young people.[99]

The range of reactions from religious communities to abstinence education demonstrates the nuances of the debates over adolescent sexual behavior in the new millennium, despite the generalizations that are often made about this period of U.S. politics, which equate progressivism with secularism, and Christian spirituality with right-wing politics.[100] Again, following the story of debates over the sexual practices of teenagers sheds new light on the fluid and unfixed boundaries of the culture wars. Luis Ricardo Torres-Rivera, who in 2005 at twenty-eight years old won Choice USA's Sex Educator Award, played a key part in bringing holistic sex education to religious communities in Washington, DC. He had started his work with churches when he was hired by the Religious Coalition for Reproductive Choice right out of college, where he had begun his work in reproductive rights organizing: "I started a chapter of FMF (Feminist Majority Foundation) on my campus at the same time as I was pledging a Latino fraternity. I wanted to have the most diverse approach I could."[101] In his work with Black churches through the Religious Coalition, Torres-Rivera learned how "to put lessons and ideas from that work" into "Latino churches and communities," and in doing so created La Iniciativa Latina.[102] This involved holding a national conference in California, which happened to fall "two days after 9/11," meaning many could not attend as expected because planes were grounded. However, this inadvertently led to the conference being attended primarily by local churches from around Los Angeles, which reminded Torres-Rivera of the importance of the "personal, one-on-one conversation" and made him shift his focus from national to local work, thereafter concentrating on the DC Campaign to Prevent Teen Pregnancy. Torres-Rivera's work on sex education in DC focused on churches and on approaching sex education and teenage pregnancy in a holistic sense. One of his major initiatives was to encourage DC churches to "open once a week to welcome local teens in, and sit down [to] have a meal together. Not to talk about sex ed or teen pregnancy, but just about, how was their day? That way we're building relationships that are really about the well-being of teens."[103]

Another important religious campaign for the well-being of teenagers in this decade was Our Whole Lives, the sexuality education program started by former president of SIECUS, Debra Haffner, through the Unitarian Church. This process began when she founded the Religious Institute in 2001 after an impassioned conversation in the cafeteria of the Union Theological Seminary with the Reverend Larry Greenfield. "I remember a fellow student stopping and asking what we were doing with such intensity," recalled Haffner. "We looked at her and said, 'perhaps creating history.'"[104] After this initial conversation, Haffner and Greenfield published the resulting manifesto, "Declaration on Sexual Morality, Justice and Healing," in the *New York Times*, and in doing so "started a movement" among like-minded people of faith.[105] The ministers' initiative would grow over the next decade to include 5,000 religious leaders from over seventy "faith traditions," all of whom were dedicated to making "resources on sexual abuse prevention, sexual and gender diversity, assisted reproductive technologies, and sexuality education" available to their communities.[106] Through the Religious Institute, Haffner and others working in the Unitarian tradition developed Our Whole Lives, a sexuality education program with modules aimed at specific age groups, from childhood through to old age. These programs differed radically from those written by evangelical abstinence groups. One major difference was the inclusion of LGBTQ+ youth. "As young people develop their adult sense of self, their understandings of their own sexual orientation and gender identity begin to emerge," it read.[107] The significance of these advocates' focus on queer and trans youth cannot be overstated— monogamous, married heterosexuality had been the only form of sexual expression that was deemed psychologically and physically healthy in federally funded sex education to date. Additionally, Haffner admitted in a talk to parents of high school students that even the culture of "hook ups" or "friends with benefits" that was emerging in this period was not necessarily harmful to young people, as long as those relationships were "consensual, honest, mutually pleasurable, and protected."[108] Haffner asserted that, despite having faith at its center, the Our Whole Lives curriculum was the kind of comprehensive sexuality education that was endorsed by "the American Medical Association, the American Academy of Pediatrics, the Society for Adolescent Medicine," and "all the former Surgeons General from the Reagan through the Clinton administrations."[109]

Scientific and research communities, meanwhile, were concerned by the Bush administration's refusal to respond to their studies. The government relied on internally produced data rather than professional researchers and institutions.[110] Thus, research became a particularly bloody battlefront in the culture wars over adolescent sexual health in the 2000s. This began within the administration. In 2001, Surgeon General David Satcher released the report *A Call to Action*, in which he presented medical findings on the importance of lifelong comprehensive sexuality education.[111] He commended the abstinence movement for its moral message, but nonetheless stressed that correct information on condom usage and concurrent access to condoms were essential components of adolescent health care.[112] Conservatives were incensed, and groups such as the Traditional Values Coalition, the

Family Research Council, and Focus on the Family called for his resignation.[113] Satcher agreed to do so at the end of the term, proving as C. Everett Koop and Jocelyn Elders had before him the unique political binds put on the surgeon generals of the United States when the medical information they promoted involved the sexual health of young people.

The surgeon general's report was followed by a series of publications by independent scientific organizations that sought to prove that abstinence-only education did not lower teenage pregnancy or sexually transmitted infection (STI) rates, and that it was actively harmful to the health of young people. This urgent flurry of research activity reflected the political significance that the Bush administration had attributed to maintaining the sexual abstinence of teenagers, which in turn inspired newly explicit advocacy for and research on the needs of young people across multiple factions of American society. The American Psychological Association concluded that not providing full sex education denied teenagers their "fundamental human rights to health, information, and life."[114] In 2004, the National Institutes of Health provided the sociologist Peter Bearman with a grant to survey 12,000 teenagers who had taken virginity pledges six years earlier. He found that 88 percent had broken their pledges and that their STI rates were "identical" to those of teenagers who had not taken pledges.[115] At the end of 2004, the Democratic California congressman Henry Waxman released a report on abstinence programs that received federal funding, which revealed that many of these organizations were "openly opposed to abortion."[116] A report in *Pediatrics & Adolescent Medicine* in 2006 produced evidence that despite being "a priority of the federal government," abstinence-only education was "supported by neither a majority of the public nor the scientific community."[117] The same study reported that most American adults wanted their children to receive some abstinence education, alongside scientifically accurate contraceptive education.[118] The findings of this report also serve as an important reminder that although the polarity of the culture wars of this era has attracted much media and historical attention, there were unexpected moments of consensus in this period of U.S. politics that are revealed in the history of adolescent sexuality.[119]

None of this research, however, would have an impact on federal policy while Bush was in the White House.[120] Abstinence campaigners, including Leslee Unruh of Abstinence Clearinghouse, claimed that the research put out by these institutions was "junk science," and the Bush administration set about creating its own data.[121] In order to circumvent the recommendations of these previously trusted institutions and experts, members of medical and policy organizations were removed from their positions as advisers to the government, and their counsel was replaced with that which reinforced the morals of the abstinence movement—for instance, CWA replaced the American Medical Association as advisers to American delegations to U.N. summits on children's issues.[122] Bush's new research appointees took measures to produce desirable data, such as changing the indicators of "successful" abstinence programs to those wherein students attended regularly and responded well to questionnaires.[123] This continued the Bush administration's tactic for ensuring only certain information was received by teenagers, particularly young women. In 2004, a congressional committee released a report that found that scientific misinformation was present in most abstinence programs receiving federal funding, and that most of the existing women's health information on government websites had been removed, replaced with conservative information about sex and sexuality.[124] In Franklin County, North Carolina, the school board ordered three chapters to be physically cut out of ninth-grade health textbooks, as they covered more information than their abstinence-only funding allowed.[125]

American sex education battles that had re-emerged in the culture wars of the 1990s gained a new urgency during the years of the Bush administration.[126] The nature of the battles also became more explicit than in previous decades: unambiguous debates over whether teenagers should be having sex formed the core of adult concerns over sex education.[127] Yet there were moments of consensus, as most adults across the political divide publicly agreed that young people should wait as long as possible before they began to have sex. Though comprehensive sex education advocates believed that young people had the right to learn about how to avoid pregnancy and STIs, and to be given information on sexual and gender identity, pleasure, and desire, most of these individuals agreed that these should be taught in addition to, not in place of, abstinence education. For instance, Susan Wilson, creator of the progressive publication *Sex Etc.*, noted that the triumph of the magazine was that "*Sex Etc.* postponed kids having sex—that was our goal."[128] Despite differing attitudes toward sex and to what information young people deserved, the desire to delay sexual initiation may have been more universal across the culture wars than it initially appeared. The ubiquitous aim to delay adolescent sex across political groups made it increasingly difficult for adult sexual health advocates or for teenagers themselves to advocate otherwise, and as a result these kinds of discussions continued to occur through underground and grassroots channels.[129] The pervasive negativity regarding teenage sex, even in liberal political circles, would lead the young director of community advocacy at SIECUS, Leslie Kantor, to lament that there was in fact "no left wing sex education in America."[130]

MEDICINE VERSUS MORALITY

Sex education, however, was not the only issue that brought medical researchers and moral warriors head to head in an explicit battle over whether young people should be having sex at all. Emergency contraception (EC), also known as the morning-after pill, was the catalyst of a major fallout at the United States Food and Drug Administration (FDA) during the Bush administration. The controversy began in late 2003, when Barr Laboratories, the manufacturer of the EC pill Plan B, applied to the FDA to gain approval for the pill to become available over the counter (OTC).[131] The EC pill had been approved for prescription use since 1998, and since 2000 major medical associations had been urging the possibility of its OTC availability.[132] In December 2000, a group of OB/GYN experts held a meeting at the FDA, during which they voted 23 to 4 in favor of Plan B becoming available over the counter to women across America. Those who objected admitted that their reasons for doing so were not based in the "demonstrated efficacy or safety" of the pill.[133] Despite this outcome, senior management at the FDA rejected Barr Laboratories' application in May 2004, citing an "absence of data on young adolescents" as the reason why they could not allow the pill to become available over the counter.[134] Over the following months, the FDA officials were unable to provide any data to support their claims that the pill might be unsafe for younger girls, while peer-reviewed medical journals published research that showed "young adolescents with improved access to EC used the method more frequently when needed, but did not compromise their use of routine contraception nor increase their sexual risk behavior."[135] In July of that year, Barr Laboratories tried again, this time amending the application to ask for the pill to become available over the counter to women over sixteen, remaining by prescription for those under that age.[136] The FDA delayed the decision for over a year.[137] Eventually, in August 2005, senior FDA officials again impeded the availability by beginning a regulatory process that would "delay the decision indefinitely."[138] Following this, the FDA was informed by concerned conservative groups about why they disapproved the drug. One letter, sent to the FDA by a law firm on behalf of a number of organizations including CWA and the Family Research Council, revealed that the reasons behind conservatives' disapproval had little to do with data. "There is no question that Plan B OTC will become the leading 'rape' drug in the country," the letter stated, as it "would give sexual predators another method to shield their abusive behavior."[139]

The Bush administration and the conservative groups that were bolstered by its policies had engendered a political climate in which adults expressed outright their moral and ethical positions on the sexual lives of teenage girls. This was also true of those within the FDA who opposed the moralizing that was taking place around teenagers' access to EC. Upon receiving news of this final delay, Dr. Susan F. Wood, the assistant FDA commissioner for women's health and director of the agency's Office of Women's Health, promptly resigned in protest.[140] "The recent decision announced by the Commissioner about emergency contraception, which continues to limit women's access to a product that would reduce unintended pregnancies and reduce abortions, is contrary to my core commitment to improving and advancing women's health," she stated. "I can no longer serve as staff when scientific and clinical evidence, fully evaluated and recommended for approval by the professional staff here, has been overruled."[141] Supporters of the Plan B application, including New York senator Hillary Clinton and members of the Reproductive Health Technologies Project, expressed distress at the delays and at Wood's leaving.[142] On the other hand, Wendy Wright, president of CWA, celebrated. "Thank goodness there is now one less political activist at the FDA," she proclaimed, "who puts radical feminist ideology above women's health."[143] But it was not long before another senior official followed Wood's example. In November 2005, Dr. Frank Davidoff, a consultant and member of the FDA's Nonprescription Drugs Advisory Committee, stepped down over the indefinite delay. "I can no longer associate myself with an organization that is capable of making such an important decision so flagrantly on the basis of political influence, rather than the scientific and clinical evidence," he stated.[144] Finally, in August 2006, the FDA made a conciliatory decision, allowing for Plan B to be purchased over the counter for women eighteen and older and only by prescription for those seventeen and under.[145] The very public fallout over EC was exemplary of the way that the enduring culture war over the potentially corrupting impact of sexual and reproductive services for young people that had raged since the 1960s had evolved in a newly sexually explicit culture, into one in which both sides spoke in overt terms about what was at stake: whether teenagers should be having sex.[146]

As the dust momentarily settled on the EC controversy in 2006, a further medical development in the area of adolescent sexual health led to a very public, heated dispute over whether teenagers should be supported in seeking safer sex—a newly developed vaccine against genital warts and the sexually transmitted human papilloma virus (HPV), some strains of which lead to cervical cancer. Marketed as Gardasil by the pharmaceutical company Merck & Co., the three doses of the vaccine were recommended by the CDC's Advisory Committee on Immunization Practices to be "routinely" administered to girls aged eleven to twelve.[147] The vaccine was hailed as a breakthrough among many in the medical community, and it was promptly introduced by forty-one states, twenty-four of which made it mandatory.[148] To many Americans, however, the vaccine represented an outright endorsement or encouragement of adolescent sexual activity.[149] Members of the CWA swiftly launched a campaign discouraging the distribution of the vaccine. Though they were pleased that the CDC had found a link between "promiscuity, STDs [sexually transmitted diseases], and cancer," they were infuriated at the release of the vaccine and at the states that made its use mandatory.[150] Among other concerns, the CWA believed that Gardasil would remove one of the consequences of extramarital sex, and thus encourage teenage girls to have sex.[151] This sentiment was echoed by various other socially conservative groups, including the Family Research Council.[152] The ability to have sex without consequence—whether that be by avoiding pregnancy or STDs—hinted at the destruction of something larger and more pivotal for the Right, in that it diminished the importance of the heterosexual family as a structure through which to experience sexuality. This had long been a driving concern of the New Right, but the frankness of the culture wars over sexuality in the 2000s empowered social conservatives to clearly articulate their position on teenage sex to an unprecedented degree.

The Right's vocal resistance to advances in reproductive and sexual health for adolescent women caused many liberals to respond just as emphatically. Katha Pollitt, a feminist writer and longtime columnist for *The Nation*, penned a furious article for the publication voicing her shock at the response to the HPV vaccine. "Just as it's better for gays to get AIDS than use condoms, it's better for a woman to get cancer than have sex before marriage," she wrote scathingly.[153] "What is it with these right-wing Christians?" she continued. "Faced with a choice between sex and death, they choose death every time."[154] Those in the medical community were equally exasperated. "I never thought that now, in the twenty-first century, we would have a debate about what to do with a vaccine that prevents cancer," one doctor exclaimed.[155] James Trusell, director of the Office of Population Research at Princeton University, presented one potential answer when he spoke to Pollitt on the topic. "It all comes down to the evils of sex. That's an ideological position impervious to empirical evidence."[156] Through these very public debates, the sexual behavior of teenage girls thus became central to the culture war between morality and medical research in the Bush administration.

However, feminists and other progressive thinkers were not unilaterally on the side of mandatory distribution of the HPV vaccine. Some feminists—and in particular, feminists of color—observed that the medical establishment and pharmaceutical companies did not always have women's best interests at heart, and that the HPV vaccine was no exception. In 2007, a representative of the Chicago Women's Health Center—a "veteran women's health collective" that was "founded on the principles of the feminist women's health movement"—wrote to *Bitch* magazine to critique their "unquestioning, 'jump on the bandwagon'" coverage of Gardasil.[157] They sent further information to the magazine in the form of a "thoughtful assessment" of the drug to counter "the current one minute TV ads" and "unreasoned legislative proposals to mandate universal vaccination of girls and young women." Further, in the newsletter of the women of color reproductive justice group SisterSong, a report mentioned 1,700 "adverse reactions" to the drug from young women who had had it administered, and brought attention to the fact that "immigrants seeking citizenship are now required to get five new vaccinations, Gardasil being one of them."[158] Jessica González-Rojas, director of policy and advocacy at the National Latina Institute for Reproductive Health, asserted that "mandating a vaccine that specifically targets young non-citizen women is both sexist and xenophobic."[159] SisterSong's reportage on the vaccine was a reminder of the ways in which medical advancements in the field of sexual health had historically been used coercively by the state to control the sexual and reproductive lives of Black, Latinx, and Indigenous young women and were not necessarily causes for blanket celebration.[160] The history of debates over girlhood sexualities proves that even the culture wars that appear most politically polarized often necessitate further interrogation.[161] The wider culture wars of this period—and indeed, today—are not always as straightforward as a battle between conservatives and progressives. The range of adults across the political spectrum who were vocal about their fear of the hypersexualization of teenage girls in the 2000s would be further proof of this.

Hypersexualization, or "Girls in Crisis" in the 2000s

Accompanying the focus on adolescent women in policy and medical debates of the 2000s was a renewed attention to the impact of popular culture on young women's sexual well-being. As indicated by the more explicit discourse on the sexual lives of teenage girls in the political sphere, American culture had become more sexually explicit in the 2000s than in any previous period. As sex in general became more speakable in popular culture, sex among young people became more speakable too. This was partly brought about by the impact of twentieth-century pro-sex feminist and queer activism on wider American culture. However, in mainstream media, those predominantly doing the speaking were not young people themselves, and straight men still controlled film, television, and news industries. This meant that much of the mainstream depiction of adolescent sexuality was not exactly feminist in nature. One notable shift was in an intensified media focus on the sex lives of young female celebrities. For instance, some internet blogs featured "countdown clocks" to the eighteenth birthdays of twin teenage TV stars Mary Kate and Ashley Olsen.[162] A 2005 magazine cover of the actress Lindsay Lohan, who had become famous at the age of eleven in 1998, bore the headline announcing that she was finally "Hot, Ready, and Legal!"[163] In recent years, the misogynistic depiction and discussion of teenage girls' sexualities in the mainstream press of the 2000s has come under public scrutiny.[164] Pop stars of this era, including Jessica Simpson and Christina Aguilera, have spoken out about their mistreatment, and some photographers and journalists have expressed regret at their "creepy" treatment of famous young women.[165] Though the newly overt discourse on young women's sexuality might at first glance have looked like a pro-sex feminist victory, it was in fact one that was predominantly designed by and for men's pleasure.

However, at the time, vocal critics of the increasingly sexualized treatment of teenage girls in the media did not target the exploitative men at the top and were instead more concerned with the increased sexual activity of teenage girls that might result from this media.[166] Despite the apparent crystallization of conservative and liberal camps of the culture wars in this era, a widespread concern over the "sexualization" or even "hypersexualization" of young women in American culture revealed unexpected intersections in the sexual politics of conservatives and many feminists.[167] As in the "pornography wars" of the 1980s and the "girls in crisis" literature of the 1990s, debates about girlhood sexualities in this era often produced ideological overlaps among adults from across the political spectrum. This was something that concerned University of Iowa women's and media studies professor Meenakshi Gigi Durham. In 2008, she described the way that the sexualized media treatment of teenage girls put feminists in a bind, in that it threatened to reopen old alliances between feminists and social conservatives and deepen existing culture war divisions. "Is it anti-sex to want to shield your child from certain kinds of sexual portrayals?" she worried. "Is it pro-sex to want high school students to have access to contraception?"[168] Durham had identified an emerging challenge for feminists: how to weigh in on the problem of exploitative media discourse on teenage girls without fueling reactionary forces in American culture. In the public conversations about hypersexualization in the 2000s, the battle between a fearful mainstream and those who advocated for frank discussions on the complexities of girlhood sexual experience became further established in the U.S. culture wars.

As the Bush administration progressed, some feminists began to notice the increasing centrality of young women's sexuality in politics and culture.[169] They also became aware of the tangible impact this was having on the young women with whom they interacted. Dagmar Herzog, for instance, observed a change in her female undergraduate students at Michigan State University. "In 1992 they were remarkably comfortable and forthright, sassy and self-confident, knowledgeable and open-minded," she remembered. However, by 2005, "students appeared far more hesitant and insecure; they communicated an astonishing lack of self-ownership and understanding when it came to sexual matters. What had happened?"[170] Though social conservatives had expressed concern over the impact of popular culture on young people for decades, the 2000s saw more "sexual liberals" converge on this position as they observed such changes in young women.[171] It was clear to them that the increasingly graphic mainstream culture, spurred by the fearmongering of a conservative government, was leading to the exploitation rather than liberation of adolescent sexuality. Unfortunately, the pervasive fear of girlhood sexuality in the American mainstream culture, particularly in the political climate engendered by a socially conservative administration, made it difficult for feminists to advocate against "sexualization" but for "sexual autonomy" without being lumped in with reactionary forces.[172]

This was partly because of how vocally socially conservative women rallied against the sexualization of young women in American media. In doing so, they often appropriated progressive feminist politics while blaming feminism for causing social problems, which is illustrative of the development of conservative forms of feminism in the twenty-first century.[173] One such voice was that of the attorney and political commentator Carol Platt Liebau, whose 2007 book *Prude* outlined how she believed the "sexualizing of America" had affected teenagers' decisions about whether to have sex. "Sex has become virtually unavoidable in every context," she contended. "The public square—from the airwaves to billboards to newspapers—is saturated with it."[174] She went on to describe how "living in an overly sexualized society takes a very real toll on girls," which included consequences such as children outside of marriage and the subsequent burden on "society" to "support both" the young mother and her child.[175] Liebau saw the tradition of what she called "radical feminism" as partly to blame for an increasingly sexually explicit culture, for insisting that "true female liberation encompasses sexual license."[176] Concern for teenage girls under the guise of a conservative "feminism" informed this critique of sexually exploitative imagery in media and advertising. In reality, socially conservative women's belief that sex and reproduction outside of marriage was a social problem rooted their politics in the racist and classist association of promiscuity and early childbearing with the economy that had been promoted by various strands of U.S. conservatism throughout the twentieth century.[177] The most vocal pundits on sexualization were white, as were most of the teenagers they wrote about. Like most of the abstinence-promoting pop stars who were upheld as models of purity, the teenage girls whose potentially increased sexual activity fueled the movement against hypersexualization were white, echoing the same dynamic that triggered the earliest panics of the culture wars.[178]

Feminism was not the only aspect of American culture blamed for the sexualization of teenagers. One major social change that troubled adults from across the

political spectrum in the 2000s was the vastly increased access to free pornography that came along with the introduction of the internet to homes and schools
across America. This was a sentiment that was also expressed by liberals and by
fierce advocates for teenage sexual health. In 2007, medical doctors Melissa Holmes
and Trish Hutchison published a book for teenage girls titled *Hang-Ups, Hook-Ups,
and Holding Out: Stuff You Need to Know about Your Body, Sex, and Dating,* in
which they attempted to discourage young women from viewing pornography
online, claiming that even "soft pornography" would "continue to haunt" them for
"weeks, months, and possibly even years."[179] Liberals and conservatives alike were
concerned by the way that sexualization occurred not only through teenage girls'
direct access to pornography online, but through the unavoidable interactions they
believed young people had with sexually graphic content in popular culture. Many
saw this as a result of the way that pornography had seeped into the mainstream.
Carol Platt Liebau, for instance, was perturbed by the availability of "subjects and
images that used to be almost impossible for them to access." Technology now provided an endless abundance in outright pornographic sites and through new forms
of sexual media including message boards, chat rooms, and personal web pages
where "cam girls" could upload their own sexually explicit images and videos of
themselves.[180] However, Liebau was equally concerned about the innate pornographic nature of teen culture beyond technology. As an example, she named the
"fantastically successful" *Gossip Girl* book series, about a group of sexually active
teenagers at an elite Manhattan high school, "where drug use and casual sex of all
sorts become the hallmarks of worldly-wise allure."[181] Liebau's conflation of emerging forms of online sex work with mass media suggests the lack of nuance in conservative concerns with sexualization, meaning they were absent of any genuine
desire to ensure the safe working conditions of young women doing this work or
the further sexual education of young people who read the *Gossip Girl* books.

Many liberals shared Liebau's concern with the influence of modern pornography on popular culture aimed at teenage girls. This demonstrated the lasting impact
of the alliance between antipornography feminists and pro-family campaigners in
the 1980s: though liberal commentators on sexualization rejected the wider politics of the Right, they shared a blanket opposition to pornography. Boston University communications professor Patrice Oppliger was one such liberal. In her 2008
publication *Girls Gone Skank: The Sexualization of Girls in American Culture,* she
demonstrated many of the same concerns as conservative critics such as Carol Platt
Liebau. She was extremely worried about cam girls and about studies that claimed
that "18–34 year old women" were "the fasting growing Internet porn users."[182] Like
Liebau, Oppliger also attributed the diffusion of "skanky" aesthetics to the availability of pornography. She gave an exhaustive list of examples, including the 2003
film *Thirteen,* an autobiographical account of director Nikki Reed's experiences
with "sexuality, cutting, and drug use" as a teenager growing up in LA, the "increasingly skanky" appearance of pop stars Christina Aguilera and Britney Spears, and
even trends in the sport of cheerleading for "dance moves that emulate strippers."[183]
Oppliger also blamed "retail marketers" for seizing on this trend, naming in par-

ticular the adolescent brand Abercrombie & Fitch's line of thong underwear bearing slogans such as "Eye Candy" and "Wink Wink" for girls as young as seven, stating that these forms of sexualization had inevitably led to increased "sexual prowess" in teenage girls.[184] Despite Oppliger's feminist concern over the increasingly exploitative and misogynist nature of teen consumer culture in the 2000s, her alarm at the increased rates of teenage sexual behavior aligned her critique with that of conservatives. In this way, the mainstream alarm over the sexualization of teenagers combined both feminist and conservative voices.[185]

Even younger, explicitly feminist women contributed to the conversations about hypersexualization, particularly in their reactions to the perceived pornographic culture of the twenty-first-century United States.[186] Most vocal on this topic was the young *New York* magazine staffer Ariel Levy, who coined the term "raunch culture" to describe the diffusion of pornographic tropes into the cultural mainstream that was unsettling women across the political spectrum. She remembered noticing this shift in the early 2000s, as a trend emerged for T-shirts bearing the bunny logo of *Playboy* magazine or even just the phrase "PORN STAR."[187] Like Patrice Oppliger, Levy ultimately was concerned with the potential impact of this raunch culture on the sexual behavior of young girls coming of age in this period. She expressed alarm at rumors of sexual trends such as "rainbow parties," in which multiple school-aged girls allegedly wore different colors of lipstick and then performed oral sex on a male peer.[188] The open discourse on the participation of teenage girls in oral sex that took place in the media over this perceived trend demonstrated the impact of the Clinton-Lewinsky affair on the ability of Americans to discuss such acts in graphic language in public.[189]

Shocking stories such as these grabbed headlines and sold books. It was certainly evident in American society in this period that young women's sexual empowerment, as started by young activists and artists calling themselves the Third Wave, had quickly been co-opted and commercialized to center the sexual young woman as an object to be desired by male consumers. It was also true that with the dawn of the internet came new ways that young people were vulnerable.[190] However, much of the popular writing on hypersexualization, as was the case amid the media discussions around child sexual abuse of the 1980s and the "girls in crisis" debates of the 1990s, perpetuated the historical focus on the sexual vulnerability of white, middle-class girls and simultaneously ignored the possibility of young women ever enacting sexual agency in such a media and political climate. This overlooked the ongoing grassroots efforts by young feminist activists themselves and by the adults who supported them to resist the racism and misogyny of policy and popular culture, and to fight for their sexual and reproductive rights. The pervasive exploitation of teenage girls in the media, and the popularity of both conservative and feminist horror stories about hypersexualization, proved that the mainstream media of the 2000s remained hostile to frank, sensitive discussions about the diverse experiences and complicated realities of young women's sexual lives across the United States. Such portrayals of adolescence could still only exist in more underground spaces in this era, despite a more sexually explicit culture than previous decades.[191]

Other feminist scholars and activists agreed that the media climate of the 2000s was toxic for young women, but still foresaw the possibility of positive sexual experiences for teenagers within such a culture.[192] These women started to take issue with the way that teenagers were being portrayed in popular discussions about sexualization. Jessica Valenti, a young feminist writer and blogger, acknowledged that "hyper-sexualization" and "porn culture" were undeniable, but criticized Ariel Levy for not showing "sympathy" for the young women she was talking about and for assuming that young women were being duped into expressing their sexuality a certain way.[193] These adult feminists also emphasized that the sexual subjectivity of girls need not be lost despite the undeniable pressures they faced. Developmental psychologist Deborah Tolman lamented in 2002 that "the possibility that girls might be interested in sexuality in their own right" was still "met with resistance and discomfort," and exhorted other researchers to resist the urge to necessarily "conflate adolescent sexuality with risky behavior."[194] The historian Dagmar Herzog, who had expressed concern over the impact of U.S. political and popular culture on the young women she taught at Michigan State by the 2000s, also joined these debates and warned against what she called "subtler variations" of antipornography feminism that had been widely accepted in the liberal media. To Herzog, it was of great concern that a consensus had formed over the idea that porn was bad for young women, and that this had become "a kind of cultural common sense" that had deadened public debate. She regretted the loss of the 1990s pro-sex push for young women to lose "their guilt about their own sexual pleasure and the stigma associated with it."[195] In this period of feminist debate over the possibility of adolescent girls' sexual pleasure, the association of some feminists with more conservative views on porn and "promiscuity" meant that there was an increased difficulty in such a climate to advocate for young women's access to sexual information, or even their own desire.[196] This reiterated the culture war that had emerged amid the 1990s girl culture, between a mainstream set of approaches to girlhood sexualities and more sexually forthright grassroots responses to the experiences of teenage girls.

In a seminar titled "Sex and American Politics" at NYU in 2004, journalism professor and pro-sex Second Wave feminist Ellen Willis reminded those attending to be wary that, in America, "sexual conservatism comes not only from the religious right but also from a certain brand of feminism."[197] Willis attributed the negative sexual culture in which young women were coming of age to the conservative politics that underpinned the sexually explicit mass media. "On the one hand, we often give the impression of being a culture of limitless permissiveness for both sexes," she told her class, "where online pornography has become a mainstream activity, where advertising which of course was always erotic is more and more boldly and explicitly sexual," and "where teenagers have sex at younger and younger ages." However, she maintained, "the United States is still deeply influenced by a historic puritanism and by the contemporary power of a religious conservative moment that is an important part of the coalition of the ruling Republican Party and the Bush administration."[198] The sexualization of adolescent women in the

United States saw otherwise warring factions of American society find consensus in their concern over a sexually explicit culture and its impact on teenage sexual behavior. In the public discourse about sexualization, debates over whether sex could ever be a positive part of adolescent life took place more explicitly than ever before. Though the culture wars that contended with girlhood sexual behavior had raged for decades, the coexistence of an outrightly religious and socially conservative government, an increasingly funded purity movement, and the most sexually explicit media culture to date in American history had led to these overt and incendiary discussions.[199] These very visible debates in turn impacted the ways in which the 2000s have been memorialized as a site of major public crises over girlhood, when in fact tensions over teenage sex had been consistently brewing over the second half of the twentieth century.

TAKING BACK GIRL CULTURE

The alternative feminist voices that countered the mainstream narrative of hypersexualized, predominantly white, teenage girls with a more intricate understanding of the sexual lives of teenagers was not only made up of adults. Teenage girls in the 2000s, led by young women of color, utilized both existing and new technologies and networks to discuss their sexual rights and to organize around them. Young women's anger over their lack of sexual and reproductive freedom had been a major component of the emergence of American feminisms under the banner of the Third Wave in the early 1990s. Over the course of the 1990s, however, the politics and aesthetics of this "girl power" were co-opted into wider popular culture and eventually codified as girl studies in the academy. By the 2000s, then, girl culture was a mainstay of popular culture, and its rebellious roots were well hidden. However, young women's activism around reproductive and sexual justice did not disappear. Despite the "mixed messages" from the exploitative media that concerned adults of all political backgrounds, the restrictions put on sexual knowledge and health care by the Bush administration, and the mass-marketing of girl culture, many young women coming of age in America in this period fought back against these forces through political engagement, social organizing, and artistic practice.[200]

Despite the pervasiveness of popular girl culture during the 2000s, it was far removed from its underground roots. In 2003, girl studies scholar Anita Harris observed that "a particular kind of young, assertive, and sassy woman selling particular kinds of girlpower-inflected products or services" had become ubiquitous, making it "cool to be a girl."[201] The cosmetics brand Bonne Belle was one such company, whose 2002 lip gloss campaign read, "I have a brain, I have lipgloss, I have a plan, I have a choice, I can change my mind, I am a girl," thus encapsulating the power of girlhood in the market and the persistence of neoliberal narratives of "self-esteem" behind the campaigns and institutions that asserted "girl power."[202]

The sexual circumstances in which young women found themselves on television also became increasingly extensive and complex in this era. There was a notable increase in the volume and detail of sex scenes in television shows. In the 2000s, a virginity-loss episode was so commonplace in teen TV series it became known in the industry as "the very special episode."[203] In the mother-daughter drama *Gilmore Girls*, which ran from 2000 to 2007, the bookish Yale undergraduate protagonist Rory Gilmore has sex for the first time with her married ex-boyfriend. In the same year, 2004, the Southern California–based teen drama *The OC* included a storyline in which one of the main characters, Marissa, has a lesbian relationship with a bartender, whom she moves in with.[204] However, it was *Gossip Girl*, a TV program based on the book series that so upset Carol Platt Liebau, that most shocked parents across the United States when it was first aired in 2007. The program portrayed a group of privileged NYC teenagers with very sophisticated sex lives. The show's producers capitalized on these reactions by taking quotes from bad reviews in local newspapers and by the Parents Television Council and blazoning them across advertisements for the second season, including the phrases "unbelievably inappropriate" and "every parent's nightmare."[205] However, American popular culture in the 2000s was not necessarily one of which the teenage feminist activists of the 1990s had dreamed. It was a stylized version of predominantly white, thin, economically privileged young women's sexualities that was dominating the mainstream, competing with a highly public abstinence campaign that made use of similar imagery in its proclamation that sex before marriage was damaging. The girls on TV whose sex lives were scandalous to parents of teenage viewers were all predominantly white, again revealing whose sexual activity white adults were predominantly preoccupied with.[206]

In the face of pervasive media depictions of girlhood sexuality in the 2000s, young women across the United States created independent, underground spaces in which they could define their sexuality on their own terms. Many of the previous generation of feminists expressed disappointment in young women's activism during this period, claiming that they lacked avenues of political engagement and that their feminism was "obscure, transitory, and disorganized."[207] While it is true that, as in the previous decade, girls who came of age in this period from a range of backgrounds remember not ever hearing feminism mentioned in their homes growing up, youth activism driven by young women of color around intersectional feminist issues continued apace throughout the 2000s.[208] While the activism of young women in this period was not made as visible as that of Riot Grrrls and young women of the early Third Wave, and was not as globally connected by social media as that which emerged in the 2010s, girls' reactions to the political and popular culture of the Bush years were significant, in that they revealed how young women resisted having their sexuality debated over and defined for them.[209] The many young people who contributed to sex education activism—from the five seniors at Cesar Chavez High School who successfully campaigned for comprehensive sex education to the teenagers who gave up their Saturdays to volunteer at the magazine *Sex Etc.*—are evidence of this. One of the well-documented dangers of feminist wave terminology is that activism that occurs "between the waves" often gets overlooked. The intersectional activism of young people, particularly that of young people of color, around the issues of sexual, reproductive, and race inequality in the United States under the Bush administration is one such movement that should not be erased.[210]

Teenage feminists were involved in a number of such pressing struggles under the Bush administration. In July 2002, a group of twelve young activists aged seventeen to twenty-eight set off in a "fifteen person van" on the Third Wave Foundation's Reaching Out Across Movements (ROAM) tour of New Mexico, Arizona, and west Texas.[211] Two high school activists participating in the trip included seventeen-year-old Endeshia Abdul-Kareem and nineteen-year-old Netta Brooks. Abdul-Kareem was "looked upon as a leader" at East Side Community High School in New York and was a part-time staff member of the Third Wave Foundation "of Native American, Jewish, Puerto Rican, and West Indian Heritage." Brooks, a "queer African Amerikan g.r.i.t.s. (Girl raised in the South)" from Louisville, Kentucky, worked "on the board of the Louisville Fairness Campaign, a broad-based local civil right organization with an emphasis on queer rights," and aspired to be a "future filmmaker" who would "revolutionize the media by making documentaries and films while wearing a red cape and silver boots!"[212] The tour encouraged the young feminist activists to "share movement building resources with organizations and individuals using a multi-issue social justice perspective in their work" and to "learn how to support groups working in regions with a strong right-wing presence."[213] They chose the Southwest for their summer 2002 tour as "it seemed particularly fitting to tour the Southwest while issues like immigration, civil liberties, border policing, and violence against women are at the forefront of policy debates." They received training in "indigenous ways of organizing" and then met "over 25 groups confronting and organizing around issues like domestic violence, border policing, youth organizing, anti-militarization, and anti-racism work." Some of these groups included Young Women United, an organization led by young women of color that fought against sexual violence, and the Southwest Alliance to Resist Militarization, which conducted "know your rights" campaigns in border communities.[214] The intersectional activist energy that young feminists brought to ROAM is just one example of the important forms of feminist action that are overlooked when we write off a decade or generation as being apolitical or between waves in our periodization of American women's movements.[215]

Adult feminists were also increasingly looking at and listening to the experiences of young women in the 2000s to inform their own sexual politics. At the 2007 conference of SisterSong Women of Color Reproductive Justice Collective, held in Chicago with the theme "Let's Talk about Sex!," the organizers created a lot of space for the voices of teenagers, who joined a program of speakers including former surgeon general Joycelyn Elders and legal scholar Dorothy Roberts. Attendee Cynthia L. Jackson, a women's health advocate, was invigorated by the way that "the potent voice of the teen, preteen and beginning-women populations was represented both creatively and culturally" at the conference, including "young socio-political activists like Claudia De la Cruz, Youth Director of the Dominican Women's Development Center in New York," and "the Illinois Caucus for Adolescent Health, represented by two powerhouses in the form of Adaku Utah and Yessenia Cervantes,"

142   TEENAGE DREAMS

who ran a workshop titled "Youth Taking Action: Organizing to Improve Sex Education in Our Schools & Communities."[216] Jackson was also "personally challenged" as she listened to young people describe their coping mechanisms following sexual violence at a "workshop for sexual assault survivors" but vowed afterward to recommit to listening to and caring for young activists. "Young people require unrelenting nurturing," she wrote following the event. "A constant and careful examination of the behavior of our young sisters remains a necessity for the continued development of our youth."[217]

Young people's organizing was also at the forefront of the March for Women's Lives in Washington, DC, held on 25 April 2004. The march was led by seven groups—the National Organization for Women, the American Civil Liberties Union, Black Women's Health Imperative, Feminist Majority, NARAL Pro-Choice America, National Latina Institute for Reproductive Health, and Planned Parenthood Federation of America—and was attended by around 1.15 million people, marching to "protect and advance abortion rights, birth control and access to a full range of reproductive health care options" that were continually under attack in this era.[218] The Third Wave Foundation reached out to their young members to encourage them to take this opportunity to stand up to the Bush administration: "Join thousands of women, men, children, activists, and hell-raisers to ensure the Bush administration, members of Congress, US Supreme Court, and local decision makers hear our voices," they urged.[219] Five "young-women led groups" met the day before the march for a session organized by Choice USA to "trade ideas, make banners, attend trainings and workshops, and get ready to show our support for reproductive freedom."[220] One young organizer was Erica Dhawan of Sewickley, Pennsylvania, who was one of "10 regional leaders organizing 3,000 young people" to take part in the march—she went on to win a place on Teen People magazine's "Teens Who Will Change the World" list for her work on reproductive rights while in high school.[221] Whether it was in workshops at local sex-positive conferences or in massive national rallies, the voices and activism of teenagers were increasingly embraced by adult feminists in their organizing work around sexual and reproductive rights in the 2000s.

Though the content of young women's activism was specific to the twin pressures of a conservative federal government and a sexualized popular culture, one method of organizing that galvanized in the 1990s remained fruitful for teenage feminists in the 2000s—the making and distributing of zines. In this way, teenagers continued to organize themselves without the need for adult support or endorsement. Despite the availability of the internet, the tangible format and punk aesthetics of this creative and political outlet continued to appeal to many young women as a way to talk about and share information on sex, and to react in subversive ways against the "mixed messages" aimed at young women in the United States.[222] For those opposed to the "objectification of teenage girls in mass culture," like the creators of the zine Go Teen Go, Theresa Molter and Gillian Beck, the low-distribution, noncommercial aspects of zine-making remained the ideal rebellion against the mainstreamed version of teenage female sexuality that appeared on televisions screens and in shopping malls across the country. Writing in their zine in 2000, Molter and Beck claimed they were "infiltrating mass teen culture" by stating that the pressure for all teen girls to "be thin/skinny/go on diets," "consume clothing, make-up, accessories, beauty products," "have a boyfriend," or "be straight in general" needed to "die."[223] They laid out their own, alternative advice for other young women: "Experimentation is fun. Sex isn't all it's hyped up to be. And remember that you have to learn to love yourself before you can truly love anyone else."[224] This topic was also covered by Maliyah Cole, editor of the zine *Pretty Girls*, in 2007, in a special sex issue in which she joined forces with the organization Health Initiatives for Youth. Cole wrote that young women in the 2000s had been forced to believe that beauty could only be found on "the cover of teen magazines." She wanted to "encourage young women to embrace their sexuality and feel empowered" in order to feel "beautiful and special," and for this empowerment to extend to girls of "all races, gender expressions, class back-grounds, abilities, sexualities, and nationalities," unlike the representations of young women in mass media.[225]

Governmental politics became an increasingly urgent theme in the writing of teenage zinesters in the 2000s. In 2002, a young zine-maker from California named Kristy Beckman made *comMOTION*, a compilation zine featuring contributions by various young women. *comMOTION*'s main focus was on teenage women's further restricted sexual citizenship under the Bush administration. The zine included an explanation of "what happens if Bush appoints an anti-choice Supreme Court Justice," a guide on how to access emergency contraception, and a list of websites teenage girls could use to find sex education resources after the introduction of new federal abstinence education funding.[226] It also reassured young women that the situation was not entirely "bleak," by drawing attention to the work of various young activists "who are making a difference in their communities." "We want to give you ideas on how you can get involved and help keep women's reproductive rights secure," the writers encouraged.[227] The activists interviewed included two young women working in California, Ome Lopez, who was Latinx and in her early 20s, and Shonell Peoples, who was African American and in her late teens. In their interview, they spoke about their work for "support groups for LGBT youth and homeless youth," about a program that "teaches twelve to twenty year olds to be peer mentors" for issues like birth control or rape crisis resources, and about their experiences volunteering for Planned Parenthood.[228] These young women's activism around issues of sexuality demonstrated the political awareness of many teenage girls in the 2000s, particularly their knowledge of the intersection of gendered oppression with sexuality, race, and class and their ability to utilize existing organizations and zine networks to enact their politics.

The grassroots activism of teenage girls in the 2000s reflected an embrace of aspects of both sides of the sex wars—they had lived experience of intersecting forms of structural harm that they and their peers faced as young women, but they also held tightly onto the possibility of liberated sexuality and ways they might be able to achieve it. "Sex shouldn't be negative, dirty, wrong or sinful," Lopez urged in her interview with *comMOTION*. "We should always be able to have pleasure, and to know about ourselves and how to care for ourselves."[229] When asked what sex would be like if "everyone received a comprehensive sexuality education," Peoples answered that young women would have sex more "because they wanted to, not to rebel."[230] As evidenced by Lopez and Peoples's involvement in *comMOTION*, zines continued to be places where young women of color built networks among zine creators and readers with similar experiences.

Teenage girls in the 2000s were also increasingly outspoken around LGBTQ+ issues. Zines remained a safe place for young women to explore their sexualities and be in contact with others who were coming of age with similar feelings. In her zine *Aperture*, Maine teenager Eleanor Whitney described having "stumbled into something healthy" with "a boy" and having "an excruciating crush on a girl who lives far away."[231] She also used the zine to express that she was "not ashamed" of her body or her sexuality.[232] Young women engaged in zine networks continued to provide sex education for one another during these years of ubiquitous abstinence education. The trading of physical zines remained an important aspect of such underground education, particularly for those who did not have home internet access or whose parents might monitor their computer use. In the zine *Pretty Girls*, one young writer wrote an article on "the ins and outs of masturbation in girlhood" and included her email address so that young readers could contact her directly if they had questions.[233] This article also demonstrated the awareness of young feminists in this era of how contentious their sexuality had become in American politics: the writer mentioned the Joycelyn Elders masturbation controversy and celebrated the work of SIECUS in promoting "positive sexuality education" in the face of abstinence campaigns.[234] The existence of these underground forms of peer sex education and open sexual expression concurrently with the perpetuation of a desired model of "prudishness" by conservatives and even liberals suggests that in the 2000s, a culture war divide continued to pit mainstream and underground discourse on adolescent sexuality against each other.[235] In this period, it was still only within such underground channels and networks that teenagers themselves could discuss what they actually desired and needed from sex education and wider sexual and reproductive health support and services.[236]

In addition to these established methods and networks, teenage girls coming of age in the 2000s utilized new technologies to enact their sexual politics. Starting in the mid-1990s, zine-makers began to extend their networks online through building electronic zines and personal websites, some taking the moniker "gURL" as a result.[237] Initially, these young women used this new format for similar purposes as they did paper zines, including creating personal diaries through the platform *LiveJournal*.[238] Eventually, young women's writing about sexuality in America started to take place in the form of blogs. Not only did young women on these sites demonstrate their political awareness, but they were also becoming more technologically savvy as a generation, and this combination of skills and knowledge enabled many young activists to use these spaces to their advantage in an era where their sexuality was so publicly debated.[239] For instance, one online group of young Asian American women used "a particular configuration of the words *Asian* and *girls* to deter surfers seeking pornography."[240] Spelman College graduate Moya Bailey also utilized the internet to connect young women of color in their activism, through her blog *Quirky Black Girls*, "all the while building bravery and challenging each other's thinking."[241] Shelby Knox, the Lubbock, Texas, high school student whose anti-abstinence education campaigning was chronicled in the 2005 documentary *The Education of Shelby Knox*, called blogs the feminist "consciousness-raising groups" of the millennial generation and noted that young women's activism in the 2000s was "inseparable from technology."[242]

One aspect of young women's activism that flourished online was peer-to-peer sex education. This had been a key component of zine-making, but the internet enabled such activists to reach far more young people than ever before. Much of this took the form of write-in questions and answers, the form allowing for a rapid response. gURL.com was a first foray into online activism for many young zine-makers and included a write-in sex education section titled "Deal With It."[243] Go Ask Alice, the sex advice website of Columbia University, was another popular online hub of sex advice and education for young people. Staffed by students and hospital doctors at Columbia, the site answered "hundreds of questions a day" from students at the university and from teenagers across "more than fifty countries," including "nervous first kissers and unsure bisexuals" and "HIV-positive teens."[244] Teenage magazines, many of which had been silent on the issue of sexuality in the 1990s, also increasingly used their websites to provide comprehensive question-and-answer sex education, including *CosmoGirl* and *Seventeen*.[245] The presence of a more vocally antifeminist president in this era had pushed some liberals to lend their voices and platforms to support underground activism protecting teenage girls' right to sexual information, at the risk of losing their readership. Though social conservatives were aware of these websites and highly critical of their content, the nature of this platform and the growing mobilization of those who fought for comprehensive sex education for teenage girls meant that the censoring tactics of previous decades could not successfully apprehend this activism.[246]

As the end of Bush's administration approached, the underground conversations by and about adolescent sexuality in all of its forms pushed consistently against the socially and religiously conservative administration, as well as the purity movement whose expansion it had enabled. Though the Bush administration had poured verbal and economic support into these conservative forces, they had been simmering since the rise of the New Right. In the run-up to the 2008 election, Loretta Ross, who was then national coordinator for SisterSong, reflected on the state of the culture wars that had developed under the past several administrations: "From the teaching of Creationism instead of evolution to the manufacturing of false claims to ban contraceptives and abortion, science has been held hostage to ideology."[247] Ross observed that, in U.S. politics, young women of color continued to be scapegoated by social and economic conservatives. The way to fight back, she contended, was for women of color and Indigenous groups to "demand the attention of elected officials and policymakers" and to build the leadership of women of color, "particularly young women."[248] The political activism Ross was encouraging had been as relentless as the conservative movements of the same era. In the 2000s, a younger generation of activists, led by young women of color, inherited and transformed ideas about sexual harm and sexual pleasure in girlhood from a previous era's feminisms. They fought back against racist and misogynist media cultures and conservative movements and laid the foundations of digital and physical networks that would continue to build throughout the early twenty-first century.

Epilogue

GIRLHOOD SEXUALITIES IN THE
CONTEMPORARY CULTURE WARS

Young people's activism for their sexual and reproductive rights in the 2000s, and their increasing sexual frankness on public platforms as a part of this action, took much of the power out of "purity" as an organizing principle for the Right. During the administration of President Barack Obama, however, a reactionary right-wing movement was refueled and reshaped, emerging as one that made even more explicit the racism and misogyny that had fueled the previous century's New Right movement. Though it could be argued that the "culture wars" have been raging for the entirety of U.S. history, they have been recharged in recent years. At first glance, it is harder to see teenage girls as being central to these culture wars than it was during the 1980s, 1990s, or 2000s. The most recent iteration of the right-wing movement has shifted its focus away from abstinence and teenage pregnancy rates. However, the sexual and gender expression of young people in the United States have remained a frequent site of moral-political debate to this day. As in the late twentieth and early twenty-first centuries, tracing debates about teenagers through the culture wars reveals that this discourse continues to be shaped by ideas about race and class, reinforcing the way in which attitudes toward racism in the United States have always underscored the multitudinous debates that are considered culture wars. As the culture wars reach their most explicit, overt form in modern history, the continued centrality of young people's gendered experiences within U.S. politics makes it crucial that we understand the history of how teenagers have been used as the nexus of a wide range of moral and political battles. Doing so not only reveals wider, shifting beliefs about youth and about sexuality in the United States, but also reveals important ways that the contours of the culture wars are not as straightforward as they initially appear.[1] Understanding the reasons that the social and political debates of the past fifty years have taken these forms is a crucial part of navigating a way forward in the recharged climate of today's culture wars.[2]

In the years since the end of the Bush administration, widespread panic over adolescent sexuality in the U.S. media continues to periodically arise, particularly as new technologies emerge. Concerns about the vulnerability of teenage girls have proliferated alongside the widespread use of smartphones in recent years, including the phenomenon of "sexting," or young people texting their own naked or semi-dressed images to each other.[3] This was the focus of a 2014 cover story in *Newsweek* magazine, "Sex and the Single Tween."[4] Despite these moments of widespread debate, which continue to reach across the political spectrum, for the most part the reality of sex among adolescents has become more speakable in the mainstream than it was in previous decades, and the heat has come out of the culture war over whether teenagers should be having sex at all.[5] New media and reproductive technologies have also made sexual information and safer sex more accessible to more teenagers, as have the efforts of activists to destigmatize using these technologies. Television and cinema increasingly represent a wider swath of adolescent sexual experiences, including those of queer and trans teenagers, and increasingly starring actors of color. The administration of President Barack Obama did not stoke the fires of any of the historical battles over young women's access to sexual information, which partially contributed to the sexual behavior of teenage girls gradually becoming a less obvious flashpoint of the culture wars in the years since 2008. As the third president in a row to enter the White House with teenage daughters, Obama strove to demonstrate a commitment to issues pertaining to young women's reproductive health rights through a measured, moderate feminism.[6] In his last year in office, Obama removed the Title V Abstinence Only Until Marriage funding introduced by Clinton and increased by Bush, ending—at least temporarily—the federal government's funding for solely abstinence-only sex education programs. The widespread, if reluctant, acceptance of premarital sex in American society has made it increasingly impossible for social conservatives to maintain the focus on teenage girls' behavior as a platform. However, perhaps sensing this, those still committed to a racialized, heteronormative ideal of the American family have pounced instead on gender itself as "under threat" in childhood and adolescence and have poured increasing vitriol into attacking the rights and lives of transgender children and teenagers.

Following a public debate over the rights of transgender students at public schools to use the bathroom that matches their gender, Obama released a memo that demonstrated that Title IX protects the rights of transgender students to use the bathroom bearing the gender that they identify with.[7] Reactionary opponents of these federal protections consistently referred without basis to the threat that they might pose to young cisgender girls in women's bathrooms.[8] Even in a public conversation about transgender youth and rights, discourse pivoted once again on the protection of the sexual purity of the innocent, presumed white, young girl, showing the lasting power of this figure for those on the right.[9] The resurgence of the Right that led to the election of the fascist forty-fifth president, Donald Trump, has only exacerbated and fueled legislative action against trans youth. Further culture war battles have grown over the rights of children to access trans health care—a report by *Democracy Now!* in January 2020 noted that, by the date of publication, twenty-five new anti-LGBTQ+ bills had been introduced around the nation, including three antitrans bills in South Dakota alone (one of which gave parents the right to deny their children access to gender-affirming treatment).[10]

Online sexual content, and its implications for LGBTQ+ teenagers, also arose as a renewed culture war during the Trump administration, most notably through the administration's introduction of the Allow States and Victims to Fight Online Sex Trafficking Act (FOSTA) and the Stop Enabling Sex Traffickers Act (SESTA) in 2018, which has had an impact on the ability of queer and trans teenagers to access information and community. FOSTA/SESTA, though purporting to punish sex trafficking online, "conflates sex trafficking survivors with consensual sex workers" and has both failed to protect people from being trafficked and made working conditions for consensual sex workers far worse.[11] The bills resulted in social networking site Tumblr, which became a hub of sexual exploration for LGBTQ+ teenagers in the 2010s, banning sexual content in response to the law and, in doing so, cutting off queer teenagers from "self-discovery and support."[12]

In February 2017, Trump took apart the "bathroom bill." This followed the public condemnation of one of his most controversial public supporters, the British "alt-Right" media personality Milo Yiannopoulos, who, despite speaking consistently from a racist, sexist, and anti-Semitic platform, was dropped by his publisher, Simon & Schuster, and barred from the Conservative Political Action Conference only following the surfacing of a video in which he admitted that intergenerational gay relationships between adult men and teenagers need not be harmful.[13] Gender and sexuality scholars Joseph Fischel and Gabriel Rosenberg noted in an op-ed for *Slate* that it is very revealing of moral priorities in the United States that it was his apparent endorsement of teenage sex that ultimately caused his downfall, not his racism or generalized sexism.[14] He attempted to mediate the media uproar by restating bigoted, unsubstantiated claims about trans women in bathrooms being a sexual threat to young girls: though it did not redeem him, it is telling that, again, young white women's sexual vulnerability was used as a political tool through which to endear oneself to as many people as possible. These events, which offer only a snapshot of the contemporary political atmosphere in the United States, again prove the sustaining legacy of using the incendiary topic of white young women's sexuality as a political bargaining tool. They demonstrate that as social movements have pushed for increasing understanding and acceptance of sexual and gender diversity, the response of the Right—and of many liberals—has continued to adapt. The gender and sexuality of young people remain an area of public debate that quickly rises to the surface of moral and political conflict in the culture wars of a changing society.

Events since the beginning of President Joe Biden's entry into the White House suggest that this pattern is not likely to change any time soon. On 20 January 2021, Biden's first day in office, he signed an executive order defending LGBTQ+ rights that read as follows: "Children should be able to learn without worrying about whether they will be denied access to the restroom, the locker room, or school sports."[15] Meanwhile, conservative legislators have sought to restrict transgender girls and women from playing on girls and women's sports teams: in the first three months of 2021, states introduced thirty-five such bills.[16] However, support for these bills has come not only from the Right. Though recent polls have shown increasing support for broader transgender rights across the United States, particular issues show more of a divided opinion from respondents, including bathroom bills and transgender girls' abilities to play on sports teams with cisgender girls.[17] These recent polls suggest that liberal adults remain more likely to express less progressive views in culture wars over gender and sexuality where children or teenagers are involved. It also suggests that the same pattern that became apparent in the Reagan administration—when the pro-life movement was far more successful in limiting teenagers' access to abortion than that of adult women because of wider support across the political spectrum for these kinds of policies—persists today.[18] As I discussed in the introduction to this book, there are a number of reasons why at many times liberals have displayed more conservative politics where young people are involved. Many liberals believe that teenagers do not or should not have the same autonomy as adults when it comes to decision-making about their gender or sexual health, and that parents should be able to make such choices for their children.[19] At other times, liberal politicians have simply performed social conservatism when it comes to teenage sex for political gain, as when Clinton passed welfare reform in 1996, knowing that it has always been a loaded, racialized, and classed issue for the Right, and that advocating publicly for teenagers' rights to sexual and reproductive information and health care has spelled the end of many a liberal's political career. Many other liberals have taken on these racialized and classed ideas about adolescent sex, and this influences their political behavior even when they see themselves as progressive in other areas. This brief review of culture war inconsistencies when it comes to teenagers is a reminder of how important it will be in coming years to follow developments in the culture wars, particularly those regarding the rights of queer and transgender teenagers, as restrictive policymaking occurs even when a Democrat is president.

However, teenagers today continue to resist having their gender or sexuality defined for them through political discord among adults, through intersectional antiracist and feminist activism, and by utilizing and influencing new technologies in order to do so. The 2016 presidential election saw young people, even those under the voting age, take part in the resistance to the rise of the Right through social activism and social media, in response to the campaigns of the first female presidential candidate for a major party, Hillary Clinton, and the racist, sexist tirade of Republican nominee Donald Trump. One moment in particular demonstrated teenage girls' stake in this election. In early October 2016, footage was unearthed of Donald Trump discussing what amounts to sexual assault with the host of *Access Hollywood*, Billy Bush. "You can do anything," Trump stated, referring to "beautiful women." "Grab them by the p-ssy. You can do anything."[20] In response to this display of outward sexual aggression by the man who would become president, teenage girls got angry. Eighteen-year-old Dallas teenager Anna Lehane traveled with friends to a Trump rally in Pennsylvania, where they wore T-shirts emblazoned with "GRAB MY P-SSY, I DARE YOU."[21] Lehane stated that it was her "civic duty" to speak out.[22] Black teenagers and other young people of color drove the online and physical backlash to Trump's election. Teenage girls attended the Women's March on Washington (and the "sister marches" in cities across the country) on 21 January 2017, the day after Inauguration. Wanting to "help parents have a voice and also help youth have a voice," Trinidadian American activist and organizer Tabitha St. Bernard-Jacobs, who was at the forefront of organizing the Women's March, launched the Women's March on Washington Youth Ambassador program.[23] The program included many young women of color dedicated to fighting against the conservative uprising in American politics. "We, the Youth, are one of the most powerful demographics in America. We control our futures," stated one such ambassador, Myra Richardson, an African American teenager from LA who was seventeen at the time of the march.[24] "President Elect Trump's campaign rhetoric invalidated my identity, degrading almost all aspects of it," stated Gabriela Orozco, a then thirteen-year-old from Washington, DC, another youth ambassador at the march. "As a Jewish Latina who is a first generation American, the way he talked about Latinos, mistreated women, and disgraced immigrants struck a blow. Instead of hiding in shame, I will continue to fight back against prejudiced policies and ignorant statements."[25]

In the years since Trump's election, teenage girls have continued to be at the forefront of social justice movements. Though, as this book has discussed, young women have been doing intersectional antiracist and feminist activism for decades, teenagers of color have increasingly become visible in this activism. Like the teenagers in the 1990s who fought back against the treatment of Anita Hill by the Senate Judiciary Committee and the violence against Rodney King by Los Angeles police officers, many young women today are organizing against the multiple, intersecting forms of social injustice in American society, including police brutality. Teenagers have been harnessing new social media technologies in their activism: many use Instagram in the way that previous generations used zines or early social networking sites like *LiveJournal* or Tumblr to seek out young people with similar experiences, and to form their politics.[26] In June 2020, in the midst of the global pandemic outbreak of COVID-19 and the structural inequalities that the virus exacerbated, the Black Lives Matter movement resurged internationally in response to the murder of George Floyd by police officers in Minneapolis, Minnesota. A group of teenage girls in Nashville, Tennessee, who met on Twitter organized a massive rally attended by "at least 10,000 protestors."[27] After finding each other online, Nya Collins, Jade Fuller, Kennedy Green, Emma Rose Smith, and Zee Thomas, who "range from 14 to 16 years old," met up and formed Teens4Equality, which then worked with Black Lives Matter Nashville to plan the event. "As teens, we are tired of waking up and seeing another innocent person being slain in broad daylight," Thomas said on 4 June, the day of the protest. "As teens, we are desensitized to death because we see videos of Black people being killed in broad daylight circulating on social media platforms. As teens, we feel like we cannot make a difference in this world, but we must."[28] Teenage activists across the country who had spent their entire adolescence engaged in protest action also went into the streets in May and

June 2020. *Teen Vogue* interviewed "veteran organizers" including Nupol Kiazolu, who at nineteen was president of Black Lives Matter of Greater New York and had in the preceding years "stood nose-to-nose with Nazis in Charlottesville" and "fled law enforcement with rifle sights set on her chest."[29] For teenagers growing up in the late 2010s and early 2020s, especially queer and trans youth, Indigenous youth, Black teenagers, and young people of color, the combination of increasingly visible activism by young people, the self-representation, community building, and organizational capacity afforded by new social media platforms, and the urgent need to fight back against the resurgence of the Far Right in American politics and society has led to the increased presence of teenagers fighting on behalf of their own lives and those of others.

As evidenced by *Teen Vogue*'s coverage of the June 2020 protest movement, online publishing has also increasingly offered teenagers more feminist and antiracist platforms and resources than ever before in American history, often accessible for free. *Teen Vogue* started to increase its political coverage in 2016, under the editorship of Black social justice advocate and writer Elaine Welteroth. It is now billed as "the young person's guide to saving the world," aims to center "the voices of the unheard," and supports teenagers "looking to make a tangible impact in their communities."[30] Meanwhile, young writers for the by-teens-for-teens online magazine *Rookie*, which ran from 2011 to 2018, consistently provided information for teenage girls about how their sexual and reproductive rights might be affected by policy and law in the new administration, and provided information on how to resist and on how to support each other, particularly for those most vulnerable, including people of color, immigrants, and queer and trans youth.[31] *Rookie* was founded by the teenage style blogger Tavi Gevinson in 2011, when she was fifteen years old. She initially planned the launch of the magazine alongside Jane Pratt, the first editor of the rebellious *Sassy* magazine in the late 1980s and early 1990s. However, it was decided by both women that Gevinson should forge forward with the publication alone.[32] The website was a virtual hub of teenage girls' political organizing around intersectional issues surrounding race, class, gender, and sexuality and centralized the voices of young women who have, throughout American history, been the most consistently silenced.

In wider American society, some forms of feminist politics have become increasingly embraced in the mainstream, and young women's formative sexual experiences and traumas have been a part of this conversation. In late 2017, the Me Too movement, which was started by activist Tarana Burke in 2006, went viral as the hashtag #MeToo. The ensuing movement—which called out abusive men and sexual harassment and abuse in industries and institutions around the world—rocked the United States. Many famous and powerful men were held accountable in public for their abuse of women, including the film producer Harvey Weinstein and comedian and actor Bill Cosby.

Following from this, in recent years, there has also been a "reappraisal" of recent decades that were viewed by many at the time as a "postfeminist" period for young women.[33] This began in early 2021 with the release of a *New York Times Presents* documentary titled *Framing Britney* that reveals the extent to which Britney Spears was worn down by a vicious, sexist tabloid media.[34] This led to a wave of commentary on the extent to which famous young women of the 2000s were sexually exploited in the marketing of their work and in the media discussions surrounding them.[35] Former *Rookie* founder and editor Tavi Gevinson contributed to this "reckoning" with the period, reflecting in an article for *The Cut* about the bind she had found herself in when she was younger as a vocal advocate for other teenagers' sexual empowerment, while simultaneously experiencing exploitation and sexual abuse: "Rookie was realistic about the challenges girls face, publishing a wealth of great writing about consent, gender dynamics, and sexual assault. But editing these articles did not make me impervious to the issues they described."[36] Gevinson's reflection is a reminder of the limitations of binary "pro-sex" and "antisex" approaches to understanding the needs and experiences of teenage girls in the late twentieth and early twenty-first centuries.[37] This recent re-evaluation of 1990s and 2000s girl cultures also suggests that understanding the history of discourse about young women is becoming an important part of both feminist history-making and of grassroots organizing around the welfare of teenage girls.

This has already been a key part of the activism in the #MuteRKelly campaign. In July 2017, two Black women—Kenyette Tisha Barnes, an activist, and Oronike Odeleye, an arts administrator—started the campaign #MuteRKelly when new details of the musician's abuse of young Black women and girls emerged: that he had a "'sex cult' where he was keeping young women under strict rules."[38] Their aim was to finally hold the musician R. Kelly accountable for the multiple allegations of "abuse, predatory behavior and pedophilia" that he had faced without conviction for over two decades, because, as Barnes stated, "it was clear that there was no attention being placed on the sexual violence against black girls by high-powered men."[39] In January 2019, Lifetime released the documentary *Surviving R. Kelly*, which details decades of abuse allegations against Kelly and includes interviews of survivors, which brought new momentum to the legal cases against him. He has since been found guilty of nine counts including "racketeering and eight violations of an anti-sex trafficking law known as the Mann Act" and awaits a further trial for producing child pornography.[40] What the activists behind #MuteRKelly and the survivors who spoke out on the documentary have brought to the fore of public conversation is the persistent lack of attention given to the sexual violence experienced by Black girls and women by white mainstream feminist campaigners.[41] This continuation of the historical racism by white Americans in which the same protections are not afforded to Black children, and in which Black girls are not considered within the same frameworks of innocence and vulnerability that white girls are afforded, shows a frightening lack of progress from the focus on the fates of white children in the public conversations about child sexual abuse in the 1980s.[42]

Discourse about girlhood sexualities in American public life has never been more open, or more explicit. Young women have also never had a more cogent, visual, global connection to each other, or more visible organization around their own oppression and that of their communities. Teenagers were central to the intense cultural and political debates of the late twentieth and early twenty-first centuries, and remain so today. The sexual and reproductive lives of teenagers entered the culture wars of the 1970s and 1980s through the racialized insinuation by the New Right that rising numbers of teenage pregnancies would have an impact on the U.S. economy, and that these numbers signified the increased sexual behavior of white teenage girls.[43] Battles over patterns in teenagers' sexual choices and cultures—and the connotations of race and class that were reproduced in these debates— proliferated in the ensuing decades, becoming central to the modern culture wars. Though the mainstream of U.S. society has become more accepting of teenage sex as a whole, young women's access to sexual, gender, and reproductive health care and education, and protection from sexual harm, is still vastly unequal, and the reactionary forces that drove the culture wars of the late twentieth century remain a powerful force in U.S. politics. At the same time, some liberals still hold more conservative opinions about teenagers' identities and behaviors than they demonstrate in other debates about gender and sexuality. This book has argued that these anomalies in the battle lines of the culture wars are important, and worthy of closer examination, because it is continually the most marginalized young people who have been excluded from positive experiences of sexuality, gender, and reproduction as a result of widespread social conservatism.[44]

What these debates have laid the ground for, however, is a public conversation on adolescent sexualities in which the young people whose gendered and sexual lives have long been flashpoints of the culture wars regularly hold adults accountable for the impact of their speech on teenagers. In future years, it will be crucial that we critically examine culture war battles over adolescent gender and sexuality with an awareness of the traps that adults have fallen into in such conversations in the past, and the effect of these conversations on the sexual, reproductive, and emotional lives of teenagers and on wider social inequalities in the United States. It is important that those adults who support an understanding of young people's sexual autonomy, safety, and health are listened to in new ways.[45] It is even more important that we listen to the voices of young people, particularly those who have been the most oppressed in the history laid out in this book, and strive to support them as they both reclaim the history and shape the future of growing up in the United States.

Acknowledgments

Completing this book has been possible because of the generosity, support, and belief of so many people. I am deeply grateful to everyone who helped take this project from its inception to landing on a library shelf—it was a truly collaborative, collective effort.

I began work on what would become *Teenage Dreams* during my doctorate at the University of Cambridge, where I was extremely lucky to have Andrew Preston as my supervisor. His guidance and encouragement have been and remain invaluable, and I hope that my work will always reflect what I have learned from his thorough, thoughtful approach to writing U.S. history. I was further supported in this research by the wider community of American historians at Cambridge. Stephen Mawdsley and Seth Archer provided thoughtful feedback on early drafts of my chapters during their time at Cambridge, Julia Guarneri provided encouragement and advice, and Gary Gerstle's insights and ideas were critically important to the development of this work. Early research toward this project was supported financially by the Arts and Humanities Research Council, the Faculty of History at Cambridge, and Emmanuel College, Cambridge. I am very grateful for the friends I studied alongside, including Will Riddington, Kate Ballantyne, and Merve Fejzula: thank you for constantly buoying me up, for the vast feedback on my work, and most of all for your friendship. Thank you to Merve for so many important conversations and ideas from the beginning to the end of this project, and beyond.

Researching this book involved many archival trips and residencies. The Dissertation Grant from the Schlesinger Library at the Radcliffe Institute for Advanced Study at Harvard University and the Mary Lily Research Grant from the Sallie Bingham Center for Women's History and Culture at Duke University made it possible to use their incredible collections. I am beyond grateful to the brilliant archivists and librarians I worked with on this project, at the Schlesinger Library, the Sallie Bingham Center, and also at the Barnard College Zine Library, the Barnard Center for Research on Women, the Fales Library at NYU, and the Sophia Smith

Collection at Smith College, for sharing their extensive knowledge of the archives themselves and of feminist research ethics more broadly. Thank you to my wonderful friend Shilpa Guha for introducing me to the BCRW's amazing resources and community, and for all of your wisdom and support throughout this project. Thank you to Che Gossett for your guidance and conversation on the archives at the BCRW, and thank you to Lisa Darms, for support with and insights into the Riot Grrrl collection at NYU. I'd also like to thank Sarah Hutcheon at the Schlesinger Library, Jenna Freedman of the Barnard Zine Library, and Kelly Wooten at the Sallie Bingham Center for their continued, generous conversations and advice over the period I was finishing this book.

This book was informed and shaped by the many places I lived and worked over the years I was working on it, and the communities I have been a part of. I was supported by a Visiting Scholarship at the History Department at Boston University: thank you to Bruce Schulman for welcoming me and for including me in the activities of U.S. historians at BU. Thank you to Megan LeBarron, Robert Shimp, Sussan Lee, and Megan McMenamin for helping to make Boston such a warm home during a historic blizzard. I will never forget your generosity and kindness. I also wish to extend my gratitude to the Fox International Fellowship at Yale University for allowing me to spend a year living and learning in New Haven. I am very grateful to the Women, Gender, and Sexuality Studies Working Group and Colloquium at Yale, within which I found an exciting community of feminist scholars and which had a huge impact on this work. In particular, I wish to thank Joseph Fischel for his invaluable mentorship and for invigorating conversations about everything from the history of sexuality to the publishing process. I'd also like to thank Leslie Dick for her kindness and support in New Haven, and for lending her apartment as a welcome writing retreat. Thank you to Tal Alexander for so much critical conversation and care in New Haven. Thank you also to Dagmar Herzog at CUNY for invaluable, thorough advice on this work, which contributed so much to its development.

My colleagues have provided so much insight and support in the writing of this book. Many thanks go to Joanna Bourke and the rest of the Sexual Harms and Medical Encounters Research Group at Birkbeck; Jonathan Bell, Nick Witham, and other members of the North American History Seminar at the Institute of Historical Research in London; Mara Keire, Stephen Tuck, Stephen Tuffnell, and Gareth Davies, who I worked with at Oxford; and Rebecca Fraser and Nicholas Grant at the University of East Anglia: they all gave me indispensable advice on the process of writing a book as a first-time author. Thank you also to Nick Grant for reading and providing feedback on my work and answering my many panicked questions. I am also very grateful for the encouragement and accountability provided by my incredible postdoc writing group that necessarily took place online in 2020–2021: thank you, Jana Mokrisova, Stephanie Wright, Matthew Laube, Sacha Hepburn, and Ruth Beecher for the community, motivation, and celebration that were vital to finishing this project during the pandemic. Thank you also to my students at Birkbeck, Oxford, and UEA for so many significant conversations about the themes of this book, and in particular Jennifer Williams, my former MA student at UEA, for the excellent ideas and information on contemporary digital activism that was so informative as I put together the epilogue. I am very grateful to the British Academy for supporting my work on this book through the British Academy Postdoctoral Research Fellowship, and I am grateful to the School of Arts, Humanities, and American Studies at UEA for the Research Fund that was crucial in financing a final archive trip for this book.

An early version of the first chapter of this book was published in the *Journal of American Studies* (as the article "Adolescent Women and Antiabortion Politics in the Reagan Administration," 2018), and I am grateful to the editors of *JAS* for encouraging me to reprint some of that research here. I have tried to do my due diligence in gaining permission to quote from as many of the unpublished sources cited in this book as I understood to be necessary, and I am very grateful to all of those who gave me that permission. If I wasn't able to get ahold of you and you wish to discuss my inclusion of a quote in this book, please do reach out to me via Rutgers University Press and I'd be happy to talk through it with you.

I have been very lucky to work with such wonderful editors at RUP, Kimberly Guinta and Jasper Chang, who have been kind and clear throughout the entire process. I am particularly grateful to them for helping me navigate the completion of this project during the pandemic. Thank you also to the fantastic production team and copyeditors that worked with me on this book. I am also very appreciative of the feedback I received from the anonymous peer reviewers of this manuscript, whose sound advice has improved this book beyond measure.

Many other friends and family members have endowed me and this manuscript with love and strength over the years that I have been researching, writing, and editing it. It would not be here without them. Thank you to my parents, Jo and Jim Jeffries, my sister, Olivia Jeffries, and my brother-in-law Tom Cumins for the constant enthusiasm and support, and the crucial reminders to take breaks, all of which I am endlessly grateful for.

My development as a feminist scholar has been expanded exponentially through friendship, research, art, and activism with Carmen Palacios-Berraquero, Caitlín Doherty, Giulia Galastro, Jenny Harris, Sarra Facey, Becca Moore, Jeremy Madrid, Jodie Mitchell, and Lauren Steele, to whom I am also very grateful for her incisive feminist thoughts on chapter drafts and for taking such great care of me throughout this project, and of our pet rabbits whenever I went away on archive trips. I am so grateful for the friendship and solidarity of Sarah Crook, Sneha Krishnan, Jess Cotton, and Madeline Michael Smith, for their invaluable insights on drafts of my chapters, and for all of their support and advice. Thank you also to Mad for hosting me for so many writing adventures together. Thank you to Claudia Andresco and Nikita Winayak for their insights, support, and love. Thank you to Genevieve van Swaay for your constant encouragement and celebration of this book. I am thankful for Alice Dunn, for her friendship and our many conversations about adolescence and about Britney Spears. Thank you to Victoria Baranetsky for sharing your brilliant feminist legal mind with me in addition to your ever-affirming and validating friendship, and to Olivia Klevorn, who has championed and inspired this project at Sunday night dinners and who saw this project over the finish line via video chat once she moved to Toronto. Thank you also to Olivia for making the most incredible piece of digital Riot Grrrl art to celebrate my completing this book. Thank you to my brilliant bandmate, Hannah Watts, for helping me think constantly and critically about the politics of the musical cultures discussed in this book and in general, and my musical comrades Anne Marie Sanguigni, for sharing your creative vision in discussing book cover ideas and your unparalleled ideas on 2000s girl culture, and Kirsty Fife and Julia Downes, for critical conversations about zines, musical cultures, and academia. Finally, I am endlessly grateful for the appearance of Christabel Williams in my life as I worked on this manuscript, and for her constant cheerleading, advice, and ideas. I am so thankful to her for filling the process of finishing this book with joy.

Notes

INTRODUCTION

1. "Teens in the Sex Trade," *The Tyra Banks Show*, 8 February 2007, https://www.youtube.com/watch?v=BxUq_zzvAaA.

2. "Teens in the Sex Trade."

3. "Teens in the Sex Trade."

4. "Teens in the Sex Trade."

5. See Jessica Valenti, *The Purity Myth: How America's Obsession with Virginity Is Hurting America's Young Women* (Berkeley, CA: Seal Press, 2009), 27; and Dagmar Herzog, *Sex in Crisis: The New Sexual Revolution and the Future of American Politics* (New York: Basic Books, 2008), xi–xiii.

6. See R. Marie Griffith, *Moral Combat: How Sex Divided American Christians and Fractured American Politics* (New York: Basic Books, 2017), xviii. There is a vast literature on girlhood in the modern United States, across multiple disciplines. Young women's sexuality has also been raised in the historical literatures on abortion, birth control, sex education, and welfare in the United States, making the story of adults' concerns over the sexual and reproductive choices of young women in the United States, and of teenagers' voices in these battles, an important one to tell. On abortion, see Rickie Solinger, *Abortion Wars: A Half Century of Struggle, 1950–2000* (Berkeley: University of California Press, 1998); and Leslie J. Reagan, *When Abortion Was a Crime: Women, Medicine, and Law in the United States, 1867–1973* (Berkeley: University of California Press, 1997). On birth control, see Linda Gordon, *The Moral Property of Women: A History of Birth Control Politics in America* (Urbana: University of Illinois Press, 2002). On sex education, see Kristin Luker, *When Sex Goes to School: Warring Views on Sex—and Sex Education—since the Sixties* (New York: W. W. Norton, 2006); and Janice Irvine, *Talk about Sex: The Battles over Sex Education in the United States* (Berkeley: University of California Press, 2002). On welfare, see Dorothy Roberts, *Killing the Black Body: Race, Reproduction, and the Meaning of Liberty* (New York: Pantheon Books, 1997); and Laura Briggs, *How All Politics Became Reproductive Politics: From Welfare Reform to Foreclosure to Trump* (Oakland: University of California Press, 2017).

7. Briggs, *How All Politics Became Reproductive Politics*, 73. See also Robert O. Self, *All in the Family: The Realignment of American Democracy since the 1960s* (New York: Hill and Wang, 2012), 368.

8. Briggs, *How All Politics Became Reproductive Politics*, 73.

9. For more on unexpected culture war positions in debates over sexuality, see E. J. Dionne, *Souled Out: Reclaiming Faith and Politics after the Religious Right* (Princeton, NJ: Princeton University Press, 2008), 48; Herzog, *Sex in Crisis*, xii–xiii; Irvine, *Talk about Sex,* 1–4, 7, 12; and Luker, *When Sex Goes to School,* 23, 92–95, 126.

10. For more on the ways in which political labels such as "traditionalist, conservative, progressive, and liberal" are "imprecise and imperfect," see Griffith, *Moral Combat*, xi. Like Griffith, I acknowledge the limitations of this terminology while still using it to gesture toward broad political groupings throughout this book.

11. For more on the political fluidity of culture wars actors, see Griffith, *Moral Combat*, xi.

12. For more on this topic, see Janet Jakobsen, *The Sex Obsession: Perversity and Possibility in American Politics* (New York: New York University Press, 2020).

13. This has been argued by a number of scholars, including Sinikka Elliot, in *Not My Kid: What Parents Believe about the Sex Lives of Their Teenagers* (New York: New York University Press, 2012), 3; and Judith Levine, in *Harmful to Minors: The Perils of Protecting Children from Sex* (Minneapolis: University of Minnesota Press, 2002).

14. See Herzog, *Sex in* Crisis, xii–xiii; and Irvine, *Talk About Sex*, 1–4, 12.

15. See Herzog, *Sex in Crisis*, xii–xiii; Irvine, *Talk about Sex,* 1–4, 7, 12; and Luker, *When Sex Goes to School,* 23, 92–95, 126.

16. See Joseph J. Fischel, *Sex and Harm in the Age of Consent* (Minneapolis: University of Minnesota Press, 2016); and Levine, *Harmful to Minors*.

17. See Briggs, *How All Politics Became Reproductive Politics*; and Griffith, *Moral Combat*, x–xi, xiii.

18. See Herzog, *Sex in Crisis*, xii–xiii; and Irvine, *Talk About Sex*, 1–4, 12.

19. See Herzog, *Sex in Crisis*, xii–xiii; and Irvine, *Talk About Sex,* 1–4, 12.

20. Though the word "queer" may not have been reclaimed as widely in the earlier era that this book explores as in the later years of this narrative, I use it throughout because of the breadth of sexualities that the term encompasses, and because it allows me to discuss the sexualities of LGBTQ+ teenagers in the past whose exact sexual identity is unknown.

21. Thank you to Dagmar Herzog and Gary Gerstle for conversations on this topic. See also Toni Morrison, ed., "Introduction: Friday on the Potomac," in *Racing Justice, Engendering Power: Essays on Anita Hill, Clarence Thomas, and the Construction of Social Reality* (New York: Pantheon Books, 1992), vii–2; and Griffith, *Moral Combat*, xviii.

22. See Briggs, *How All Politics Became Reproductive Politics*, 54; Robin Bernstein, *Racial Innocence: Performing American Childhood and Race from Slavery to Civil Rights* (New York: New York University Press, 2012); Renee Romano, *Race Mixing: Black-White Marriage in Postwar America* (Cambridge, MA: Harvard University Press, 2003), 168; Andrew Hartman, *A War for the Soul of America: A History of the Culture Wars* (Chicago: University of Chicago Press, 2015), 63, 85; and Griffith, *Moral Combat*, 118–119.

23. The racial divide in how adults discuss adolescent sexuality has arisen in many studies, most recently in Sarah Projansky, *Spectacular Girls: Media Fascination and Celebrity Culture* (New York: New York University Press, 2014), 7.

24. See Annette Lawson and Deborah L. Rhode, *The Politics of Pregnancy: Adolescent Sexuality and Public Policy* (New Haven, CT: Yale University Press, 1993), 3; Carolyn Cocca, "From 'Welfare Queen' to 'Exploited Teen': Welfare Dependency, Statutory Rape, and Moral Panic," *NWSA Journal* 14 (2002): 58; Zillah Eisenstein, *The Color of Gender: Reimaging Democracy* (Berkeley: University of California Press, 1994), 40; Jessica Fields, "'Children Having Children': Race, Innocence, and Sexuality Education," *Social Problems* 52 (November 2005): 549–550; Jeffrey Moran, *Teaching Sex: The Shaping of Adolescence in the 20th Century*

(Cambridge, MA: Harvard University Press, 2000), 223; and Stephanie Coontz, *The Way We Never Were: American Families and the Nostalgia Trap* (New York: Basic Books, 2010), 204.

25. See Kimberly Springer, "Third Wave Black Feminism?," *Signs* 27 (Summer 2002): 1062; and Nancy Hewitt, introduction to *No Permanent Waves: Recasting Histories of U.S. Feminism*, ed. Nancy Hewitt (New Brunswick, NJ: Rutgers University Press, 2010), 1–14. For another example of a feminist history of a period that is sometimes seen as "between" waves, see Lisa Levenstein, *They Didn't See Us Coming: The Hidden History of Feminism in the Nineties* (New York: Basic Books, 2020).

26. Springer, "Third Wave," 1062.

27. Springer, "Third Wave," 1062.

28. Springer, "Third Wave," 1062; and Hewitt, *No Permanent Waves.*

29. For more on this history, see Irvine, *Talk About Sex.*

30. See Hartman, *A War for the Soul of America*, 63, 75; and Bernstein, *Racial Innocence*, 241–242.

31. See Irvine, *Talk About Sex*, 1–4, 12.

32. See Irvine, *Talk About Sex*, 196.

33. For a discussion of the impact of the sexual revolution on U.S. society, see, for example, Griffith, *Moral Combat*; Elaine Tyler May, *America and the Pill: A History of Promise, Peril, and Liberation* (New York: Basic Books, 2010), 71–92; and John D'Emilio and Estelle B. Freedman, *Intimate Matters: A History of Sexuality in America*, 2nd ed. (Chicago: University of Chicago Press, 2012), 301–325.

34. For a wider history of the inception of the culture wars, see Hartman, *A War for the Soul of America*; Robert M. Collins, *Transforming America: Politics and Culture in the Reagan Years* (New York: Columbia University Press, 2009); Matthew Avery Sutton, "Reagan, Religion and the Culture Wars of the 1980s," in *A Companion to Ronald Reagan*, ed. Andrew L. Johns (Hoboken, NJ: John Wiley and Sons, 2014)), 204–220; Donald T. Critchlow, "Mobilizing Women: The 'Social Issues,'" in *The Reagan Presidency: Pragmatic Conservatism and Its Legacies*, ed. W. E. Brownlee and H. D. Graham (Lawrence: University of Kansas Press, 2003), 293–326; Seth Dowland, *Family Values and the Rise of the Christian Right* (Philadelphia: University of Pennsylvania Press, 2015), 4–6; and Griffith, *Moral Combat*, xi.

35. Hartman, *A War for the Soul of America*, 2. See also Griffith, *Moral Combat*, xi.

36. Hartman, *A War for the Soul of America*, 1.

37. As Hartman admits, "The history of America, for better and worse, is largely a history of debates about the idea of America." Hartman, *A War for the Soul of America*, 2.

38. Hartman, *A War for the Soul of America*, 2.

39. Projansky, *Spectacular Girls*, 11; Briggs, *How All Politics Became Reproductive Politics*, 53. Thank you to Nicholas Grant for conversations on this topic.

40. Emily Owens, "Keyword: Consent," *differences: A Journal of Feminist Cultural Studies* 30, no. 1 (May 2019): 151. See also Bernstein, *Racial Innocence.*

41. Owens, "Keyword: Consent," 151.

42. Argued by Crystal Feimster, in *Southern Horrors: Women and the Politics of Rape and Lynching* (Cambridge, MA: Harvard University Press, 2009), 5. For an autobiographical account of this experience, see Harriet A. Jacobs, *Incidents in the Life of a Slave Girl* (New York: Open Road, 2016), originally published in 1861.

43. Crystal Feimster documents how the journalist and early civil rights leader Ida B. Wells exposed and fought against the racist sexual politics of lynching in *Southern Horrors.*

44. On rape and white girlhood in Reconstruction-era media, see Estelle B. Freedman, "'Crimes Which Startle and Horrify': Gender, Age, and the Racialization of Sexual Violence in White American Newspapers, 1870–1900," *Journal of the History of Sexuality* 20,

no. 3 (September 2011): 483, 497. On white men perpetuating the idea of the Black male rapist, see Feimster, *Southern Horrors*, 5. For a history of these issues in the mid-twentieth century, see Danielle L. McGuire, *At the Dark End of the Street: Black women, rape and resistance—a new history of the civil rights movement from Rosa Parks to the rise of Black Power* (New York: Alfred A. Knopf, 2010).

45. See Projansky, *Spectacular Girls*, 11, and Mary E. Odem, *Delinquent Daughters: Protecting and Policing Adolescent Female Sexuality in the United States, 1885-1920* (Chapel Hill, NC: University of North Carolina Press, 1995).

46. D'Emilio and Freedman, *Intimate Matters*, 260; and Projansky, *Spectacular Girls*, 11.

47. Briggs, *How All Politics Became Reproductive Politics*, 28. See also Hartman, *A War for the Soul of America*, 85, 63.

48. On segregation and the construction of racial innocence, see Bernstein, *Racial Innocence*, 21-22, 241-242. On anti-desegregationists, see Romano, *Race Mixing*, 168; Hartman, *A War for the Soul of America*, 63, 85; Briggs, *How All Politics Became Reproductive Politics*, 28, 54; and Griffith, *Moral Combat*, 118-119.

49. See D'Emilio and Freedman, *Intimate Matters*, 287; and Griffith, *Moral Combat*, 155.

50. D'Emilio and Freedman, *Intimate Matters*, 276.

51. D'Emilio and Freedman, *Intimate Matters*, 300.

52. D'Emilio and Freedman, *Intimate Matters*, 345. See also Self, *All in the Family*, 310.

53. Griffith, *Moral Combat*, xviii, 156-157.

54. See D'Emilio and Freedman, *Intimate Matters*, 276; Dowland, *Family Values*, 7; and Griffith, *Moral Combat*, xi.

55. Dowland, *Family Values*, 6. See also Levenstein, *They Didn't See Us Coming*, 121; and Self, *All in the Family*, 153.

56. D'Emilio and Freedman, *Intimate Matters*, 299. I use the term "Blackness" in this book to refer to stereotypes constructed by white Americans, what Devon W. Carbado calls "the social construction of blackness" in the United States, in "(E)racing the Fourth Amendment," *Michigan Law Review* 100, no. 5 (2002), 949.

57. Roberts, *Killing the Black Body*, 56. See also Self, *All in the Family*, 148-149.

58. Roberts, *Killing the Black Body*, 56.

59. D'Emilio and Freedman, *Intimate Matters*, 314.

60. Roberts, *Killing the Black Body*, 93. See also Self, *All in the Family*, 150.

61. Roberts, *Killing the Black Body*, 94.

62. D'Emilio and Freedman, *Intimate Matters*, 315.

63. D'Emilio and Freedman, *Intimate Matters*, 328.

64. See Griffith, *Moral Combat*, 157.

65. D'Emilio and Freedman, *Intimate Matters*, 346.

66. See D'Emilio and Freedman, *Intimate Matters*, 348; and Self, *All in the Family*, 311, 351-354.

67. Briggs, *How All Politics Became Reproductive Politics*, 8-9.

68. For a description of the factions that made up the New Right, see Briggs, *How All Politics Became Reproductive Politics*, 38.

69. Briggs, *How All Politics Became Reproductive Politics*, 73.

70. Briggs, *How All Politics Became Reproductive Politics*, 73.

71. See Self, *All in the Family*, 367.

72. D'Emilio and Freedman, *Intimate Matters*, 348.

73. Briggs, *How All Politics Became Reproductive Politics*, 73.

74. Joseph J. Fischel, *Sex and Harm in the Age of Consent* (Minneapolis: University of Minnesota Press, 2016), 15, 132.

75. Fischel, *Sex and Harm*, 132.

76. This is similar to the framing put forward by Briggs in *How All Politics Became Reproductive Politics*, 5.

77. For more on this, see the introductions to Sophie Lewis, *Full Surrogacy Now! Feminism against Family* (New York: Verso, 2019); Loretta J. Ross and Rickie Solinger, *Reproductive Justice: An Introduction* (Oakland: University of California Press, 2017); and Briggs, *How All Politics Became Reproductive Politics*.

78. Briggs, *How All Politics Became Reproductive Politics*, 5.

79. Definition of the origins of the culture wars from James Davison Hunter, *Culture Wars: The Struggle to Define America* (New York: Basic Books, 1991), 1–7. The subtitle was a rewording of Pat Buchanan's speech on the presidential campaign for George H. W. Bush, wherein he described the United States as being engaged in "a religious war" for "the soul of America." Pat Buchanan, "1992 Republican National Convention Speech," 17 August 1992, http://buchanan.org/blog/1992-republican-national-convention-speech-148, cited in Hunter, *Culture Wars*, 46.

80. See Herzog, *Sex in Crisis*, xii–xiii; and Irvine, *Talk About Sex*, 1–4, 12. For more on the ways that adults discuss adolescent sexual autonomy, see Fischel, *Sex and Harm in the Age of Consent*, 15; and Joseph J. Fischel, "Pornographic Protections? Itineraries of Childhood Innocence," *Law, Culture and the Humanities* 12, no. 2 (June 2016): 206–220.

CHAPTER 1 — TEENAGE GIRLS AND THE NEW RIGHT

Ellen Willis, "Teen Lust," *Ms. Magazine*, July/August 1987, Ellen Willis Papers, folder 7.11: *Ms.* Articles 1973–1987, Schlesinger Library, Radcliffe Institute, Harvard University. James Baldwin, "To Crush a Serpent," originally published in *Playboy*, January 1987, reprinted in James Baldwin, *The Cross of Redemption: Uncollected Writings*, ed. Randall Kenan (New York: Vintage, 2010), 195–204.

1. See Laura Briggs, *How All Politics Became Reproductive Politics: From Welfare Reform to Foreclosure to Trump* (Oakland: University of California Press, 2017), 28, 38, 53–54.

2. See, for example, Annette Lawson and Deborah L. Rhode, *The Politics of Pregnancy: Adolescent Sexuality and Public Policy* (New Haven, CT: Yale University Press, 1993), 3; Carolyn Cocca, "From 'Welfare Queen' to 'Exploited Teen': Welfare Dependency, Statutory Rape, and Moral Panic," *NWSA Journal* 14 (2002): 58; Zillah Eisenstein, *The Color of Gender: Reimaging Democracy* (Berkeley: University of California Press, 1994), 40; Jessica Fields, "'Children Having Children': Race, Innocence, and Sexuality Education," *Social Problems* 52 (November 2005): 549–550; Jeffrey Moran, *Teaching Sex: The Shaping of Adolescence in the 20th Century* (Cambridge, MA: Harvard University Press, 2000), 223; and Stephanie Coontz, *The Way We Never Were: American Families and the Nostalgia Trap* (New York: Basic Books, 2010), 204.

3. Briggs, *How All Politics Became Reproductive Politics*, 8.

4. Kristin Luker, *Dubious Conceptions: The Politics of Teenage Pregnancy* (Cambridge, MA: Harvard University Press, 1996), 106.

5. See Alesha E. Doan and Jean Calterone Williams, *The Politics of Virginity: Abstinence in Sex Education* (Westport, CT: Praeger, 2008), 122; Briggs, *How All Politics Became Reproductive Politics*, 53; and Seth Dowland, *Family Values and the Rise of the Christian Right* (Philadelphia: University of Pennsylvania Press, 2015), 6–7.

6. See Briggs, *How All Politics Became Reproductive Politics*, 54; Robin Bernstein, *Racial Innocence: Performing American Childhood and Race from Slavery to Civil Rights* (New York: New York University Press, 2012); Renee Romano, *Race Mixing: Black-White Marriage in Postwar America* (Cambridge, MA: Harvard University Press, 2003), 168; Andrew Hartman, *A War for the Soul of America: A History of the Culture Wars* (Chicago: University of

Chicago Press, 2015), 63, 85; and R. Marie Griffith, *Moral Combat: How Sex Divided American Christians and Fractured American Politics* (New York: Basic Books, 2017), 118–119.

7. See Kristin Luker, *When Sex Goes to School: Warring Views on Sex—and Sex Education—since the Sixties* (New York: W.W. Norton, 2006), 92–93; and Dagmar Herzog, *Sex in Crisis: The New Sexual Revolution and the Future of American Politics* (New York: Basic Books, 2008), xii–xiii.

8. See Rickie Solinger, ed., *Abortion Wars: A Half Century of Struggle, 1950–2000* (Berkeley: University of California Press, 1998), 215; Sara Diamond, *Roads to Dominion: Right Wing Movements and Political Power in the United States* (New York: Guildford Press, 1995), 235; and Daniel K. Williams, "Reagan's Religious Right," in *Ronald Reagan and the 1980s: Perceptions, Policies, Legacies*, ed. Cheryl Hudson and Gareth Davies (Basingstoke: Palgrave Macmillan, 2008), 143; and Fields, "'Children Having Children,'" 551.

9. For more on the difficulty of advocating for sex education in this era, see Janice Irvine, *Talk about Sex: The Battles over Sex Education in the United States* (Berkeley: University of California Press, 2002), 1–4, 12.

10. Alan Guttmacher Institute, *Teenage Pregnancy: The Problem That Hasn't Gone Away* (New York: Alan Guttmacher Institute, 1981), Schlesinger Library, Radcliffe Institute, Harvard University, 5.

11. Maris Vinovskis, *An "Epidemic" of Adolescent Pregnancy? Some Historical and Policy Considerations* (New York: Oxford University Press, 1988), 22.

12. Guttmacher Institute, *Teenage Pregnancy*, 4.

13. Guttmacher Institute, *Teenage Pregnancy*, 5. The fact that teenage birth rates were actually falling in this period has been described in Stephanie Coontz, *The Way We Never Were: American Families and the Nostalgia Trap* (New York: Basic Books, 2010), 202; Moran, *Teaching Sex*, 203; Sinikka Elliot, *Not My Kid: What Parents Believe about the Sex Lives of Their Teenagers* (New York: New York University Press, 2012), 11; Dorothy Roberts, *Killing the Black Body: Race, Reproduction, and the Meaning of Liberty* (New York: Pantheon Books, 1997), 116; and Luker, *Dubious Conceptions*, 81.

14. Guttmacher Institute, *Teenage Pregnancy*, 4.

15. This argument has been put forward in Roberts, *Killing the Black Body*, 116; and Nancy Lesko, *Act Your Age! A Cultural Construction of Adolescence* (New York: Routledge/Falmer, 2001), 144.

16. This has been argued in Luker, *Dubious Conceptions*, 86; and John D'Emilio and Estelle B. Freedman, *Intimate Matters: A History of Sexuality in America*, 2nd ed. (Chicago: University of Chicago Press, 2012), 341.

17. Marie Winn, "What Became of Childhood Innocence?," *New York Times*, 25 January 1981, SM4.

18. Willis, "Teen Lust."

19. Willis, "Teen Lust."

20. I use the term "Blackness" in this chapter to refer to stereotypes constructed by white Americans, what Devon W. Carbado calls "the social construction of blackness" in the United States, in "(E)racing the Fourth Amendment," *Michigan Law Review* 100, no. 5 (2002): 949.

21. This history has been explored by many feminist scholars. See Lawson and Rhode, *The Politics of Pregnancy*, 3; Cocca, "From 'Welfare Queen' to 'Exploited Teen,'" 58; Eisenstein, *The Color of Gender*, 40; Fields, "'Children Having Children,'" 549–550; Moran, *Teaching Sex*, 223; Coontz, *The Way We Never Were*, 204; and Briggs, *How All Politics Became Reproductive Politics*.

22. See Fields, "'Children Having Children,'" 549–550; and Cocca, "From 'Welfare Queen' to 'Exploited Teen,'" 57.

23. Guttmacher Institute, *Teenage Pregnancy*, 9.

24. Nadine Brozan, "More Teenagers Are Pregnant Despite Rise in Contraception," *New York Times*, 12 March 1981, C1.

25. Briggs, *How All Politics Became Reproductive Politics*, 54.

26. Briggs, *How All Politics Became Reproductive Politics*, 54.

27. Charles Murray, cited in Briggs, *How All Politics Became Reproductive Politics*, 54.

28. June Dobbs Butts, "Adolescent Sexuality and Teenage Pregnancy from a Black Perspective," in *Teenage Pregnancy in a Family Context: Implications for Policy*, ed. Theadora Ooms (Philadelphia: Temple University Press, 1981), 308.

29. Dobbs Butts, "Adolescent Sexuality," 327.

30. Peggy Taylor, "Teen Moms: Are We to Blame?," *Essence*, February 1985, 125. For a critique of respectability politics, see Brittney Cooper, *Beyond Respectability: The Intellectual Thought of Race Women* (Urbana: University of Illinois Press, 2017).

31. Dorothy I. Height, "What Must Be Done about Children Having Children," *Ebony*, July 1985, 76

32. Taylor, "Teen Moms," 125.

33. For more on the "restriction of sexual speech" in this era, see Irvine, *Talk About Sex*, 1–4, 12.

34. "Loretta Ross," from "The Power of Women's Voices: Selection from the Voices of Feminism Project," Sophia Smith Collection, Women's History Collection at Smith College, https://www.smith.edu/libraries/libs/ssc/pwv/pwv-ross.html. For further biographical details on Loretta Ross, see Lisa Levenstein, *They Didn't See Us Coming: The Hidden History of Feminism in the Nineties* (New York: Basic Books, 2020), 82.

35. Loretta Ross, "Women of Color and the Reproductive Rights Movement" (speech, October 17, 1987), Loretta Ross Papers, box 4, file: "'The Politics of Color in the Feminist Movement' at the 9th annual Anti-Rape Week POWER Panel," Smith College Special Collections, 1.

36. Information packet, Pyramid Communications International, Loretta Ross Papers, box 43, Smith College Special Collections.

37. Letter from Loretta Ross to Karen Epstein of NOW, 30 April 1986, Loretta Ross Papers, box 43, Smith College Special Collections.

38. Flyer, Conference: "Teens Taking Charge (on Teen Pregnancy)," 10 May 1986, Loretta Ross Papers, box 43, Smith College Special Collections.

39. "NOW News Release: Seminar for Teens, by Teens, about Teens to Be Held Saturday May 10," 5 May 1996, Loretta Ross Papers, box 43, Smith College Special Collections.

40. Ann Welbourne-Moglia, cited in Sharon Johnson, "School Sex Education Enters a New Phase," *New York Times*, 9 January 1986, C1.

41. Briggs, *How All Politics Became Reproductive Politics*, 53–54.

42. Jerry Falwell, evangelical pastor and founder of the Moral Majority, had identified and admonished the work of Mary Calderone and other advocates for sex education in an essay for *The SIECUS Circle: A Humanist Revolution*, ed. Claire Chambers (Belmont, MA: Western Islands, 1977) as early as 1977. See also "Mary Calderone: Godmother of the New Sexuality?," interview in *Christopher Street* magazine, 31, carton 2, Clippings of Magazine Articles, 1981–2 Folder, Schlesinger Library, Radcliffe Institute, Harvard University.

43. Phyllis Schlafly, "What's Wrong with Today's Sex Education?," *Christian Life*, March 1982, Fundamentalism file: Bob Jones University Archives.

44. This is discussed in Irvine, *Talk about Sex*, 133; and in Bonnie Nelson Trudell, *Doing Sex Education: Gender Politics and Schooling* (New York: Routledge, 1993), x.

45. "Mary Calderone: Godmother of the New Sexuality?," 32.

46. Griffith, *Moral Combat*, xi.

47. For more on this history, see Irvine, *Talk About Sex*, 1–4, 12.

48. Frank F. Furstenberg, Richard Lincoln Jr., and Jane Menken, eds., *Teenage Sexuality, Pregnancy, and Childbearing* (Philadelphia: University of Pennsylvania Press, 1981), 15.

49. Ross, "Women of Color and the Reproductive Rights Movement."

50. The connection between Ross's experiences and her activism are discussed in "Loretta Ross," from "The Power of Women's Voices: Selection from the Voices of Feminism Project."

51. Flyer, date unknown, National Latina Health Organization Records, box 1, Smith College Special Collections. For more details on the founding of the NLHO, see Levenstein, *They Didn't See Us Coming*, 171.

52. Sonia M. Perez and Luis A. Duany, "Reducing Hispanic Teenage Pregnancy and Family Poverty: A Replication Guide," National Council of La Raza, Publications Department, July 1992, National Latina Health Organization Records, box 4, Smith College Special Collections.

53. Ann Welbourne-Moglia and Sharon R. Edwards, "Sex Education Must Be Stopped!," *SIECUS Report*, November/December 1986, 1.

54. "A Generation in Jeopardy: Children and AIDS," a Report of the Select Committee on Children, Youth, and Families, U.S. House of Representatives, 100th Congress, December 1987, 26.

55. Robert O. Self, *All in the Family: The Realignment of American Democracy since the 1960s* (New York: Hill and Wang, 2012), 387–393.

56. D'Emilio and Freedman, *Intimate Matters*, 354–355.

57. On the radical potential of political collaboration between young Black women on welfare and LGBTQ+ communities, see Cathy Cohen, "Punks, Bulldaggers, and Welfare Queens: The Radical Potential of Queer Politics?," *GLQ* 3, no. 4 (1997): 437–465.

58. D'Emilio and Freedman, *Intimate Matters*, 355.

59. Furstenberg, Lincoln, and Menken, *Teenage Sexuality*, 6.

60. The Therapeutic Abortion Act is discussed in Williams, "Reagan's Religious Right," 135; and the Briggs Initiative in Robert M. Collins, *Transforming America: Politics and Culture in the Reagan Years* (New York: Columbia University Press, 2009), 137. See also Matthew Avery Sutton, "Reagan, Religion and the Culture Wars of the 1980s," in *A Companion to Ronald Reagan*, ed. Andrew L. Johns (Hoboken, NJ: John Wiley and Sons, 2014), 205. I published an earlier version of this section in the following form: Charlie Jeffries, "Adolescent Women and Antiabortion Politics in the Reagan Administration," *Journal of American Studies* 52, no. 1 (February 2018): 193–213.

61. As seen in "Letter from Ronald Reagan to Robert L. Mauro, 11 Oct. 1979," in *Reagan: A Life in Letters*, ed. Kiron K. Skinner, Annelise Anderson, and Martin Anderson (New York: Free Press, 2003), 197–198. This rhetorical support is also discussed in Williams, "Reagan's Religious Right," 142.

62. For more on Reagan's priorities as president, see Sutton, "Reagan, Religion, and the Culture Wars of the 1980s," 213–218; Williams, "Reagan's Religious Right," 141–142; Gil Troy, *Morning in America: How Ronald Reagan Invented the 1980s* (Princeton, NJ: Princeton University Press, 2007), 8, 14; Robert Mason, *The Republican Party and American Politics from Hoover to Reagan* (Cambridge: Cambridge University Press, 2012), 260; and Self, *All in the Family*, 368–369, 376–377.

63. Diamond, *Roads to Dominion*, 229.

64. Argued in Solinger, *Abortion Wars*, 215; Diamond, *Roads to Dominion*, 235; and Williams, "Reagan's Religious Right," 143.

65. For a longer discussion of the impact of these social movements on young women's increased social and sexual freedoms, see Joan Jacobs Brumberg, *The Body Project: An Intimate History of Teenage Girls* (New York: Random House, 1997); Carol Dyhouse, *Girl Trouble: Panic and Progress in the History of Young Women* (New York: Zed Books, 2013); and Herzog, *Sex in Crisis.*

66. Gil Troy, "A Historiography of Reagan and the 1980s," in Hudson and Davies, *Ronald Reagan and the 1980s,* 237; Neil J. Young, *We Gather Together: The Religious Right and the Problem of Interfaith Politics* (New York: Oxford University Press, 2016), 214; and Self, *All in the Family,* 370.

67. Fields, "'Children Having Children,'" 551. See also Irvine, *Talk About Sex,* 1–4, 12.

68. Collins, *Transforming America,* 129–130.

69. Briggs, *How All Politics Became Reproductive Politics,* 73.

70. See Mason, *The Republican Party,* 249, for a discussion of the widespread unpopularity of welfare in this period. For an exploration of the panic around an "epidemic" level of teenage pregnancies in the 1980s, see Vinovskis, *An "Epidemic" of Adolescent Pregnancy?,* 76. For more on the emerging idea among conservatives of an "underclass" in American society, see Stephen Tuck, "African American Protest," in Hudson and Davies, *Ronald Reagan and the 1980s,* 122; and Collins, *Transforming America,* 124.

71. Peter G. Bourne, "Drug Abuse Policy," in Hudson and Davies, *Ronald Reagan and the 1980s,* 49.

72. Collins, *Transforming America,* 130. See also Levenstein, *They Didn't See Us Coming,* 121. For details of Reagan's campaign speech, see "'Welfare Queen' Becomes Issue in Reagan Campaign," *New York Times,* 15 February 1976.

73. See Roberts, *Killing the Black Body,* 94. See also Self, *All in the Family,* 148–150.

74. Irvine, *Talk about Sex,* 91. See also Williams, "Reagan's Religious Right," 143; and Matthew C. Moen, *The Christian Right and Congress* (Tuscaloosa: University of Alabama Press, 1989), 106.

75. Quote from Irvine, *Talk about Sex,* 91. The success that Senators Denton and Hatch had in introducing the AFLA is discussed in Robert Pear, "Reagan Backs Plan to Limit Abortion Counseling," *New York Times,* 26 October 1985, 10. Denton's role specifically is mentioned in Moen, *The Christian Right and Congress,* 106. Hatch's previous work on the Hatch Amendment, a constitutional amendment that would have given states and Congress the power to form their own abortion laws, circumventing *Roe,* is discussed in Young, *We Gather Together,* 212.

76. The Adolescent Family Life Act, Title XX of the Public Health Service Act, 1981, 580 (hereafter cited as AFLA).

77. Lawson and Rhode, *The Politics of Pregnancy,* 285.

78. Lawson and Rhode, *The Politics of Pregnancy,* 285.

79. D'Emilio and Freedman, *Intimate Matters,* 343. See also Dowland, *Family Values,* 4–5; and Griffith, *Moral Combat,* xi.

80. Williams, "Reagan's Religious Right," 143; and Steven F. Hayward, *The Age of Reagan: The Conservative Counterrevolution, 1980–1989* (New York: Crown Forum, 2009), 278.

81. Ronald Reagan, "Abortion and the Conscience of a Nation," 1983, reprinted in *The Human Life Review* 30 (Summer 2004): 65.

82. For a discussion of how the Christian Right celebrated "Abortion and the Conscience of a Nation," see Williams, "Reagan's Religious Right," 143; and Hayward, *The Age of Reagan,* 278. The description of Reagan's propensity for "phoning in" his support for the pro-life movement can be found in Troy, *Morning in America,* 159.

83. States News Service, "U.S. Expands Fight on Teenage Pregnancy," *New York Times*, 19 October 1982, A15.

84. "U.S. Expands Fight on Teenage Pregnancy," A15.

85. Vinovskis, *An "Epidemic" of Adolescent Pregnancy?*, 81.

86. AFLA, 580.

87. A number of sources reveal the varied sites of opposition to AFLA. On sexual health advocates, Moran, *Teaching Sex*, 215; on the clergy, Linda Gordon, *The Moral Property of Women: A History of Birth Control Politics in America* (Urbana: University of Illinois Press, 2002), 350; and on Congress, Doan and Williams, *The Politics of Virginity*, 28.

88. Robert Pear, "Planned Parenthood Groups Investigated on Use of U.S. Funds," *New York Times*, 6 December 1981, 30.

89. Pear, "Planned Parenthood Groups," 30.

90. Loretta J. Ross, book review, "Faye Wattleton: A Life on the Line," Loretta Ross Papers, box 4, Smith College Special Collections, 3.

91. Faye Wattleton, *Life on the Line* (New York: Ballantine Books, 1996), first quote from 213 and second from 212.

92. Elliot, *Not My Kid*, 11.

93. Moran, *Teaching Sex*, 214.

94. "About Us: History," Project Reality: Leader in Abstinence Education since 1985, www .comriva.com.

95. Marcela Howell, updated by Marilyn O'Keefe, *The History of Federal Abstinence-Only Funding*, Advocates for Youth, July 2007, https://www.advocatesforyouth.org/wp-content /uploads/storage//advfy/documents/fshistoryabonly.pdf.

96. AFLA, 579.

97. For example, see Briggs, *How All Politics Became Reproductive Politics*; Linda Gordon, *Women, the State, and Welfare* (Madison: University of Wisconsin Press, 1990); Theda Skocpol, *Protecting Soldiers and Mothers: The Political Origins of Social Policy in the United States* (Cambridge, MA: Belknap Press of Harvard University Press, 1992); Michael B. Katz, *In the Shadow of the Poorhouse: A Social History of Welfare in America* (New York: Basic Books, 1996); and James T. Patterson, *America's Struggle against Poverty in the Twentieth Century* (Cambridge, MA: Harvard University Press, 2000).

98. There are a number of important scholarly works on the ways that adolescent African American women have been blamed and punished through federal policy for having children outside of marriage. See Roberts, *Killing the Black Body*; Patricia Hill Collins, *Black Sexual Politics: African Americans, Gender, and the New Racism* (New York: Routledge, 2005); Fields, "'Children Having Children'"; Doan and Williams, *The Politics of Virginity*; Lawson and Rhode, *The Politics of Pregnancy*; Nancy Kendall, *The Sex Education Debates* (Chicago: University of Chicago Press, 2013); Cris Mayo, "Gagged and Bound: Sex Education, Secondary Virginity, and the Welfare Reform Act," *Philosophy of Education Archive* (1998): 309–317; and Rhonda Y. Williams, *The Politics of Public Housing: Black Women's Struggles against Urban Inequality* (New York: Oxford University Press, 2004).

99. For more on the Moynihan Report and its legacy, see Roberts, *Killing the Black Body*; Briggs, *How All Politics Became Reproductive Politics*; Self, *All in the Family*, 153; Lee Rainwater, *The Moynihan Report and the Politics of Controversy* (Cambridge, MA: MIT Press, 1967); Carl Ginsburg, *Race and Media: The Enduring Life of the Moynihan Report* (New York: Institute for Media Analysis, 1989); James T. Patterson, *Freedom Is Not Enough: The Moynihan Report and America's Struggle over Black Family Life from LBJ to Obama* (New York: Basic Books, 2010); Daniel Geary, *Beyond Civil Rights: The Moynihan Report*

and Its Legacy (Philadelphia: University of Pennsylvania Press, 2015); and Susan D. Greenbaum, *Blaming the Poor: The Long Shadow of the Moynihan Report on Cruel Images about Poverty* (New Brunswick, NJ: Rutgers University Press, 2015).

100. Hortense Spillers, "Mamas Baby, Papa's Maybe: An American Grammar Book," *Diacritics* 17, no. 2 (Summer 1987): 65, 66.

101. Spillers, "Mama's Baby," 68. For more on "the social construction of blackness," see Carbado, "(E)racing the Fourth Amendment," 949.

102. AFLA, 578.

103. Melvin Anchell, "Dedication," in *What's Wrong with Sex Education?* (Selma, AL: Hoffman Center for the Family, 1991).

104. Thank you to Dagmar Herzog for conversations on this topic.

105. Susan F. Rasky, "New Battle at Family Planning Office," *New York Times*, 13 July 1985, 6.

106. Roberts, *Killing the Black Body*, 232–233.

107. For more on the responsibility of the parental role emphasized by the Moynihan Report, see the texts listed in notes 92–94, notably Gordon, *Women, the State, and Welfare*; Skocpol, *Protecting Soldiers and Mothers*; and Patterson, *Freedom Is Not Enough*.

108. Gordon, *Moral Property*, 310; and Vinovskis, *An "Epidemic" of Adolescent Pregnancy?*, 87.

109. Bellotti v. Baird, 443 U.S. 622 (1979).

110. Wattleton, *Life on the Line*, 213.

111. Wattleton, *Life on the Line*, 213.

112. H. L. v. Matheson, 450 U.S. 398, 1981.

113. H. L. v. Matheson.

114. H. L. v. Matheson.

115. Planned Parenthood v. Ashcroft, 462 U.S. 476 (1983).

116. Planned Parenthood v. Casey, 505 U.S. 833 (1992).

117. For more on these overlaps in the culture wars over sexuality, See Irvine, *Talk About Sex*, 7; Herzog, *Sex in Crisis*; xii, and Luker, *When Sex Goes to School*, 92–93.

118. Wattleton, *A Life on the Line*, 215.

119. Kristin A. Moore and Martha R. Burt, *Private Crisis, Public Cost* (Washington, DC: Urban Institute Press, 1982), 130.

120. Moore and Burt, *Private Crisis, Public Cost*, 139.

121. "Family Planning Programs," *New York Times*, 4 April 1984, C15.

122. "Ambivalence" described in Wattleton, *A Life on the Line*, 215.

123. State of New York v. Heckler, 719 F. 2d 1191 (1983).

124. For more on "the social construction of blackness," see Carbado, "(E)racing the Fourth Amendment," 949.

125. Discussed in Nadine Brozan, "Birth Control Rule: Clinics Ponder Effects," *New York Times*, 29 January 1983, 11. Opposition to the squeal rule is also discussed in Joan Jacobs Brumberg, *The Body Project: An Intimate History of American Girls* (New York: Random House, 1997), 172; and Lucy Rollin, *Twentieth Century Teen Culture by the Decades* (Westport, CT: Greenwood Press, 1999), 290.

126. First quotation is Marjory Mecklenburg quoted in Brozan, "Adolescents, Parents, and Birth Control," *New York Times*, 8 March 1982, B6; and the second is Kathleen Carscallen quoted in Brozan, "Birth Control Rule," 11.

127. Faye Wattleton, quoted in Brozan, "Birth Control Rule," 11

128. Brumberg, *The Body Project*, 172.

129. C. Everett Koop, *Koop: The Memoirs of America's Family Doctor* (New York: Random House, 1991), 195–224. See also Alexandra M. Lord, *Condom Nation: The U.S. Government's*

Sex Education Campaign from World War I to the Internet (Baltimore: Johns Hopkins University Press, 2010). See also Self, *All in the Family*, 388, 390.

130. For more on how the Reagan "revolution" is defined by "the relationship between success and failure," see Self, *All in the Family*, 368.

131. See Williams, "Reagan's Religious Right," 143; and Hayward, *The Age of Reagan*, 277.

132. For more on this, see Briggs, *How All Politics Became Reproductive Politics*, 28, 38, 53–54; Lawson and Rhode, *The Politics of Pregnancy*, 3; Cocca, "From 'Welfare Queen' to 'Exploited Teen,'" 58; Eisenstein, *The Color of Gender*, 40; Fields, "'Children Having Children,'" 549–550; Moran, *Teaching Sex*, 223; and Coontz, *The Way We Never Were*, 204.

133. For more on this history, see Irvine, *Talk About Sex*, 1–4, 12.

134. For more on these overlaps in the culture wars over sexuality, see Irvine, *Talk About Sex*, 7; Herzog, *Sex in Crisis*, xii–xii; and Luker, *When Sex Goes to School*, 92–93.

CHAPTER 2 — WOMEN AND CHILDREN?

1. Janice Irvine, *Talk about Sex: The Battle over Sex Education in the United States* (Berkeley: University of California Press, 2002), 132.

2. Irvine, *Talk about Sex*, 136.

3. For more on consensuses over sexuality and unexpected culture war positions, see E. J. Dionne, *Souled Out: Reclaiming Faith and Politics after the Religious Right* (Princeton, NJ: Princeton University Press, 2008), 48; Kristin Luker, *When Sex Goes to School: Warring Views on Sex—and Sex Education—since the Sixties* (New York: W. W. Norton, 2006), 92–93; Dagmar Herzog, *Sex in Crisis: The New Sexual Revolution and the Future of American Politics* (New York: Basic Books, 2008), xii–xiii; and Irvine, *Talk about Sex*, 1–4, 7, 12.

4. Irvine, *Talk about Sex*, 136.

5. See Kathryn Bond Stockton, *The Queer Child, or Growing Sideways in the Twentieth Century* (Durham, NC: Duke University Press, 2009), 62; and Irvine, *Talk About Sex*, 1–4, 12.

6. See James R. Kincaid, *Erotic Innocence: The Culture of Child Molesting* (Durham, NC: Duke University Press, 1998), 18–19; Joseph J. Fischel, "Catharine MacKinnon's Wayward Children," *differences* 30, no. 1 (2019): 48, 35; and Lauren Berlant, "Live Sex Acts," *Feminist Studies* 21, no. 2 (Summer 1995): 388.

7. For a longer discussion of this history, see Robin Bernstein, *Racial Innocence: Performing American Childhood and Race from Slavery to Civil Rights* (New York: New York University Press, 2012). For more on "innocence" and "vulnerability," see Joseph J. Fischel, "Pornographic Protections? Itineraries of Childhood Innocence," *Law, Culture and the Humanities* 12, no. 2 (June 2016): 206–220; and Jennifer C. Nash, "Pedagogies of Desire," *differences* 30, no. 1 (May 2019): 197–217. Further, Dagmawi Woubshet has asserted that the antiracist activist and writer James Baldwin was thinking this about his own adolescence at the end of his life in the 1980s, in the context of the culture wars—and in particular the ways that innocence was constructed through whiteness in the United States. Dagmawi Woubshet, "The Fierce Legacy of James Baldwin: On Love, Race, Religion, and Sexuality" (public lecture, Queer@King's, King's College London, 7 November 2019).

8. For more on the privileging of whiteness in the protection of children, see Fischel, "Pornographic Protections?," 206–220.

9. Lucy Rollin, *Twentieth-Century Teen Culture by the Decades: A Reference Guide* (Westport, CT: Greenwood Press, 1999), 266.

10. Rollin, *Teen Culture*, 266.

11. Mallory Szymanski, "Adolescence, Literature, and Censorship: Unpacking the Controversy Surrounding Judy Blume," *The Neo-Americanist* 3 (Spring/Summer 2007): 6.

12. Fred M. Hechinger, "Wave of Censors Hit the Schools," *New York Times*, 8 May 1979, C1.

13. Judy Blume, *Places I Never Meant to Be: Original Stories by Censored Writers* (New York: Simon Pulse, 2001), 5.

14. Alexa Tsoulis-Reay, "Tracing the Career of Tween-Lit Doyenne Judy Blume," *New York Magazine*, 27 May 2013.

15. Judy Blume, "Is Puberty a Dirty Word?," *New York Law School Law Review* 38 (1993): 38 (adapted from a speech given at the conference "The Sex Panic: Women, Censorship, and Pornography," 7-8 May 1993).

16. Colin Campbell, "Book Banning in America," *New York Times*, 20 December 1981, BR1.

17. For more on the history of the Gablers, see Seth Dowland, "Textbook Politics," chapter 2 in *Family Values and the Rise of the Christian Right* (Philadelphia: University of Pennsylvania Press, 2015), 49-77.

18. Ann McFeatters, "Children's Author Spars with Moral Majority," *Pittsburgh Post-Gazette*, 26 October 1981.

19. Judith F. Krug, quoted by Leonard S. Marcus, *The Minders of Make Believe: Idealists, Entrepreneurs, and the Shaping of American Children's Literature* (Boston: Houghton Mifflin Harcourt, 2008), 303.

20. Tsoulis-Reay, "Tracing the Career."

21. Campbell, "Book Banning." See also Dowland, "Textbook Politics," 49-77.

22. Marcus, *The Minders of Make Believe*, 303.

23. Marcus, *The Minders of Make Believe*, 303.

24. "School Board Reverse Blume Book Ban," *Southeast Missourian*, 6 December 1984.

25. Marcus, *The Minders of Make Believe*, 303.

26. Alleen Pace Nilsen and Kenneth L. Donelson, *Literature for Today's Young Adults* (New York: Longman, 2000), 424.

27. Blume, "Is Puberty a Dirty Word?," 38.

28. Blume "Is Puberty a Dirty Word?," 38.

29. Blume, "Is Puberty a Dirty Word?," 38.

30. Blume, "Is Puberty a Dirty Word?," 38.

31. Blume, *Places I Never Meant to Be*, 7.

32. Irvine, *Talk about Sex*, 132.

33. Norma Klein, "On Being a Banned Writer," *Lion and the Unicorn* 10 (1986): 19.

34. Letter from parent, cited in Klein, "On Being a Banned Writer," 19.

35. For more on vulnerability and race in youth, see Fischel, "Pornographic Protections?"

36. Joan Jacobs Brumberg, *The Body Project: An Intimate History of Teenage Girls* (New York: Random House, 1997), 185.

37. Judy Blume, "The Giddy/Sad, Flighty/Solid Life of Judy Blume," interview by Peter Gorner, *Chicago Tribune*, 15 March 1985.

38. Norma Klein, *It's OK If You Don't Love Me* (London: Futura, 1978), 27.

39. Nicholas J. Karolides, "*It's OK If You Don't Love Me*: Evaluating Anticipated Experiences of Readers," in *Censored Books: Critical Viewpoints*, ed. Nicholas J. Karolides, Lee Burress, and John M. Kean (Metuchen, NJ: Scarecrow Press, 1993), 328.

40. Frank Battaglia, "'If We Cannot Trust . . .' The Pertinence of Judy Blume's in Karolides, Burress, and Kean, *Censored Books*, 259.

41. Barbara Nosanchuk, "Is Weetzie Bat a Good Role Model?," *New York Times*, 25 June 1989, BR38.

42. Nosanchuk, "Is Weetzie Bat a Good Role Model?"

43. Robin F. Brancato, "In Defense of *Are You There God? It's Me! Margaret, Deenie,* and *Blubber*—Three Novels By Judy Blume," in Karolides, Burress, and Kean, *Censored Books,* 89.

44. Nilsen and Donelson, *Literature for Today's Young Adults*, 424.

45. This shift is described in Irvine, *Talk about Sex*, 133.

46. Campbell, "Book Banning."

47. Melvin Anchell, cited by Irvine, *Talk about Sex*, 133.

48. Phyllis Schlafly, "What's Wrong with Sex Education?," *Phyllis Schlafly Report* 14 (February 1981).

49. Michael W. Apple, "Series Editor's Introduction," in Bonnie Nelson Trudell, *Doing Sex Education: Gender Politics and Schooling* (New York: Routledge, 1993), x.

50. Irvine, *Talk about Sex*, 133.

51. Apple, "Series Editor's Introduction," x.

52. Lottie Beth Hobbs, "Is Humanism Molesting Your Child?," Christian Faith in America, 1980, http://christianfaithinamerica.com/culture-war/is-humanism-molesting-your -child/. For more on secular humanism, see Seth Dowland, "Christian Schools," chapter 1 in *Family Values*, 23–48; and Robert O. Self, *All in the Family: The Realignment of American Democracy since the 1960s* (New York: Hill and Wang, 2012), 344.

53. Blume, "Is Puberty a Dirty Word?," 38.

54. For a description of the factions that made up the New Right, see Briggs, *How All Politics Became Reproductive Politics*, 38.

55. Klein, "On Being a Banned Writer," 20.

56. Blume, "Is Puberty a Dirty Word?," 43.

57. For more on sexual autonomy and adolescence, see Joseph J. Fischel, *Sex and Harm in the Age of Consent* (Minneapolis: University of Minnesota Press, 2016). For more on the "restriction of sexual speech" in this era, see Irvine, *Talk About Sex*, 1–4, 12.

58. Lisa Duggan and Nan Hunter, *Sex Wars: Sexual Dissent and Political Culture* (New York: Routledge, 1995), 1.

59. See Kincaid, *Erotic Innocence*, 18–19; Fischel, "Catharine MacKinnon's Wayward Children," 48, 35; and Berlant, "Live Sex Acts," 388.

60. Duggan and Hunter, *Sex Wars*, 3.

61. Alix Kates Shulman, "Sex and Power: Sexual Bases of Radical Feminism," *Signs: Journal of Women in Culture and Society* 5, no. 4 (Summer 1980): 591.

62. This included Andrea Dworkin, *Intercourse* (New York: Simon & Schuster, 1987); and Dworkin, *Pornography: Men Possessing Women* (London: Women's Press, 1981).

63. Joanna Fateman, introduction to *Last Days at Hot Slit: The Radical Feminism of Andrea Dworkin* (South Pasadena, CA: Semioxt(e), 2019), 9.

64. Andrea Dworkin, "Suffering and Speech," in *In Harm's Way: The Pornography Civil Rights Hearings*, ed. Catharine A. MacKinnon and Andrea Dworkin (Cambridge, MA: Harvard University Press, 1997), 27.

65. The connection between Ross's experiences and her activism are discussed in "Loretta Ross," from "The Power of Women's Voices: Selection from the Voices of Feminism Project," Sophia Smith Collection, Women's History Collection at Smith College, https://www .smith.edu/libraries/libs/ssc/pwv/pwv-ross.html.

66. "Loretta Ross," from "The Power of Women's Voices: Selection from the Voices of Feminism Project."

67. Susan Brownmiller, *Against Our Will: Men, Women, and Rape* (New York: Simon & Schuster, 1975), 273.

68. Robin Morgan, cited in Carolyn Bronstein, *Battling Pornography: The American Feminist Anti-pornography Movement, 1976–1986* (New York: Cambridge University Press, 2011), 4.

69. Alice Walker, "Fable," reprinted in her collection, *You Can't Keep a Good Woman Down: Stories* (New York: Harcourt Brace Jovanovich, 1981), 80.

70. Walker, "Fable," 83.

71. For more on the work of Black antipornography feminists, see LaMonda Horton-Stallings, *Funk the Erotic: Transaesthetics and Black Sexual Cultures* (Urbana: University of Illinois Press, 2015), 65–66; and Jennifer Nash, "Strange Bedfellows: Black Feminism and Antipornography Feminism," *Social Text* 26, no. 4 (2008): 51–76. Jennifer Nash describes the unlikely intersection of Black feminist thought with antipornography feminism but acknowledges that these two branches of feminist thought share "a normative goal of eradicating sexualized representations, at least those that are produced for the voyeuristic consumption of the dominant white male subject" (63).

72. See Andrea Dworkin Papers, box 104, folder 5, "Children: Newspaper Clippings Re Porn 1981–85"; and Catharine MacKinnon Papers, box 217 no. 2 vol. 1, "Content analysis of magazines portraying children, crime, and violence, 1986," both at the Schlesinger Library, Radcliffe Institute, Harvard University.

73. Barbara Varro, "Are Sexy Ads, Movies, Exploiting Teen Stars?," *Pittsburgh Press*, in Florence Rush Papers, carton 1, Schlesinger Library, Radcliffe Institute, Harvard University.

74. Leah Lamson, "Author Says Sexual Child Abuse Increasing," *Evening Gazette* (Worcester), 12 December 1980, 6, Florence Rush Papers, carton 1, Schlesinger Library, Radcliffe Institute, Harvard University.

75. See Kincaid, *Erotic Innocence*, 18–19; and Fischel, "Catharine MacKinnon's Wayward Children," 48, 35.

76. For more on this history, see Sarah Projansky, "Pint-Sized and Precocious," chapter 1 in *Spectacular Girls: Media Fascination and Celebrity Culture* (New York: New York University Press, 2014).

77. Tracey A. Gardner, "Racism in Pornography and the Women's Movement," in *Take Back the Night: Women on Pornography*, ed. Laura Lederer (New York: William Morrow, 1980), 72. See also Nash, "Strange Bedfellows."

78. See Jill Lewis, "The Subject of Struggle: Feminism and Sexuality," chapter 8 in Gloria I. Joseph and Jill Lewis, *Common Differences: Conflicts in Black and White Feminist Perspectives* (Garden City, NY: Anchor Press/Doubleday, 1981), 234; and Stallings, *Funk the Erotic*, 65.

79. Nash, "Strange Bedfellows," 54. Nash also notes that this argument has been made by Angela Harris, in "Race and Essentialism in Feminist Legal Theory," *Stanford Law Review* 42 (1989): 592.

80. Stallings, *Funk the Erotic*, 65.

81. Luisah Teish, "A Quiet Subversion," in Lederer, *Take Back the Night*, 116.

82. Nash, in "Strange Bedfellows," describes this body of writing as including Patricia Hill Collins, "Pornography and Black Women's Bodies," in *Making Violence Sexy*, ed. Diana Russell (New York: Teacher's College Press, 1993), 97–104; Audre Lorde, "Uses of the Erotic," in *Sister Outsider: Essays and Speeches* (Trumansburg, NY: Crossing Press, 1984), 53–59; Alice Walker, "Coming Apart," in Lederer, *Take Back the Night*, 95–104; and Gardner, "Racism in Pornography and the Women's Movement." Some contemporary pro-pornography Black feminist scholars have asserted that they do not relinquish the involvement of African American feminists in antipornography organizing in the 1980s. See Stallings, *Funk the Erotic*, 65–66; and Mireille Miller-Young, *A Taste for Brown Sugar: Black Women in Pornography* (Durham, NC: Duke University Press, 2014), preface.

83. Nona Willis Aronowitz, "Introduction: Transcendence," in *The Essential Ellen Willis*, ed. Nona Willis Aronowitz (Minneapolis, University of Minnesota Press, 2014), xii.

84. Ellen Willis, "Feminism, Moralism, and Pornography," *Village Voice*, 15 October 1979, reprinted in Aronowitz, *The Essential Ellen Willis*, 351.

85. Ellen Willis, "To Emma with Love," *Newsday*, 19 December 1989, Ellen Willis Papers, box 7, file 6, "*Newsday* articles," Schlesinger Library, Radcliffe Institute, Harvard University.

86. bell hooks, *Feminist Theory from Margin to Center* (Boston: South End Press, 1984), 148.

87. hooks, *Feminist Theory*, 150.

88. Gloria I. Joseph, "Styling, Profiling, and Pretending: The Games Before the Fall," in *Common Differences*, 181.

89. Joseph, "Styling, Profiling, and Pretending," 182.

90. Amber Hollibaugh and Cherríe Moraga, "What We're Rolling Around in Bed With," *Heresies* 12 (1981): 59–60.

91. Hollibaugh and Moraga, "What We're Rolling Around in Bed With," 62. For the history of the forced sterilization of young women of color, see Dorothy Roberts, *Killing the Black Body: Race, Reproduction, and the Meaning of Liberty* (New York: Pantheon Books, 1997). See also Self, *All in the Family*, 148–150. Hollibaugh and Moraga's use here of "Third World women" refers to the reclaimed use of the term as a part of the Third World feminism of this era. See also *This Bridge Called My Back: Writings By Radical Women of Color*, ed. Cherríe Moraga and Gloria Anzaldúa (New York: Kitchen Table, Women of Color Press, 1983).

92. For more on the "restriction of sexual speech" in this era, see Irvine, *Talk About Sex*, 1–4, 12.

93. "Minutes from the Scholar and Feminist Planning Committee," from Janie Kritzman and Carole Vance, 24 September 1981, Ann Snitow Papers, box 22, David M. Rubenstein Rare Book & Manuscript Library, Duke University.

94. "Minutes from the Scholar and Feminist Planning Committee."

95. Duggan and Hunter, *Sex Wars*, 24.

96. Women Against Pornography "We Protest" Letter, Ellen Willis Papers, box 1, Scholar and Feminist 1982 Folder, Schlesinger Library, Radcliffe Institute, Harvard University.

97. See a collection of the conference talks reprinted in *Pleasure and Danger: Exploring Female Sexuality*, ed. Carole S. Vance (Boston: Routledge & K. Paul 1984); and "Diary of a Conference," reprinted in *GLQ: A Journal of Lesbian and Gay Studies* 17 (2010): 49–78.

98. Bronstein, *Battling Pornography*, 232.

99. Duggan and Hunter, *Sex Wars*, 32.

100. Catharine MacKinnon, "Not a Moral Issue," reprinted in *Feminism Unmodified: Discourses on Life and Law* (Cambridge, MA: Harvard University Press, 1987), 156.

101. MacKinnon, "Not a Moral Issue," 157.

102. Bronstein, *Battling Pornography*, 324.

103. See Fischel, "Catharine MacKinnon's Wayward Children"; and Berlant, "Live Sex Acts." Comment on Brooke Shields from Louise Armstrong, testifying at the Minneapolis hearings, reprinted in MacKinnon and Dworkin, *In Harm's Way*, 244.

104. Charlotte Kasl, testifying at the Minneapolis hearings, reprinted in MacKinnon and Dworkin, *In Harm's Way*, 172.

105. Melinda Vadas, "A First Look at the Pornography/Civil Rights Ordinance," *Journal of Philosophy* 84 (September 1987): 489.

106. See Victoria Baranetsky, "The Economic-Liberty Approach of the First Amendment: A Story of American Booksellers v. Hudnut," *Harvard Civil RightsCivil Liberties Law Review* 47 (January 2012): 205. For a description of the use of graphic materials by antipornography feminists, see Harriet Gilbert, "So Long as It's Not Sex and Violence: Andrea Dworkin's *Mercy*," in *Sex Exposed: Sexuality and the Pornography Debate*, ed. Lynne Segal and Mary McIntosh (London: Virago, 1992), 219.

107. Baranetsky, "The Economic-Liberty Approach," 196.

108. Katrina Forrester, "Making Sense of Modern Pornography," *New Yorker*, 26 September 2016.

109. See Baranetsky, "The Economic-Liberty Approach," 172; and Forrester, "Making Sense of Modern Pornography."

110. Thanks to Sneha Krishnan for conversations on this topic.

111. Patricia Hill Collins, *From Black Power to Hip Hop: Racism, Nationalism, and Feminism* (Philadelphia: Temple University Press, 2006), 179.

112. Kimberlé Crenshaw, "Demarginalizing the Intersection of Race and Sex: A Black Feminist Critique of Antidiscrimination Doctrine, Feminist Theory and Antiracist Politics," *University of Chicago Legal Forum* (1989), no. 1: 154.

113. Thanks to Joe Fischel for conversations on this topic. See also Fischel, "Catharine MacKinnon's Wayward Children," 37.

114. See Nash, "Strange Bedfellows"; Fischel, "Pornographic Protections?"; and Bernstein, *Racial Innocence*.

115. Bronstein, *Battling Pornography*, 327.

116. "Child Victims," from the Final Report of the Attorney General's Commission on Pornography (hereafter cited as the Meese Report), part 1, chapter 3, 855.

117. "Exposure of Children to Explicit and Violent Materials," from the Meese Report, part 1, chapter 3.

118. For a definition of a "moral panic," see Jeffrey Weeks, *Sex, Politics and Society: The Regulation of Sexuality since 1800* (New York: Pearson Education, 2012), 14.

119. See *Caught Looking: Feminism, Pornography, and Censorship*, ed. Kate Ellis et al. (East Haven, CT: Long River, 1992).

120. Ellen Willis, "Toward a Sexual Revolution," reprinted in Willis, *No More Nice Girls: Countercultural Essays* (Hanover, NH: University Press of New England for Wesleyan University Press, 1992), 23.

121. Published as Pat Califia, "Among Us, against Us—the New Puritans," in *Caught Looking*.

122. Califia, "Among Us, against Us—the New Puritans," 20.

123. Published as Pat Califia, "The Obscene, Disgusting, and Vile Meese Report," 1986, reprinted in Califia, *Public Sex: The Culture of Radical Sex* (San Francisco: Cleis Press, 1994), 102.

124. Califia, "The Obscene, Disgusting, and Vile Meese Report," 102.

125. Kincaid, *Erotic Innocence*, 18–19.

126. See Berlant, "Live Sex Acts"; and Lisa Duggan, "Appendix," in Duggan and Hunter, *Sex Wars*, 240. Some feminist scholars are exploring the impact and legacy of the sex wars, including Brenda Cossman, in "#MeToo, Sex Wars 2.0 and the Power of Law," *Asian Yearbook of Human Rights and Humanitarian Law* 3 (September 2018): 18–37.

127. Lisa Duggan, "Feminist Historians and Anti-pornography Campaigns: An Overview," in Duggan and Hunter, *Sex Wars*, 68.

128. For more on the flexibility of culture wars actors when it comes to issues of sexuality, see Luker, *When Sex Goes to School*, 92–93; Herzog, *Sex in Crisis*, xii–xiii; and Irvine, *Talk about Sex*, 7.

129. Fischel, "Catharine MacKinnon's Wayward Children," 50. See also Phillip Jenkins, *Moral Panic: Changing Concepts of the Child Molester in Modern America* (New Haven, CT: Yale University Press, 1998).

130. See Fischel, *Sex and Harm in the Age of Consent*, 132.

131. Judith Levine, *Harmful to Minors: The Perils of Protecting Children from Sex* (Minneapolis: University of Minnesota Press, 2002), 33.

132. Gayle Rubin, "Thinking Sex: Notes for a Radical Theory of the Politics of Sexuality," reprinted in *The Lesbian and Gay Studies Reader*, ed. Henry Abelove, Michele Aina Barale, and David M. Halperin (New York: Routledge, 1993), 146.

133. Daniel S. Moretti, *Obscenity and Pornography: The Law under the First Amendment* (London: Oceana, 1984); and Judith Levine, *Harmful to Minors: The Perils of Protecting Children from Sex* (Minneapolis: University of Minnesota Press, 2002), 33.

134. Levine, *Harmful to Minors*, 33.

135. New York v. Ferber, 458 U.S. 747 (1982).

136. The history of public awareness about child abuse in the United States has been discussed by a number of scholars, including Richard Beck, *We Believe the Children: A Moral Panic in the 1980s* (New York: Public Affairs, 2015); Judith Sealander, *The Failed Century of the Child: Governing America's Young in the Twentieth Century* (New York: Cambridge University Press, 2003); Lela B. Costin, Howard Jacob Karger, and David Stoesz, *The Politics of Child Abuse in America* (New York: Oxford University Press, 1996); and Barbara Nelson, *Making an Issue of Child Abuse: Political Agenda Setting for Social Problems* (Chicago: University of Chicago Press, 1984).

137. On the collapsing of adolescence into childhood, see Kincaid, *Erotic Innocence*, 18–19; Fischel, "Catharine MacKinnon's Wayward Children," 48, 35; and Berlant, "Live Sex Acts," 388.

138. Costin, Karger, and Stoesz, *The Politics of Child Abuse in America*, 16.

139. Philip Jenkins, *Pedophiles and Priests: Anatomy of a Contemporary Crisis* (New York: Oxford University Press, 1996).

140. *Body & Soul: The Black Women's Guide to Physical Health and Emotional Well-Being*, ed. Linda Villarose, foreword by Angela Y. Davis and June Jordan (1994), Black Women's Health Imperative Records, box 4, Smith College Special Collections.

141. Sealander, *The Failed Century of the Child*, 78.

142. Kincaid, *Erotic Innocence*, 10.

143. Costin, Karger, and Stoesz, *The Politics of Child Abuse in America*, 34. See also Beck, who has contributed a lengthy exposition on this in *We Believe the Children*.

144. Elaine Showalter, *Hystories: Hysterical Epidemics and Modern Culture* (New York: Columbia University Press, 1997), 172.

145. For a description of the use of graphic materials by antipornography feminists, see Gilbert, "So Long as It's Not Sex and Violence," 219.

146. Michel Foucault, *The History of Sexuality*, vol. 1, *An Introduction* (New York: Pantheon Books, 1978), 18.

147. For more on this, see Irvine, *Talk About Sex*, 1–4, 12.

148. Richard Wexler, *Wounded Innocents: The Real Victims of the War against Child Abuse* (Buffalo: Prometheus Books, 1990), 18.

149. For more on this, see Briggs, *How All Politics Became Reproductive Politics*.

150. Mary Pride, *The Child Abuse Industry: Outrageous Facts & Everyday Rebellions against a System That Threatens Every North American Family* (Westchester, IL: Crossway Books, 1986), 36.

151. This topic has been the subject of increasing popular interest, most recently explored by Katrina Forrester for the *New Yorker*. See Forrester, "Making Sense of Modern Pornography."

152. Kim Murphy, "Lords Video Agent Convicted on Child Porno Charges," *Los Angeles Times*, 16 June 1989.

153. Kim Murphy, "Three in Traci Lords Sex Film Case Indicted," *Los Angeles Times*, 6 March 1987, D1.

154. Carol Jacobsen, "Redefining Censorship: A Feminist View," *Art Journal* 50 (December 1991): 42.

155. Florence Rush, "Speech re. Court of Appeals Decision on Section 263.15," 1981, Florence Rush Papers, carton 1, Schlesinger Library, Radcliffe Institute, Harvard University.

156. Steven C. Dubin, *Arresting Images: Impolitic Art and Uncivil Actions* (New York: Routledge, 1992), 141.

157. Philip Brookman and Deborah Singer, "Chronology," in *Culture Wars: Documents from the Recent Controversies in the Arts*, ed. Richard Bolton (New York: New Press, 1992), 335.

158. Brookman and Singer, "Chronology," 334.

159. For more on sexuality and unexpected culture wars positions, see Luker, *When Sex Goes to School*, 92–93; Herzog, *Sex in Crisis*, xii–xiii; and Irvine, *Talk about Sex*, 7.

160. Tipper Gore, *Raising PG Kids in an X-Rated Society* (Nashville, TN: Parthenon Press, 1987), 19.

161. These bands are mentioned by name in Gore, *Raising PG Kids*, 16, 17, 88.

162. Gore, *Raising PG Kids*, 17. For more on the use of graphic materials by antipornography feminists, see Gilbert, "So Long as It's Not Sex and Violence," 219.

163. Gore, *Raising PG Kids*, 89.

164. Gore, *Raising PG Kids*, 15.

165. Brookman and Singer, "Chronology," 335.

166. Thanks to Andrew Preston for conversations on this topic.

167. Ice-T, "Freedom of Speech," from the album *The Iceberg/Freedom of Speech . . . Just Watch What You Say!* (Sire, Warner Bros., 1989).

168. Miller v. California, 413 U.S. 15 (1973).

169. Susan G. Caughlan, "Private Possession of Child Pornography: The Tensions between Stanley v. Georgia and New York v. Ferber," *William and Mary Law Review* 29 (1987): 193.

170. Court Decision in Ferber, cited in Caughlan, "Private Possession," 172.

171. New York v. Ferber.

172. Miller v. California.

173. Brookman and Singer, "Chronology," 334.

174. The Child Sexual Abuse and Pornography Act of 1986.

175. The Child Protection and Obscenity Enforcement Act of 1988.

176. Carole Vance, "The Pleasures of Looking: The Attorney General's Commission on Pornography versus Visual Images," in *The Critical Image: Essays on Contemporary Photography*, ed. Carol Squiers (London: Lawrence & Wishart, 1991), 41.

177. Dubin, *Arresting Images*, 140.

178. Brookman and Singer, "Chronology," 341.

179. Dubin, *Arresting Images*, 138.

180. Vance, "The Pleasures of Looking," 41.

181. Vance, "The Pleasures of Looking," 41.

182. Vance, "The Pleasures of Looking," 41.

183. Vance, "The Pleasures of Looking," 41.

184. Vance, "The Pleasures of Looking," 41; and Brookman and Singer, "Chronology," 341.

185. Brookman and Singer, "Chronology," 341.

186. Information about Reisman comes from "North Carolina 'Prevention of Child Sexual Abuse' Conference Guide," Florence Rush Papers, carton 1, Schlesinger Library, Radcliffe Institute, Harvard University; and see Califia, "The Obscene, Disgusting, and Vile Meese Report," 100.

187. Judith Reisman, "Promoting Child Abuse as Art," *Washington Times*, 7 July 1989, quoted in Brookman and Singer, *Culture Wars*, 57.

188. Reisman, "Promoting Child Abuse as Art," 57.

189. Ann Beattie, introduction to *At Twelve: Portraits of Young Women*, by Sally Mann (New York: Aperture, 1988), 10.

190. Mann, *At Twelve*.

191. For more on this history, see Projansky, *Spectacular Girls*.

192. Richard B. Woodward, "The Disturbing Photography of Sally Mann," *New York Times Magazine*, 27 September 1992, SM1.

193. Charles Hagen, "Childhood without Sweetness," *New York Times*, 5 June 1992, C30.

194. Hagen, "Childhood without Sweetness," C30.

195. Woodward, "The Disturbing Photography of Sally Mann," SM1.

196. Sally Mann, *Hold Still: A Memoir with Photographs* (New York: Little, Brown, 2015), xi.

197. Mann, *Hold Still*, 100.

198. For more on this topic, see Fischel, *Sex and Harm in the Age of Consent*.

199. Connie Samaras, "Feminism, Photography, Censorship and Sexually Transgressive Imagery," *New York Law School Law Review* 38 (1993): 79–90.

200. Woodward, "The Disturbing Photography of Sally Mann," SM1.

201. Jacobsen, "Redefining Censorship: A Feminist View," 42.

202. Ellen Willis, "Child Abuse: The Search for Scapegoats," *Newsday*, 1990 Ellen Willis Papers, box 7, file 6, "*Newsday* Articles," Schlesinger Library, Radcliffe Institute, Harvard University.

203. Jacobsen, "Redefining Censorship: A Feminist View," 45.

204. For more on consensuses over sexuality in the culture wars, see Luker, *When Sex Goes to School*, 92–93; Herzog, *Sex in Crisis*, xii–xiii; and Irvine, *Talk about Sex*, 1–4, 7, 12.

205. For more on the "restriction of sexual speech" in this era, see Irvine, *Talk About Sex*, 1–4, 12.

206. Ellen Willis, "The Sex Panic Conference Report, 1993," 13, Ellen Willis Papers, box 5, folder 6, Schlesinger Library, Radcliffe Institute, Harvard University.

207. Judy Blume, quoted by Willis, "The Sex Panic Conference Report, 1993," 16.

208. This sentiment is expressed by Ellen Willis in "Toward a Feminist Sexual Revolution," in Willis, *No More Nice Girls*, 20.

209. For more on this history, see Projansky, *Spectacular Girls*.

CHAPTER 3 — EXPLICIT CONTENT

1. Thanks to Dagmar Herzog for conversations on this topic.

2. For more on unexpected culture war positions in debates over sexuality, see Kristin Luker, *When Sex Goes to School: Warring Views on Sex—and Sex Education—since the Sixties* (New York: W. W. Norton, 2006), 92–93; Dagmar Herzog, *Sex in Crisis: The New Sexual Revolution and the Future of American Politics* (New York: Basic Books, 2008), xii–xiii; and Janice Irvine, *Talk about Sex: The Battle over Sex Education in the United States* (Berkeley: University of California Press, 2002), 1–4, 7, 12.

3. For more on the history of this categorization in the postwar period, see Sarah Projansky, *Spectacular Girls: Media Fascination and Celebrity Culture* (New York: New York University Press, 2014), 11; and John D'Emilio and Estelle B. Freedman, *Intimate Matters: A History of Sexuality in America*, 2nd ed. (Chicago: University of Chicago Press, 2012), 260.

4. For more on the difficulty facing advocates of sex education in the United States, see Irvine, *Talk About Sex*, 1–4, 12.

5. Sarah Projansky addresses this in *Spectacular Girls*, 11.

6. See Marnina Gornick, "Between 'Girl Power' and 'Reviving Ophelia': Constituting the Neoliberal Girl Subject," *NWSA Journal* 18, no. 2 (2006): 1–23.

7. The title of this section is from Sara Marcus, *Girls to the Front: The True Story of the Riot Grrrl Revolution* (New York: Harper Perennial, 2010).

8. Melissa Klein, "Duality and Redefinition: Young Feminism and the Alternative Music Community," in *Third Wave Agenda: Being, Doing Feminism*, ed. Leslie L. Heywood and Jennifer Drake (Minneapolis: University of Minnesota Press, 1997), 208.

9. For more on the "restriction of sexual speech" in this era, see Irvine, *Talk About Sex*, 1–4, 12.

10. Kate Eichhorn, *The Archival Turn in Feminism: Outrage in Order* (Philadelphia: Temple University Press, 2013), 95.

11. Marcus, *Girls to the Front*, 56.

12. Marcus, *Girls to the Front*, 56.

13. Marcus, *Girls to the Front*, 57–58.

14. Marcus, *Girls to the Front*, 58–59.

15. Klein, "Duality and Redefinition," 213.

16. Melissa Klein, "Interview with Kathleen Hanna," *Off Our Backs*, February 1993, vol. 23, no. 2, p. 7, Schlesinger Library, Radcliffe Institute, Harvard University.

17. "Riot Grrrl Test Patterns," date unknown, Kathleen Hanna Papers, MSS 271, box 2, folder 22, Fales Library and Special Collections, New York University Libraries.

18. Alison Piepmeir, *Girl Zines: Making Media, Doing Feminism* (New York: New York University Press, 2009), 43

19. Marcus, *Girls to the Front*, 14.

20. Marcus, *Girls to the Front*, 14.

21. Klein, "Duality and Redefinition," 213.

22. Klein, "Duality and Redefinition," 213.

23. Klein, *Off Our Backs*, 6.

24. Klein, *Off Our Backs*, 6; and Klein, "Duality and Redefinition," 213. Mimi Thi Nguyen cites the descriptions of Klein in *Off Our Backs* and Marcus in *Girls to the Front* of the uncomfortable realizations of young white women at the convention in "Riot Grrrl, Race, and Revival," *Women & Performance: A Journal of Feminist Theory* 22 (July–November 2012): 179–180.

25. Klein, "Duality and Redefinition," 213.

26. Klein, *Off Our Backs*, 6.

27. Marcus, *Girls to the Front*, 16.

28. Kathleen Hanna, quoted in Klein, *Off Our Backs*, 7.

29. Kathleen Hanna, quoted in Denise Shepard, "Bikini Kill," in *Ray Gun*, Riot Grrrl Publicity Collection, MSS 316, box 1, folder 3, Fales Library and Special Collections, New York University Libraries.

30. Marcus, *Girls to the Front*, 134.

31. Bikini Kill / Huggy Bear flyer, date unknown, Kathleen Hanna Papers, MSS 271, box 2, folder 23, Fales Library and Special Collections, New York University Libraries.

32. Unnamed flyer, date unknown, Kathleen Hanna Papers, MSS 271, box 2, folder 23, Fales Library and Special Collections, New York University Libraries.

33. Klein, "Duality and Redefinition," 212.

34. Marcus, *Girls to the Front*, 14.

35. Erika Reinstein, quoted in Lauren Spencer, "Grrrls Only," *Outlook, The Washington Post*, 3 January 1993, Riot Grrrl Publicity Collection, MSS 316, box 1, folder 4, Fales Library and Special Collections, New York University Libraries.

36. Klein, "Duality and Redefinition," 215.

37. Anonymous, in *Bikini Kill* zine no. 1, date unknown, Kathleen Hanna Papers, MSS 271, box 1, folder 10, Fales Library and Special Collections, New York University Libraries.

38. Klein, "Duality and Redefinition," 216.

39. "Revolution, Girl Style," *Newsweek*, 23 November 1992, 85, Riot Grrrl Publicity Collection, MSS 316, box 1, folder 1, Fales Library and Special Collections, New York University Libraries.

40. *Bikini Kill* zine no. 1.

41. Klein, "Duality and Redefinition," 216.

42. Kathleen Hanna, quoted in Gina Arnold, "Bikini Kill: Revolution Girl-Style," *Option Music Alternatives*, May/June 1992, 46, Riot Grrrl Publicity Collection, MSS 316, box 1, folder 2, Fales Library and Special Collections, New York University Libraries.

43. Emily White, *Fast Girls: Teenage Tribes and the Myth of the Slut* (New York: Scribner, 2002), 147.

44. Kathleen Hanna, interview, "The Feminism Issue," *Bust*, Winter 2000, 52, Schlesinger Library, Radcliffe Institute, Harvard University.

45. *Bikini Kill* zine no. 1.

46. Descriptions of Riot Grrrl style taken from Jennifer Baumgardner and Amy Richards, *ManifestA: Young Women, Feminism, and the Future*, excerpted in *The Women's Movement Today: An Encyclopedia of Third-Wave Feminism*, ed. Leslie L. Heywood (Westport, CT: Greenwood Press, 2006), 303; and Natasha Stovall, "Adult Crash," *Village Voice*, 30 April 1996, Riot Grrrl Publicity Collection, MSS 316, box 1, folder 6, Fales Library and Special Collections, New York University Libraries.

47. "Revolution, Girl Style," 84.

48. Shepard, "Bikini Kill."

49. For a discussion of the politics of reclaiming language, see Farah Godrej, "Spaces for Counter-Narratives: The Phenomenology of Reclamation," *Frontiers: A Journal of Women's Studies* 32 (January 2011): 111–133.

50. Shepard, "Bikini Kill."

51. *Hungry Girl* zine, cited in "Revolution, Girl Style," 67.

52. Nguyen, "Riot Grrrl, Race, and Revival," 179.

53. Ani Mukherji, originally published in Daisy Roos's *Not Even 5*, featured in *Evolution of a Race Riot*, ed. Mimi Thi Nguyen, 1997, Barnard Zine Collection, Barnard College Library.

54. Lauren Martin, "On Being Critical," in *Race Riot 2*, Mimi Thi Nguyen Zine Collection, in Collaboration with the People of Color Zine Project, MSS 365, Series I: Zines, box 2, folder 10, Fales Library and Special Collections, New York University Libraries.

55. "Revisiting the Riot: An Interview with Punk Veteran Mimi Thi Nguyen by Tina Vasquez," *Bitch* (Summer 2013).

56. Mimi Thi Nguyen, introduction to *Evolution of a Race Riot*, ed. Mimi Thi Nguyen, 1997, Barnard Zine Collection, Barnard College Library, 6.

57. Mimi Thi Nguyen, flyer for contributions to compilation zine, *Evolution of a Race Riot*, ed. Mimi Thi Nguyen, 1997, Barnard Zine Collection, Barnard College Library, 82.

58. Nguyen, "Riot Grrrl, Race, and Revival," in order of citation: 174, 167, 181, 175.

59. Marcus, *Girls to the Front*, cited in Eichhorn, *The Archival Turn in Feminism*, 116.

60. As suggested by Lisa Darms in conversations on this topic. See *Frighten the Horses*, issues 7, 11, and 13, 1991–1993, Kelly Marie Martin Riot Grrrl Collection, MSS 349, box 3, folder 3, Fales Library and Special Collections, New York University Libraries.

61. This is discussed in Marcus, *Girls to the Front*, 32; and in Eichhorn, *The Archival Turn in Feminism*, 116.

62. Eichhorn, *The Archival Turn in Feminism*, 116.

63. This has been noted by a number of scholars, including Nguyen in "Riot Grrrl, Race, and Revival"; and most recently Janice Radway, "Girl Zine Networks, Underground Itineraries, and Riot Grrrl History: Making Sense of the Struggle for New Social Forms in the 1990s and Beyond," *Journal of American Studies* (February 2016): 1–31.

64. *Eracism*, Mimi Thi Nguyen Zine Collection, in Collaboration with the People of Color Zine Project, MSS 365, Series I: Zines, box 1, folder 11, Fales Library and Special Collections, New York University Libraries.

65. "Riot Grrrl Test Patterns."

66. Jen Angel, *Fucktooth*, no. 17, 1995, Ann Marie Wilson Zine Collection, Schlesinger Library, Radcliffe Institute, Harvard University.

67. Sex education restrictions are discussed in Marcus, *Girls to the Front*, 259; and White, *Fast Girls*, 147.

68. *Bikini Kill* zine, no. 1.

69. Belissa Cohen, "LADEEDA," *LA Weekly*, 9–15 October 1992, Riot Grrrl Publicity Collection, MSS 316, box 1, folder 2, Fales Library and Special Collections, New York University Libraries.

70. "Pleasure" and "pain" from Marcelle Karp and Debbie Stoller, eds., *The BUST Guide to the New Girl Order* (New York: Penguin, 1999), 186. See also Irvine, *Talk About Sex*, 1–4, 12.

71. Mary Celeste Kearney, "Riot Grrrl: It's Not Just Music, It's Not Just Punk," in *The Girls' History and Culture Reader: The Twentieth Century*, ed. Miriam Forman-Brunell and Leslie Paris (Urbana: University of Illinois Press, 2011), 303.

72. Anonymous, in *Riot Grrrl* zine, no. 4, date unknown, Molly Neuman Riot Grrrl Collection, MSS 289, box 3, folder 2, Fales Library and Special Collections, New York University Libraries.

73. Mary P. Sheridan-Rabideau, *Girls, Feminism, and Grassroots Literacies: Activism in the GirlZone* (Albany: State University of New York Press, 2008), 45.

74. Anonymous, in *Girl Germs* zine, no. 3, date unknown, ed. Molly Neuman and Allison Wolfe, Molly Neuman Riot Grrrl Collection, MSS 289, box 3, folder 3, Fales Library and Special Collections, New York University Libraries.

75. Eleanor Whitney, *Aperture* zine, 2000, Barnard Zine Collection, Barnard College Library.

76. *Growing Pains* zine, no. 1, 1996, Barnard Zine Collection, Barnard College Library.

77. Anonymous, in *Girl Germs* zine, no. 4, 1992, ed. Molly Neuman and Allison Wolfe, Tammy Rae Carland Zine Collection, MSS 320, box 4, folder 11, Fales Library and Special Collections, New York University Libraries.

78. This is noted in much of the scholarship on Riot Grrrl. See, for example, Nguyen in "Riot Grrrl, Race, and Revival"; and Radway, "Girl Zine Networks, Underground Itineraries, and Riot Grrrl History."

79. Sel Hwahng, "For Colored Girls Who Have Considered Homicide," from *Bamboo Girl 3*, featured in *Evolution of a Race Riot*, ed. Mimi Thi Nguyen, 1997, Barnard Zine Collection, Barnard College Library.

80. Hwahng, "For Colored Girls."

81. Nguyen, "Riot Grrrl, Race, and Revival," 179.

82. Ramdasha Bikceem, in *Gunk*, no. 4, Fales Library and Special Collections, New York University Libraries, cited in Gabby Bess, "Alternatives to Alternatives: The Black Grrrls Riot Ignored," *Broadly*, 3 August 2015, https://broadly.vice.com/en_us/article/alternatives -to-alternatives-the-black-grrrls-riot-ignored.

83. Lauren Martin, from *You Might As Well Live 4*, featured in *Evolution of a Race Riot*, ed. Mimi Thi Nguyen, 1997, Barnard Zine Collection, Barnard College Library, 16.

84. Description of Riot Grrrl as "white-dominated" is from Bess, "Alternatives to Alternatives."

85. Bess, "Alternatives to Alternatives."

86. Mimi Thi Nguyen, "Fales Library Donation Statement," Mimi Thi Nguyen Collection in Collaboration with the POC Zine Project, 13 January 2012, https://poczineproject.tumblr .com/post/40517982011/poczp-news-mimi-collection-donation-statement-fales.

87. Tasha Fierce, *Bitchcore* zine, no. 1, 1999, Barnard Zine Collection, Barnard College Library.

88. *i love you (queerly not dearly)* zine, no. 1, 1997, Barnard Zine Collection, Barnard College Library.

89. *i love you (queerly not dearly)*.

90. Karen Friedland, Cathy Miner, Angela Taylor, and Nancy Deutsch, "Out Loud: The Queer Sensibility of Rock's Third Wave," *Sojourner: The Women's Forum* (June 1997), Amy Richards Papers, box 1, Smith College Special Collections.

91. John Sanchez, "Meet the Butchies," *The Advocate*, 9 November 1999, 90, https://books .google.co.uk/books?id=-mQEAAAAMBAJ&pg=PA90&lpg=PA90&dq=meet+the+butchie s+john+sanchez&source=bl&ots=jMcDEMXTh_&sig=ACfU3U1ukMXRMQt75Ih8ZwGnr w3CvDpT4A&hl=en&sa=X&ved=2ahUKEwian8PNmKXqAhWEZxUIHfoWDdkQ6AEw AXoECAoQAQ#v=onepage&q=meet%20the%20butchies%20john%20sanchez&f=false.

92. Bess, "Alternatives to Alternatives."

93. Bess, "Alternatives to Alternatives."

94. Bess, "Alternatives to Alternatives."

95. Bess, "Alternatives to Alternatives."

96. Martin, "On Being Critical."

97. For more on the whiteness of mainstream girl cultures in the 1990s, see Projansky, *Spectacular Girls*.

98. For more on the difficulty of discussing sexuality in public in this era, see Irvine, *Talk About Sex*, 1–4, 12.

99. Erika Reinstein, writing in the Riot Grrrl Press Catalogue, Riot Grrrl Zines/Flyers, Series I, box 2, folder 23, Fales Library and Special Collections, New York University Libraries.

100. Hanna, "Riot Grrrl Test Patterns," 3.

101. Piepmeier, *Girl Zines*, 94.

102. Kim France, "at War," *Rolling Stone*, 8–22 July 1993, Riot Grrrl Publicity Collection, MSS 316, box 1, folder 3, Fales Library and Special Collections, New York University Libraries.

103. Ann Powers, "No Longer Rock's Playthings," *New York Times: Arts and Leisure*, 14 February 1993, Riot Grrrl Publicity Collection, MSS 316, box 1, folder 3, Fales Library and Special Collections, New York University Libraries.

104. "Revolution, Girl Style," 84.

105. Quotes from "Revolution, Girl Style," 84. Marcus describes the Grrrls' mixed reaction to this description of Love in *Girls to the Front*, 7.

106. Marcus, *Girls to the Front*, 206, 212.

107. Paula Kamen, *Her Way: Young Women Remake the Sexual Revolution* (New York: New York University Press, 2000), 31.

108. Marcus, *Girls to the Front*, 212.

109. Kearney, "Riot Grrrl," 306.

110. Stovall, "Adult Crash."

111. For more on the politics of sexual speech in US culture, see Irvine, *Talk About Sex*.

112. Marcus, *Girls to the Front*, 325.

113. Marcus, *Girls to the Front*, 325.

114. See Lisa Levenstein, *They Didn't See Us Coming: The Hidden History of Feminism in the Nineties* (New York: Basic Books, 2020), 65.

115. Described in *i love you (queerly not dearly)* zine and by Marcus in *Girls to the Front*, 326.

116. *Riot Grrrl NYC* zine, no. 5, March 1993, Kathleen Hanna Papers, MSS 271, box 2, folder 23, Fales Library and Special Collections, New York University Libraries.

117. Elana Levine, "Buffy and the 'New Girl Order': Defining Feminism and Femininity," *Undead TV: Essays on Buffy the Vampire Slayer*, ed. Elana Levine and Lisa Parks (Durham, NC: Duke University Press, 2007), 177.

118. Bridget Lee, "Punk Feminism: Riot Grrrl Zines as a Feminist Movement," undergraduate thesis, 1998–2001, 22, Kathleen Hanna Papers, MSS 271, box 8, folder 11, Fales Library and Special Collections, New York University Libraries.

119. Joan Jacobs Brumberg, *The Body Project: An Intimate History of American Girls* (New York: Random House, 1997), 132–136.

120. Lee "Punk Feminism," 22; and White, *Fast Girls*, 150.

121. Marcus, *Girls to the Front*, 327.

122. For more on the "restriction of sexual speech" in this era, see Irvine, *Talk About Sex*, 1–4, 12.

123. Kara Jesella and Marissa Meltzer, *How Sassy Changed My Life: A Love Letter to the Greatest Teen Magazine of All Time* (New York: Faber and Faber, 2007), viii.

124. Jesella and Meltzer, *How Sassy*, viii.

125. Sandra Yates, cited in Jesella and Meltzer, *How Sassy*, 6.

126. Jesella and Meltzer, *How Sassy*, 6.

127. Jesella and Meltzer, *How Sassy*, 8.

128. As suggested by Linda Gordon, in a meeting at New York University, March 2015.

129. Elizabeth Larsen, "Censoring Sex Information: The Story of *Sassy*," *Utne Reader*, July/August 1990, Widener Library, Harvard University.

130. Larsen, "Censoring."

131. Larsen, "Censoring."

132. Larsen, "Censoring."

133. Subscription Advertisement, *Sassy*, June 1988, Schlesinger Library, Radcliffe Institute, Harvard University.

134. Karen Catchpole, "Getting Turned On," *Sassy*, June 1988, 50, Schlesinger Library, Radcliffe Institute, Harvard University.

135. Christina Kelly, "Hot for Teacher," *Sassy*, August 1988, 94, Schlesinger Library, Radcliffe Institute, Harvard University.

136. Jesella and Meltzer, *How Sassy*, 31–32.

137. Jesella and Meltzer, *How Sassy*, 32. The collections of popular teen magazines *Seventeen* and *YM* in the same period at the Schlesinger Library, Radcliffe Institute, Harvard University, both confirm the lack of queer sexualities in other publications.

138. "Lesbian Dilemma," *Sassy*, March 1994, Schlesinger Library, Radcliffe Institute, Harvard University.

139. Catherine Gysin, "Laurel and Lesli and Alex and Brian are your basic kids. They're dating. They go to movies and concerts. They fight over stupid things. They make up. They're sad sometimes. They're happy. AND THEY'RE GAY," *Sassy*, July 1988, Schlesinger Library, Radcliffe Institute, Harvard University.

140. For example, the January 1992 issue of *YM* featured an "Intimacy Report" that summarized from its poll: "When you sleep with someone you sleep with everyone they've ever

slept with" (106). This could also be seen in the May 1990 issue of *Seventeen*, in the article titled "Teens and AIDS," and in the same magazine's June 1990 article "Hazards of Early Sex."

141. Catherine Gysin, "Real Stories about Incest," *Sassy*, June 1989, 79, Schlesinger Library, Radcliffe Institute, Harvard University.

142. Larsen, "Censoring."

143. Larsen, "Censoring."

144. Sonic Youth, "Personality Crisis" flexi-disc, recorded for *Sassy*, November 1990. See Karp and Stoller, *The BUST Guide to the New Girl Order*, 186.

145. Jesella and Meltzer, *How Sassy*, viii.

146. This is described by Baumgardner and Richards in *ManifestA*, excerpt in Heywood, *The Women's Movement Today*, 298–301.

147. Kim France, "Girl of a Certain Age: Christina Kelly," *Girls of a Certain Age*, 3 April 2012, http://old.girlsofacertainage.com/2012/04/03/girl-of-a-certain-age-christina -kelly/

148. See Christina Kelly, "Cute Band Alert," *Sassy*, March 1992; and Kelly, "What Now?," *Sassy*, May 1992, Riot Grrrl Publicity Collection, MSS 316, box 1, folder 2, Fales Library and Special Collections, New York University Libraries.

149. Kelly, "Cute Band Alert"; and Kelly, "What Now?"

150. Sarah Maitland, quoted in "My Life in Zines: Zine of the Sallie Bingham Center for Women's History and Culture," 8, Third Wave Foundation Records, box 1, David M. Ruben- stein Rare Book & Manuscript Library, Duke University.

151. Kake, "Who Is Choking and Dying," *Riot Grrrl NYC* zine, no. 5, March 1993, Riot Grrrl Zines/Flyers, Series I, box 2, folder 23, Fales Library and Special Collections, New York University Libraries.

152. Gina Arnold, "Bikini Kill: Revolution Girl Style," *Option Music Alternatives*, May/ June 1992, 46, Riot Grrrl Publicity Collection, MSS 316, box 1, folder 2, Fales Library and Special Collections, New York University Libraries.

153. Arnold, "Bikini Kill," 46.

154. Arnold, "Bikini Kill," 46.

155. For more on this history, see Irvine, *Talk About Sex*, 1–4, 12.

156. Larsen, "Censoring."

157. Larsen, "Censoring."

158. Jesella and Meltzer, *How Sassy*, 33.

159. *The Citizen*, cited in Jesella and Meltzer, *How Sassy*, 33.

160. *The Citizen*, cited in Jesella and Meltzer, *How Sassy*, 34.

161. Larsen, "Censoring." See also Carlene Bauer, "How *Sassy* (Should Have) Changed My Life," *N+1*, July 2007, https://nplusonemag.com/online-only/online-only/how-sassy-should -have-changed-my-life/.

162. Jesella and Meltzer, *How Sassy*, 34.

163. Larsen, "Censoring." Also see Lisa Jervis, "Kicking Sass," *Salon*, 18 November 1996, http://www.salon.com/1996/11/18/media961118/.

164. Jesella and Meltzer, *How Sassy*, 34. See also Leandra Zarnow, "From Sisterhood to Girlie Culture: Closing the Great Divide between Second and Third Wave Cultural Agen- das," in *No Permanent Waves: Recasting Histories of U.S. Feminism*, ed. Nancy Hewitt (New Brunswick, NJ: Rutgers University Press, 2010), 280.

165. Jesella and Meltzer, *How Sassy*, 36.

166. Kearney, "Riot Grrrl," 303. See also Irvine, *Talk About Sex*.

167. Jesella and Meltzer, *How Sassy*, 32.

168. Jesella and Meltzer, *How Sassy*, 36. See also Bauer, "How *Sassy* (Should Have)."

169. For more on the flexibility of culture wars actors in debates over sexuality, see Luker, *When Sex Goes to School*, 92–93; Herzog, *Sex in Crisis*, xii–xiii; and Irvine, *Talk about Sex*, 7.

170. "Bait & Switch *Sassy*," *Bitch* zine, no. 1, Schlesinger Library, Radcliffe Institute, Harvard University.

171. Jervis, "Kicking Sass."

172. For more on this history, see Irvine, *Talk About Sex*.

173. Lee, "Punk Feminism," 22. For more on the history of *Bitch*, see Levenstein, "Making a Living from Social Change," chapter 5 in *They Didn't See Us Coming*, 93.

174. Lee, "Punk Feminism," 22.

175. Zarnow, "From Sisterhood to Girlie Culture," 278–279.

176. Jesella and Meltzer, *How Sassy*, 111.

177. Jesella and Meltzer, *How Sassy*, 111. A description of how the name of the publication was chosen is in Zarnow, "From Sisterhood to Girlie Culture," 283.

178. Zarnow, "From Sisterhood to Girlie Culture," 283.

179. Zarnow, "From Sisterhood to Girlie Culture," 282.

180. Karp and Stoller, *The BUST Guide to the New Girl Order*, 186.

181. Zarnow, "From Sisterhood to Girlie Culture," 283.

182. Jesella and Meltzer, *How Sassy*, 111.

183. Jennifer Baumgardner and Amy Richards, *ManifestA: Young Women, Feminism, and the Future* (New York: Farrar, Straus and Giroux, 2010), 136.

184. Debbie Stoller and Marcella Karp, "Editors' Letter," *BUST*, no. 5, Winter/Spring 1995, "My Life as a Girl Issue," 3, Schlesinger Library, Radcliffe Institute, Harvard University.

185. Buffy Watch, *BUST*, no. 13, Fall 1999, 10, Schlesinger Library, Radcliffe Institute, Harvard University.

186. Karp and Stoller, *The BUST Guide to the New Girl Order*, 184.

187. Jesella and Meltzer, *How Sassy*, 112.

188. Zarnow, "From Sisterhood to Girlie Culture," 290; Jesella and Meltzer, *How Sassy*, 112; and "Profile: Lisa Jervis, Co-Founder," Bitch Media, https://bitchmedia.org/profile/lisa-jervis.

189. Lee, "Punk Feminism," 22.

190. Zarnow, "From Sisterhood to Girlie Culture," 291.

191. Lisa Jervis and Andi Zeisler, "Editor's Letter," *Bitch*, vol. 3, no. 1, 1998, "The Puberty Issue," 2, Schlesinger Library, Radcliffe Institute, Harvard University.

192. Andi Zeisler, "Baby Tease," *Bitch*, vol. 2, issue 2, 1997, 25, Schlesinger Library, Radcliffe Institute, Harvard University.

193. Rachel Fudge, "The Buffy Effect: Or, a Tale of Cleavage and Marketing," *Bitch*, vol. 3, no. 10, 1998, Schlesinger Library, Radcliffe Institute, Harvard University.

194. Fudge, "The Buffy Effect."

195. Letter, 5 June 2000, Bitch: Feminist Response to Pop Culture Records, box 2, David M. Rubenstein Rare Book & Manuscript Library, Duke University.

196. Letter to *Bitch*, Bitch: Feminist Response to Pop Culture Records, box 2, David M. Rubenstein Rare Book & Manuscript Library, Duke University.

197. Letter to *Bitch*.

198. Ophira Edut, "HUES Magazine," http://www.ophira.com/mags_hues.html.

199. Edut, "HUES."

200. Edut, "HUES."

201. Edut, "HUES."

202. "Magazines Written by Youth," BUST Magazine Records, 1993–2015, box 3, David M. Rubenstein Rare Book & Manuscript Library, Duke University.

203. Titles from Spring 1998 and Summer 1998, http://www.ophira.com/mags_hues.html. Quote from Letter to *Bitch*.

204. Edut, "HUES." For more on the "restriction of sexual speech" in this era, see Irvine, *Talk About Sex*, 1–4, 12.

205. Maureen, "Watch this Girl," *Sassy*, August 1994, Schlesinger Library, Radcliffe Institute, Harvard University; Stoller and Karp, *The BUST Guide to the New Girl Order*, 186.

206. Kathleen Sweeney, *Maiden USA: Girl Icons Come of Age* (New York: Peter Lang, 2008), 29–30.

207. Sweeney, *Maiden USA*, 33.

208. Sweeney, *Maiden USA*, 34–35.

209. Susan Driver, *Queer Girls and Popular Culture: Reading, Resisting, and Creating Media* (New York: Peter Lang, 2007), 62.

210. Tanya R. Cochran, "Complicating the Open Closet: The Visual Rhetoric of Buffy the Vampire Slayer's Sapphic Lovers," in *Televising Queer Women: A Reader*, ed. Rebecca Beirne (New York: Palgrave Macmillan, 2008), 54.

211. For more on the whiteness of the girls at the center of media cultures in this era, see Projansky, *Spectacular Girls*.

212. In *Spectacular Girls*, Projansky surveyed the covers of *Time*, *Newsweek*, and *People* magazines from January 1990 to July 2012, and found that "78 percent" of the young women "appear to be white." For a longer exploration of this see Projansky, *Spectacular Girls*, 63, 72–73.

213. On the whiteness of young women in media cultures, see Projansky, *Spectacular Girls*. For a longer history of race, childhood, and the conception of innocence, see Robin Bernstein, *Racial Innocence: Performing American Childhood and Race from Slavery to Civil Rights* (New York: New York University Press, 2012). See also Joseph J. Fischel, "Pornographic Protections? Itineraries of Childhood Innocence," *Law, Culture and the Humanities* 12, no. 2 (June 2016): 206–220.

214. Sweeney, *Maiden USA*, 46.

215. Sweeney, *Maiden USA*, 52.

216. See, for example, Maria Cramer, "For 'Buffy' Fans, Another Reckoning with the Show's Creator," *New York Times*, 15 February 2021, https://www.nytimes.com/2021/02/15/arts/television/joss-whedon-charisma-carpenter.html; "The Long Fight to 'Free Britney,'" *New York Times*, 12 February 2021, https://www.nytimes.com/article/framing-britney-spears.html; Mara Wilson, "The Lies Hollywood Tells about Little Girls," *New York Times*, 23 February 2021, https://www.nytimes.com/2021/02/23/opinion/britney-spears-mara-wilson-hollywood.html; and Tavi Gevinson, "Britney Spears Was Never in Control," *The Cut*, 23 February 2021, https://www.thecut.com/2021/02/tavi-gevinson-britney-spears-was-never-in-control.html. See also *Framing Britney*, produced and directed by Samantha Stark (The New York Times Presents, FX/Hulu, 2021).

217. See Astrid Henry, "From a Mindset to a Movement: Feminism since 1990," in *Feminism Unfinished: A Short, Surprising History of American Women's Movements*, ed. Dorothy Sue Cobble, Linda Gordon, and Astrid Henry (New York: Liveright / W.W. Norton, 2014), 180; Marcus, *Girls to the Front*, 56.

218. This is argued by Kimberly Springer in "Third Wave Black Feminism?," *Signs* 27 (Summer 2002): 1078–1079; and in Andi Zeisler, *We Were Feminists Once: From Riot Grrrl to CoverGirl, the Buying and Selling of a Political Movement* (New York: BBS, Public Affairs, 2016), 159.

219. On the whiteness of the girlhoods represented in mainstream media cultures, see Projansky, *Spectacular Girls.*

220. Springer discusses Queen Latifah's decision not to identify as a feminist in "Third Wave Black Feminism?," 1078; and Molly Neuman's admiration of the artist is described in Marcus, *Girls to the Front,* 56.

221. For a discussion of the influence of porn on Lil' Kim, see bell hooks, "Hardcore Honey: bell hooks Goes on the Down Low with Lil' Kim," *Paper,* May 1997, http://www.papermag .com/hardcore-honey-bell-hooks-goes-on-the-down-low-with-lil-kim-1427357106.html.

222. hooks, "Hardcore Honey."

223. Lil' Kim, quoted in hooks, "Hardcore Honey."

224. For more on the whiteness of mainstream girl cultures in this era, see Projansky, *Spectacular Girls.*

225. Gornick, "Between 'Girl Power' and 'Reviving Ophelia,'" 4–5.

226. This two-sided discussion of teenage girls has been described by a number of scholars, including Projansky in *Spectacular Girls;* Gornick in "Between 'Girl Power' and 'Reviving Ophelia'"; Carol Dyhouse, *Girl Trouble: Panic and Progress in the History of Young Women* (London: Zed Books, 2013); and Anita Harris, "Not Waving or Drowning: Young Women, Feminism, and the Limits of the Next Wave Debate," in Heywood, *The Women's Movement Today.*

227. The "Girl Power" rhetoric is explored at length by Gornick in "Between 'Girl Power' and 'Reviving Ophelia.'" Publications that appear to support the idea of, or the possibility of, the sexually empowered teenage girl include the special "Feminisms and Youth Cultures" issue of *Signs* (*Signs: A Journal of Women and Culture* 23 [Spring 1998]). In "Not Waving or Drowning," Harris also cites the following examples of "Girl Power" feminism: Karen Green and Tristan Taormino, *A Girl's Guide to Taking Over the World: Writings from the Girl Zine Revolution* (New York: St. Martin's Griffin, 1997); Hilary Carlip, *Girl Power* (New York: Warner Books, 1995); Kathy Bail, *DIY Feminism* (St. Leonard's, NSW: Allen & Unwin, 1996); and Stoller and Karp, *The BUST Guide to the New Girl Order.*

228. Sweeney, *Maiden USA,* 47.

229. Dyhouse, *Girl Trouble,* 212.

230. See Projansky, *Spectacular Girls;* and Gornick, "Between 'Girl Power' and 'Reviving Ophelia.'"

231. Mary Pipher, *Reviving Ophelia: Saving the Selves of Adolescent Girls* (New York: Putnam, 1994), 11.

232. Kathleen Sweeney, "Maiden USA: Representing Teenage Girls in the '90s," *Afterimage* 26 (January/February 1999): 10.

233. Quote from Lorna Jowett, *Sex and the Slayer: A Gender Studies Primer for the Buffy Fan* (Middletown, CT: Wesleyan University Press, 2005), 97. This included publications such as Barbara Littman, *Everyday Ways to Raise Smart, Strong, Confident Girls: Successful Teens Tell Us What Works* (New York: St. Martin's Griffin, 1999); Mindy Bingham and Sandy Stryker, *Things Will Be Different for My Daughter: A Practical Guide to Building Her Self-Esteem and Self-Reliance from Infancy through the Teen Years* (New York: Penguin Books, 1995); Carol J. Eagle and Carol Colman, *All That She Can Be: Helping Your Daughter Achieve Her Full Potential and Maintain Her Self-Esteem during the Critical Years of Adolescence* (New York; Simon & Schuster, 1993); Judy Mann, *The Difference: Growing Up Female in America* (New York: Warner Books, 1994); and Sara Shandler, *Ophelia Speaks: Adolescent Girls Write about Their Search for Self* (New York: Harper Perennial, 1999). These and others are listed in Jowett, *Sex and the Slayer,* 97.

234. Dyhouse, *Girl Trouble,* 221.

235. See Alyssa Harad, "Reviving Lolita; or, Because Junior High Is Still Hell," in *Catching a Wave: Reclaiming Feminism for the 21st Century*, ed. Rory Cooke Dicker and Alison Piepmeier (Boston: Northeastern University Press, 2003), 87; Projansky, *Spectacular Girls*, 7–8; and Fischel, "Pornographic Protections?"

236. Pipher, *Reviving Ophelia*, 13.

237. For more on unexpected overlaps in the culture wars over sexuality, see Luker, *When Sex Goes to School*, 92–93; Herzog, *Sex in Crisis*, xii–xiii; and Irvine, *Talk about Sex*, 1–4, 7, 12.

238. See, for instance, American Association of University Women, "Shortchanging Girls, Shortchanging America: Executive Summary," https://www.aauwbakersfield.com/uploads/9/6/2/5/96257912/shortchanging_girls_shortchanging_america.pdf See also Harris, "Not Waving or Drowning," 86; Gornick, "Between 'Girl Power' and 'Reviving Ophelia'"; and Nancy Lesko, *Act Your Age: A Cultural Construction of Adolescence* (New York: Routledge, 2001), 103.

239. Mann, *The Difference*, 161.

240. In addition to the commentators mentioned in note 214.

241. Baumgardner and Richards, *ManifestA*, 132; and Dyhouse, *Girl Trouble*, 213.

242. Naomi Wolf, "Two Traditions", excerpt in Heywood, *The Women's Movement Today*, 15

243. Wolf, "Two Traditions," 15.

244. Naomi Wolf, *Promiscuities: The Secret Struggle for Womanhood* (New York: Random House, 1997), 74.

245. White, *Fast Girls*, 150.

246. For more on this phenomenon, see Gornick, "Between 'Girl Power' and 'Reviving Ophelia'"; and Levenstein, *They Didn't See Us Coming*, 4–5.

247. For more on the whiteness of media girl cultures, see Projansky, *Spectacular Girls*, 7–8.

248. See Janice Irvine, *Sexual Cultures and the Construction of Adolescent Identities* (Philadelphia: Temple University Press, 1994), 4–5.

249. Sharon Thompson, *Going All the Way: Teenage Girls' Tales of Sex, Romance, and Pregnancy* (New York: Hill and Wang, 1995), 11, 15.

250. Brumberg, *The Body Project*, 192.

251. For more on the "restriction of sexual speech" in this era, see Irvine, *Talk About Sex*, 1–4, 12.

CHAPTER 4 — THE THIRD WAVE AND THE THIRD WAY

1. Ann Powers, "No Longer Rock's Playthings," *New York Times: Arts and Leisure*, 14 February 1993, Riot Grrrl Publicity Collection, MSS 316, box 1, folder 3, Fales Library and Special Collections, New York University Libraries.

2. Powers, "No Longer Rock's Playthings."

3. Anonymous letter writer, *Girl Germs* zine, no. 4, 1992, ed. Molly Neuman and Allison Wolfe, Tammy Rae Carland Zine Collection, MSS 320, box 4, folder 11, Fales Library and Special Collections, New York University Libraries.

4. Thanks to Dagmar Herzog for conversations on this topic. For more on the 1990s as a point of tension for young women in the United States, see Joan Jacobs Brumberg, *The Body Project: An Intimate History of American Girls* (New York: Random House, 1997), 249.

5. Wahneema Lubiano, "Black Ladies, Welfare Queens, and State Minstrels: Ideological War by Narrative Means," in *Race-ing Justice, En-gendering Power: Essays on Anita Hill, Clarence Thomas, and the Construction of Social Reality*, ed. Toni Morrison (New York: Pantheon Books, 1992), 323–363.

6. Sarah Projansky, *Spectacular Girls: Media Fascination and Celebrity Culture* (New York: New York University Press, 2014), 7.

7. Projansky, *Spectacular Girls*, 7.

8. For more on unexpected positions within the culture wars, see Kristin Luker, *When Sex Goes to School: Warring Views on Sex—and Sex Education—since the Sixties* (New York: W. W. Norton, 2006), 92–93; Dagmar Herzog, *Sex in Crisis: The New Sexual Revolution and the Future of American Politics* (New York: Basic Books, 2008), xii–xiii; and Janice Irvine, *Talk about Sex: The Battle over Sex Education in the United States* (Berkeley: University of California Press, 2002), 1–4, 7, 12.

9. See Irvine, *Talk About Sex*, 1–4, 7, 12.

10. Astrid Henry, "From a Mindset to a Movement: Feminism since 1990," in *Feminism Unfinished: A Short, Surprising History of American Women's Movements*, ed. Dorothy Sue Cobble, Linda Gordon, and Astrid Henry (New York: Liveright, 2014), 148.

11. Henry, "From a Mindset to a Movement," 148.

12. Henry, "From a Mindset to a Movement," 148.

13. Shirley Gutierrez, "A Woman's Place Is . . . ," *Frighten the Horses* 9 (Spring 1992), 46, Tammy Rae Carland Riot Grrrl Zine Collection 1988–2002, MSS 320, box 4, folder 1, Fales Library and Special Collections, New York University Libraries.

14. For more on the varied receptions of sexual harassment cases in this era, see R. Marie Griffith, *Moral Combat: How Sex Divided American Christians and Fractured American Politics* (New York: Basic Books, 2017), 241–244; and Robert O. Self, *All in the Family: The Realignment of American Democracy since the 1960s* (New York: Hill and Wang, 2012), 415–418.

15. Letter to Senate, printed in Anita Hill, *Speaking Truth to Power* (New York: Doubleday, 1997), 69.

16. Hill, *Speaking Truth to Power*, 69–70.

17. Hill, *Speaking Truth to Power*, 78–79.

18. Hill, *Speaking Truth to Power*, 2.

19. This is discussed by Deborah Siegel in *Sisterhood, Interrupted: From Radical Women to Grrrls Gone Wild* (New York: Palgrave Macmillan, 2007), 111–114; and in Henry, "From a Mindset to a Movement," 147–151.

20. First quote on "terrain" from Leslie Heywood and Jennifer Drake, introduction to *Third Wave Agenda: Being Feminist, Doing Feminism* (Minneapolis: University of Minnesota Press, 1997), cited by Catherine M. Orr, in "Charting the Currents of the Third Wave," *Hypatia* 12, no. 3 (August 1997): 29–45. Second, longer quotation from Kimberly Springer, "Third Wave Black Feminism?," *Signs* 27, no. 4 (Summer 2002): 106. See also Lisa Levenstein, *They Didn't See Us Coming: The Hidden History of Feminism in the Nineties* (New York: Basic Books, 2020), 189.

21. See Kimberlé Crenshaw, "Demarginalizing the Intersection of Race and Sex: A Black Feminist Critique of Antidiscrimination Doctrine, Feminist Theory and Antiracist Politics," *University of Chicago Legal Forum* 140 (1989), 139–167.

22. For more on this, see Levenstein, *They Didn't See Us Coming*, 189.

23. For more on this, see Levenstein, *They Didn't See Us Coming*, 189.

24. Becky Thompson, "Multiracial Feminism: Recasting the Chronology of Second Wave Feminism," *Feminist Studies* 28 (Summer 2002): 345.

25. Toni Morrison, "Introduction: Friday on the Potomac," in *Race-ing Justice, Engendering Power: Essays on Anita Hill, Clarence Thomas, and the Construction of Social Reality*, ed. Toni Morrison (New York: Pantheon Books, 1992), vii–xxx.

26. Lubiano, "Black Ladies, Welfare Queens, and State Minstrels," first quote from 344 and second from 350.

27. Lubiano, "Black Ladies, Welfare Queens, and State Minstrels," 350.

28. Ellen Willis, "Typed speech about Monica Lewinsky," Ellen Willis Papers, folder 10.31, Schlesinger Library, Radcliffe Institute, Harvard University.

29. Debra Haffner, interview by Janice M. Irvine, 2010–2011, Schlesinger Library, Radcliffe Institute, Harvard University.

30. Henry, "From a Mindset to a Movement," 147; and Siegel, *Sisterhood Interrupted*.

31. Henry, "From a Mindset to a Movement," 151.

32. For more problems with feminist wave theory, see Springer, "Third Wave Black Feminism?"; and Nancy Hewitt, ed., *No Permanent Waves: Recasting Histories of U.S. Feminism* (New Brunswick, NJ: Rutgers University Press, 2010).

33. Henry, "From a Mindset to a Movement," 159–161.

34. Siegel, *Sisterhood Interrupted*, 111.

35. Henry, "From a Mindset to a Movement," 147.

36. Rebecca Walker, "Becoming the Third Wave," *Ms. Magazine* 11 (1992): 39, https://teachrock.org/wp-content/uploads/Handout-1-Rebecca-Walker-%E2%80%9CI-Am-the-Third-Wave%E2%80%9D.pdf?x96081.

37. Walker, "Becoming the Third Wave," 39.

38. Walker, "Becoming the Third Wave," 41.

39. For more history of the organization, see "Third Wave History" at http://www.thirdwavefund.org/history--past-initiatives.html.

40. This was true of many women of color activist groups in this period; see Levenstein, *They Didn't See Us Coming*, 165.

41. Rebecca Walker, "Editor's Letter," *3Wave News* (Summer 1994), Third Wave Foundation Records, box 1, David M. Rubenstein Rare Book & Manuscript Library, Duke University. See also Levenstein, *They Didn't See Us Coming*, 13.

42. See Brenda E. Stevenson, *The Contested Murder of Latasha Harlins: Justice, Gender, and the Origins of the LA Riots* (New York: Oxford University Press, 2013), xvii.

43. Brenda Stevenson discussed how Harlins was not considered a victim in the trial for her murder on a panel at "Latasha Harlins and the Victimization of Black Girls," Hammer Museum, Los Angeles, 29 March 2017, https://hammer.ucla.edu/programs-events/2017/03/latasha-harlins-the-victimization-of-black-girls. For more on race, youth, and vulnerability, see Joseph J. Fischel, "Pornographic Protections? Itineraries of Childhood Innocence," *Law, Culture and the Humanities* 12, no. 2 (June 2016): 206–220.

44. Walker, "Editor's Letter."

45. "Third Wave History," Third Wave Fund, https://www.thirdwavefund.org/history--past-initiatives.html.

46. Ellen Willis, "Contradictions of Late Feminism: In Internal Debate (drafts)," 1992, Ellen Willis Papers, folder 7.25, Schlesinger Library, Radcliffe Institute, Harvard University.

47. Faye Wattleton, *Life on the Line* (New York: Ballantine Books, 1996), 213.

48. Quote from Wattleton, *Life on the Line*, 214. See also Feminist Majority Foundation, "Abortion Denied: Shattering Young Women's Lives," 1991, Nicole Armenta Collection, Schlesinger Library, Radcliffe Institute, Harvard University.

49. Wattleton, *Life on the Line*, 214.

50. Siegel, *Sisterhood Interrupted*, 118.

51. Sara Marcus, *Girls to the Front: The True Story of the Riot Grrrl Revolution* (New York: Harper Perennial, 2010), 18, 20–21.

52. Ellen Willis to *Glamour* Magazine, Ellen Willis Papers, box 3, Schlesinger Library, Radcliffe Institute, Harvard University.

53. For more on the Moynihan Report and its legacy, see Dorothy Roberts, *Killing the Black Body: Race, Reproduction, and the Meaning of Liberty* (New York: Vintage Books, 1999); Laura Briggs, *How All Politics Became Reproductive Politics: From Welfare Reform to Foreclosure to Trump* (Oakland: University of California Press, 2017); Lee Rainwater, *The Moynihan Report and the Politics of Controversy* (Cambridge, MA: MIT Press, 1967); Carl Ginsburg, *Race and Media: The Enduring Life of the Moynihan Report* (New York: Institute for Media Analysis, 1989); James T. Patterson, *America's Struggle against Poverty in the Twentieth Century* (Cambridge, MA: Harvard University Press, 2000) and Patterson, *Freedom Is Not Enough: The Moynihan Report and America's Struggle over Black Family Life from LBJ to Obama* (New York: Basic Books, 2010); Daniel Geary, *Beyond Civil Rights: The Moynihan Report and Its Legacy* (Philadelphia: University of Pennsylvania Press, 2015); Susan D. Greenbaum, *Blaming the Poor: The Long Shadow of the Moynihan Report on Cruel Images about Poverty* (New Brunswick, NJ: Rutgers University Press, 2015); Linda Gordon, *Women, the State, and Welfare* (Madison: University of Wisconsin Press, 1990); Theda Skocpol, *Protecting Soldiers and Mothers: The Political Origins of Social Policy in the United States* (Cambridge, MA: Belknap Press of Harvard University Press, 1992); and Michael B. Katz, *In the Shadow of the Poorhouse: A Social History of Welfare in America* (New York: Basic Books, 1996).

54. "Dan Quayle vs. Murphy Brown," *Time*, 1 June 1992, http://content.time.com/time /magazine/article/0,9171,975627,00.html.

55. See Bill Carter, "Back Talk from 'Murphy Brown' to Dan Quayle: The First Fall Episode Is to Wreak Something Like Revenge," *New York Times*, 20 July 1992, C14. Ellen Willis discusses the negative impact of the "Murphy Brown" speech in Willis to *Glamour* Magazine, Ellen Willis Papers, box 3: Correspondence, Schlesinger Library, Radcliffe Institute, Harvard University. Evidence of the continued support for the TV show and for its retort to Quayle's remarks can be seen in Rick Du Brow, "'Murphy Brown' to Dan Quayle: Read Our Ratings: Television: The Series' Response to the Vice President Draws 70 Million Viewers, Keying a Big Monday Night for CBS," *Los Angeles Times*, 23 September 1992. Further discussion of the criticism leveled against the speech can be seen in Steve Proffitt, "Los Angeles Times Interview: Dan Quayle: The Vice President on Values, Clinton, and the Campaign," *Los Angeles Times*, 11 October 1992.

56. See "Family Values: Editorial," *Ms.* 5, no. 1 (1994); and Nancy Lesko, *Act Your Age! A Cultural Construction of Adolescence* (New York: Routledge, 2012), 178.

57. Briggs, *How All Politics Became Reproductive Politics*, 70–71, 73.

58. Alesha Doan and Joan Calterone Williams, *The Politics of Virginity: Abstinence in Sex Education* (Westport, CT: Praeger, 2008), 30. See also Self, *All in the Family*, 414.

59. The "welfare" whiteboard can be seen in *The War Room*, directed by Chris Hegedus and D. A. Pennebaker (October Films, 1992). The second quote here is from Bill Clinton's autobiography, *My Life* (New York: Knopf, 2004), 271–272.

60. Clinton, *My Life*, 271–272.

61. Hegedus and Pennebaker, *The War Room*.

62. Hegedus and Pennebaker, *The War Room*.

63. Siegel, *Sisterhood Interrupted*, 117.

64. Siegel, *Sisterhood Interrupted*, 117.

65. Hegedus and Pennebaker, *The War Room*.

66. Siegel, *Sisterhood Interrupted*, 118.

67. Siegel, *Sisterhood Interrupted*, 117.

68. Siegel, *Sisterhood Interrupted*, 118.

69. See Siegel, *Sisterhood Interrupted*, 117; and Gil Troy on her "messy melange of symbols" as a feminist in Gil Troy, *Hillary Rodham Clinton: Polarizing First Lady* (Lawrence: University Press of Kansas, 2006), 43.

70. Barbara Burrell, "The Clintons and Gender Politics," in *The Postmodern Presidency: Bill Clinton's Legacy in U.S. Politics*, ed. Steven E. Schier (Pittsburgh: University of Pittsburgh Press, 2000), 239.

71. This is discussed by a number of contributors to *The Postmodern Presidency*, including Burrell, "Gender Politics," 239; and James L. Guth, "Clinton and the Culture Wars," 208.

72. Donald T. Critchlow, *Intended Consequences: Birth Control, Abortion, and the Federal Government in Modern America* (New York: Oxford University Press, 1999), 221.

73. Burrell, "Gender Politics," 240.

74. Critchlow, *Intended Consequences*, 221.

75. "Don't Ask, Don't Tell" is used as shorthand to refer to the Department of Defense Directive 1304.26, 21 December 1993, The Climate Change and Public Health Law Site, LSU Law Center, Louisiana State University http://biotech.law.lsu.edu/blaw/dodd/corres/html2 /d130426x.htm.

76. Adam Clymer, "The 1994 Elections: Congress the Overview; G.O.P. Celebrates Its Sweep to Power; Clinton Vows to Find Common Ground," *New York Times*, 10 November 1994.

77. Clymer, "The 1994 Elections."

78. Clymer, "The 1994 Election." See also Self, *All in the Family*, 413.

79. Levenstein, *They Didn't See Us Coming*, 5.

80. For more on the history of organizing against welfare reform in this era led by women of color, see Levenstein, "Tackling Women's Poverty from Global Perspectives," chapter 7 in *They Didn't See Us Coming*.

81. Linda Burnham, "Taking It Out on Women and Children," *Sister to Sister/S2S: Newsletter of the Women of Color Resource Center*, vol. 1, no. 4, Winter 1995, Women of Color Resource Center Records, box 1, Smith College Special Collections, 1. Biographical detail from Linda Burnham, interview by Loretta J. Ross, transcript of video recording, 18 March 2005, Voices of Feminism Oral History Project, Sophia Smith Collection, Smith College, ii, https://www.smith.edu/libraries/libs/ssc/vof/transcripts/Burnham.pdf. For further biographical details on Linda Burnham, see Levenstein, *They Didn't See Us Coming*, 82.

82. Burnham, "Taking It Out on Women and Children," 4.

83. "Flyer: Rally for Women's Lives," Mandy Carter Papers 1970–2013, box 120, David M. Rubenstein Rare Book & Manuscript Library, Duke University.

84. See Luker, *When Sex Goes to School*, 92–93; Herzog, *Sex in Crisis*, xii–xiii; and Irvine, *Talk about Sex, 7*.

85. See Irvine, 1–4, 7, 12.

86. Douglas Jehl, "Surgeon General Forced to Resign by White House," *New York Times*, 10 December 1994.

87. Jehl, "Surgeon General Forced to Resign."

88. Dan Burton, cited in Judith Levine, *Harmful to Minors: The Perils of Protecting Children from Sex* (Minneapolis: University of Minnesota Press, 2002), 185.

89. "Political Irony: Joycelyn Elders Fired by Clinton," ACT UP NY, http://www.actupny .org/reports/elders.html.

90. See Irvine, *Talk About Sex*, 1–4.

91. See Irvine, *Talk About Sex*.

92. All biographical information on Elders from Joycelyn M. Elders, *Joycelyn Elders, M.D.: From Sharecropper's Daughter to Surgeon General of the United States of America* (New York: Morrow, 1996).

93. Jehl, "Surgeon General Forced to Resign."

94. ACT UP NY, "Political Irony."

95. William J. Clinton, "Statement on Senate Action Confirming Joycelyn Elders as Surgeon General," 7 September 1993, in *Public Papers of the Presidents of the United States*, book 2 (Washington, DC: Government Printing Office, 1993), 1448.

96. See Jehl, "Surgeon General Forced to Resign"; Siegel, *Sisterhood Interrupted*, 118; and Guth, "Clinton and the Culture Wars," 208. See also Elders, *From Sharecropper's Daughter to Surgeon General*, 1–8.

97. The wording of "sexual welfare" is used in Fischel, "Pornographic Protections."

98. Letter to President Clinton, signed by Women of African Descent for Reproductive Justice: A national Pro-Choice Coalition, 13 February 1995, SisterSong Women of Color Reproductive Justice Collective Records, box 1, Smith College Special Collections.

99. 140 Cong. Rec. H47 (28 September 1994) (statement of Rep. John Doolittle).

100. Haffner, interview.

101. M. Joycelyn Elders, "Joycelyn Elders Puts Congress on Blast," interview by Cynthia Gordy, *The Root*, 18 April 2011, http://www.theroot.com/views/root-interview-jocelyn-elders.

102. See Irvine, *Talk About Sex.*

103. Irvine, *Talk about Sex*, 197.

104. Jehl, "Surgeon General Forced to Resign."

105. Jehl, "Surgeon General Forced to Resign."

106. Guth, "Clinton and the Culture Wars," 205.

107. Guth, "Clinton and the Culture Wars," 205.

108. Ellen Willis, "With Friends Like These," *Village Voice*, 2 August 1994, Ellen Willis Papers, Schlesinger Library, Radcliffe Institute, Harvard University.

109. Leora Tanenbaum, *Slut! Growing Up Female with a Bad Reputation* (New York: Seven Stories Press, 1999), 241.

110. Jehl, "Surgeon General Forced to Resign."

111. Willis, "With Friends Like These."

112. For more on the long history of this, see Briggs, *How All Politics Became Reproductive Politics*, 53.

113. See Briggs, *How All Politics Became Reproductive Politics*, 53.

114. President William Jefferson Clinton's proposal for welfare reform to the 103rd Congress, cited in A. T. Geronimus, "Teen Childbearing and Personal Responsibility: An Alternative View," *Political Science Quarterly* 112 (Fall 1997): 406.

115. Doan and Williams, *The Politics of Virginity*, 32.

116. Geronimus, "Teen Childbearing," 408.

117. Congressional Record of the 104th Congress, "Recognizing Successful Teen Pregnancy Prevention Programs," House of Representatives, 17 April 1996, p. H3548; and "Conference Report on HR 3734, Personal Responsibility and Work Opportunity Act of 1996," House of Representatives, 30 July 1996, p. H8831.

118. Doan and Williams, *The Politics of Virginity*, 32.

119. Geronimus, "Teen Childbearing," 407.

120. This has been argued in Cris Mayo, "Gagged and Bound: Sex Education, Secondary Virginity, and the Welfare Reform Act," in *Philosophy of Education 1998*, ed. Steve Tozer (Urbana: Philosophy of Education Society, 1999), 408; and Geronimus, "Teen Childbearing," 407–408. For a longer discussion on the racist history of work-based models of welfare, see Briggs, *How All Politics Became Reproductive Politics*. See also Luker, *When Sex Goes to School*, 92–93; Herzog, *Sex in Crisis*, xii–xiii; and Irvine, *Talk about Sex, 7.*

121. See Geronimus, "Teen Childbearing," 406.

122. For more on the treatment of young women of color on welfare in this era, see Cathy Cohen, "Punks, Bulldaggers, and Welfare Queens: The Radical Potential of Queer Politics?," *GLQ* 3, no. 4 (1997): 437–465.

123. Senator Howell Heflin (D-AL), in the Congressional Record, "Personal Responsibility and Work Opportunity Reconciliation Act of 1996—Conference Report," Senate, 1 August 1996, p. S3987.

124. The Personal Responsibility and Work Opportunity Reconciliation Act of 1996, Title I—Block Grants for Temporary Assistance for Needy Families (TANF), 22 August 1996, 2110.

125. TANF, 2111.

126. Briggs, *How All Politics Became Reproductive Politics*, 53.

127. See Joseph J. Fischel, *Sex and Harm in the Age of Consent* (Minneapolis: University of Minnesota Press, 2016), 91; and Briggs, *How All Politics Became Reproductive Politics*, 54.

128. Fischel, *Sex and Harm in the Age of Consent*, 92.

129. TANF, 2111.

130. Fischel, *Sex and Harm in the Age of Consent*, 92.

131. Carolyn E. Cocca, "From 'Welfare Queen' to 'Exploited Teen': Welfare Dependency, Statutory Rape," *NWSA Journal* 14 (Summer 2002): 58.

132. Senator Barbara Mikulski (D-MD), "Personal Responsibility and Work Opportunity Reconciliation Act of 1996—Conference Report," S3988.

133. Alan Guttmacher Institute, *Sex and America's Teeangers* (1994), cited in Cocca, "From 'Welfare Queen' to 'Exploited Teen,'" 62.

134. Michelle Oberman, cited in Cocca, "From 'Welfare Queen' to 'Exploited Teen,'" 67.

135. Quote from Fischel, *Sex and Harm in the Age of Consent*, 92; see also Cocca, citing Joycelyn Elders, in "From 'Welfare Queen' to 'Exploited Teen,'" 67.

136. Fischel, *Sex and Harm in the Age of Consent*, 91–92.

137. Janet R. Jakobsen, "'He Has Wronged America and Women': Clinton's Sexual Conservatism," in *Our Monica, Ourselves: The Clinton Affair and the National Interest*, ed. Lauren Berlant and Lisa Duggan (New York: New York University Press, 2000), 300.

138. H.R. 4, sec. 100 (104th Congress), cited in Mayo, "Gagged and Bound," 310.

139. Linda Burnham, "Racism in US Welfare Policy—a Human Rights Issue," in *Report to the UN World Conference Against Racism, Racial Discrimination, Xenophobia and Related Intolerance*, Durban, South Africa, 28 August–7 September 2001, 101, Women of Color Resource Center Records, box 1, Smith College Special Collections.

140. Herzog, *Sex in Crisis*, 121.

141. Roberts, *Killing the Black Body*, 18–19.

142. Jakobsen, "He Has Wronged America and Women," 300. See also Self, *All in the Family*, 413.

143. Patricia Hill Collins, *Black Sexual Politics: African Americans, Gender, and the New Racism* (New York: Routledge, 2004), 78.

144. Roberts, *Killing the Black Body*, 18.

145. Cohen, "Punks, Bulldaggers, and Welfare Queens," first quote from 438 and second from 442.

146. Nina Perales, "A Welfare System Check-Up," *Instantes: Latina Initiative Quarterly Newsletter*, vol. 3, no. 4, December 1994, 9, National Latina Health Organization Records, box 4, Smith College Special Collections.

147. Linda Burnham, writing in *Sister to Sister/S2S: Newsletter of the Women of Color Resource Center*, 4, Women of Color Resource Center Records, box 1, Smith College Special Collections. For more on the significance of the United Nations Fourth World Conference on Women in Beijing in 1995, see Levenstein, *They Didn't See Us Coming*.

148. Burnham, in *Sister to Sister*, 4.

149. "WISE Reaches Out to Our Girls," *Sister to Sister/S2S: Newsletter of the Women of Color Resource Center*, 4, Women of Color Resource Center Records, box 1, Smith College Special Collections.

150. Brigette M. Moore, "Envisioning a Black Grrrl Revolution: A Problackgrrrl-Feminist Founders Statement," *See It? Tell It. Change It!*, Newsletter of the Third Wave Foundation, Third Wave Foundation Records, box 1, David M. Rubenstein Rare Book & Manuscript Library, Duke University.

151. "Voices, Power, Choices: National Young Women's Day of Action 1998," *The Fight for Reproductive Freedom: A Newsletter for Student Activists*, Produced by the Civil Liberties and Public Policy Program at Hampshire College, Fall 1998, vol. 13, no. 1, 3, Third Wave Foundation Records, box 3, David M. Rubenstein Rare Book & Manuscript Library, Duke University.

152. Teen Outreach Reproductive Challenge of New York City, in "Voices, Power, Choices," 8.

153. For more on this history, see Michelle Alexander, *The New Jim Crow: Mass Incarceration in the Age of Colorblindness* (New York: New Press, 2010).

154. Elizabeth Martinez, "Be Down with the Brown: Thousands of Raza Youth Blowout of School to Protest Racism," *Z Magazine*, November 1994, 40, National Latina Health Organization Records, box 7, Smith College Special Collections.

155. Martinez, "Be Down with the Brown," 40.

156. Martinez, "Be Down with the Brown," 40.

157. Flyer: Third Wave Remembers Amadou Diallo, 1999, Third Wave Foundation Records, box 1, David M. Rubenstein Rare Book & Manuscript Library, Duke University.

158. For more on unexpected positions within the culture wars on sexuality, see Luker, *When Sex Goes to School*, 92–93; Herzog, *Sex in Crisis*, xii–xiii; and Irvine, *Talk about Sex*, 7.

159. Brendan O'Connor, "Policies, Principles, and Polls: Bill Clinton's Third Way Welfare Politics, 1992–1996," *Australian Journal of Politics and History* 48, no. 3 (September 2002): 396–411. See also Levenstein, *They Didn't See Us Coming*, 122; and Self, *All in the Family*, 411.

160. For more on this, see Briggs, *How All Politics Became Reproductive Politics*. See also Self, *All in the Family*, 399.

161. Mayo, "Gagged and Bound," 310.

162. Mindy Bingham and Sandy Stryker, *Things Will Be Different for My Daughter: A Practical Guide for Building Her Self-Esteem and Self-Reliance* (New York: Penguin Books, 1995), xi.

163. For more on this, see Projansky, *Spectacular Girls*.

164. See Projansky, *Spectacular Girls*, introduction.

165. Annette Lawson and Deborah L. Rhode, *The Politics of Pregnancy: Adolescent Sexuality and Public Policy* (New Haven, CT: Yale University Press, 1993), 105.

166. Lesko, *Act Your Age!*, 137.

167. Roberts, *Killing the Black Body*, 104–149; and Briggs, *How All Politics Became Reproductive Politics*, 128.

168. Roberts, *Killing the Black Body*, 114.

169. "Depo-Provera Research/Survey Project," National Latina Health Organization, December 1995, National Latina Health Organization Records, box 7, Smith College Special Collections.

170. "Depo-Provera Research/Survey Project."

171. Eleanor Hinton Hoytt quoted in a news article by LaTicia D. Greggs in the *Chicago Defender*, 23 January 1993, 5, Black Women's Health Imperative Records, box 3, Smith College Special Collections.

196 NOTES TO PAGES 105–108

172. Barbara Karkabi, "Minority Women Stress Health Choices," *Houston Chronicle*, 24 January 1993, Black Women's Health Imperative Records, box 3, Smith College Special Collections.

173. Olga Morales Aguirre, quoted in Karbaki, "Minority Women Stress Health Choices."

174. Doan and Williams, *The Politics of Virginity*, 33.

175. U.S. Department of Health and Human Services, Health Resources and Services Administration, Maternal and Child Health Bureau, "Understanding Title V of the Social Security Act" (1996), 14.

176. The Personal Responsibility and Work Opportunity Reconciliation Act of 1996, Title V, Section 510 (b) of Title V, Separate Program for Abstinence Education, 2354.

177. See Self, *All in the Family*, 412.

178. "Understanding Title V," 14.

179. For an expansive history on the role of welfare within the rise of neoliberalism, see Briggs, *How All Politics Became Reproductive Politics*, 9.

180. Nancy Kendall, *The Sex Education Debates* (Chicago: University of Chicago Press, 2013), 5.

181. Bonnie Nelson Trudell, *Doing Sex Education: Gender Politics and Schooling* (New York: Routledge, 1993), 2; and Mayo, "Gagged and Bound," 311.

182. This is explored in Christine Gardner, *Making Chastity Sexy: The Rhetoric of Evangelical Abstinence Campaigns* (Berkeley: University of California Press, 2011). See also Herzog, "Saved from Sex," chapter 4 in *Sex in Crisis*, and Irvine, *Talk About Sex*.

183. Mayo, "Gagged and Bound," 314.

184. Michel Foucault, *The History of Sexuality* (New York: Pantheon Books, 1978), 18.

185. Trudell, *Doing Sex Education*, 3.

186. Sex Respect: The Option of True Sexual Freedom, *Student Workbook*, Kristen Luker Papers, carton 1, Schlesinger Library, Radcliffe Institute, Harvard University.

187. "Sex, Lies, and Politics—Abstinence-Only Curricula in California Public Schools," a joint report from the Public Media Center and the Applied Research Center, 1997, Kristen Luker Papers, carton 2, Schlesinger Library, Radcliffe Institute, Harvard University, 21.

188. "Sex Lies and Politics," 21.

189. Haffner, interview.

190. Haffner, interview.

191. Debra Haffner, *Facing Facts: Sexual Health for America's Adolescents* (National Commission on Adolescent Sexual Health: Sexuality Information and Education Council of the United States, 1995), Debra Haffner Papers, carton 1, Schlesinger Library, Radcliffe Institute, Harvard University.

192. Haffner, *Facing Facts*.

193. For more on the histories of sexual speech and sex education, see Irvine, *Talk About Sex*.

194. Haffner, interview.

195. Leslie Kantor, interview by Janice M. Irvine, 2010–2011, Schlesinger Library, Radcliffe Institute, Harvard University.

196. Haffner, interview.

197. Haffner, interview.

198. These studies are discussed in "Sex Lies and Politics," 56; and "The California Wellness Foundation Teenage Pregnancy Prevention Initiative: 1997 Public Education Campaign," Debra Haffner Papers, carton 1, Schlesinger Library, Radcliffe Institute, Harvard University.

199. Kantor, interview; Haffner, interview.

200. See Irvine, *Talk About Sex*, 1–4, 12.

201. Kantor, interview.

202. Kantor, interview.

203. Haffner, interview; and Debra Haffner, "The Third Special Issue on HIV/AIDS Education and Prevention in Rural Communities," Health Education Monograph series 16 (1998), 48, Debra Haffner Papers, carton 1, Schlesinger Library, Radcliffe Institute, Harvard University.

204. Siegel, *Sisterhood, Interrupted*, 114.

205. Siegel, *Sisterhood Interrupted*, 114.

206. Siegel, *Sisterhood Interrupted*, 114.

207. Berlant and Duggan, introduction to *Our Monica, Ourselves*, 4.

208. Simone Weil Davis, "The Door Ajar: The Erotics of Hypocrisy in the White House Scandal," in Berlant and Duggan, *Our Monica, Ourselves*, 89.

209. Berlant and Duggan, introduction, 4.

210. Monica Lewinsky, "Emerging from 'The House of Gaslight' in the Age of #MeToo," *Vanity Fair*, 25 February 2018, https://www.vanityfair.com/news/2018/02/monica-lewinsky -in-the-age-of-metoo.

211. Lewinsky, "Emerging from 'The House of Gaslight.'"

212. Lewinsky, "Emerging from 'The House of Gaslight.'" For more on how the dichotomy between "victim" and "empowered" was discussed at the time in relation to Anita Hill and Monica Lewinsky, see Self, *All in the Family*, 418.

213. Franklin Foer, "Feminism, Clinton, and Harassment," *Slate*, 19 April 1998.

214. Ellen Willis, "Moralism and the Body Politic," *Newsday*, 1 February 1998, Ellen Willis Papers, folder 7.6, Schlesinger Library, Radcliffe Institute, Harvard University.

215. Willis, "Moralism and the Body Politic."

216. Ellen Willis, "Typed speech about sexuality of Monica Lewinsky," Ellen Willis Papers, folder 10.31, Schlesinger Library, Radcliffe Institute, Harvard University.

217. Foer, "Feminism, Clinton, and Harassment."

218. Quote from Catharine Mackinnon, "Harassment Law under Siege," *New York Times*, 5 March 1998, A29; see also Foer, "Feminism, Clinton, and Harassment."

219. Mackinnon, "Harassment Law under Siege."

220. Mackinnon, "Harassment Law under Siege."

221. Foer, "Feminism, Clinton, and Harassment."

222. Gloria Steinem, "Why Feminists Support Clinton," *New York Times*, 22 March 1998.

223. Steinem, "Why Feminists Support Clinton."

224. Steve Dunleavy in the *New York Post*, cited in Willis, "Moralism and the Body Politic."

225. "Memo: Young Women Speak Out!," 8 October 1998, Third Wave Foundation Records, box 3, David M. Rubenstein Rare Book & Manuscript Library, Duke University.

226. Fax from Liz Schiller of the Institute for Women's Policy Research to Vivien Labaton, "Re: young women on Clinton + election-proposed coalition," 9 October 1998, Third Wave Foundation Records, box 3, David M. Rubenstein Rare Book & Manuscript Library, Duke University.

227. See Judith Levine, *Harmful to Minors: The Perils of Protecting Children from Sex* (Minneapolis: University of Minnesota Press, 2002), 100.

228. Willis, "Moralism and the Body Politic."

229. Weil Davis, "The Door Ajar," 89.

230. Weil Davis, "The Door Ajar," 89.

231. Weil Davis, "The Door Ajar," 89.

232. Tomasz Kitlinski, Pawel Leszkowicz, and Joe Lockard, "Monica Dreyfus," in Berlant and Duggan, *Our Monica, Ourselves*, 204.

233. The *National Examiner*, cited by Kitlinski, Leszkowicz, and Lockard in "Monica Dreyfus," 205.

234. Tanenbaum, *Slut!*, 96–97.

235. Laura Kipnis, "The Face That Launched a Thousand Jokes," in Berlant and Duggan, *Our Monica, Ourselves*, 55.

236. Troy, *Hillary Rodham Clinton*, 191.

237. Kitlinski, Leszkowicz, and Lockard, "Monica Dreyfus," 204; and Sex Respect: The Option of True Sexual Freedom.

238. Self, *All in the Family*, 418.

239. Quote from Tanenbaum, *Slut!*, 97, see also Jakobsen, "He Has Wronged America and Women," 306.

240. See Projansky, *Spectacular Girls*, 7; and Briggs, *How All Politics Became Reproductive Politics*, 53, 73.

241. See Irvine, *Talk About Sex*, 1–4, 12.

242. Tanenbaum, *Slut!*, 241. See also see Troy, *Hillary Rodham Clinton*, 191.

243. Troy, *Hillary Rodham Clinton*, 191.

244. Clinton, *My Life*, 809.

245. Susan Wilson, "Talking about the Presidential Scandal in the Classroom," *Education Week*, September 1998, Kristen Luker Papers, carton 2, Schlesinger Library, Radcliffe Institute, Harvard University.

246. Wilson, "Talking about the Presidential Scandal in the Classroom."

CHAPTER 5 — MEDICINE, EDUCATION, AND SEXUALIZATION

1. FBI, "FBI Announces List of 19 Hijackers," press release, 14 September 2001, https://www.fbi.gov/news/pressrel/press-releases/fbi-announces-list-of-19-hijackers.

2. Leslie Dorrough Smith, *Righteous Rhetoric: Sex, Speech, and the Politics of Concerned Women for America* (New York: Oxford University Press, 2014), 56.

3. Smith, *Righteous Rhetoric*, 56.

4. Jerry Falwell, interview by Pat Robertson, *The 700 Club*, Christian Broadcasting Network, 13 September 2001, https://www.youtube.com/watch?v=kMkBgA9_0Q4.

5. Falwell, interview.

6. Smith, *Righteous Rhetoric*, 113.

7. For more on the role of sexuality in the 2000 election, see R. Marie Griffith, *Moral Combat: How Sex Divided American Christians and Fractured American Politics* (New York: Basic Books, 2017), 271–272.

8. The Bushes' discussion of Middle Eastern women is found in Barbara Finlay, *George W. Bush and the War on Women* (New York: Zed Books 20060), 5; and feminist response to this in Deborah Siegel, *Sisterhood Interrupted: From Radical Women to Grrrls Gone Wild* (New York: Palgrave Macmillan 2007), 159.

9. Siegel, *Sisterhood Interrupted*, 159.

10. The description of sexual liberalism and conservatism in this context is laid out in Kristin Luker, *When Sex Goes to School: Warring Views on Sex—and Sex Education—since the 1960s* (New York: W. W. Norton, 2006), 98.

11. Janice Irvine, *Talk about Sex: The Battles over Sex Education in the United States* (Berkeley: University of California Press, 2002), 196.

12. Unexpected ideologies in culture wars over sexuality are discussed in Luker, *When Sex Goes to School*, 92–93; Irvine, *Talk about Sex*, 1–4, 7, 12; and Dagmar Herzog, *Sex in Crisis: The New Sexual Revolution and the Future of American Politics* (New York: Basic Books, 2008), xii–xiii.

13. Kevin M. Kruse, "Compassionate Conservatism: Religion in the Age of George W. Bush," in *The Presidency of George W. Bush: A First Historical Assessment*, ed. Julian Zelizer (Princeton, NJ: Princeton University Press, 2010), 228–230.

14. Discussed in Kruse, "Compassionate Conservatism," 230; and Finlay, *War on Women*, 2.

15. Lauren F. Turek, "Religious Rhetoric and the Evolution of George W. Bush's Political Philosophy," *Journal of American Studies* 48 (November 2014): 976.

16. Finlay, *War on Women*, 2.

17. Kruse, "Compassionate Conservatism," 239.

18. Kruse, "Compassionate Conservatism," 239.

19. These two policy moves are discussed, respectively, in Kruse, "Compassionate Conservatism," 240, and Finlay, *War on Women*, 74.

20. Dorothy Roberts, "Background Paper—'Black Women and Reproductive Health,'" in the conference magazine for the National Coalition on Black Women's Health, 11 April 2003, Washington, DC, Black Women's Health Imperative Records, box 3, Smith College Special Collections, 8.

21. Delores Huerta and Rocio Córdoba, "Parental Notification of Abortions Will Hurt California's Latinos," 4 November 2005, in *Collective Voices: SisterSong Women of Color Reproductive Health Collective*, volume 2, issue 5 (2006), SisterSong Women of Color Reproductive Justice Collective Records, Acc. #11S-09, box 1, Smith College Special Collections.

22. Huerta and Córdoba, "Parental Notification."

23. The precedent set in this area by Clinton is discussed in Sinikka Elliot, *Not My Kid: What Parents Believe about the Sex Lives of Their Teenagers* (New York: New York University Press, 2012), 11; Esther Kaplan, *With God on Their Side: How Christian Fundamentalists Trampled Science, Policy, and Democracy in George W. Bush's White House* (New York: New Press, 2004), 39; E. J. Dionne, *Our Divided Political Heart: The Battle for the American Idea in an Age of Discontent* (New York: Bloomsbury, 2012), 87, 90; Alesha Doan, *The Politics of Virginity: Abstinence in Sex Education* (Westport, CT: Praeger, 2008), 30; and Sara Moslener, *Virgin Nation: Sexual Purity and American Adolescence* (New York: Oxford University Press, 2015), 112.

24. Elliot, *Not My Kid*, 12.

25. Consolidated Appropriations Act 2001, Title II Department of Health and Human Services, 763a-13–14.

26. Sexuality Information and Education Council of the United States, "A History of Abstinence-Only-Until-Marriage (AOUM) Funding," 2019, https://siecus.org/wp-content/uploads/2019/05/AOUM-Funding-History-Report-5.2019.pdf.

27. SIECUS, "A History of AOUM Funding."

28. Kaplan, *God on Their Side*, 52.

29. Finlay, *War on Women*, 50.

30. Jonathan Zimmerman, *Too Hot to Handle: A Global History of Sex Education* (Princeton, NJ: Princeton University Press, 2015), 131.

31. Zimmerman, *Too Hot to Handle*, 131.

32. George W. Bush, State of the Union Address, 2003, http://georgewbush-whitehouse.archives.gov/news/releases/2003/01/20030128-19.html.

33. Bush, State of the Union, 2003.

34. One Hundred and Eighth Congress of the United States of America, "United States Leadership Against HIV/AIDS, Tuberculosis, and Malaria Act of 2003," 5, https://www.govinfo.gov/content/pkg/BILLS-108hr1298enr/pdf/BILLS-108hr1298enr.pdf

35. See John W. Dietrich, "The Politics of PEPFAR: The President's Emergency Plan for AIDS Relief," *Ethics and International Affairs* 21 (September 2007): 277–292.

36. Rosemary Radford Ruether, "Sexual Illiteracy," *Conscience*, Summer 2003, 16, Debra Haffner Papers, carton 1, folder: Press Coverage 2003, Schlesinger Library, Radcliffe Institute, Harvard University.

37. See Herzog, *Sex in Crisis*, 94.

38. SIECUS, "Federal Funding for Abstinence."

39. Department of Health and Human Services, Administration for Children and Families, Community-Based Abstinence Education Program, 2005, 12.

40. Administration for Children and Families, 9.

41. See Herzog, *Sex in Crisis*, 94.

42. Administration for Children and Families, 6.

43. Jessica Valenti, *The Purity Myth: How America's Obsession with Virginity Is Hurting America's Young Women* (Berkeley, CA: Seal Press, 2009), 109.

44. See National Youth Advocacy folder and LGBT Youth Summit folder, Mandy Carter Papers, box 139, David M. Rubenstein Rare Book & Manuscript Library, Duke University.

45. Application Information and Form, the Audre Lorde Project Young Women's Leadership Training Program, 2000, Southerners on New Ground Records, 1993–2015, box 1, David M. Rubenstein Rare Book & Manuscript Library, Duke University.

46. "Make a Difference Now!," *See It? Tell It. Change It!*, Newsletter of the Third Wave Foundation, Fall/Winter 2003, Third Wave Foundation Papers, box 1, David M. Rubenstein Rare Book & Manuscript Library, Duke University.

47. "Happy Summer from 3rd Wave!," *See It? Tell It. Change It!*, Newsletter of the Third Wave Foundation, Summer 2006, vol. 1, issue 2, Third Wave Foundation Papers, box 1, David M. Rubenstein Rare Book & Manuscript Library, Duke University.

48. "I Spy Transphobia," *See It? Tell It. Change It!*, Newsletter of the Third Wave Foundation, Summer 2006, vol. 1, issue 2, Third Wave Foundation Papers, box 1, David M. Rubenstein Rare Book & Manuscript Library, Duke University.

49. Department of Health & Human Services, Administration for Children and Families, Healthy Marriage Demonstration Grants 2006, https://www.healthymarriageinfo.org/wp-content/uploads/2017/12/federalrfp_4.3.pdf; also discussed in Valenti, *The Purity Myth*, 138.

50. Political Research Associates & Women of Color Resource Center, "Pushed to the Altar," Report on Marriage Promotion, Women of Color Resource Center Records, box 1, Smith College Special Collections.

51. The emergence of an abstinence "movement" in this period is considered in Doan, *Politics of Virginity*, 17; Valenti, *The Purity Myth*, 23; and Christine J. Gardner, *Making Chastity Sexy: The Rhetoric of Evangelical Abstinence Campaigns* (Berkeley: University of California Press, 2011), 3.

52. Leslee Unruh cited in Irvine, *Talk about Sex*, 99.

53. Moslener, *Virgin Nation*, 112.

54. Leslie Kantor, interview by Janice M. Irvine, 2010–2011, Schlesinger Library, Radcliffe Institute, Harvard University.

55. The extent of the abstinence movement is discussed in Doan, *Politics of Virginity*, 7; and in Gardner, *Making Chastity Sexy*.

56. Moslener, *Virgin Nation*, 130.

57. Moslener, *Virgin Nation*, 116–117.

58. Moslener, *Virgin Nation*, 145.

59. Valenti, *The Purity Myth*, 65.

60. Discussion of musical appropriation in Valenti, *The Purity Myth*, 100; discussion of consumerism in Moslener, *Virgin Nation*, 131.

61. Valenti, *The Purity Myth*, 110.

62. See Irvine, *Talk About Sex*.

63. This is argued in Gardner, *Making Chastity Sexy*; Valenti, *The Purity Myth*, 65; Irvine, *Talk About Sex*; Herzog, *Sex in Crisis*; and Cris Mayo, "Gagged and Bound: Sex Education, Secondary Virginity, and the Welfare Reform Act," in *Philosophy of Education 1998*, ed. Steve Tozer (Urbana: Philosophy of Education Society, 1999).

64. Valenti, *The Purity Myth*, 65. See also Herzog, "Saved from Sex," chapter 4 in *Sex in Crisis*.

65. Michel Foucault, *The History of Sexuality*, vol. 1, *An Introduction* (New York: Pantheon Books, 1978), 18.

66. From Gardner, *Making Chastity Sexy*, 1.

67. Doan, *Politics of Virginity*, 149.

68. Leslee Unruh, quoted in Herzog, *Sex in Crisis*, 99.

69. See Hazel Cills, "The Rise and Fall of the Pop Star Purity Ring," *Jezebel*, 25 January 2018, https://jezebel.com/the-rise-and-fall-of-the-pop-star-purity-ring-1822170318.

70. See Sarah Projansky, *Spectacular Girls: Media Fascination and Celebrity Culture* (New York: New York University Press, 2014), 5–6; and Valenti, *The Purity Myth*, 30. See also recent commentary on the obsession with famous young women's behavior in this period, such as Jessica Bennett, "Speaking of Britney . . . What about All Those Other Women?," *New York Times*, 27 February 2021, https://www.nytimes.com/2021/02/27/style/britney-spears-documentary-jackson-celebrity-reappraisal.html.

71. On delay, see Doan and Williams, *The Politics of Virginity*, 122. For more on the long history of these racist constructions, see Briggs, *How All Politics Became Reproductive Politics*, 53. See also Marnina Gornick, "Between 'Girl Power' and 'Reviving Ophelia': Constituting the Neoliberal Girl Subject," *NWSA Journal* 18, no. 2 (2006): 1–23.

72. Projansky, *Spectacular Girls*, 7–11.

73. Projansky, *Spectacular Girls*, 7–11.

74. Projansky, *Spectacular Girls*, 1.

75. Valenti, *The Purity Myth*, 27.

76. Valenti, *The Purity Myth*, 27. See also Sophie Lewis, introduction to *Full Surrogacy Now! Feminism against Family* (New York: Verso, 2019). 1–29.

77. Jessica Simpson, with Kevin Carr O'Leary, "Eyeshadow Abs," chapter 8 in *Open Book* (New York: HarperCollins, 2021).

78. Doan, *Politics of Virginity*, 122.

79. See Irvine, *Talk About Sex*; Herzog, *Sex in Crisis*; Gardner, *Making Chastity Sexy*; Valenti, *The Purity Myth*; and Mayo, "Gagged and Bound."

80. Debra Haffner, interview by Janice M. Irvine, 2010–2011, Schlesinger Library, Radcliffe Institute, Harvard University

81. Debra Haffner, *A Time to Speak: Why Progressive Religious Leaders Must Find Their Voice on Sexual Justice*, Center for American Progress, 9 June 2006, Debra Haffner Papers, carton 1, folder: Media 2006, Schlesinger Library, Radcliffe Institute, Harvard University.

82. Finlay, *War on Women*, 71.

83. Finlay, *War on Women*, 71.

84. Letter from Kaiser Family Foundation to Kristin Luker, 8 October 2000, Kristin Luker Papers, carton 2, folder on Alliance between Kaiser Family Foundation and *Seventeen* Magazine, 2000–2002, Schlesinger Library, Radcliffe Institute, Harvard University.

85. *Seventeen*, October 2000, Kristin Luker Papers, carton 2, folder on Alliance between Kaiser Family Foundation and *Seventeen* Magazine, 2000–2002, Schlesinger Library, Radcliffe Institute, Harvard University.

86. Sarah Cordi, "Fight for Your Right . . . to Sex Ed," *Girl's Life*, a Choice USA Newsletter, October/November 2002, Choice USA Records, box 3, Smith College Special Collections.

87. Cordi, "Fight for Your Right."

88. "Choice USA Awards Young Reproductive Rights Leaders," press release, 11 March 2005, Choice USA Records, box 2, Smith College Special Collections.

89. Susan Wilson, interview by Janice M. Irvine, 2010–2011, Schlesinger Library, Radcliffe Institute, Harvard University.

90. Wilson, interview.

91. Wilson, interview.

92. *Answers* (formerly *Sex Etc.*), Spring 2006, 7 and 14, Kristin Luker Papers, carton 2, Schlesinger Library, Radcliffe Institute, Harvard University.

93. *Answers*, 7.

94. Wilson, interview.

95. Carol Platt Liebau, *Prude: How the Sex-Obsessed Culture Damages Girls (and America, too!)* (New York: Center Street, 2007), 39.

96. Carlton W. Veazey, "Faith-Based Sexuality Education Breaks the Silence in Black Churches," in *Sacred Places, Civic Purposes: Should Government Help Faith-Based Charity?*, ed. E. J. Dionne Jr. and Ming Hsu Chen (Washington, DC: Brookings Institution Press, 2001), 55. This history has also been addressed, most notably, in Patricia Hill Collins, *Black Sexual Politics: African Americans, Gender, and the New Racism* (New York: Routledge, 2005), 34–44.

97. Veazey, "Faith-Based Sexuality Education Breaks the Silence," 55.

98. Veazey, "Faith-Based Sexuality Education Breaks the Silence," 55.

99. Veazey, "Faith-Based Sexuality Education Breaks the Silence," 56.

100. See E. J. Dionne, *Souled Out: Reclaiming Faith and Politics after the Religious Right* (Princeton, NJ: Princeton University Press, 2008), 48; Luker, *When Sex Goes to School*, 93–95; Herzog, *Sex in Crisis*, xii–xiii; and Irvine, *Talk About Sex*, 7.

101. Choice USA, "Faith and Reproductive Rights: Interview with Luis Ricardo Torres-Rivera," politicalaffairs.net: Marxist Thought Online, 12 June 2005, Choice USA Records, box 3, Smith College Special Collections.

102. Choice USA, "Faith and Reproductive Rights: Interview with Luis Ricardo Torres-Rivera."

103. Choice USA, "Faith and Reproductive Rights: Interview with Luis Ricardo Torres-Rivera."

104. Religious Institute, *A Decade of Dedication, 2001–2011: Celebrating 10 Years Advocating for Sexual Health, Education, and Justice in Faith Communities and Society*, 1, Debra Haffner Papers, carton 1, folder: Religious Institute, Schlesinger Library, Radcliffe Institute, Harvard University.

105. Religious Institute, *A Decade of Dedication, 2001–2011*, 2.

106. Religious Institute, *A Decade of Dedication, 2001–2011*, 1.

107. Religious Institute, *A Time to Speak: Second Edition*, 2005, 23, Debra Haffner Papers, carton 1, folder: Religious Institute 2006–2012, Schlesinger Library, Radcliffe Institute, Harvard University.

108. Leslie Long, *Larchmont Gazette*, 20 May 2005, Debra Haffner Papers, carton 1, folder: 2005 Press Coverage, Schlesinger Library, Radcliffe Institute, Harvard University.

109. W. Evan Golder, "Sex Education for Teens: How Much and How Soon?," *United Church News*, October 2003, Debra Haffner Papers, carton 1, folder: 2003 Press Coverage, Schlesinger Library, Radcliffe Institute, Harvard University.

110. Sara I. McClelland and Michelle Fine, "Embedded Science: Critical Analysis of Abstinence-Only Education Research," *Cultural Studies←—→Critical Methodologies* 8 (2008): 50–81.

111. David Satcher, "The Surgeon General's Call to Action to Promote Sexual Health and Responsible Sexual Behavior," *American Journal of Health Education* 32 (2001), discussed in Deborah Tolman, *Dilemmas of Desire: Teenage Girls Talk about Sexuality* (Cambridge, MA: Harvard University Press, 2002), 3.

112. Kaplan, *God on Their Side*, 213.

113. Kaplan, *God on Their Side*, 213.

114. Valenti, *The Purity Myth*, 118. This issue is also covered in Tolman, *Dilemmas of Desire*, 18.

115. Peter Bearman and Hannah Bruckner, "After the Promise: The STD Consequences of Adolescent Virginity Pledges," *Journal of Adolescent Health* 36 (April 2005), discussed in Kaplan, *God on Their Side*, 216.

116. Representative Henry Waxman (D-CA), *The Content of Federally Funded Abstinence-Only Education Programs*, U.S. House of Representatives Committee on Government Reform, 1 December 2004, discussed in Finlay, *War on Women*, 68–69.

117. Amy Bleakley et al., "Public Opinion on Sex Education in US Schools," *Archives of Pediatric & Adolescent Medicine* 160 (November 2006): 1151.

118. Bleakley et al., "Public Opinion," 1151.

119. For more on consensuses over sexuality and unexpected culture war positions, see Dionne, *Souled Out*; Herzog, *Sex in Crisis*; Irvine, *Talk about Sex*; and Luker, *When Sex Goes to School*.

120. Doan, *Politics of Virginity*, 14.

121. Doan, *Politics of Virginity*, 13.

122. Kaplan, *God on Their Side*, 64.

123. Finlay, *War on Women*, 71.

124. U.S. House of Representatives Committee on Government Reform/Minority Special Investigations Division, "The Content of Federally Funded Abstinence-Only Education Programs," http://www.democrats.reform.house.gov/Documents/20041201102153-50247 .pdf, cited in Siegel, *Sisterhood Interrupted*, 164.

125. Katy Kelly, "Just Don't Do It!," *U.S. News and World Report*, 17 October 2005, 46, Debra Haffner Papers, carton 1, folder: 2005 Press Coverage, Schlesinger Library, Radcliffe Institute, Harvard University.

126. Kelly, "Just Don't Do It!," 46.

127. See Herzog, "Saved from Sex"; and Luker, *When Sex Goes to School*, 98–99.

128. Wilson, interview.

129. For more on the "restriction of sexual speech" in this era, see Irvine, *Talk About Sex*, 1–4, 12.

130. Leslie Kantor, cited in Judith Levine, *Harmful to Minors: The Perils of Protecting Children from Sex* (Minneapolis: University of Minnesota Press, 2002), 93.

131. Alastair J. J. Wood et al., "A Sad Day for Science at the FDA," *New England Journal of Medicine* 353 (2005): 1197.

132. Valenti, *The Purity Myth*, 122.

133. Wood et al., "Sad Day," 1197.

134. Cynthia Harper et al., "The Effect of Increased Access to Emergency Contraception among Young Adolescents," *Obstetrics and Gynecology* 106 (September 2005): 483.

135. Harper et al., "Increased Access," 484. See also American Academy of Pediatrics, "Policy Statement: Emergency Contraception," *Pediatrics* 116 (2005), 1026–1035.

136. Wood et al., "Sad Day," 1198.

137. Wood et al., "Sad Day," 1199.

138. Reproductive Health Technologies Project, "Senior FDA Official Steps Down over Announcement to Stall Plan B OTC Approval," press release, 31 August 2005, 1,

139. Letter to the FDA signed by members of Concerned Women for America, the Family Research Council, American Association of Pro-Life Obstetricians and Gynecologists, and Christian Medical and Dental Associations, prepared by Kirkpatrick & Lockhart Nicholson Graham LLP, "Comment to Docket No. 2005N-0345, 'Circumstances under Which an Active Ingredient May Be Simultaneously Marketed in Both a Prescription Drug Product and an Over-the-Counter Drug Product,'" 1 November 2005, 27, http://concernedwomen.org /images/content/planbfiling_CWA_%20FRC_e_%20al_11-01-2005.pdf.

140. Wood et al., "Sad Day," 1199.

141. Reproductive Health Technologies Project, "Senior FDA Official Steps Down," 1.

142. See Marc Kaufman, "FDA Official Quits over Delay on Plan B: Women's Health Chief Says Commissioner's Decision on Contraceptive Was Political," *Washington Post*, 1 September 2005; and Reproductive Health Technologies Project, "Senior FDA Official Steps Down."

143. Kaufman, "FDA Official Quits."

144. Sexuality Information and Education Council of the United States, "Another FDA Expert Resigns in Protest over Plan B Non-decision; Legislators Urge Acting FDA Commissioner to Approve Over-the-Counter Status," November 2005, http://www.siecus.org /index.cfm?fuseaction=Feature.showFeature&featureID=1246.

145. Office of Population Research & Association of Reproductive Health Professionals at Princeton University, "History of Plan B OTC," http://ec.princeton.edu/pills/planbhistory .htmlhttp://ec.princeton.edu/pills/planbhistory.html It was not until June 2013 that the FDA finally conceded and allowed for unrestricted OTC access to EC, without age restriction, a decision that followed two years of discursive and legal disputes.

146. For the longer history of sex education battles, see Luker, *When Sex Goes to School*; and Irvine, *Talk about Sex*.

147. Michelle M. Mello, Sara Abiola, and James Colgrove, "Pharmaceutical Companies' Role in State Vaccination Policymaking: The Case of Human Papillomavirus Vaccination," *American Journal of Public Health* 102 (May 2012): 893.

148. Mello, Abiola, and Colgrove, "Pharmaceutical Companies," 893.

149. Mello, Abiola, and Colgrove, "Pharmaceutical Companies," 893.

150. Concerned Women for America, 2005 article, cited in Smith, *Righteous Rhetoric*, 87.

151. Smith, *Righteous Rhetoric*, 87.

152. Katha Pollitt, "Virginity or Death! Is the Threat of Cervical Cancer at Age 60 Really Keeping Teenage Girls Virgins?," *The Nation*, 30 May 2005, http://www.thenation.com/article /virginity-or-death/.

153. Pollitt, "Virginity or Death!"

154. Pollitt, "Virginity or Death!"

155. Herzog, *Sex in Crisis*, 116.

156. James Trusell, quoted in Pollitt, "Virginity or Death!"

157. Letter to *Bitch* from Chicago Women's Health Center, 10 April 2007, Bitch: Feminist Response to Pop Culture Records, box 14, David M. Rubenstein Rare Book & Manuscript Library, Duke University.

158. "Health Officials Report Pain, Fainting among Girls Receiving Merck's HPV Vaccine Gardasil," *Collective Voices: SisterSong Women of Color Reproductive Health Collective*, volume 2, issue 8 (2008), 19, SisterSong Women of Color Reproductive Justice Collective

Records, Acc. #11s-09, box 1, Smith College Special Collections. For more on the history of the founding of SisterSong, see Lisa Levenstein, "Heart Communities: SisterSong, SONG, and Incite!," chapter 9 in *They Didn't See Us Coming: The Hidden History of Feminism in the Nineties* (New York: Basic Books, 2020).

159. "Health Officials Report Pain, Fainting."

160. For the longer history of this, see Dorothy Roberts, *Killing the Black Body: Race Reproduction, and the Meaning of Liberty* (New York: Pantheon Books, 1997).

161. See Luker, *When Sex Goes to School*, 92–93; Irvine, *Talk about Sex*, 1–4, 7, 12; and Herzog, *Sex in Crisis*, xii–xiii.

162. Kathleen Sweeney, *Maiden USA: Girl Icons Come of Age* (New York: Peter Lang, 2008), 53–55.

163. Sweeney, *Maiden USA*, 53–55.

164. See, for example, Bennett, "Speaking of Britney."

165. In Bennett, "Speaking of Britney." See also Julia Jacobs, "'Sorry, Britney': Media Is Criticized for Past Coverage, and Some Own Up," *New York Times*, 12 February 2021, https:// www.nytimes.com/2021/02/12/arts/music/britney-spears-documentary-media.html.

166. See Bennett, "Speaking of Britney."

167. This was first historicized in Carol Dyhouse, *Girls in Trouble* (London: Zed Books, 2013), 223. On unexpected overlaps in the culture wars over sexuality, see See Luker, *When Sex Goes to School*, 92–93; Irvine, *Talk about Sex*, 1–4, 7, 12; and Herzog, *Sex in Crisis*, xii–xiii.

168. Meenakshi Gigi Durham, *The Lolita Effect: The Media Sexualization of Young Girls and What We Can Do about It* (Woodstock, NY: Overlook Press, 2008), 35.

169. This can be seen in Gornick, "Between 'Girl Power' and 'Reviving Ophelia,'" 115; Isabel Sawhill, "Framing the Debate: Faith-Based Approaches to Teenage Pregnancy," in Dionne and Chen, *Sacred Places, Civic Purposes*, 23; Herzog, *Sex in Crisis*, x; Ellen Willis, "Sex and American Politics," Seminar 2004, Ellen Willis Papers, folder 10.40, Schlesinger Library, Radcliffe Institute, Harvard University; and Wilson, interview.

170. Herzog, *Sex in Crisis*, x.

171. For more on a conservative consensus on sexuality, see Herzog, *Sex in Crisis*; Irvine, *Talk about Sex*; and Luker, *When Sex Goes to School*.

172. For an articulation of youth and "sexual autonomy," see Joseph J. Fischel, *Sex and Harm in the Age of Consent* (Minneapolis: University of Minnesota Press, 2016).

173. For more on the conservative women's movement, see Ronnee Schreiber, *Righting Feminism: Conservative Women and American Politics* (New York: Oxford University Press, 2008). Thank you to Merve Fejzula for conversations on this topic.

174. Liebau, *Prude*, 5.

175. Liebau, *Prude*, 8.

176. Liebau, *Prude*, 8.

177. For more on this, see Briggs, *How All Politics Became Reproductive Politics*, 53, 70–71, 73; and Robert O. Self, *All in the Family: The Realignment of American Democracy since the 1960s* (New York: Hill and Wang, 2012), 399.

178. Projansky, *Spectacular Girls*, 7–8.

179. Melissa Holmes and Trish Hutchison, *Hang-Ups, Hook-Ups, and Holding Out: Stuff You Need to Know about Your body, Sex, and Dating* (Deerfield Beach, FL: Health Communications, 2007), 142.

180. Liebau, *Prude*, 42, 51.

181. Liebau, *Prude*, 65.

182. Patrice Oppliger, *Girls Gone Skank: The Sexualization of Girls in American Culture* (Jefferson, NC: McFarland, 2008), 3, 47.

183. Oppliger, *Girls Gone Skank*, 4, 36, 31.

184. Oppliger, *Girls Gone Skank*, 1.

185. For more on these unexpected overlaps in the culture wars over sexuality, see see Luker, *When Sex Goes to School*, 92–93; Irvine, *Talk about Sex*, 1–4, 7, 12; and Herzog, *Sex in Crisis*, xii–xiii.

186. This shift is described in Herzog, *Sex in Crisis*, 21–25.

187. Ariel Levy, *Female Chauvinist Pigs: Women and the Rise of Raunch Culture* (New York: Free Press, 2005), 2.

188. Levy, *Female Chauvinist Pigs*, 139.

189. See Troy Gil, *Hillary Rodham Clinton: Polarizing First Lady* (Lawrence: University of Kansas, 2006), 191. Thanks to Joe Fischel for conversations on this topic.

190. For more on this, see Fischel, *Sex and Harm in the Age of Consent*, 8.

191. For more on the history of sexual speech in this era, see Irvine, *Talk About Sex*, 1–4, 12.

192. See, for example, Levine, *Harmful to Minors*; and Tolman, *Dilemmas of Desire*.

193. Valenti, *The Purity Myth*, 50, 82, 197.

194. Tolman, *Dilemmas of Desire*, 7–9.

195. Herzog, *Sex in Crisis*, 25.

196. For more on this history, see Irvine, *Talk About Sex*, 1–4, 12.

197. Willis, "Sex and American Politics."

198. Willis, "Sex and American Politics."

199. On the "mixed messages" that resulted within such a culture, see Durham, *The Lolita Effect*, 3. This was previously argued in Hill Collins, *Black Sexual Politics*.

200. Durham, *The Lolita Effect*, 3. This was previously argued in Hill Collins, *Black Sexual Politics*.

201. Anita Harris, *Future Girl: Young Women in the Twenty-First Century* (New York: Routledge, 2004), 21.

202. Harris, *Future Girl*, 21. On plasticity and the neoliberal brain, see Victoria Pitts-Taylor, "The Plastic Brain: Neoliberalism and the Neuronal Self," *Health* 14, no. 6 (2010): 635–652.

203. "Doing It in Prime Time," *U.S. News and World Report*, 20 May 2005, 50, Debra Haffner Papers, carton 1, folder: 2005 Press Coverage, Schlesinger Library, Radcliffe Institute, Harvard University.

204. "Doing It in Prime Time," 50. This storyline is also discussed at length in Susan Driver, *Queer Girls and Popular Culture: Reading, Resisting, and Creating Media* (New York: Peter Lang, 2007), 221.

205. Richard Lawson, "New Ad Campaign Flaunts *Gossip Girl*'s Bad Self," Gawker.com, 18 July 2008, http://gawker.com/5026817/new-ad-campaign-flaunts-gossip-girls-bad-self.

206. Projansky, *Spectacular Girls*, 7–8.

207. Anita Harris, "Introduction: Youth Cultures and Feminist Politics," in *Next Wave Cultures: Feminism, Subcultures, Activism*, ed. Anita Harris (New York: Routledge, 2008), 1.

208. Astrid Henry, "From a Mindset to a Movement: Feminism since 1990," in *Feminism Unfinished: A Short, Surprising History of American Women's Movements* (New York: Liveright, 2014), 159–160.

209. Siegel, *Sisterhood Interrupted*, 170.

210. For more on the pitfalls of wave theory, see Kimberly Springer, "Third Wave Black Feminism?," *Signs* 27 (Summer 2002):1059–1082; and Nancy Hewitt, ed., *No Permanent Waves: Recasting Histories of U.S. Feminism* (New Brunswick: Rutgers University Press, 2010).

211. "Dear Third Wavers," *See It? Tell It. Change It!*, Newsletter of the Third Wave Foundation, Fall 2002, Third Wave Foundation Papers, box 1, David M. Rubenstein Rare Book & Manuscript Library, Duke University.

212. "Participant Biographies," *See It? Tell It. Change It!*, Newsletter of the Third Wave Foundation, Fall 2002, Third Wave Foundation Papers, box 1, David M. Rubenstein Rare Book & Manuscript Library, Duke University.

213. "Dear Third Wavers."

214. Alexandra Teixera, "Patrolling the Border," *See It? Tell It. Change It!*, Newsletter of the Third Wave Foundation, Fall 2002, Third Wave Foundation Papers, box 1, David M. Rubenstein Rare Book & Manuscript Library, Duke University.

215. See Hewitt, *No Permanent Waves*.

216. Cynthia L. Jackson, "Let's Talk about Sex! Conference Perspectives," *Collective Voices: SisterSong Women of Color Reproductive Health Collective*, volume 2, issue 8 (2008), 8, SisterSong Women of Color Reproductive Justice Collective Records, Acc. #11S-09, box 1, Smith College Special Collections.

217. Jackson, "Let's Talk about Sex!," 8.

218. Lisa Bennett, "Over One Million March for Women's Lives," *National Times: National Organization for Women*, Spring 2004, Black Women's Health Imperative Records, box 3, Smith College Special Collections. For more on how the multiracial feminist organizations leading the march navigated working with "white-dominated pro-choice organizations" (164), see Levenstein, *They Didn't See Us Coming*, 183.

219. "Make a Difference Now!"

220. Kalpana Krishnamurthy, "Get on the Bus! March for Women's Lives," *See It? Tell It. Change It!*, Newsletter of the Third Wave Foundation, Spring/Summer 2004, Third Wave Foundation Papers, box 1, David M. Rubenstein Rare Book & Manuscript Library, Duke University.

221. Bob Batz Jr., "Sewickley Teen on Magazine's List of World-Changers," *Pittsburgh Post Gazette*, 10 March 2004, Choice USA Records, box 3, Smith College Special Collections.

222. On "mixed messages," see Durham, *The Lolita Effect*, 3; and Hill Collins, *Black Sexual Politics*.

223. Theresa Molter and Gillian Beck, *Go Teen Go: Co-Ed Teen Magazine to Fuel the Revolution* zine, no. 3, Winter 2000, Barnard Zine Collection, Barnard College Library.

224. Molter and Beck, *Go Teen Go*.

225. Maliyah Cole with Health Initiative for Youth, *Pretty Girls* zine, October 2007, 2, Schlesinger Library, Radcliffe Institute, Harvard University.

226. Kristy Beckman, *comMOTION* zine, 2002, Barnard Zine Collection, Barnard College Library.

227. Beckman, *comMOTION* zine.

228. Beckman, *comMOTION* zine.

229. Beckman, *comMOTION* zine.

230. Beckman, *comMOTION* zine.

231. Eleanor Whitney, *Aperture* zine, 2000, Barnard Zine Collection, Barnard College Library.

232. Whitney, *Aperture*.

233. "The Ins and Outs of Masturbation in Girlhood," in Cole, *Pretty Girls*, 7.

234. "The Ins and Outs of Masturbation in Girlhood," in Cole, *Pretty Girls*, 10.

235. See Kantor, cited in Levine, *Harmful to Minors*, stating that there is "no left-wing sex education in America" (93).

236. For more on the history of sex education and sexual speech, see Irvine, *Talk About Sex*, 1–4, 12.

237. Harris, *Future Girl*, 161. See also Levenstein, *They Didn't See Us Coming*, 65.

238. Katie Davis, "Coming of Age Online: The Developmental Underpinnings of Girls' Blogs," *Journal of Adolescent Research* 1 (January 2010): 146.

239. Harris, *Future Girl*, 162; and Durham, *Lolita Effect*, 222.

240. Harris, *Future Girl*, 162.

241. Moya Bailey, cited in Henry, "From a Mindset to a Movement," 178.

242. Shelby Knox, cited in Henry, "From a Mindset to a Movement," 176.

243. Levine, *Harmful to Minors*, 144, 147.

244. Levine, *Harmful to Minors*, 144.

245. Liebau, *Prude*, 40–41.

246. Liebau, *Prude*, 40–41.

247. Loretta J. Ross, "The 2008 Elections and Women of Color," *Collective Voices: Sister-Song Women of Color Reproductive Health Collective*, volume 2, issue 8 (2008), 10, SisterSong Women of Color Reproductive Justice Collective Records, Acc. #11s-09, box 1, Smith College Special Collections.

248. Ross, "The 2008 Elections and Women of Color," 11.

EPILOGUE

1. For more on this history, see Kristin Luker, *When Sex Goes to School: Warring Views on Sex—and Sex Education—since the Sixties* (New York: W. W. Norton, 2006), 92–93; Dagmar Herzog, *Sex in Crisis: The New Sexual Revolution and the Future of American Politics* (New York: Basic Books, 2008), xii–xiii; and Janice Irvine, *Talk about Sex: The Battle over Sex Education in the United States* (Berkeley: University of California Press, 2002), 1–4, 7, 12.

2. For more on the importance of understanding this history, see R. Marie Griffith, *Moral Combat: How Sex Divided American Christians and Fractured American Politics* (New York: Basic Books, 2017), 321.

3. Concern over sexting is discussed by Peggy Orenstein in *Girls & Sex: Navigating the Complicated New Landscape* (New York: Harper/Harper Collins, 2016), 1; and the social panic surrounding this issue is explored in Sarah Projansky, *Spectacular Girls: Media Fascination and Celebrity Culture* (New York: New York University Press, 2014), 6, and in Kathryn Bond Stockton, "The Queer Child Now and Its Paradoxical Global Effects," *GLQ: A Journal of Lesbian and Gay Studies* 22 (2016): 505, 507.

4. Abigail Jones, "Sex and the Single Tween," *Newsweek*, 22 January 2014, cited in Stockton, "The Queer Child Now," 507.

5. For more on this see Stockton, "The Queer Child Now," 505–539.

6. Orenstein, *Girls & Sex*, 2.

7. Catherine E. Lhamon and Vanita Gupta, "Dear Colleague Letter on Transgender Students," U.S. Department of Justice, Civil Rights Division, and U.S. Department of Education, Office for Civil Rights, 13 May 2016, https://www2.ed.gov/about/offices/list/ocr/letters/colleague-201605-title-ix-transgender.pdf.

8. See, for example, Ann Coulter, speaking on *Real Time with Bill Maher*, in May 2016, cited by Hilary Hanson in "Dan Savage Takes on Ann Coulter over Transgender Bathroom Rights," *Huffington Post*, 8 May 2016, http://www.huffingtonpost.com/entry/dan-savage-ann-coulter-transgender-bathroom-rights_us_572f9c74e4b0bc9cb0472f03.

9. See Joseph Fischel and Gabriel N. Rosenberg, "Milo Was the Wrong Voice on the Real Complexity of Age, Sex, and Consent," *Slate*, 24 February 2017, http://www.slate.com/blogs

/outward/2017/02/24/what_the_milo_yiannopoulos_case_teaches_us_about_sex_age
_and_consent_in.html.

10. "South Dakota May Criminalize Lifesaving Healthcare for Trans Youth in Latest Attack on LGBTQ Rights," *Democracy Now!*, 29 January 2020, https://www.democracynow.org /2020/1/29/south_dakota_anti_trans_bill_1057.

11. Kitty Stryker, "What the FOSTA/SESTA Anti-Sex Trafficking Bill Means," *Teen Vogue*, 27 March 2018, https://www.teenvogue.com/story/fosta-sesta-anti-sex-trafficking -bill.

12. Stefanie Duguay, "Why Tumblr's Ban on Adult Content Is Bad for LGBTQ Youth," *The Conversation*, 6 December 2018, https://theconversation.com/why-tumblrs-ban-on-adult -content-is-bad-for-lgbtq-youth-108215. For more on this topic, see Alexander Cho, "Queer Reverb: Tumblr, Affect, Time," in *Networked Affect*, ed. Susanna Paasonen, Ken Hillis, and Michael Petit (Cambridge, MA: MIT Press, 2015), 43–58. Thanks to Jennifer Williams for conversations on this topic.

13. Fischel and Rosenberg, "Milo Was the Wrong Voice."

14. Fischel and Rosenberg, "Milo Was the Wrong Voice."

15. Joseph R. Biden Jr., "Executive Order on Preventing and Combating Discrimination on the Basis of Gender Identity or Sexual Orientation," White House, 20 January 2021, https://www.whitehouse.gov/briefing-room/presidential-actions/2021/01/20/executive -order-preventing-and-combating-discrimination-on-basis-of-gender-identity-or-sexual -orientation/.

16. Danielle Kurtzleben, "Political Dispute over Transgender Rights Focuses on Youth Sports," *NPR*, 11 March 2021, https://www.npr.org/2021/03/11/974782774/political-dispute -over-transgender-rights-focuses-on-youth-sports?t=.

17. Justin McCarthy, "In U.S., 71% Support Transgender People Serving in Military," Gallup, 20 June 2019, https://news.gallup.com/poll/258521/support-transgender-people-serving -military.aspx, cited in Kurtzleben, "Political Dispute."

18. See chapter 1 of this book. See also Luker, *When Sex Goes to School*, 92–93; Herzog, *Sex in Crisis*, xii–xiii; and Irvine, *Talk about Sex*, 1–4, 7, 12.

19. See Faye Wattleton, *Life on the Line* (New York: Ballantine Books, 1996), 215. See also Irvine, *Talk About Sex.*

20. Ben Mathis-Lilley, "Trump Was Recorded in 2005 Bragging about Grabbing Women 'by the Pussy,'" *Slate*, 7 October 2016, http://www.slate.com/blogs/the_slatest/2016/10/07 /donald_trump_2005_tape_i_grab_women_by_the_pussy.html.

21. Chelsea Stone, "Anna Lehane Wears a 'Grab My P*ssy' Shirt to a Trump Rally," *Teen Vogue*, 11 October 2016, http://www.teenvogue.com/story/grab-my-pussy-shirt-trump-rally -anna-lehane.

22. Stone, "Anna Lehane."

23. Quote from Kate Dwyer, "How to Get Involved with the Women's March on Washington," *Teen Vogue*, 30 December 2016, https://www.teenvogue.com/story/how-to-get -involved-with-womens-march-on-washington; biographical information from Tabitha St. Bernard-Jacobs, personal website, http://www.tabithastbernard.com.

24. Tabitha St. Bernard, "32 Kids and Teens Tell Us Why They're Getting Involved with the Women's March," *Teen Vogue*, 19 January 2017, https://www.teenvogue.com/gallery/kids -teens-youths-ambassadors-womens-march.

25. St. Bernard, "32 Kids and Teens."

26. For more on this, see Lisa Levenstein, *They Didn't See Us Coming: The Hidden History of Feminism in the Nineties* (New York: Basic Books, 2020), 190.

27. Brooke Seipel, "Six Teen Girls Who Met on Twitter Were Behind Nashville's Massive Black Lives Matter Protest," *The Hill*, 5 June 2020, https://thehill.com/homenews/state-watch /501450-six-teen-girls-who-met-on-twitter-were-behind-nashvilles-massive-black.

28. Seipel, "Six Teen Girls."

29. Sarah Emily Baum, "Black Lives Matter Protests Bring Teen Activists into the Streets," *Teen Vogue*, 3 June 2020, https://www.teenvogue.com/story/black-lives-matter-protests -teens.

30. "Teen Vogue," Condé Nast, https://www.condenast.com/brands/teen-vogue/.

31. See Savana Ogburn, "Daily Links: Birth Control Edition," *Rookie*, 6 February 2017, http://www.rookiemag.com/2017/02/daily-links-birth-control-edition/; and Sarah Gouda, "What to Do with That Fiery Ball of Post-election Anger Raging inside of You: Ways to Fight Islamophobia, Self-Soothe, and Create Community," *Rookie*, 8 December 2016, http:// www.rookiemag.com/2016/12/post-election-anger/.

32. Anaheed, "Why Can't I Be You: Jane Pratt," *Rookie*, 25 October 2013, http://www .rookiemag.com/2013/10/wciby-jane-pratt/2/.

33. See, for example, Jessica Bennett, "Speaking of Britney . . . What about All Those Other Women?," *New York Times*, 27 February 2021, https://www.nytimes.com/2021/02/27/style /britney-spears-documentary-jackson-celebrity-reappraisal.html.

34. *Framing Britney*, produced and directed by Samantha Stark (The New York Times Presents, FX/Hulu, 2021).

35. See, for example, Bennett, "Speaking of Britney"; Mara Wilson, "The Lies Hollywood Tells about Little Girls," *New York Times*, 23 February 2021, https://www.nytimes.com/2021 /02/23/opinion/britney-spears-mara-wilson-hollywood.html; and Tavi Gevinson, "Britney Spears Was Never in Control," *The Cut*, 23 February 2021, https://www.thecut.com/2021/02 /tavi-gevinson-britney-spears-was-never-in-control.html.

36. Gevinson, "Britney Spears Was Never in Control."

37. Gevinson, "Britney Spears Was Never in Control."

38. Charlie Brinkhurst-Cuff, "Could the Black Women behind the #muteRKelly Campaign Finally Bring the Monster Down?," *gal-dem*, 1 May 2018, https://gal-dem.com/could -the-black-women-behind-the-muterkelly-campaign-finally-bring-the-monster-down/.

39. Brinkhurst-Cuff, "Could the Black Women Behind the #muteRKelly Campaign"; and allegations details from "Surviving R. Kelly: New Doc Says Time's Up for Singer Accused of Abusing Black Girls for Decades," *Democracy Now!*, 7 January 2019, https://www .democracynow.org/2019/1/7/surviving_r_kelly_new_doc_says.

40. Bobby Allyn and Anastasia Tsioulcas, "R. Kelly Arrested on Federal Charges, Including Child Pornography and Kidnapping," *NPR*, 12 July 2019, https://www.npr.org/2019/07 /12/741008967/federal-prosecutors-arrest-and-charge-r-kelly-in-new-child-pornography -case?t=1591879816880.

41. Brinkhurst-Cuff, "Could the Black Women behind the #muteRKelly Campaign."

42. On the political importance of vulnerability, see Jennifer C. Nash, "Pedagogies of Desire," *differences* 30, no. 1 (May 2019): 197–217; and Joseph J. Fischel, "Pornographic Protections? Itineraries of Childhood Innocence," *Law, Culture and the Humanities* 12, no. 2 (June 2016): 206–220. See also Projansky, *Spectacular Girls*.

43. Laura Briggs, *How All Politics Became Reproductive Politics: From Welfare Reform to Foreclosure to Trump* (Oakland: University of California Press, 2017); Annette Lawson and Deborah L. Rhode, *The Politics of Pregnancy: Adolescent Sexuality and Public Policy* (New Haven, CT: Yale University Press, 1993), 3; Carolyn Cocca, "From 'Welfare Queen' to 'Exploited Teen': Welfare Dependency, Statutory Rape, and Moral Panic," *NWSA Journal* 14 (2002): 58; Zillah Eisenstein, *The Color of Gender: Reimaging Democracy* (Berkeley:

University of California Press, 1994), 40; Jessica Fields, "'Children Having Children': Race, Innocence, and Sexuality Education," *Social Problems* 52 (November 2005): 549–550; Jeffrey Moran, *Teaching Sex: The Shaping of Adolescence in the 20th Century* (Cambridge, MA: Harvard University Press, 2000), 223; and Stephanie Coontz, *The Way We Never Were: American Families and the Nostalgia Trap* (New York: Basic Books, 2010), 204.

44. For more on anomalies in the culture wars over sexuality, see Luker, *When Sex Goes to School*, 92–93; Herzog, *Sex in Crisis*, xii–xiii; and Irvine, *Talk about Sex*, 1–4, 7, 12.

45. For more on adolescence and sexual autonomy, see Joseph J. Fischel, *Sex and Harm in the Age of Consent* (Minneapolis: University of Minnesota Press, 2016).

Index

AAUW. *See* American Association of University Women

Abdul-Kareem, Endeshia, 141

Abercrombie & Fitch, 137

abortion: access to, 3, 9, 20, 27–28, 35, 150; adolescent girls and antiabortion policy, 14, 20–26, 86, 118; culture war battle, 14; endorsement of, 13; fetal personhood, 118; financial support, 118, 143; legal, 15, 92; loss of Medicaid funding, 17; parental notification laws, 92; pro-choice, 86, 97; rights, 36, 88, 94; safe alternatives, 65; schism over, 19–20, 108, 129

"Abortion and the Conscience of a Nation" (Reagan), 22–23

abstinence campaigns: A-H definition of, 105–106, 107, 120; celebrity promotions, 123, 135; contraceptive education versus, 21–24; fear tactics, 75; funding sources, 122; global efforts, 119–120; growth of campaign, 90, 98, 117; legislation to promote, 21, 71; media attention, 122; outlandishness of, 2; programs, 119–124; racism, 117, 124; sex education and, 3, 95–96, 105–107, 119, 124–130, 144–145; Title V funding, 119, 120, 148; virginity pledges, 129; welfare reform bill, 24–25, 87, 98–109, 120–122. *See also* sex education

Abstinence Clearinghouse, 129

Abstinence Education Grant Program, 105

Access Hollywood, 150

AC/DC, 51

ACF. *See* U.S. Administration for Children and Families

Acker, Kathy, 64

ACLU. *See* American Civil Liberties Union

activism, grassroots, 59–69, 80, 140–146, 151–153

adolescent, use of term, 11

Adolescent Family Life Act (AFLA), 21–26, 27, 36, 105, 122

Adolescent Health, Services, and Pregnancy Prevention Act, 14

adolescent sexual behavior. *See* New Right movement; teenage girls of color; white teenage girls

adoption, 23

adult business zones, 44

advertising, 8, 9, 137

Advocates for Youth, 125

Adweek, 74

Afghanistan, 116

AFLA. *See* Adolescent Family Life Act

African American Women in Defense of Ourselves, 90

Against Our Will: Men, Women, and Rape (Brownmiller), 39

Aguilera, Christina, 80, 134, 136

Aguirre, Olga Morales, 105

AIDS epidemic: ABC model, 119–120; importance of sex education, 3, 19, 71, 84, 96, 107, 108, 119–120; literature censorship and, 36; prevention, 94; virus spread, 29, 35

Alan Guttmacher Institute. *See* Guttmacher Institute

Albright, Madeleine, 94

Alexander, Michelle, 103

Allen, Woody, 48

Allow States and Victims to Fight Online Sex Trafficking Act (FOSTA), 149

"Alternatives to Alternatives" (Bess), 67

American Academy of Pediatrics, 128

Union Theological Seminary, 128
Unitarian Church, 3, 128
United Farm Workers, 118
United Nations: Special Session on
  Children, 119; summits on children's
  issues, 129; World AIDS Day, 96; World
  Conference Against Racism, Racial
  Discrimination, Xenophobia and Related
  Intolerance, 100
University of California at Berkeley, 102
University of California at Los Angeles
  (UCLA), 102
University of Pennsylvania, Institute of
  Contemporary Art, 53
Unruh, Leslee, 121–122, 123, 129
U.S. Administration for Children and
  Families (ACF), 120, 122
U.S. Commission on Pornography, 45–47
U.S. Congress, Select Committee on
  Children, Youth, and Families, 19
U.S. Congressional Black Caucus Health
  Braintrust, 118
U.S. Department of Education, 88; Office of
  Civil Rights, 88
U.S. Department of Health and Human
  Services, 125
U.S. Equal Employment Commission, 88
U.S. Food and Drug Administration,
  130–132; Nonprescription Drugs Advisory
  Committee, 131; Office of Women's
  Health, 131
U.S. Maternal and Child Health Bureau,
  120
U.S. Office of Adolescent Pregnancy
  Programs, 23
U.S. Office of Faith-Based Initiatives, 122
U.S. Senate: Black Legislative Staff Caucus,
  118; Committee on Commerce, 51
U.S. Student Association, 112
U.S. Supreme Court, 87, 88–91
Utah, Adaku, 141

Valenti, Jessica, 123, 138
Vance, Carole, 44–45
Vanity Fair, 110
Veazey, Carlton W., 126–127
victim feminism, 83–84
Village Voice, 69
Violence Against Women Act, 94
Violent Crime Control and Law Enforce-
  ment Act, 103
virginity movement. See abstinence
  campaigns
visual arts, 50

Walker, Alice, 40, 41, 79, 91
Walker, Rebecca, 91–92

Wall Street Journal, 16
WAP. See Women Against Pornography
Wattleton, Faye, 24, 27, 28, 29, 92
wave terminology, 6, 140–141
wave theory. See feminists/feminism
WAVPM. See Women Against Violence in
  Pornography and the Media
Waxman, Henry, 28, 129
websites, personal, 144–145
Weetzie Bat (Block), 37
Weinstein, Harvey, 152
Welbourne-Moglia, Ann, 17, 19
"welfare queen" trope, 10, 15, 21, 87, 90,
  99, 106
welfare reform: abstinence policies, 24–25,
  87, 98–109, 118–122; Clinton and, 3, 24–25,
  87, 93–94, 98–109, 118–119, 150; neoliberal-
  ism and, 2; New Right social and fiscal
  factions, 9–10, 20–21, 93–95
Wellesley College, Center for Research on
  Women, 83
Welteroth, Elaine, 152
Werkler, Henry F., 29
Wetlands (New York City, New York,
  nightclub), 73
Wexler, Richard, 49
"What Must Be Done about Children
  Having Children" (Height), 16
What's Wrong with Sex Education
  (Anchell), 26
"What's Wrong with Sex Education"
  (Schlafly), 37
"What We're Rolling Around in Bed With"
  (Hollibaugh and Moraga), 42
Whedon, Joss, 80
White House Interns, 112
white supremacy, 4, 41, 93
white teenage girls: centrality within media,
  55, 83, 140; debates over sexuality, 109–115;
  increased sexual habits, 9, 13; parental
  control, 26–27; protective politics toward,
  4, 7–8, 41, 87, 95–96, 104, 124; reproductive
  and marital conformity, 2, 25; Riot Grrrls
  movement, 64, 66, 78–79; rise in pregnancies, 16; sexual innocence, 47, 97, 117, 148;
  sexual morality and family structure, 8
  (see also family practices); victimization
  of, 7, 47, 63, 84, 87, 106, 110, 111–112, 113;
  vulnerability to sexual harm, 6, 7, 14, 40,
  45, 57, 83–84, 137, 149
Whitney, Eleanor, 65, 144
"Why Feminists Support Clinton"
  (Steinem), 112
Wildmon, Donald, 74
Williams, Wendy O., 51
Willis, Ellen, 15, 42, 46, 56, 90, 98, 111–112,
  138

About the Author

Charlie Jeffries (she/her) is a British Academy Postdoctoral Research Fellow in the Department of History, Classics and Archaeology at Birkbeck, University of London. Her research focuses on the history of sexuality and the history of social movements in the modern United States.